Anonymus

The Pilgrim Of Our Lady Of Martyrs

Vol. XV.

Anonymus

The Pilgrim Of Our Lady Of Martyrs
Vol. XV.

ISBN/EAN: 9783741179099

Manufactured in Europe, USA, Canada, Australia, Japa

Cover: Foto ©Andreas Hilbeck / pixelio.de

Manufactured and distributed by brebook publishing software (www.brebook.com)

Anonymus

The Pilgrim Of Our Lady Of Martyrs

THE PILGRIM

OF

Our Lady of Martyrs

A MONTHLY MAGAZINE

DEVOTED TO

The Interests of the Shrine of Our Lady of Martyrs
at Auriesville, to the Cause of the Martyrs
who died there, to the American and
other Missions, past and present.

FIFTEENTH YEAR. VOL. XV.

JANUARY—DECEMBER, 1899

INDEX

The Pilgrim of Our Lady of Martyrs

VOLUME XV.—1899.

An Instance of Gratitude 287
Annals of the Shrine 85, 237, 275, 291, 321
Contributions to the Missions 32, 64, 96, 192, 224, 256, 286, 320, 352
Contributions to the Shrine 12, 57, 85, 117, 144, 188, 216 239, 282, 301, 330, 370
Copts of Upper Egypt, Movement Towards Conversion of the 288

Fiction :
    Sister Stephanie. D. S. Béni. 42, 87, 118
    Through the Pieta. T. M. Joyce. 122, 144
    Térèse and Pierre. K. A. Hennessy. 179, 216, 246, 264, 302, 331, 354
    Morad. Charles J. Mullaly, S. J 370

If It Be the Will of God. L. W. Reilly 14
Iroquois Maiden, An—Life of Catharine Tegakwitha. From the French of
    P. Chauchetiere 2, 50, 75, 105, 130, 162, 203, 227, 258
Jesuits and New France in the Seventeenth Century, The. Translated from the
    French of Rev. Camille de Rochemonteix, S. J., by K. A. Hennessy .
    .... 34, 66, 59, 156, 168, 194, 232

Missions, From the :
    Conawoody, India—Calcutta, India—Bela Kasaragod, India—Cœur D'Alene
    Indians to the Director of the Association for the Propagation of the
    Faith (Correspondence) 26
    Dunbrody, South Africa—St. Mary's Mission, Wash.—Key West, Fla.—Salon-
    ique, Turquie D'Europe (Correspondence) 58
    Juneau, Alaska—Death of Father Judge, S. J. (Correspondence) 95
    Death Place of Fathers Brébeuf and Lalemant, Coldwater, Ontario—Manga-
    lore Magazine (Correspondence)—Death of an American Missionary,
    Rev. Maurice D. Sullivan 189
    A Brief Account of the Incipient Mission of Nellikunja (Correspondence)... 252
    Consecration of a Bishop in China—A New Publication, *Les Missions Catho-
    lique Françaises, au XIXe Siecle*—Martyrdom of the Franciscan Father
    Victorin at Che-Keon-Chau 283
    Ultal, Mangalore—Account of What Is Being Done by Our Missionaries on
    the Island of Syra in Greece (Correspondence) 314
    St. Mary's Mission, Wash. (Correspondence) 383

Mission Notes :
    Massacre of a Missionary in the Ubanghi District, Central Africa—Missions
    in China 29
    Precis Historiques—Missions of the Belgian Province—Ceylon—Mission of
    the German Jesuits—India—Congo Mission—Mission of Uganda—War
    Between England and France and the Missions—A New Catholic
    Church in Dawson City, Alaska 62

Quang-Binh—Blessed Father Perboyre, Lazarist, Martyred in China—Kiatcheon and Wei-Hai-Wei—Lazarists in Abyssinia—Marist Fathers go to Solomon Islands—Amazonia, Brazil	94
Chinese Missions	127
Rev. Frederick Hopkins, S. J., Named Vicar-Apostolic of British Honduras—Emperor of China Issues a Decree—Danger of Our Missionaries in China—Statistics from *L'Univers*	319
"Missions in the Far East," from *London Tablet*—Father Escande from Pondicherry and Father Guéno of Annam in Cochin-China to *Les Missions Catholiques*	348
Letter from Angora in *L'Univers*—Bourbaki, the leader of the Turks in Africa, at Lourdes, from *Semaine Religieuse* of Auch—Some South African Missionary Statistics, from *Les Missions Catholiques*—Mme. Isabelle Massieu writes in the *Revue des deux Mondes* on Burmah	378
Notes of Interest	374
Poetry.	
Bethlehem. E. S. B.	1
A Tribute to St. Francis de Sales.	23
Your Tears Shall Be Turned Into Joy. Rev. Ernest R. Ryan, S. J.	33
Candlemas Day. Patrick Rafferty, S. J.	49
Good Friday. J. F. X. Burns, S. J.	65
Mater Dolorosa. John J. Branin.	86
Resurrexit Sicut Dixit. E. M. Smith.	97
Altar Flowers. H. M	129
May. J. G.	142
Resignation. C. M. Girardeau.	161
Monstra Te Esse Matrem. A. E. Sullivan	193
Janua Coeli. Rev. C. W. Barraud, S. J.	225
Mater Amabilis. Rev. C. W. Barraud, S. J.	257
Courage. S. T. Smith	274
Causa Nostræ Laetitiæ. Rev. C. W. Barraud, S. J.	289
Aspirations. James Raymond Perry	348
Aftermath. Edwin L. Sabin	352
Transeamus Usque Bethlehem. H. M	353
Shrine, Annals of the	85, 237, 275, 291, 321
Shrine, Contributions to the	12, 57, 85, 117, 144, 188, 216, 239, 282, 302, 330, 370
Shrine Notes	13, 56, 115, 143, 177, 210, 366
Tegakwitha, Life of Catharine. From the French of P. Chauchetière	2, 50, 75, 105, 130, 162, 203, 227, 258
Thanksgiving, A	176

THE PILGRIM
OF
OUR LADY OF MARTYRS

XV. YEAR. JANUARY, 1899. NO. 1.

BETHLEHEM.

BY E. S. B.

THEY search through Bethlehem's storm-swept lanes,
    Nor shelter find;
Their earnest quest no answer gains,
    Save words unkind.
Cheerful the hearth-fire lights that throw
A glory on the frost below;
But on they move through blinding snow
    With hearts resigned.

Behind them glimmer Bethlehem's lights
    In solitude,
Like fays that lure benighted wights
    Through mists fen-brewed:
Before them, on the moon-bathed wold,
By frosty sprites in crystal scrolled,
A ruined stable they behold,
    A shelter rude.

And there, within those stable walls,
    The Infant lies,
While meek-eyed tenants of the stalls
    Look mute surprise;
With minstrelsy of voice and string,
And bursts of joy, the angels sing
The advent of the new-born King
    In humble guise.

Copyright, 1898, by APOSTLESHIP OF PRAYER.

Jesus! to-day how many hearts
  Are filled with sin;
Sweet, gentle Babe, Thy loving arts
  No love can win;
Still, coming as a Christmas guest,
Each feels Thee knocking at his breast:
In vain! Few heed Thy meek request
  To enter in.

Let my heart, then, Thy manger be
  This Christmas morn,
Though rude as that which sheltered Thee
  From Winter's scorn.
I'll garnish well for Christmas shrine,
Mean though it be, this heart of mine
To hold Thy Housel gift divine,
  My new-born King.

AN IROQUOIS MAIDEN.

OR

Life of Catharine Tegakwitha.

(*Continued.*)

CHAPTER VII.

Mission of the Saut.—Its Origin.—Its Fervor.

THIS mission, named at first for its patron, "Iroquois Mission of St. Francis Xavier du Près," then "Iroquois Mission of St. Francis Xavier du Saut," and later "Mission of the Saut St. Louis," the name which it still bears, only counted, at the date of Catharine's arrival, a few years of existence. Its origin is connected with the foundation of the village of La Prairie de la Magdeleine, which was its first cradle (1681).

Its history must be told.

On the banks of the great stream St. Lawrence, two leagues above the city of Montreal, but on the opposite shore, there is a flat and fertile stretch of land, known as "the Prairie de la

Magdeleine." The vast curve which this coast describes, from the foot of the Saut St. Louis, forms a large basin, which has sometimes borne the name of Lake St. Paul, into which empty the abundant waters of the Saut St. Louis.

This place attracted the attention of the first settlers of Montreal (1). In 1643 Father Poncet gave this description of it: "This position is favorable for hunting and fishing because of the prairies. The trees are fine, the soil good, but the enemy is to be feared, and to convey provisions thither at low water appears difficult."

During the entire period of the war with the Iroquois this shore was uninhabitable. Nothing could shield it from the incursions of those terrible savages, so that they reigned as masters on this coast. On the peace of 1667, security began to revive, and Father Raffeix was sent to the Prairie de la Magdeleine to prepare the way for French occupation. It was the intention to gather there also those Iroquois Christians willing to expatriate themselves; for, after an experience of several years, the necessity was recognized of separating the Christian Iroquois from their pagan countrymen, in order to protect them from the seduction of bad example and root from their hearts even the very least traces of idolatry and superstition.

Francis Xavier Tonsohoten and his wife were the first to accept the benevolent proposition. They were also to become the first founders of this celebrated Mission. Their name and their history deserve to be preserved. Tonsohoten was of Huron origin; he had been taken prisoner by the Oneidas, and owed his life less to the humanity than to the cupidity of his master. Guarded as a slave, Tonsohoten attracted the attention of the Iroquois chiefs by the nobility of his character, by his courage, fidelity, and devotion. It was resolved that he should be incorporated into the Nation. It is not unusual among these savages to see the vanquished thus adopted by the vanquishers and admitted amongst them, to equal rights with themselves.

---

(1) Montreal was founded in 1642.

This custom, which had become a law, so to speak, was imposed upon them as a necessity, as, in consequence of cruel wars, carried on incessantly, they saw their ranks thinned each day without being able to fill the gaps. It was, therefore, their sole means of recruiting, and, strange to say, one then saw these men, so long irreconcilable enemies, all at once forget their name, their country and their hereditary hatreds, in order to espouse the interests of their new country, to such a point as to become its most intrepid defenders.

Tonsohoten, having become an Iroquois, thought of taking a wife. His choice, which no one had a right to control, fixed itself upon a young slave named Ganneaktena (1), who had been taken captive by the Iroquois during their war against the Eries or Cats (2), and he espoused her.

She had escaped from the complete destruction of her village, named Gentaienton, and the misfortune was, by a secret dispensation of Providence, the cause of her happiness, since her captivity obtained for her the knowledge of the faith, and marriage restored her to liberty. Nature had endowed her with the best qualities, and her great innocence in youth and amid the seductions of her captivity, seemed to call down on her the best blessings of heaven.

Father Bruyas, then missionary to the Oneidas, struck by her qualities, undertook to instruct her in the Christian religion. He thereby paid a debt of gratitude, for this good pagan with rare amiability served him as interpreter with the sick, and, by her lessons, smoothed for him the difficulties of the Iroquois language.

After some years, Tonsohoten was attacked by an illness which affected his limbs, and which the most skilful *juggler* was powerless to relieve. He resolved to profit by the peace, and go to the French colony, in search of a remedy, which, in his own country he had been unable to procure. His wife was to accompany him, and everything was favorable for the accomplishment of the project she meditated. She thereby

---
(1) Gandeaktessa.
(2) This nation, entirely destroyed by the Iroquois, occupied the shores of Lake Erie, to which it owed its name.

found an easy way of being instructed, and sooner receiving baptism, the object of her most ardent desires. By force of entreaty, she obtained that her mother, her brother-in-law, and five others of their friends, should accompany them. They reached the Island of Montreal in 1667.

On its southern shore, arose the French town, then better known as *Ville Marie*. It had received this sacred name, as a touching proof of the devotion of its founders to the Mother of God. It already counted twenty-nine years of existence. Seated at the foot of the mountain, whose name it has since taken, and on the banks of the great River St. Lawrence, it already appeared destined for the great development which it was to receive later. The piety which had presided at its foundation, and with which its first inhabitants were animated gave the rising city a religious zeal that one could not weary of admiring.

Our Iroquois voyagers were singularly edified, at the sight this happy city offered them. The governor and his officers set an example of all the Christian virtues, and, for the happiness of humanity, every species of self-devotion was emulously practised there, under the influence of religion.

Pious virgins (1) had braved a thousand dangers coming from France, to devote themselves to the alleviation of all sorts of infirmity, and all kinds of pain. A poor and humble girl whose name, blessed by angels and men, will be as immortal as her works, Sister Bourgeois (2), there consecrated herself to the needs of children. With that pious perseverance that characterizes religious works and assures their success, she formed in virtue and useful knowledge both French and pagan children. In a word, virtuous priests sustained by their zeal those touching foundations which they had themselves inspired, and watched over the spiritual and temporal interests of the growing flock. They belonged to the fervent community of St. Sulpice of Paris.

---

(1) The Religious of S. Joseph de la Flèche.
(2) Catharine Bourgeois of Troyes in Champagne founded the Congregation of Sisters of Our Lady of Montreal, in 1653, for the education of young girls. The institution grew with the colony and in proportion to its needs.

This was more than sufficient to produce the most favorable impression on the wife of Tonsohoten. Her desire to become a Christian was but the more lively.

Father Raffeix, who then presided over the first establishments of the Prairie, frequently came to visit Montreal. As he spoke the Iroquois language very well, he was placed in communication with the travellers, who were all the more closely drawn to him, for being so happy as to be able to converse with a *Black Robe* in their own language. The missionary saw in the meeting a manifestation of the designs of Providence.

To begin with, he invited these good Iroquois to accompany him to the village of La Prairie and to give more time to their instruction. They readily and without difficulty decided to go and pitch their tent of bark near the missionary.

Some months later, in the spring of 1668, Father Raffeix, being obliged to go as far as Quebec, thought that in order to complete and consolidate the work of God nothing could be more salutary for these good neophytes, than to witness what savages like themselves could become under the influence of religion. He therefore proposed that they should accompany him, and he conducted them to the celebrated Mission of the Hurons : Our Lady of Faith, near Quebec.

This Mission had always been one of the brilliant triumphs of the faith. Under the direction of Father Chaumonot, its founder, it recalled by its fervor the happy days of the early Church, and what must forever be its chief title to glory. Those Christian Hurons became the most active instruments in the conversion of those who had formerly been their most cruel enemies. When an Iroquois came to visit them, they spared nothing to inspire him with love and esteem for the Christian religion, and induce him to embrace it.

The conquest of Tonsohoten, and especially that of his wife, had been easier than that of many others. Every cabin had been thrown open to them, and every one found pleasure in offering them the best they had of everything. It was soon evident that the wife was worthy of baptism, and that the ceremony might be more imposing, the Bishop of Quebec, we are informed by the annals of that time, desired to confer it himself on the catechumen. She received the name of *Catharine*, that she was to bear so gloriously.

Tonsohoten, though Christian in heart, dared not declare it. He had been happily cured of his infirmity (*mal de jambe*), and thought always of returning to the Iroquois country. With this design he quitted the mission, his wife at first not daring to oppose him. But on reaching Montreal, she could no longer conceal her regret, and conjured him to settle near the missionary of La Prairie, who spoke their language, and who would help them to keep their faith. He consented after much urging, and twelve other baptized Iroquois who were aware of his project, joined them. Together they came and settled near Father Raffeix, at the Prairie de la Magdeleine.

"It is an admirable thing," remarks Father Dablon, "that God willed the Iroquois should preserve the life of that captain, in order that he should afterwards procure for them eternal life, and that their slave (his wife), should thus become their mistress in the faith. She was that in fact, not only at the beginning of her conversion, but for the remainder of her life, by the example of rare virtue that she set them."

The news of the foundation of this Iroquois Mission, in the French Colony, excited lively interest in France, and some pious souls immediately desired to have a share in the good work. There is still preserved in the village of the Saut St. Louis, the beautiful silver ostensorium that was sent from Paris for this occasion. It bears this inscription: "Claude Prevost, ex-Alderman of Paris, and Elizabeth le Gendre, his wife, have presented this ostensorium to the Reverend Jesuit Fathers, for their first church of the Iroquois, in the year 1668, for the honor of God."

On the death of his wife (May 6, 1673), Tonsohoten, who was still only a neophyte, gave a remarkable example of the change that the faith had already worked in his mind. Far from conforming to the custom general among the savages, of burying with their dead whatever had belonged to them, he assembled the great council of the elders (ancients), and thus addressed them: "In quality of first Captain, I am resolved to renounce a practice which is of no use to the dead, and unjust to the living. I will be the first to set you an example. I will clothe the body of my wife with her richest garments; but all else that belonged to her I will bestow upon the poor." All applauded this resolution, which became a law among the Christian savages. As to Tonsohoten himself, after receiving baptism, he continued for the space of twenty years to edify the Mission, and there died in 1688.

To make the first Christians of this Mission better known, we will cite another example, that of Martin Skandegourhakten. He was a near relative of the *great Anié*, who had drawn him thither. He distinguished himself so greatly among the neophytes, that Father Frémin, at his oft repeated request, abridged his term of probation, and admitted him to baptism. He was only to be seen at church, or in the woods or fields, at work. Up to his death, which occurred two years later, he had preserved his baptismal innocence. In spite of his youth, his zeal prompted him to make a long voyage to preach the faith in his own country. The rude attacks he was forced to sustain, were a new triumph for his virtue. During the autumn hunt when near Fort Lamothe, not far from Chambly, he fell seriously ill, in the midst of the woods, December 1, 1675. This misfortune did not overcome him. He had immediate recourse to prayer, and declared that he was willing to die although still so very young. He only feared one thing, and that was to displease God. His beads constantly in his hands, the names of Jesus and Mary on his lips, he often repeated acts of faith, hope, charity and contrition. His delirium, even, was a succession of acts of piety. His companions wished to carry him to the Mission. The great Anié, who was chief of the band, was the first to undertake this service. "My brothers," said the sick man, "offer to God what you are doing for me. It is difficult for you to carry me, but God will reward you for this charity." Then he tried to hide his sufferings, in order to lessen the pain he was causing to others. Three times they were obliged to stop on the road to give him rest. At the first station Martin, turning to the great Anié, said "I see a very beautiful person coming to seek me, and at the same time who fills me with consolation." A third time this beautiful being appeared to him, told him her name was Mary, and that he would soon be in heaven. Then, having, under the form of a testament, recommended his affairs to the great Anié, and exhorted those around him, always to esteem the faith, and live good Christians, he died at the age of twenty years, December 29, 1675. (Mss. of Father Chauchetière, p. 30.)

The little flock of Christians of the Prairie increased so rapidly that from 1672 this Mission counted two hundred neophytes, and its light begun to shine forth. In their journeyings, the savages often had occasion to visit it. During the autumn of 1675 alone, one counted more than eight hundred visitors, who had sojourned there. That hospitality, which the savage regards as a sacred duty, became even more so for the neophytes, who there found an opportunity of instructing infidels in our faith, and the means of detaining some of them amongst them. All the provisions they had amassed during the two previous years were exhausted, for the savage utterly forgets his own interest, when a guest is to be received. They act without any hope of payment, and often the stranger whom they have lodged and fed, departs without a word of thanks, as they themselves do in their turn.

Such were the first Christians, and the happy commencement of this Mission, which, in the beginning, occupied the southern portion of the Prairie. The place still bears the name of *la Borgnesse*, thus called because of the cabin of a poor blind Indian woman. It was in the little wooden chapel, constructed for the French settlers in the missionaries' own house, that the savages heard Mass, and it was in order to supply for its insufficiency, as well as to obviate the inconvenience of a mixture of French and savages, that a second service was celebrated for the latter.

It was soon evident that the spot chosen for the Mission was little favorable for the savages, not only by reason of its proximity to the French, but because of the too great dampness of the soil, which rendered it unfavorable for the cultivation of Indian corn, their only resource. It was, however, important for the cause of religion, not to allow the savages to withdraw. The interest of the whole colony demanded it also. In case of hostilities, always to be feared from the Iroquois, this Mission, situated at the actual limits of the Colony, might serve as a barrier, and hold them at a distance.

The Intendant, Duchesne, understood these grave reasons, and permitted the Christian Iroquois to establish their village on a neighboring ground, that had not, as yet, been conceded. It was on the same shore of the river, but a league higher up, and precisely at the foot of the Saut St. Louis. The little river *du Portage*, which, at this place empties its waters into the St. Lawrence, forms at its mouth a peninsula easily fortified, and most advantageous for a village. The removal took place in 1676, and the Mission took the name of St. Francis Xavier du Saut St. Louis (1).

A wooden fort was there constructed, defended by four bastions (bulwarks), to enclose the church, and the house of the missionaries, and, in case of attack, to serve as place of retreat from the Iroquois. In the meantime, all the people contended in zeal to erect and embellish the house of the Prairie. The brave Christian, Francis Xavier Tonsohoten, desired to have the consolation of donating the ground on which it was built.

Begun by fervent Christians, this church soon offered the

---

(1) Here are the changes of location which this Mission underwent.

About fifteen years after the translation of 1676, it was carried a little further, to a place called *Chez Catho*. In 1696, it was planted opposite the Rapids of the Saut St. Louis, on the banks of the river *Susanne*. This place, still named "le Vieux Saut (the Old Fall), still bears traces of the constructions of that epoch. Charlevoix wrote that the Mission of the Saut was at the latter place, while he was professor at the College of Quebec, 1705–1708.

The last translation, to the spot where it may be seen to-day, took place in 1716. (Letter of Father Lafitan.) The village took the name of Caughmerouaga or Kahnasake (Saut or Rapid). The king had given to the Christian savages, a vast territory covered with wood, on this coast. It was about two leagues in length and four in depth.

In his second voyage to Canada, Father Charlevoix stopped at this Mission, and dated from it one of his letters.

most edifying spectacle. Not content with fulfilling the Commandments of God, several neophytes found happiness in following the way of Evangelical counsel. Many cabins were real schools of virtue and sanctity. "Among our neophytes," wrote a missionary of this village in 1678, "there are perfect Christians. They know how to make war against their bad habits, and to quell their passions by study and reflection. Their purity of conscience is admirable, their communions frequent. One sees here examples of virtue, capable of humiliating the best Christians among the French. *Vere non inveni tantem fidem in Israel.* Verily I have not found so much faith in Israel."

The Captain of the Mohawks of the Saut, named Touatescon, gave a beautiful example of forgiveness of injury. One of the Huron Captains of the Saut, in a voyage to Montreal, had spoken against him, and even against the Mission. His words were reported. They were sufficient to cause angry dissension, and, above all, to cause great scandal. The missionary resolved to prevent it. At the first meeting he spoke to the Christians on the pardon of injuries, its importance for the glory of God, and the good of souls. His words bore fruit; our Captain not only smothered all resentment, but he also prepared a solemn feast to which he invited his detractor, and gave him the place of honor. Such were the victories that these generous souls gained over themselves.

The peace, order, and joy that reigned in this happy sojourn, made a profound impression on the stranger savages who passed by. The sight of it alone was sufficient to induce some to settle here, or, at least, to become the panegyrists of The Prière (The Prayer). One cause for untiring admiration, was the perfect harmony that reigned among these savages, drawn together from all directions, although the Iroquois element predominated. There were, in fact, at this Mission, Iroquois, Hurons, savages of Neutral Nations, Eries, etc., without being in any way prejudicial to the action of the Gospel through this mixture of nationalities.

Admirable economy of the Church of God, which does not distinguish between the Greek and the Roman, the Jew and the Gentile, but which embraces all men, without distinction of origin, and leads them happily to the same end, as one sees mingle and lost in the bosom of the same ocean, the waters of rivers flowing in such different directions and from such various countries.

The Captains of the villages, chosen according to custom, to watch over the public interests, admirably seconded the missionaries, who confided in them, for the execution of those wise rules, which they had in concert established.

In this wise subjection, there was to be seen neither superstitious interpretation of dreams, nor gambling, dangerous to morals. The instability of marriage and drunkenness, ordinarily a source of such great disorders amongst the savages, were severely banished. The stranger desirous of settling at this Mission, was first obliged to pledge himself to follow its rules, and to abandon all practices contrary to them.

More than once exemplary chastisement gave its sanction to this wise legislation, and savages addicted to evil habits, and drunkenness, were heard to declare loudly, in the Iroquois country, "that they would not go to the Saut Mission, as they would not there be free to do as they liked."

(*To be continued.*)

Contributions to the Shrine.

G. L. D., Philadelphia $5 00
M. C. 1 00
M. M. 1 00
K. C.   25
A Friend, Chelsea, Mich 1 00
M. L. S. H., Buffalo, N. Y. . . 5 00
J. J. W., Harris Lot, Md. . . . 1 50
J. M. J. B., Flushing, N. Y. . . 40
From ten contributors, per A. M.
 R., Providence, R. I. 1 00
Miss M. C. K., Philadelphia . . 1 00
Miss O'N., Philadelphia 1 00
Miss McC., Philadelphia 1 00
A J. S., New York, in thanksgiving 5 00
A. H., Boston, Mass., per B. L.   50
M. E. C., Boston, Mass., per B. L. 50

M. McA., Augusta, Ga. $1 00
J. J. P., Mexico 2 30

FOR THE CROWN.

M. C., Somerville, Mass. . . 5 00
Mr. D., New York, two gold cuff buttons.
Anon, Philadelphia, a gold medal.
K. L. S., Boston, Mass., five gold rings, six mosaic earrings, two mosaic brooches, four gold earrings and one silver thimble.
E. A. H., Schenectady, N. Y., gold chain and locket, one badge, two breast pins, six pairs of earrings, two studs, one pencil and a silver thimble and two gold rings.

THE SHRINE.

The early approach of the winter season and the heavy snow storms along the Mohawk valley, prevented the workmen from completing their labors at Auriesville, and some of the improvements in the Ravine cannot be made until spring. The important change in the roadway to the Ravine was successfully made, and there was time to save the bank under the grotto from the erosion threatened by the force of the stream in its new course.

January the sixth has been set as the day for handing over to the goldsmiths all the gold and precious stones contributed for the crowns that are to adorn the statues of our Lady and her Divine Son, representing them in the group known as the Pietà. This day, the feast of the Epiphany, has been chosen, because it is the day when the Kings of the East laid their crowns with other gifts at the feet of the King of Kings.

There is but one announcement to make in this issue, and it is that, to meet the repeated request of our readers, we shall continue the series of articles on the early missions in Canada, which was begun last year from Rochemonteix's history of "The Jesuits and New France," but interrupted for a time to make room for the Life of Catherine Tegakwitha, which we have been publishing the past five months. In February we shall have the story of the Missions in Arcadia, and we are sure that our readers will be glad to have in English this first complete account of that happy but unfortunate mission. It is fashionable nowadays to weave into romances the wonderful incidents narrated in the *Relations*, but with all the interest of the stories thus invented, the simple truth of the history is still stranger than the fiction.

As an instance of strange things that appear in the romances just referred to, we quote the following from the *Providence Visitor*, a Catholic weekly well worth reading:

"There is an odd paragraph in the Christmas number of Harper's, page 87. We invite attention to it as a sample of the absurd things outsiders say when they undertake to write of Catholic ceremonials. And the full page picture illustrative of the manger is in strict keeping with demands of the text:

"'These matters being settled we were made spectators to surely the strangest sight my eyes had ever looked upon. Andre brought forth a small folding table, and the priest, still in his rusty soutane, recited the holy office of the mass to the kneeling savages under the shade of the great pines, and only the ripple of the water broke the pauses in the service. To my astonishment, the Indians recited the *Venite* but this was the extent of their knowledge, apart from the *Pater-Noster*, the *Confiteor*, and some of the responses.'

"What an astonishing performance this is. There is no 'holy office of the mass' as far as we are aware. If it means that the priest said mass be it known that no priest may say mass without the sacred vestments. If it means that he reads the mass prayers, well and good, only what is the '*Venite*?' But the allusion to the 'small folding table' which was brought out, reminds us of the fact that the black robes of the Indian missions were always provided with conveniences for saying mass and said it as often as they could. The passage deserves to go on record as a choice example in its line."

IF IT BE THE WILL OF GOD!

BY L. W. REILLY.

TWO members of the St. Vincent de Paul Society were making a round of visits to some of its clients in a squalid tenement district of a large city. One of them was a veteran worker for the Conference to which he belonged; the other was a novice in the field of personal charity. They walked rapidly through the dingy streets, noisome with foul gutters and festering garbage boxes; they ascended gingerly the narrow stairways in the malodorous houses, taking care not to touch the grimy handrails of the balustrades; they felt oppressed by the suffocating air in the crowded apartments, and they took a deep breath when they emerged from every residence in which they had to make a call.

In one building, five stories in height, in which the visitors found four families on every floor, they had six households on their list of relief. As they came out of one of the rear flats at the top of the dwelling, in which they had succored a family, consisting of a paralyzed father, a cancer-stricken wife and two small children, they passed by the door of the opposite tenement, which happened to be opened. Even at a glance they saw a clean room, the floor of which was covered with an ingrain carpet, at the two windows of which hung scrim curtains and which contained a set of furniture that looked as if it had seen better days. A woman nearly sixty, dressed in blue-dotted calico, with a little three-cornered wine-colored shawl about her shoulders, sat in a rocker near the mantelpiece knitting a stocking. As the gentlemen passed down the reeking hallway, the younger motioned over his shoulder, and in a low tone remarked :

"That looks like an oasis of neatness in a desert of dirt!"

"Yes," responded the other, "and there's a pathetic story in the woman's life that I'll tell you when we get down stairs."

This is the story.

Eleven years ago there were few pleasanter homes among plain people than the Breslins'. They lived far up town in a cosy dwelling which they intended to buy with the help of a building and loan association in which they had several shares. The father was a salesman. One of the three sons was a bookkeeper in a factory, the second was a commercial "drummer," and the third, named Francis, was at college. One of the two daughters was a school teacher, while the other one staid at home to help with the housework.

Of all her children, the mother loved most the lad at college. "He looks so like his Uncle James," she would say. This Uncle James had been Mrs. Breslin's favorite brother, had studied for the priesthood, and had died a few weeks before his ordination.

Nothing would do the mother but that Francis must take up his uncle's career. She set her heart on it. Under her abiding influence, the impulsive youth had been persuaded to harbor the notion of devoting himself to the service of the altar. Now in his twentieth year, he was in the graduating class at college and he expected to enter the diocesan seminary in the following September.

When all the Breslin plans were prosperous and all their ways were peace, Francis fell critically ill. The family doctor, recognizing the gravity of the case, brought in a consulting physician. Despite all their lore and all their drugs, the patient rapidly grew worse.

The mother was seized with a nervous chill when her darling took to his bed. She got wan and hollow-eyed when his illness increased. She was almost desperate when the two medical men gave her the disquieting assurance, "while there's life there's hope." She had the orphans in the asylum begin a novena for his recovery; she sent an entreaty to the Sisters at the academy where her Anna had made her studies, to pray for him at the devotions of the community; and she distributed alms in order to win the favor of heaven for her intention.

All this happened in a day or two. Then, as it was evident, against the hope of the mother, that the youth was in danger of death, word of his condition was hurried to the parish priest. Father D—— came within half an hour. After hearing the confession of Francis, who was then quite rational, administering the Viaticum, and giving him Extreme Unction, the priest, cheering him with a few words of encouragement, left him in the care of his father, and accompanied mother and daughter to their sitting-room to offer them his sympathy. He spoke from his heart, but the woman would not be comforted.

"We must hope for the best," went on the priest, "but if his time has come, well, he's a good boy and he'll die a good death."

At this the mother burst into a passion of grief and cried out: "Don't speak of him dying, Father; he musn't die; O, I don't want him to die. God would have forgotten to be merciful if He were to take my Francis from me!"

"Hush, hush, my good woman," replied the priest, "you musn't talk that way. Where is your Christian training? Where's your resignation to the will of God? Francis must die some time, and if the Lord wants him now, now is the best time for him to die."

"O not now, Father, not now, not now!" sobbed the mother, while the daughter Margaret, sitting over by the window, hid her face in her apron, and cried convulsively.

The priest pulled out his watch and made a pretense of looking at the time in order to gain a moment in which to ask Divine inspiration for his next words. Then he said slowly and impressively:

"It might be better for Francis to go now when he is ready than to go later when he will have more to answer for and possibly be unprepared. Still we must leave the decision to Almighty God. He knows what is best. To His judgment we should submit. So, Mrs. Breslin, like the pious woman that you are, give up your youngest son, if necessary, as the Blessed Virgin gave up her only Son. No doubt, as she stood under His cross on Calvary, although it almost broke her heart to see Him die, she still kept saying in her heart, 'Thy will be done! Thy will be done!' to give her strength to be resigned."

The mother had quieted down by this. The example of our Blessed Lady in her agony, had struck home. But the thought of her boy lying pallid in his bed and the idea of him laid out stiff and cold in death, quickly obliterated that impression and darkened her soul again with grief.

"Please take this offering, Father," she said, handing the priest an envelope, "and say a Mass that he may get well."

"I will," he replied, "provided you add—'if it be the will of God.'"

"O, don't ask me to do that, Father," she wailed, bursting out again into a storm of tears and inarticulate cries, "my poor heart cannot stand it. I cannot bear to see my dear boy die in the bloom of his youth. I can't, I can't, I can't!"

Reluctant to add to the woman's misery by a refusal, the priest hesitated an instant, and then said: "I'll not insist on your uttering those words with your lips, but you know without my telling you that in your heart you are bound to mean them; and I will celebrate the Mass only on condition that you try to feel them and that you let me say them for you at the foot of the altar."

"Say it, Father," she whispered faintly, weak from her emotion.

The priest took this answer as, at least apparently, a half consent to his condition, and, unwilling to press her afflicted spirit then for a more explicit act of submission, he arose, bade her and Margaret good-bye, promising to come again the next day, and departed.

That same afternoon the doctors called in a specialist. After a long consultation the family physician informed the father that Francis would likely live out the night, but that he would certainly expire before noon the next day.

Mrs. Breslin was made frantic by the sad announcement. She began to walk from room to room and back again in pitiful bewilderment, wringing her hands and moaning to herself. All night long she sat by the bed of the lad, holding his hand in hers, except when she gave him his medicine. She could not be persuaded to try to get some sleep. The others took turns in watching and resting—all but Edward, the commercial traveller, who had been in the far West on a business trip, and who was now hurrying home in obedience to a telegram from his brother William. Towards five o'clock the mother was dozing in her chair, overcome with the long strain as well as drowsiness, when she awoke with a start, to find Francis seemingly at the point of death. She hastily called to Margaret, who was in the kitchen preparing to get breakfast, and the latter aroused the other members of the family. They gathered around the bedside, did what they could for the patient, and then knelt down to recite the prayers for the dying. While the father was hunting for them in the prayer book, Margaret whispered to her mother:

"Father D—— will be beginning Mass now."

The woman only nodded her head in hopeless wretchedness.

"Do try, Mother, to say what he told you."

With one fond, lingering look of affection at the pale face on the pillow, she shook her head. "I can't," she said, half aloud. "I can't give my consent to his death."

Anna had lighted a blessed candle, which the mother now

held within the cold clasp of Francis. The father commenced the prayers for the dying, but before he had gone far his voice broke, and he had to hand over the book to William. Before the end was reached, the invalid seemed to collapse utterly, and they thought he was dead. At this the mother emitted a shriek of anguish and fell over in a faint. Her swoon caused considerable confusion, and she was carried into the next apartment. As soon as she revived she made her way back, tottering, to the bedside of Francis to kiss his beloved corpse.

But the youth was not dead. There was still some warmth in him, and his breathing, even if low and irregular, was yet easy. William rushed out for the doctor, while the others set about applying restoratives. Before the physician arrived Francis was gently sleeping.

"Perhaps Father D——'s Mass brought him back to us, Mother," said Margaret; "and maybe he'll get well."

"May God grant it!" was the fervent response.

Francis recovered. His return to health was not made in a day, but by steady stages he got back a measure of strength. That recuperation took several months. Then, as the heated term was approaching, the doctor ordered him to be sent as soon as he could bear the fatigue of the journey, to a popular resort on the Atlantic coast.

In the invigorating air from the ocean the young man speedily became as robust as ever. In a fortnight after his arrival he went boating and bathing, driving and bicycle riding. He sent home glowing reports of his enjoyment and marvellous tales of the rapacity of his appetite. In one of these letters he wrote: "The hotel man isn't going to make anything off this boarder."

The other members of the family who were at work, sacrificed the cost of a vacation for themselves to keep him at the seashore and to let him enjoy every luxury of recreation.

Shortly after the middle of August, Francis unexpectedly came home. While his folks were still making a great to-do over him, rejoicing in his erect carriage, his bronzed cheeks, and his clear eyes, he sheepishly announced that he was engaged to be married, that his sweetheart was a non-Catholic girl, the only child of a widower, whom he had met at the seaside resort, and that they intended to wed in the following month. Imagine the amazement of the family! Think of their indignation! Mrs. Breslin was the one most shocked. Her dream of her son a priest, was shattered. Yet that disappointment, for he had no vocation, could have been cheerfully endured, particularly in the joy of his convalescence. But for him to make such a wantonly selfish return for all their love, to forsake them for a stranger, and to marry out of the Church—all this baseness smote her to the quick and made her hot with anger. She kept her pain and her indignation pretty well to herself, although she could not resist the fury of her first inclination to give Francis a piece of her mind. In the course of her deliverance she inquired:

"On what do you expect to support a wife?"

"Her father has a dairy in Philadelphia and he'll employ me to go live on his place in New Jersey and superintend the care of the stock and the shipment of the milk."

"Nice work for a college graduate!" she sneered.

When Father D—— was informed by Mrs. Breslin of the projected marriage and of the vain, wilful, extravagant, and worldly character of the young woman with whose pretty face and jaunty manners Francis had become infatuated, the gray-haired pastor shook his head sadly and said:

"Forgive me for being frank, Mrs. Breslin, but the truth is that I'd sooner see him happily dead than a party to such a mixed marriage."

Near the close of September, the month in which Francis was to have entered the seminary, he rushed into wedlock instead and quit the home of his parents to live with his bride on her father's farm.

Time went on for the Breslins as well as for the rest of the world. It brought them more than a fair share of reverses. On the very first anniversary of Francis's recovery, the father lost his employment; a few weeks later he was carried off by pneumonia. Seven months after that bereavement, William was killed by the explosion of a boiler in the factory where he worked. Two years or so further on, Anna fell into consumption and after lingering for many weary months she passed away. In the third year following her demise, Edward was fatally injured in a railroad collision and expired after four months of suffering in a hospital in Chicago. Last of all, Margaret, who had clung to her mother during all these troubles and who then had married well, yielded to the pangs of childbirth some ten months later. In the course of nine years, misfortune followed misfortune, until only the mother was left and she was reduced from a condition of comfort to a state of destitution.

The savings of the family had all to be taken from the bank to meet the expenses of repeated sickness and death, and, as less and less income came in, no money could be put back in their place.

During all these years of affliction, Francis was practically estranged from the family. What his hasty marriage had begun, his wife shortly completed—she turned against his kindred. Frivolous and ill-bred, she did not feel at ease among them from the start and she hated them for objecting to his marriage to her. She used every pretext to prejudice him against them. She succeeded so well that after the first year or so, there was no visiting done between the two families and only at Christmas was there a brief letter from Francis to his mother. To this sorely tried woman, too, there came rumors that her son was drifting away from the Faith—his home was remote from a church and his wife put every possible obstacle she could in the way of his practising his religion. More than once, in the bitterness of her soul, Mrs. Breslin exclaimed:

"Would that I had said, 'If it be the will of God!'"

Eventually tribulation entered the home of Francis also. His wife's father was drowned at Atlantic City. Then it transpired that the farm and the dairy were mortgaged, through bad management, almost up to their full value. The creditors seized the property, sold it off at auction, took the proceeds, and left the daughter without any inheritance.

Next Francis, who had to take the first job that he could get after being evicted from the farm, for he had by this a family of seven to support, and had no funds accumulated, went out to work for a railroad as brakeman on a freight train, and soon afterwards he slipped on an ice-covered car that was speeding along a down grade, lost his footing, rolled off and broke his neck.

His sudden and unprovided-for death seemed the culmination of Mrs. Breslin's sorrows. In her affliction she cried out:

"O, would that he had died when he was prepared! Woe is me, woe is me! How wicked I was to want to keep him even if against the will of God!"

The wife of Francis, after a short struggle to support her children, put the eldest two in a non-Catholic asylum, brought herself and the three others to Mrs. Breslin's door, then, alas, in a far humbler locality than of yore, invited herself to stay, then settled down to live upon her mother-in-law. But the income made by an unfashionable dressmaker was not sufficient to procure luxuries for five persons, and the home was dull that was presided over by a grief-stricken woman beset with melancholy memories. The young widow, after much fretting and many complaints, took all her things, abandoned her three little ones, and disappeared.

"In the hope of preserving them to the Faith and of saving their souls," concluded the St. Vincent de Paul man, "Mrs. Breslin from that day to this has striven to earn bread for those forsaken children. She has turned her hand to every sort of work that she could get to do for them. She has moved from house to house in a descending scale of respectability in order to keep them with her. She has become attached to them, especially to the little Francis, who has his father's eyes as well as his name. She cannot bear to put them into an orphanage, for one reason, lest she should shirk a duty imposed upon her by Providence. She has accepted her cares as a penance and has rather cherished them than sought to evade them. She has learned by frequent practice to say easily, 'Thy will be done!' That act of submission has indeed been a great comfort to her in her years of distress and expiation. It has taken the sting out of them. It has given her ground for the expectation not only of pardon but also of reward, for the hope that the Father who sees her penitential patience, will yet wipe away the tears from her eyes and take her to His own. She has been loth to ask assistance from us in the past, but now that rheumatism is crippling her hands and making remunerative labor nigh impossible, that last humiliation will shortly have to be endured by her strong spirit. Yet even so, she will make the sacrifice of parting with her grandchildren and eating the bread of charity, if it be the will of God!"

There were tears in the eyes of the younger man as the story was brought to an end.

"I am humbled and edified," he said, "by the virtues of the poor. In the lowliest places the sweetest flowers bloom. If ever I am again tempted to revolt against the Almighty or to murmur at His dispensations, I shall certainly recall the story of Mrs. Breslin, and taking fresh courage from her beautiful example, I shall easily exclaim: 'Thy will my God, be done!'"

A TRIBUTE TO SAINT FRANCIS DE SALES.

Hail Switzerland!
Thou'rt fair, thou'rt free, thou art a noble land,
   And many a heart beats loyally for thee.
We love thy Alps, snow-capped and veiled in mist,
   That reach up in their freedom to the skies;
That wrap their sides in icy coat of mail,
   And stand like armèd guards. We love thy rocks,
Thy cataracts by snowy fountains fed;
   Thy joyous bounding streams of glaciers born:
Thy lakes that gleam; thy silent solemn heights,
   That bear no trace of desecrating man;
Thy crystal spires; thy glittering icy domes,
   Where gale and avalanche with mighty voice,

Their great Creator praise ; thy torrents wild,
   Thy sweet delicious pastures, and thy skies,
That ever low and friendly seem to bend,
   Thy eagles—Freedom's types—that sail thy air ;
Thy peopled vales, thy feeding flocks, thy snows,
   Thy very storms, we hail, we love them all !
No land like thee so happily doth link,
   Its scenes of awe with those of tender grace,
Doth like thee mingle so familiarly,
   Sublimity with charming loveliness.
Above thy dreadful rock-piled chasm-mouths,
   The wild goat and the timid chamois leap ;
The wind that howls across thy barren steeps,
   Is soft and pleasant music in thy vales ;
Thy peaks that reach up to the thunder's home,
   And fling its bolts reverberating down,
Repeat as well the shepherd's cheery song,
   The boat-man's call, or bleating of the flocks.
The pilgrim resting on his Alpine-stock,
   Awed by the thought of God's omnipotence,
As swift and direful down its glistening track,
   As if in rage, the avalanche is hurled,
Plucks at his feet a tender flower and feels,
   God's all-upholding providence.

                              Dear land !
Methinks some charm, some secret influence,
   Doth in thy still and cloistered vales abound,
Some hidden power that makes thy children all,
   Grow like thy face as to their mother's own !
Is't with thy winds that wander wild and free
   They from their birth drink Freedom's spirit in ?
Thy lakes serene, is't from their waters clear
   They drink the draught of purity and peace ?
Is't from thy heights, uplifting thought and soul,
   Their spirits like thy eagles nobly rise ?
O fair and free ! O lovely Switzerland !
   Where blended awe and beauty sweetly dwell,

How like to thee was one who called thee "home,"
    Who loved thy scenes; who, when thy sheltered flock
Didst leave its folds, didst wander far away,
    Searched for it long, and led it gently back,
Geneva's gentle Bishop!

                                How serene,
And level spreads Geneva's cradled lake!
    How bright its wave, how sunny is its strand!
How do the sweet, blue, bending skies above
    Lie mirrored in its bosom! Ah, as still,
As bright, as calm, as peaceful was his soul.
    A beauty more enduring than the sky's,
The beauty of God's holiness was there,
    Of God's eternal sunshine; and o'er thee,
O'er thee, his darkened, desolated land,
    He cast a ray refulgent and serene
That e'er will be thy glory.

                              Grand and fair
Within his soul were mountain heights of joy
    Snow-covered like thine own, that reached the skies,
And depths of love and tenderness as deep
    As are thy mountain-chasms. Noble, true,
Strong as thy streams, unsullied as thy snows,
    High as thy heights, and humble as thy depths,
As lofty as thy eagles' dizzy flight,
    As full of sweet and soothing harmonies
As are the winds that sigh within the vale
    Of lovely Chamouni; so was his life,
Geneva's gentle saint!

ST. MARY'S OF THE WOODS.

FROM THE MISSIONS.

CONNAWOODY, NEAR LALGUDI, TRUHY DT,
MADRAS PRESIDENCY, INDIA.

MY DEAR REV. FATHER:

No words are eloquent enough to express the pleasure I feel in reading the *Messenger*, and with what avidity I wait for the next number month after month. The plain truth, it is with unabated pleasure and with increasing interest, I put every number aside very carefully till I shall find for them a conspicuous place in a good library.

It may not be pleasant for you to hear, nor for the Sacred Heart of Jesus to see, that the Methodists as you call them there in your distant country, Wesleyans as they call themselves here, cause a good deal of trouble amongst our easy-going Catholic population—as if they have not millions and hundreds of millions of pagans to whom to preach their heresies. They take great pleasure in converting, as they say, but perverting, I must say, with money, of course, some of our ignorant poor Catholics, who are ready to sell their immortal souls for Mammon. It is worse than the bubonic plague now raging in some parts of India, and the novelty is that when they admit our Catholics into their sect, they pour water upon them, and thus rebaptize them.

Not one Hindoo, nor one pagan, nor one Turk, have they made their followers, but the refuse of the Catholic population they receive with open arms, and help with money. I hope you will excuse me, my dear Rev. Father, if you find my letter tedious.

Recommending myself to your prayers.

I beg to remain, my dear Rev. Father,
Your most obedient servant in Christ,
M. ARDKIANADER.

CALCUTTA, November 15, 1898.

DEAR REV. FATHER:

Calcutta, or "the City of Palaces," is, like every great capital of a large Empire, a perfect mixture of races and nationalities. The predominant part of the population is composed of Hindoos. After them follow the Mussulmans. There are a goodly number of Chinamen, but those I wanted to speak about in a special manner are the Christians, whom it would be difficult to count indeed, and who are far outnumbered by the disciples of Khrishna and the followers of Mohammed. If we take Christians of every denomination together we might perhaps venture to say that they are in the proportion of one to twenty Mussulmans, and one to sixty Hindoos. What may interest your readers more is to know that Catholics are the lesser part of the Christians. Now let us see what are the different elements that compose our Catholic community. Among them we count comparatively few pure Europeans; most of them are the offspring of mixed races, namely of Europeans and inhabitants of the country, whose children have come to form a race quite distinct from any thing that surrounds them. Among them is the bulk of our Catholics and as a rule the best and staunchest Christians are found in their midst. It is among them especially lies the ministry of the Catholic priest. There are also some converts from Hindooism, especially; fewer from Mohammedanism. The greater number of these last are not from Calcutta itself but come from the surrounding missions.

It may prove useful to mention the reason of the emigration of these Christians from their native villages into Calcutta. As a rule all the cooks employed in Christian families, are Catholics and come from Dacca. The term "Dacca cook" is proverbial. It is unnecessary to add that being separated from wife and children, those poor Christians are far from leading a very exemplary life. To endeavor to keep them in their native place would be nearly the same as to try to keep people in America from going to Klondyke. It would be better to get them to bring their families and possessions to the city, and some do this. But too often the priest is told that life is too expensive in Calcutta. Leaving aside this drawback, which is a very great one indeed, these people are religiously inclined and the priest has no difficulty in bringing them together and getting them to frequent the sacraments. Another class of natives are those that come from Chittayong. Most of them are on board the steamers and other vessels as servants, or cooks, or firemen, and it is interesting to hear them relate the impressions produced on them by the different parts of the world they have been visiting in their journeys. They are absent sometimes for a whole year or fourteen months, but the first thing they do before beginning their tour of the world, or when they come back from it, is to make their confession and have their candles lit in honor of the Blessed Virgin or some saint. There is another part of the mission that furnishes especially the innumerable *ayahs* or nurses for the English speaking families, that is Kh mayore. Most of the Catholics there were brought over from M. hammedanism, and Mussulman nurses are very much appreciated. It is clear that these women run great risks in a town like Calcutta, where corruption is rampant, but it is the hope of earning some money and providing for their families at home that prompts them to come to Calcutta. A great many families have settled down in Calcutta with all they possess, and form the best portion of the Bengali portion of my parish. Yours sincerely, A. J. MAENE, S.J.

BELA KASARAGOD, S. CANARA, INDIA.

DEAR REV. FATHER :

As the general intention for this month is "Charity to the Poor," I think this is high time to come forward with my humble petition on behalf of my poor parish. I confidently hope persons of generous heart will not be wanting to respond to my request in honor of the Sacred Heart of our Lord.

This Church of Bela is one of the last in the diocese of Mangalore. Some five years before there was not even a decent building for the parishioners. It is due to the indefatigable labors of my predecessor that the present building (a substantial one) has been built. All the surrounding people, even pagans, have liberally subscribed for the construction of the building. Other well-to-do persons of the diocese have also contributed for it. Nevertheless the church is still incomplete, and many necessary articles for the decorations of the altar are required; a school for the parish is of absolute necessity. As the people are very poor, and with great difficulty manage to get their daily bread, it is beyond their power, to supply for the wants of their church. Since I do not expect to get any more help here, I am obliged to seek help abroad.

I remain, yours sincerely in Christ,

R. P. B. LUIS, Vicar of Bela, Kasaragod, India.

LETTER FROM THE CŒUR D'ALENE INDIANS TO THE DIRECTOR OF THE ASSOCIATION FOR THE PROPAGATION OF THE FAITH.

DE SMET MISSION, IDAHO, November 23, 1898.

GOOD BLACKGOWN, our Father in Maryland :

We have been told by our Father Joseph,* our spiritual guide

---

* Rev. Joseph Caruana, S.J., the present Superior of De Smet Mission.

here, that some wondered greatly at our generosity in contributing last May to the Propagation of the Faith as members of that Association. But the wonder would be if we had not done so. It is true, we are not rich, but who is so poor as not to be able to give sixty cents a year for such a great and charitable purpose? We did it with all our heart, even though some had to make sacrifices. We owe this little charity to the Sacred Heart of Jesus, who in His mercy sent us, fifty-six years ago, His own ministers to instruct us, His children, through baptism, given to us by our fathers, supported by the Propagation of the Faith, of which we are now, though unworthy, members. Is it not our strict duty to contribute the little we did and will do? Is it not, moreover, the duty of every Christian to help the propagation of our Christian Faith? We wondered when we heard that we did contribute more than many other white congregations. Yes, we see many white people squandering money for their comfort, and sometimes also in foolish things; and then they have no means, they say, to support the ministers of God in propagating His Faith, to which we owe everything. This is what people should wonder at, not for showing our gratitude to the Merciful Heart of our Lord Jesus Christ, to which both this Mission and Indian tribe are consecrated.

Praying and hoping that God will give light to those blind Catholics, that they may be more grateful to God and His Church on earth, we beg of you to ask our Holy Father, Pope Leo XIII., to bless his Indian children at De Smet.

Head Chief,
SETTISE.

In behalf of all the Cœur d'Alene Indians, and all the other Indians on this De Smet Reservation.

MISSION NOTES.

Out of twenty-one rebels of the Matabele tribe lately executed at Bulawayo, Africa, all but two embraced Christianity and were baptized before their death. Many of the condemned Mashonas received the same grace, among them, Kabuki, their leader and famous witch-doctor.

Among the recently deceased missionary bishops are the Right Reverend Valentin Garnier, S.J., Vicar Apostolic of Kiang-Nan, China; Monsignor Michael Castelli, Bishop of Tinos in Greece, remarkable for his vast erudition and valuable works in the cause of science and religion, and Monsignor Lépierre of the Society of Foreign Missions, Vicar Apostolic of Western Cochin, China.

The island of Ceylon numbers 275,000 Catholics out of a total population of 3,200,000 souls. Two new bishops have lately been appointed to that distant field. Monsignor Coudert has has been made Coadjutor to his Lordship, Mgr. Melizan, Archbishop of Columbo, with the right of succession, and the Right Reverend Charles Lavigne, S.J., formerly Vicar Apostolic of Kottayam in India, has been appointed Bishop of Trincomalee.

A dispatch from China announces the death of Sister Perboyre, the youngest and sole surviving member of the family of the Blessed Martyr of that name. She became a Sister of Charity when eighteen years old, and lived to the age of eighty-three, fifty-five of which she spent in China. Another sister of the Martyr, who was likewise a Sister of Charity, died a few years ago at Naples, where she had spent the greater part of her life. She had the consolation of being present at the solemn beatification of Blessed Perboyre, on the tenth of November, 1889, together with her youngest brother, who was also a missionary and died at Paris in 1896. Blessed Perboyre was strangled to death at Ou-tchang-fou, the chief city of the province of Houpe, on the eleventh of September, 1840, after enduring with heroic constancy, for more than a year, most frightful tortures for the faith he had preached.

MASSACRE OF A MISSIONARY IN THE UBANGHI DISTRICT, CENTRAL AFRICA.

A letter from Monsignor Augouard, Vicar Apostolic of Ubanghi, announces the recent massacre of one of his missionaries, Brother Severin, of the Congregation of the Holy Spirit. The Brother was killed by the ferocious Bondjos as he stepped into the boat on which he was to set out from the Holy Family Station. His body, torn by four horrible wounds, was fortunately recovered and brought to the Mission for burial. A Christian boy, who accompanied the missionary, was killed with him, and was afterward eaten by the murderers, who are among the fiercest cannibals of Africa. Father Gourdy, who set out on a journey by land at the same time as Brother Severin, was likewise attacked by the savages, and was only saved from death by the special protection of heaven. Four of his men were severely wounded.

In his last letter written to one of his religious brethren, Brother Severin gives the following account of the difficulties and dangers of his missionary life. "Our Bondjos are still very troublesome. One of our children has just been killed, cut to pieces and eaten for having ventured a few steps away from the Mission. Another captured in like manner, was fortunate enough to make his escape. Several times these ferocious savages have attacked our children who were working quietly in the garden, guarded by me and armed Senegalese soldiers. They steal from us everything they can lay their hands on, and have made frequent attempts to break into my room, and to set fire to the Mission buildings. Day and night we must be on the watch against their attacks. Ever since the death of Fathers Leclercq and Goblet a year ago, I have lived in this wild region alone with Father Sollaz amid sufferings and annoyances of every kind. But since God wants me to be here, I am happy to do His holy will. Did He not die also for these poor savage Bondjos? If the work of their salvation is more laborious, the reward will be the greater. Pray with me for their converson and . . . . farewell!"

MISSIONS IN CHINA.

In spite of persecution and obstacles of every kind, the true faith is making admirable progress in China. The statistics of the two missions of Kiangnan and South Eastern Tcheu-li, entrusted to the Society of Jesus, have been published, giving the state of these missions on July 1, 1898. Last year we gave a brief account of the state of the same missions on July 1, 1897. Most consoling are the results obtained in one year.

The mission of Kiangnan has its headquarters at Shanghai. It is divided into sixteen sections comprising in all ninety-one districts. Each district is attended to by one missionary, and is composed of a certain number of Christian communities. Each section comprises several districts, and has at its head a superior who directs both missionaries and Christians. The whole mission forms a Vicariate Apostolic, but is at the present moment without a Vicar Apostolic, owing to the recent death of the venerable Bishop, Monsignor Garnier.

The number of the missionary priests in Kiangnan has during the past year increased from 149 to 156, the catechists of both sexes including school teachers from 1,065 to 1,230, the Christian communities from 661 to 725, and the Christians from 111,605 to 115,177, giving a net gain of 3,572 souls. The catechumens number 34,481. In the course of the year, 48,997 baptisms were administered, more than two-thirds of the whole number being administered to children of infidel parents. The Mission supports 390 schools for boys, and 449 schools for girls, numbering 11,262 and 5,309 scholars respectively. It directs moreover a large and a small seminary, several colleges for the higher education of youth, and a considerable number of hospitals, orphan asylums and dispensaries. The missionaries also direct a magnetic and meteorological observatory, a semi-weekly Chinese journal and a Messenger of the Sacred Heart in Chinese. The Apostleship of Prayer numbers 22,988 associates.

In the mission of the South-Eastern Tcheu-li similar progress has been made during the past year. The missionary priests number fifty-seven instead of fifty-three a year ago. The number of catechists of both sexes has risen from 627 to 688, 423 of these being also school teachers. The Christian communities have increased from 611 to 668, the Christian population from 45,508 to 47,086, a gain for the year of 1,578 souls. There are 637 churches and chapels in the mission, 12,980 children of infidel parents were baptized at the point of death, 1,342 confirmations and 648 extreme unctions were administered, and 314 marriages were blessed. There are 212 schools for boys and 189 schools for girls, frequented by 2,848 and 2,126 scholars respectively. The Apostleship of Prayer numbers 8,207 Associates.

Acknowledgment is made of the following contributions:

For the most Needy Mission.
M. C., St. Paul, Minn $2 30
J. B., National Military Home, Ind. 1 00
J. McC., Ardoch. N. D 3 00

For the Ursuline Nuns, Montana.
J. R. J., ... $1.00

For St. Anthony's Bread.
T. P. M., Rich Patch, Mo. . . . $1 00

THE PILGRIM
OF
OUR LADY OF MARTYRS

XV. YEAR.   FEBRUARY, 1899.   No. 2.

YOUR TEARS SHALL BE TURNED INTO JOY.

BY REV. ERNEST R. RYAN, S.J.

FLOW, flow, flow
   As a torrent of Spring, O Tears,
   For never again till the Judgment Day
My Saviour in flesh appears.

'Tis well for the guards in white
That their eyes are heavenly flame,
They see Him throned in the utmost height
Of the bright realm whence He came.

'Tis well they have hearing tuned
To the music of speech divine.
The Master's voice o'er-floods their lives
With the bliss that is gone from mine.

Flow, flow, flow
As a torrent of Spring, O Tears,
For flesh shall not see nor hear Him more,
Till the dawn of eternal years.

Oh! would 't were no fault to care
For the poor bruised corpse of shame.
Is it fault? Oh Love! I would all things dare
For one glance at thy shattered frame—

Copyright, 1898, by APOSTLESHIP OF PRAYER

Ah ! Gardener, sir, be kind,
Show me where my Lord they've laid—
Mary !—I knew Him not—How blind !
He is risen as He said.

Flow, flow, flow
For joy, as a flood, O Tears,
Our Love His temple of flesh reclaims,
And in endless life appears.

THE JESUITS AND NEW FRANCE

In the Seventeenth Century.

From the French of Rev. Camille de Rochemonteix, S.J.

BY K. A. HENNESSY.

IN Part First, Chapter Seventh, of the work entitled *L'Histoire de la Colonie française en Canada*, we read : "The Franciscans—convinced of the necessity of bringing up the savage children in order, by this means, to lead them to Christianity ; aware of the ill-will borne this work by the Company of Merchants who also opposed Catholicity and proved faithless to their engagements ; and fully conscious of the futility of the voyages they themselves had made to Court in the hope of finding a remedy for the sad state of affairs then existing—determined to resort to prayer, and thereby obtain a divine inspiration as to how they had best proceed. The result was that, feeling themselves unable to hold out unaided against the Company and being too indifferently protected by the Court to expect any support from it, they thought that they should summon to their assistance a community that would share with them the labor of the missions. . . . They had learned from experience that, in order to succeed among the savages, it was necessary to have wherewith to supply their wants ; and they concluded that since, as disciples of Saint Francis, their rule forbade them an income, they should invite to their missions a community not only capable of sustaining itself by its own revenues, but also of furnishing support for the Indian children who would be gathered into a seminary, and of assisting the new converts. They finally decided that, of all the religious orders in receipt of revenues, the Society of Jesus would, because of its zeal and power, be best equipped for the contemplated work, and therefore, the Franciscans resolved to appeal to the Jesuits."

The Abbé Faillon here tells us on the testimony of Father Le Clercq and of Brother Sagard, an eye-witness, the motives by which the Franciscans were actuated in calling upon the Jesuits. The latter were supposed to be very wealthy—a silly prejudice, a thousand times refuted!—and above all, more influential than they were in reality. But, be all that as it may, the Franciscans, once resolved upon their course of action, sent Father Irénée Piat and Brother Sagard to France in 1624, with orders to negotiate this important affair.

Father Coton was then in charge of the Paris province. He had been one of the promoters of the Acadian Mission and its staunch advocate at Court, and when, at length, the good cause was dropped, his thoughts frequently reverted to the shores of the St. Lawrence, where he would have been happy to select a missionary battle-field for the religious of his order. The Jesuits of the Paris province were, for their part, very anxious once more to set foot upon Canadian territory and see again a land of which they had had but a glimpse; they had read Father Biard's letters and *Relations*, and the perusal of these rousing recitals had filled their apostolic hearts with an ardent yearning for the mission.

Upon his return from the Isle of Monts-Déserts, Father Massé, had, as we know, been sent to the College of Henri IV. at La Flèche, and his duties brought him daily into contact with many young Jesuits who were there following courses in Philosophy and Theology. Among these students were Charles Lalemant, Nicolas Adam, Anne de Nouë, Paul Le Jeune, Barthélemy Vimont, Alexandre de Vieuxpont, Claude Quentin, Charles du Marché, François Ragueneau and Jaques Buteux.

Father Massé remained ten years at La Flèche and he often entertained his fellow religious with accounts of all that he had seen and done while on the Acadian Peninsula and at Saint-Sauveur, and talked at length to them of the great harvest of souls to be reaped from a mission in New France. These interviews stimulated their courage and ardor, and kindled within their hearts a desire for sacrifice and, if needs be, martyrdom.

Two of their number, Paul Le Jeune and Barthélemy Vimont, were sent, a few years after completing their course in Philosophy, to the Clermont College at Paris, there to follow theological instruction under Louis le Mairat, François Gandillon and the celebrated Denys Petau. It was the month of October, 1622, and Father Jean de la Bretesche was acting in the capacity of spiritual director at the College. Born at Braine in the diocese of Soissons in 1570, he entered the Society of Jesus at Verdun, May the 12th, 1592. Rector of the Jesuit novitate at Rouen, then Master of Novices at Paris and Instructor of the third year fathers, he was, later, at the opening of the Clermont College, appointed spiritual director of the young religious studying Philosophy and Theology.

Father de la Bretesche was neither brilliant nor an orator, but he was a man of God, who had, coupled with a knowledge of heavenly things, an admirable aptitude for directing valiant souls and gradually elevating them to the acquirement of exalted virtue and the achievement of the noblest acts of self-abnegation. Under his holy tutelage generous hearts were quickly attracted to the apostolic life; he loved and strove to make others love souls ransomed by the blood of Jesus Christ.

Both before and after this saintly man's entrance into the Society of Jesus, our Lord, who reveals Himself to whomsoever He will, had favored him with choicest graces, while he, ever ready to follow in the path indicated for him, walked dauntlessly on, constantly responsive to the faintest whisperings of divine inspiration. He seemed predestined to make known to his brethren the will and ways of God, and for twenty years was their guide and unwavering support.

However, his sanctity savored not of austerity. Distinguished, carefully and highly educated, he studied how to temper his natural sternness by sweetness and affability, and his virtue was cheerful and attractive. He fairly magnetized men of the world, and those religious who lived under his government or followed his advice yielded him with ready and implicit confidence their most profound secrets, and told him unreservedly of all their aspirations.

When the two theological students, Vimont and Le Jeune, reached Paris, they were quickly and irresistibly drawn toward this man of God. There is a mutual attraction of souls—as of bodies which are drawn together through the invisible power of a magnet—and it was under a superior influence that Le Jeune had taken his first steps in the religious life.

The two students related to Father de la Bretesche all that they had learned from Father Massé, and did not conceal from him their most ardent desire to one day go forth and labor in an unexplored quarter of New France and, if necessary, there meet death in God's holy cause. Le Jeune told his spiritual guide that a long time previously he had had a dream in which he suddenly found himself in the midst of the Iroquois, whose name he then heard for the first time. These savages were preparing to put him to death amid most cruel torments, when he called Father Vimont to his aid. The earnest young man's faith deduced from this dream the assurance that God called him to Canada, and he firmly hoped to reach there some day in company with Father Vimont.

Father de la Bretesche could not but encourage such noble aspirations, and yet his wisdom and delicacy of sentiment were quick to discover difficulties to which, in their pious ardor, his spiritual sons were blind. And here was the chief obstacle that presented itself to the tactful, far-seeing priest. The Jesuits could not be sent to Canada without the authorization or formal invitation of the Franciscans, and, therefore, how could they discreetly offer their services? Moreover, it hardly seemed probable that the Franciscans would seek the assistance of a religious order.

But these objections, though serious, dampened not the ardor of the two students, who said: "Undoubtedly the place is taken; the Franciscans have received a portion of the Lord's field to till, but that field is vast, and surely there is room for more than one religious order. Think of the tribes throughout the immense territory of New France whom the zeal of the Franciscans can never reach! What are ten missionaries when scattered among so many different peoples, especially when several of the laborers must remain at Quebec to minister to the wants of the colonists?"

They firmly believed that God would overcome all these obstacles and at some future day it would please His omnipotence to open to the Society of Jesus the portals of New France, already closed against them for ten years.

Father de la Bretesche advised the two young men to pray, and the three religious established amongst themselves a sort of league of prayer. Le Jeune and Vimont communicated to their companions their own burning zeal for the conversion of the Indians, and Father de la Bretesche recommended the good work to all his friends, endeavored to interest his penitents in its favor, and solicited many prayers for its success.

At that time he was directing the conscience of Henri de Lévis, Duc de Ventadour, a noble Christian gentleman and nephew of the Duc de Montmorency. De Ventadour, disgusted with the glamor and empty vanities of the world, and aspiring to a higher and calmer life far from the noise and distractions of the Court, had retired for a time and taken Holy Orders. The *Monumenta Historiæ Canadiensis* tell us that he had a great and generous heart entirely devoted to holy undertakings, and that he was capable not only of approving but of doing, according to the measure of his strength and resources, all that would contribute to the glory of God and the extension of His earthly kingdom. Therefore, when Father de la Bretesche spoke to him of the mission of Canada he seemed to realize immediately all that was grand and beautiful in the enterprise, and, admiring the work, associated himself with it.

But, in the meantime, death deprived him of his pious director. It would, perhaps, be imprudent to affirm that, in his last moments, Father de la Bretesche had a revelation from on high concerning the approaching return of the Society of Jesus to New France; but, if deprived of revelation, it seems certain that he did not lack intuition. On his death-bed, Father Vimont and François Ragueneau begged him, when in heaven, not to forget his dear mission in Canada, and, in reply, the dying man told them that they would both carry the light of faith to the Canadian tribes. Then, addressing Father Vimont, he continued : " I am not in the habit of prophesying, but I assure you that you will see a Jesuit house in Quebec."

Father de la Bretesche died November 20, 1624, and was deeply lamented. Charles Lalemant, Le Jeune, Vimont, de Quen, Le Moyne, de Noué, Ragueneau, Le Mercier, Charles Garnier, Jérôme Lalemant and others, all active members in Clermont College of the league of prayer for the Canadian mission, lost, in Father de la Bretesche, the soul of the organization.

On the day of the obsequies the Duc de Ventadour, who attended the funeral, met Father Philibert Noyrot, Procurator ot the college at Bourges. Father Noyrot was born in 1592, and entered the Paris novitiate of the Society at the age of twenty-five, and Father de la Bretesche, who was there at the time, was the first instructor of his religious career. The novice thought of becoming a missionary in China, but, by dint of reasoning, his director deterred him from that purpose, and turned his aspirations towards Canada. After two years novitiate the young man was put to studying theology for two years more, and made Procurator at the college at Bourges.

He was not a gifted speaker but expressed himself slowly and with great effort, betraying much embarrassment at not being able to find words in which to readily convey his meaning. His intellect was more solid than brilliant, he had excellent judgment, was eminently practical, a fine manager and indefatigable worker, and, if he had not the quick, lively imagination nor subtle penetration of his fellow-countrymen, at least he resembled them in point of activity, affability, and being pleasantly accessible. His uncomeliness of feature was amply compensated by his genuine benevolence, and his goodness of heart, constantly in evidence, had a refining effect upon his natural brusqueness. It has been said, and truly, that character is worth more than intelligence. Men of intellect are frequently met with: men of character, rarely. Father Noyrot had character, and in it strength and generosity, self-forgetfulness and love of duty, patience and courage shone conspicuous. When there was question of undertaking anything conducive to God's greater glory, his manly nature could not be thwarted, and often he paused not to try to solve difficulties but went straight ahead, risking rough contact with the obstacles in his path. While at Bourges, he divided his day between the duties of his charge and the direction of souls, and at night, after the community had retired, he would repair to the chapel and spend long hours in prayer and meditation. On Sundays and feast days he was accustomed to start out early in the morning in company with a young religious, each taking with him a piece of bread which he would eat at noon seated near some well or spring. Thus, Father Noyrot went from village to village teaching Catechism to the children and the poor. For six years he continued this course with admirable regularity, returning home late at night well spent with hunger and fatigue after his long fast and constant preaching and catechizing. He himself said that it was thus he served his apprenticeship of missionary among the savages. He was known and loved in all the suburbs of Bourges, being called "Father of the Little Ones," and this permitted him to give free rein to his zeal by sometimes resorting to extreme measures which called into play both his industry and originality. Despite the impediment in his speech his hearers loved to listen to him, and it is related that the shepherds who were obliged to remain in the field to guard their flocks, were ever on the alert for the passing of their clerical friend, and would often waylay him in the field or by the roadside to seek instruction.

From the first days of Father Noyrot's novitiate, Father de Bretesche, his spiritual director, conceived the greatest esteem for him, and indeed, it was mutual. Though opposites in point of character and education, the master and disciple closely resembled each other in their ardent love of souls, and in their letters as well as during their interviews, these two men delighted in referring to apostolic work and foreign missions, notably those of Canada.

The Duc de Ventadour had learned from Father de la Bretesche of the strong friendship existing between the two religious, and, out of regard for the beloved director whom he had lost, begged Father Noyrot to become his spiritual guide. The new adviser was not accustomed to use indirect means in leading souls to the accomplishment of good and, being quick to discern the elevated and apostolic spirit of his penitent, he soon realized what great impetus the Duke could give to the evangelization of the savages of New France, if he might be induced to accept the viceroyalty of Canada. Consequently, upon learning that the Duc de Montmorency, tired of the constant bickerings of his Company of Merchants, contemplated relinquishing and selling out his charge, Father Noyrot advised the Duc de Lévis to purchase it. "There is in this lofty position," he said, "a magnificent cause to sustain: the conversion of savage tribes to the faith by your intervention." The Duke did not hesitate but bought out his uncle and, at the beginning of January, 1625, the king ratified the transfer by letters patent.

Scarcely had the new Viceroy been named when Father Irénée Piat, the Franciscan, who had lately arrived in France, called on him at his residence and begged him, in the name of the sons of St. Francis, to send the Jesuits to New France. During the course of the interview Father Noyrot appeared upon the scene, and immediately Father Piat renewed his request, and as no proposition could be more agreeable to the Viceroy and the Jesuit, both readily accepted it.

(To be continued.)

SISTER STEPHANIE.

BY D. S. BÉNI.

WHEN I was about eighteen years of age, reverses in fortune compelled my father to sell our beautiful home in Philadelphia, hallowed by many sweet associations, and to remove to the city of B———. My father was already bowed down by the death of my good mother, which had occurred scarcely six months before, and wishing to be of some practical assistance to him, whom I loved more than life itself, I determined to accept a position as governess in the family of an old friend. To make myself more competent for this position, I went to the Convent in B——— to take private lessons in French and Italian, and later on, in vocal music.

I shall never forget the first impression which Sister Stephanie made upon me, as she entered the class-room and addressed me in Italian, and although I could not perfectly understand what she said, the gentle tone of her voice fell upon my ear like the sweetest music. She was rather above medium height, dignified in her bearing and graceful in her movements, and beyond the meridian of life. Her features were faultless, and the expression of her face beautiful, though very pale.

While her sweet affability made me feel perfectly at home, her religious manner showed that she was a superior person, with whom familiarity would have been impossible. When she found that I did not speak Italian, she addressed me in French, and it was then decided that we should use that language as a medium of conversation until I would be able to speak Italian, which she hoped would be very soon. The hour passed so quickly that it seemed only a few minutes, and I bade adieu to my gentle teacher, carrying with me the sweetest impressions, which deepened in each succeeding lesson.

In a short time I felt so free with her, that I told her of my mother's death, and our pecuniary misfortunes, and why I wished to perfect myself in these branches. She praised me for my laudable undertaking, but told me that I must not look upon reverses as misfortunes, for on the contrary, they were often blessings in disguise, as they made us think less of men and more of God, they filled the soul with nobler thoughts, and aspirations after higher and holier things, and gave a strength and nobility to the character, which could hardly be attained amid the luxury of an easy life.

In theory, I concurred in all she said, but practically the thought of leaving home, of beginning life under circumstances so different, the diffidence I felt in myself and my attainments, made me tremble, and I almost shrank back from my duty, and my self-imposed task.

Sister Stephanie smiled sweetly and said:

"When'er we cross a river at a ford,
 If we would pass in safety, we must keep
 Our eyes fixed steadfast on the shore beyond,
 For if we cast them on the flowing stream,
 The head swims with it; so if we would cross
 The running flood of things here in this world,
 Our souls must not look down, but fix their sight
 On the firm land beyond."

"Or in other words, my dear child, we must keep our eyes fixed upon God, who must be the beginning and end of all our actions. Were we to lose sight of Him and allow ourselves to be troubled by the accidents of life, if we may so speak, for nothing happens without His permission, we would waste our precious time and our opportunities, and accomplish nothing. Life would pass away in unavailing sorrow; we should be disturbed and saddened by the apprehension of things that may never come to pass; whereas, if we place all our confidence in God, feeling sure that He will guide, direct and sustain us, He will strengthen us in all trials, and give us that peace which the world can neither give nor take away. The past is no longer ours, the future is in the hands of God, who will always give us sufficient grace, so

"Do thy duty; that is best,
 Leave unto thy Lord, the rest."

Every day I learned a spiritual lesson from my gentle teacher, and every day my interest in her increased and my affection for her became more profound. She spoke no idle words, and what she said impressed me so deeply that I repeated it all to my father and sister. I wished so much to know something of her antecedents, where was her home, who was her father? who was her mother? but delicacy would not allow me to ask these questions; finally I ascertained from one of the pupils "that she was a Philadelphian, Miss Emily Clarkson, a great belle; her father's name was Robert Clarkson, and she is a convert."

When I told this to my father, he started from his chair. "Miss Emily Clarkson a Catholic and a nun, impossible! If Sister Stephanie is my conscientious friend Miss Emily C., I will become a Catholic myself!"

"Take care, father, you know you never break your word, and I think my Sister Stephanie can be no other than your Miss Emily Clarkson." My father said: "Robert Clarkson was one of the most cultivated gentlemen I ever knew, and his beautiful home on the banks of the Delaware, was the resort of the most cultured men of his day. It was under his roof I had the pleasure of meeting at different times, such men as Washington Irving, Bryant and Longfellow. He had a lovely family, two sons and two daughters by the first wife, and an almost innumerable circle of relatives as honorable and highly cultured as himself.

"They were High Church Episcopalians, or rather, they were Episcopalians with ritualistic tendencies, for there were no such distinctions as High and Low Church in that day, but the Clarksons were all upright and scrupulously conscientious in their religious belief, and if Sister Stephanie was Miss Emily, I can believe everything good and beautiful of her.

"Her mother died when she was quite a child, but she was brought up with the tenderest care, provided with an accomplished governess, the best professors of music and the languages that could be found in Philadelphia, and her education was carefully superintended by Mr. Clarkson himself. Both sisters had beautiful voices. In conversation her voice was as soft and sweet as music. But how did *she* become a Catholic and a nun? They had no Catholic friends, and though her love of music frequently attracted her to the Catholic churches, she never went to them on Sunday, nor on any day that her own church was open. For conscientious reasons she never went to the theatre, but she made a distinction between the theatre and opera, which she attended to improve herself by hearing the best music. She was well versed in Latin, French and German, and on hearing her uncle incidentally remark, that if he was not conversant with Italian, he would be repaid for learning it by reading, "I Promessi Sposi," in the original, Miss Emily procured an Italian teacher and soon acquired that mellifluous tongue. As a conversationalist she was unrivalled, not that she indulged in any showy outburst of wit, but her improving conversation was always full of absorbing interest. About the year 1853, her older sister married her first cousin, a young Episcopal minister named Edmund M., and after Mr. Clarkson married a second time, Miss Emily spent the greater part of her time with Mrs. M. and her many aunts and uncles, each of whom claimed her time, for she was always the centre of an admiring circle, and was considered an oracle on points of religion or literature. The gentle sweetness of her disposition, and her simplicity of manner made her accessible to all; she had many advantageous matrimonial offers, and her disregard for them was a subject of wonder to her friends. But how did she ever become a Catholic and a nun? Surely no one can say *she* left the world because of any disappointment in life."

I said to my father: "I think she was just the kind of a person that ought to be a nun, for she was too good for the world."

"But think of all she sacrificed by going to a convent," said my father. "First, she had every personal charm of head and heart, she was admired, she was rich, for her father, as president of the ———— Company, had a princely income and might have made millions in a way which in this day would be called perfectly legitimate, but he preferred his unstained honor to all the world could offer.   He scorned the empty applause of the world.   His doors were always open, and the hospitality which was there dispensed was not fettered by foolish, meaningless ceremonies, and no one sat at Robert Clarkson's table without finding food for the intellectual and nobler part of his being, while he partook of the meaner food which is necessary to sustain life.   He cared not a straw for public opinion; he lived up to what he believed to be just and true before God and man, and he was in every sense a nobleman. And to say you were a friend of Robert Clarkson, or had dined at his board, was sufficient to give you the entrée into the most cultivated society in Philadelphia."

I said: "I think Sister Stephanie was just the one to make the heroic sacrifice, and, as she was conscientious and good as an Episcopalian, no doubt God recompensed her fidelity to the light she then had by giving her the true faith."

My father was not a Catholic, and did not dwell so much on the spiritual side, and he said to me:

"And I think she was just the person to do good in the world, for she had so much influence."

One day, shortly after this conversation, while I was taking my lesson in Italian, I said:

" Sister, were you ever in Rome?"

" Yes, dear, I spent the Lent of 1869 there, and attended magnificent ceremonies at St. Peter's."

" Sister, were you always a Catholic?"

" No, my family were Episcopalians, and when my sister Mrs. M. became a Catholic, it almost broke my heart."

" Oh! dear Sister, if I am not asking too much, won't you please tell me about your conversion?   My mother was a convert, and there is something so fascinating in hearing about conversions and vocations, because it shows in how many different ways, God leads souls to Himself, for

'Not by one portal or by one path alone,
  God's holy messages to men are known.' "

" Well, dear child, if you ask me to speak of myself I hope I may be excused for doing so, though in truth I speak only of what God has done for me. I was an Episcopalian, conscientiously devoted to my religion. My brother, near my own age, was an Episcopal minister, and we had not a thought or an aspiration that we did not share with each other. At heart I am sure he was a Catholic, but we never doubted that we were *real Catholics*, and that our church alone had the Apostolic succession. Once I went to New Brunswick to visit my sister, Mrs. M., who then had two lovely little boys, who were the joy of my life. Her husband had charge of an Episcopal church there, and I never dreamed that they had any Romanistic proclivities. To my surprise, when I arrived I found no one at home, but the servant told me they would be back that evening and that they were expecting me. I made so many inquiries about them, that at last, the servant, herself a Catholic, told me that they had all gone to New York to be baptized in the Catholic Church. I could not comprehend her words, it was such an overwhelming shock to me. It was the 10th of August, the Feast of St. Lawrence, and even now, I am sure that the martyrdom of that Saint was not more severe than mine. What could my sister mean? I viewed it in every light, but the one thought that she was unfaithful to God, that she was untrue to the faith of her fathers, that God was displeased with her—seemed like a two-edged sword of sorrow piercing my heart and my soul. When they returned, my silence and my tears spoke more than words. Mr. and Mrs. M. had themselves gone through an intense agony beyond the pen of mortal man to describe. They saw the truth, they weighed all the consequences of their step, which they knew would be followed by the displeasure of their relatives and friends, and contempt and opprobrium on all sides. More than this, they were first cousins, and wrongly believing that their marriage would not be recognized by the Church, they had made all their arrangements, the heroic sacrifice was to be consummated, they were to separate, and thus sever the dearest family ties. They had passed through this mental anguish, and the crucifixion of soul had left its impression on their exterior. I knew not their agony—only my own, and to be truthful, I felt a bitterness in my heart that no explanations or excuses could remove. I soon returned home, and Mr. M. seeing that there would be no peace whilst he was in reach of his relatives, and hoping to educate his sons with less expense in Europe, the little family set sail, and for several years lived in the suburbs of Lyons.

"Their expatriation added to my anguish, for my sister had been the better part of myself. I thought she was inexcusable, and now there was but little congeniality between us. I heard her censured on every side, and to add to my burden of sorrow, my brother to whom I had been especially devoted was accidentally drowned in the Ohio River. This accumulated grief and suffering had completely broken down my health, and I was physically a wreck. As soon as I was able to travel I went to Wisconsin, where my brother had begun to build a church at his own expense, which I completed and presented to his congregation. I will pass over many excruciating things which wrung my heart, and will tell you that according to the advice of physicians I went to California, where I stayed about eighteen months, travelling especially in the southern part of the State.

"The sight of the old churches, and the old monasteries, the cloisters of which were then used for shops and market places, impressed me greatly, and above all the beautiful old Spanish epitaphs which I found in the cemeteries. Could bad, ignorant people have such high and holy thoughts? I pondered over this day and night, and one day at the dinner table when an Episcopal minister spoke in an abusive manner of the Church and the Pope I left the table, because I felt that he was in a passion and was uncharitable in his remarks. After reaching my room I said to myself with energy: 'I am a reasonable being, I will accept my sister's invitation and see the Church in Europe and judge for myself,' though I had not the slightest idea of becoming a Catholic, but I would at least gratify my natural inclination for travel.

"I joined them in France in October, but there was an insuperable barrier between us; we had no longer the same thoughts or the same hopes. When we visited the churches I went to gratify my pardonable curiosity—the M's. went to pray. When we passed a statue or a shrine along the street my little nephews, now five in number, wondered that I did not kneel down to pray as they did—and after telling me what prayers to say, they gently pulled me down on my knees, and rather than give them pain, I submitted, but my heart did not bend with my body.

(To be continued.)

CANDLEMAS DAY.

BY PATRICK RAFFERTY, S.J.

BEHOLD, O sons of men, this humble deed,
   Which doth humility itself exceed,
     A lesson for our pride;
She who in spotlessness bore Christ our Lord,
Is cleansed tho' clean, and of her own accord
     The pure is purified!

And see! the babe whom in her arms she holds,
And to her loving breast so warmly folds,—
     Our Saviour, Jesus Christ,—
The glory of God's people and a light
To guide poor sinners wand'ring in the night,
     To God is sacrificed!

Will ye be haughty now, O proud of earth,
When Mary, pure and spotless from her birth,
     Humbleth herself so low?
Ungenerous souls, what answer can ye make,
When ye behold your Saviour, for your sake,
     His all on God bestow?

AN IROQUOIS MAIDEN,

OR

Life of Catharine Tegakwitha

(*Continued.*)

CHAPTER VIII.

Catharine at the Saut Mission.

ON her arrival at the Mission of the Saut, Catharine found that it had been established for about one year at the mouth of the Portage river. She had been provided with a letter of recommendation from Father de Lamberville to Father de Cholenec, who, with Fathers Chauchetière and Frémin were in charge of the Mission. She hastened to present her letter to them. It contained these lines: " Catharine Tegakwita is going to live at the Saut. Will you kindly undertake to direct her? You will soon know what a treasure we have sent you. Guard it well! May it profit, in your hands, for the glory of God and the salvation of a soul that is certainly very dear to Him." This brief praise was worth a long discourse. Its truth was soon proved.

Father Cholenec at once set about finding a pious family who would take charge of Catharine, and he thought he could not do better than to confide her to a savage who was related to her, and who had served as her guide and protector in her flight. On finding herself amongst faithful servants of God, Catharine could not believe her eyes. It seemed to her that she was in an earthly paradise. Far from domestic persecution and the scandals of her village, she at length found herself free to give herself up as much as she wished to the sweet inclination of her heart towards virtue, like the bird that escapes from the snare of the fowler, and can take its flight freely towards heaven.

Catharine was received like an angel, in the cabin of her relation, whom she called her brother-in-law. She was to become to this family a new source of blessings. Under that humble roof of bark there was also to be found an aged Christian woman, named Anastasia Tegonhatsiongo, who had been one of the first among the Iroquois to receive baptism, and who had become one of the pillars of the Mission of the Saut. Her zeal and her skill in instructing neophytes, had won for her universal esteem, and a well-merited reputation. Her daily occupation was to prepare persons of her own sex for baptism. She welcomed with especial benevolence the good Catharine, who found in her a worthy friend of her mother. It was thus that began between these two hearts, that intimate friendship, of wholly supernatural charity, from which both the one and the other gathered most precious fruit.

The first sentiment that arose in Catharine's heart, at the thought of the many benefits she had received from heaven, was one of lively gratitude to God for having withdrawn her from the midst of paganism, and for having placed her among such good Christians.

Endowed with a generous heart, an ardent soul, a mind prompt and active, she placed all these rare qualities at the service of her Divine Master, and thenceforth her only thought was, how to respond faithfully to the blessings of Heaven, with which she found herself as if inundated. These gifts of God fell on a ground well prepared. One may say that this pious girl had never been a novice, on a road where so many others, even after many years, are still only beginners. At an age, when, ordinarily, one has such great need of being formed, she could serve as model for the oldest. Her principal, her only maxim was: to seek in everything what appeared to be the most agreeable to God. Regardless of creatures, without thought of self, she always exacted from her will the most complete and most generous sacrifice. Whence had she drawn principles so pure, and of such high perfection? From the high idea she had formed of the Divine Majesty, and a lively gratitude for the benefits with which she had been filled.

In this virtuous shelter, Catharine could follow, and without danger, her attraction for visiting our Lord often in His Temple, and what sweet happiness for her to converse freely with

Him there! At four o'clock A. M., as soon as the doors of the chapel were open, Catharine was sure to be seen entering, even in the most rigorous season, and she remained in prayer till the last Mass. Several times a day, when her work permitted, she saluted her Saviour hidden in the Tabernacle, and, when heavy rains, or the cold of winter, rendered work in the fields impossible, she multiplied her visits to the church, for, in spite of the example of other savage girls, she would never give her precious time to frivolous visits, prolonged games, or useless conversation. In the evening she was again to be found in the church, at the prayers recited in common, but she arrived before the others, and only withdrew when the doors were about to be closed. Catharine was soon familiar with the religious exercises followed at the Mission. She hastened to learn by heart the prayers, always recited by the savages at church in two choirs ; as well as the canticles they chant during the Office.

We find in a letter of Father Cholenec's dated 1678, curious details about the order and nature of Sunday religious exercises, at this Mission. " From a very early hour, the savages came to the church in great numbers, to approach the tribunal of Penance. Mass was said at eight o'clock. The men ranged on the Gospel side, the women on the Epistle side, alternately sang in two choirs, the Kyrie, the Gloria, the Credo, sacred hymns and canticles, all translated into the Iroquois language, and this practice has been retained at this Mission till our own day. The missionary delivered a familiar instruction on the Gospel. From time to time he yielded his place to some good Christian Captain, and the words of the savage often had weighty influence with his fellow-countrymen. At ten o'clock the church bell again sounded, and if there was not to be a second Mass the beads were recited. At one o'clock P. M. took place the meeting of the Confraternity of the Holy Family, composed of the élite of these good Christians. They recited the usual prayers, and received an instruction from the missionary, or some salutary advice to excite their zeal and fervor. Edifying traits more than once proved the attachment these associates felt for their title of membership, and the esteem in which they were held by the other savages.

At three o'clock they met to sing vespers, or rather for an exercise that took its place. The psalms were, in fact, replaced by a series of prayers in Iroquois, which Father Frémin had set to the tones of the various psalms: First, the usual morning prayer to the 8th tone; second, prayer for the Elevation at Holy Mass, to the 1st tone; third, prayer to the Guardian Angel, to the 4th tone; fourth, thanksgiving for the gift of faith, 1st tone; fifth, Commandments of God, to the chant of *In Exitu*.

Then followed the hymn in Iroquois to the chant of *Iste Confessor*, then the *Ave Maria* to the 8th tone, to replace the *Magnificat*. At the end Benediction of the Blessed Sacrament was given. The sun often set before all these were ended.

All these chants and pious practices soon became familiar to Catharine. She was always the first at them. She found a singular consolation in thus proclaiming aloud the praises of God, in the assembly of saints, and in consecrating to His glory the gifts of nature which she owed to His bounty.

Without Catharine's suspecting it, the Lord had already initiated her into the secrets of the interior life. Prayer, or rather meditation, her almost habitual occupation, she made such great progress in, that, without difficulty, she attained to a high degree of contemplation. God is prodigal of His gifts in proportion to the generosity with which the heart responds. One often saw her eyes overflow with tears and on her face the impress of the holy ardor that animated her. A stranger to all that was passing around her, she might be seen motionless, her eyes cast down or fixed on the altar. Nothing had power to distract her. Without other master than the Holy Ghost, she thus attained to the prayer of the perfect, and God permitted her to find in this celestial converse so much sweetness and charm that the hours seemed too short to satisfy her desires.

Catharine's devotion was all the more praiseworthy that it did not resemble those ill-comprehended devotions, in which self-love has a part, nor those strange devotions that please through their singularity. Her piety, far from being a prejudice to her daily work, only caused her to acquit herself of it with greater ardor. She learned to sanctify it by uprightness of intention, while at the same time it served her as a means of conversing with God and nourishing in her heart throughout the day the sentiments she had imbibed at the foot of the altar. Thus, in the woods or fields, or in the house, she found God everywhere, and never lost sight of Him. Although Catharine had avoided the noisy meetings of companions likely to distract her, she understood the succor she could find in the relations of a truly Christian friendship.

It was for this reason, that she formed a close friendship with good Anastasia, whose disposition and tastes harmonized so well with her own. They mutually sustained each other's fervor by pious conversation, which turned, for the most part, on the mysteries of the faith, the goodness of God, the means of pleasing Him, and advancing in His holy service, conversations with which were intermingled incidents of the life and virtues of the saints, their generosity towards God, their hatred of sin, and the rigor of their penance.

Days thus passed, were full days, that is to say, in the words of Holy Writ, days filled with virtues and merits. Yet all this was not enough for Catharine's generous soul. Each week she strove to acquire a new degree of purity and love, by severe examination of her conscience, and the frequentation of the Sacrament of Penance. She then set before herself the exact account of all her actions. The least infidelity was a crime in her eyes, because it displeased her God. She prepared herself to approach the holy tribunal by prayer and mortification. She already comprehended the powerful succor that virtue finds in the holy severity with which the soul treats the body, in order to recall this revolted slave to its primitive condition, and to conquer its evil inclinations. Her confession was often accompanied by sobs and tears.

It was by this fervent and exemplary conduct that Catharine showed herself worthy of a favor, only accorded to strangers from the Iroquois country after several years of probation. These precautions were necessary in order to give to these souls, so rude and so ignorant of supernatural things, a high idea of the Church, and especially of the Holy Eucharist. But the virtue of this neophyte was too extraordinary to confound her with the others. For a long time she had ardently anticipated the happy moment, when her heart should become the living Tabernacle of her Saviour.

Some time before Christmas, the missionary made known to her the grace she was to receive on that happy day. Her joy was great at this happy news, and her fervor redoubled. Eager desires, holy aspirations, even greater purity of conscience, such were Catharine's preparations for embellishing the sanctuary she destined for her God.

What a beautiful day for heaven, for the whole mission, and especially for the holy maiden herself was that on which, with angelic modesty, and an ardor wholly celestial, she came to approach the Holy Table for the first time. God permitted the feast of Christmas to be celebrated this year, with more than usual pomp and ceremony. Never before had the savages congregated in such numbers.

This first communion of our young savage, which was for her so great a source of grace and benediction, implanted in her heart, as its first fruit, the desire of often partaking of the same happiness.

She obtained this favor, in fact, and on each occasion found therein new devotion. They had such an idea of her fervor that at each epoch of General Communion, the most devout women loved to find themselves beside her in the Church. They declared that the sight of her modest and pious exterior at this moment, was, of itself alone, sufficient to animate their fervor, and serve them as preparation for making a good Communion.

(*To be continued.*)

SHRINE NOTES.

"The Shrine must look so much like Bethlehem at this season," wrote one at Christmas, who knows it quite well enough to imagine how it looks at any time of year. The hills and roads about Auriesville did remind one of Bethlehem the day after Christmas, and of a Bethlehem, which in the pious imagination of most Christians, of those at least who live in northern countries, was covered with snow and ice. One who had the privilege of visiting the Shrine on that day, and the good fortune to be driven to it over roads slippery as glass by the neighboring pastor, Rev. Father Dolan, of Fonda, thought of snow shoes as he paced the paths about the Shrine, and descended into the Ravine by the road which was finished early in December. The weather may make a place like Auriesville very bleak, but never dreary to those who know the country and its associations. The very atmosphere is so exhilarating as to keep alive the most pleasant sentiments. It is a fit place for a shrine, to which the pilgrim can go with profit in spirit when the actual visit is not possible.

* * *

So many of our readers have asked us to continue the chapters from Rochemonteix's history, "The Jesuits and New France," that we have decided to have the task of translating it taken up again, or, at least, its most interesting chapters. We interrupted it, our readers will remember, in order to publish a good biography of Catharine Tegakwitha, whose life had never been properly told in the PILGRIM. Now that we have published most of the life of this saintly Indian maiden, we can continue the history of the early missions in New France as narrated by Rochemonteix. The value of this history may not be appreciated at first, especially when read in short chapters at one month's interval, but it is a story of undying interest, and we are confident that our readers will like it more than anything we have as yet published in the PILGRIM.

* * *

Subscribers to the PILGRIM should renew their subscriptions as promptly as possible and induce others to subscribe to it. As subscribers increase, not only will they furnish a slight revenue for the Shrine and the Cause of the Martyrs, but they will also enable the editor to improve the PILGRIM itself.

CONTRIBUTIONS TO THE SHRINE.

The Shrine was incorporated last August under the title of "The Shrine of Our Lady of Martyrs, of Auriesville, New York," and the various properties formerly held in trust for the Shrine by the Apostleship of Prayer, have been formally transferred to the new corporation as their proper owner. Donations, legacies, contracts, and all business of importance with the Shrine should henceforth be transacted under the title "The Shrine of Our Lady of Martyrs, New York," the officers of the corporation being Rev. John J. Wynne, President; Rev. Francis J. Lamb, Vice-President; and Rev. William F. Cunningham, Secretary.

* * *

As announced in our last issue, the gold and jewels which have been collected from pious clients of Our Lady of Martyrs, for the past five years, have at length been handed over to the goldsmith who is to make with them the crowns for the statue to be erected and blessed at Auriesville. Whilst the jeweler is still preparing his designs and material, contributions of gold or silver will still be accepted, as also donations of money for the manufacture of the crowns and for the statue.

CONTRIBUTIONS TO THE SHRINE.

J. C. S., Wilkesbarre, Pa. . . . $5.00
A. D., Chicago, Ill. 1.00
S. C., " " 1.00
R. R., Buffalo, N. Y. 50
A Friend of Our Lady. . . . 1.00
K. A., Maysville, Ky. 50
M. L. S. H., Buffalo, N. Y. . 5.00
N. G., Bunker Hill, Ill. . . . 10.00
A. F., Wheeling, W. Va. . . 1.00
T. M., New York. 5.00
K. McK., Pittsburg, Pa. . . . 2.40
    FOR THE CROWN.

M. R., Boston, a gold breast-pin.
F. H. McC., Albany, New York, two gold brooches, three earrings, four rings, a silver chain and a medal.
M. B., Phila., five earrings, a necklace, two rings, and a chain and locket.
M. K., Pittsburg, Pa., two gold earrings, a silver thimble, a silver ring with emerald, and sundry pieces of jewelry.
A. N., Kittell, N. C., a gold ring, two cuff buttons, a cross and a gold badge.

T. P. K., Utica, N. Y., an earring and a piece of gold chain.

FROM THE MISSIONS.

DUNBRODY, BLUECLIFF, S. AFRICA,
November 21, 1898.

DEAR REV. FATHER, P.C.:

Our work here is the dull monotonous work of routine, and wonderful incidents can't even be invented. Our comfort is that we are preparing the ground for our successors and that our reward will not be measured by success but by fidelity.

One of those galling facts which Catholics have to endure at times has come to pass in Bulawayo. The Sisters who worked through the Matabele war, nursing the sick and wounded with unflagging care and who have been decorated for their services, are reported by the papers to have *resigned*. That means that some meddlers, using the technical wording of the law that all nurses must be certified, have morally forced them out and of course substituted Protestant nurses in their place.

ST. MARY'S MISSION, ALMA P. O., WASHINGTON,
December 11, 1898.

DEAR REV. FATHER, P. C.:

Thanks for your kind letter, thanks to the charitable person who sends me the $5 for Masses. Anything is a great help to me. I have now another Father with me and it is a great help in the immense territory over which our Indian missions extend; it is at the same time an increased burden to find means of support for two. Our school is started but I have to refuse children for we have no help from any source. The Indians themselves are bringing the food and clothing to their children. But so many parents will not do it and their children would come if I could take charge of them. So they are scattered all over this country, too far to come even to church regularly and are only baptized but without Christian instruction. What will become of our new generation mixed up with the whites, worse than Indians here on the frontier?

In case any one should ask what can be done for us, you can say any thing would be welcome, even old clothing for our boys, small or large.

KEY WEST, FLORIDA, November 7, 1898.

REV. DEAR FATHER, P.C.:

We are trying to do some good here, and so far we have reason to hope that our efforts will be partially successful. There is not a town in the South where there have been so many apostasies. This is inexplicable to me. It cannot be attributed to ignorance, not to mixed marriages, not to social standing. I do not mean apostasies of Cubans; few could be called apostates, having nothing to fall off from. Many Cubans became *nominal* Protestants. Some few of them are good Catholics, the rest are nothing, not even infidels. The mass of Cubans here have just enough religion to be extremely superstitious.

As far as I can learn, no preacher in Key West uses a cassock in the streets. One Episcopal negro preacher, however, is seen occasionally in a cassock in the streets. The other Episcopal preacher uses a cassock in all his services, funerals included.

All the preachers of all the denominations call themselves Catholic when speaking to the Cubans. They do not call themselves Roman Catholics, but the *real true* Catholics. When Cubans who know a little more and have some little faith left, come for a baptism, they explicitly ask whether we are Roman Catholics and Catholics like those in Cuba. I believe that there are many good Catholics in Cuba amongst the ladies of all classes, very few amongst the men.

A woman in Jamaica, W. I., who had long neglected her religious duties, was suddenly stricken down by paralysis, and became unconscious. The priest put the scapular of our Lady of Mount Carmel together with a scapular of the Sacred Heart upon her with the result that she not only regained sufficient consciousness to make her confession, but at last accounts was fast recovering. Her physician, who is a Protestant, called on the priest to request special prayers of thanksgiving for a cure in which he could not fail to recognize the hand of the Almighty.

A letter from Calcutta informs us that an establishment of the Third Order Apostolate of our Lady of Mount Carmel is to be begun in or near that city at a place called St. Thomas' Mount. The bishop has generously donated the house and grounds. But the great difficulty is the want of religious. There are only two European nuns to begin the establishment and the reverend missionary who writes earnestly prays that God may inspire some zealous ladies in Europe or America to devote their lives to His service in this apostolic work.

MISSION DES FILLES DE LA CHARITÈ,
SALONIQUE, TURQUIE D'EUROPE, December 27, 1898.

MY DEAR SISTER:—

I have no doubt you are anxious at not hearing from me for so long a time, but am sure you will pardon my seeming forgetfulness, when you hear the cause of it. It is owing to a dreadful hail-storm that passed over this town during October last. For some time the weather had been very hot; suffocating, I may say, but a few days before the storm took place, the sky was covered with black clouds, that indicated anything but good. On the 20th the firmament was blacker than ever, and that night the storm burst upon us with dreadful flashes of lightning and great thunder. It was frightful to hear. The night was as light as day, with the flashes of lightning that succeeded each other uninterruptedly. It was then eight o'clock, the hour we go to chapel for night prayers, when suddenly we heard a great noise, that made us tremble with fear. We had barely courage enough to reach the chapel, and fall on our knees to beg God's mercy, for we thought our last hour had come. Happily this terror lasted only the space of five or six minutes, had it been longer the whole population of Salonica must have been buried beneath the ruins of their own dwellings, for even in that brief space of time, there took place dreadful disasters. The hail-stones that fell were larger than an orange, and each one had points all around it, that did not spare the windows nor the roofs, but pierced large holes in the latter, through which for three whole days the rain came pouring in without cessation, filling the apartments with water. We were kept busy emptying it from our upper rooms, trying, if possible, to prevent it making its way to the lower story, and destroying all our belongings, which had been transported thither and thrown down pell-mell. On the second day, while I was trying to move out the beds and speaking with a sick sister for a moment, we were suddenly shocked by an awful noise that frightened us the more, because we could not account for it, or tell whence it came. Almost at the same moment there was a cry in the street: "Fly, Sisters, fly for your lives, your house is falling." A hasty glance around the room showed nothing worse than a little bend in the roof, but we obeyed the voice without an instant of hesitation and to this promptitude no doubt we owe our lives, for when we reached the street we saw the beam that supported the roof, broken in two and poised high in air instead of falling in and crushing down on our heads. A miracle of God's mercy, indeed, this, to give us time to leave the house and thereby save our lives. We were then forced to carry all the things we had saved to the new church, which also had its share in the general disaster. It was a sad sight for us to behold its roof all broken. With what difficulty had we not collected the money for its construction! We were expecting to have Mass there on December 8th, and now we do not know how long it will be before we can have it restored.

In this extremity, will you believe it, we could not get workmen to help us. They demanded such an exorbitant price that we were unable to employ them, and were forced to do all the work ourselves; to carry, not only our furniture and clothing, but even the stones, wood and mortar of our demolished house. It was necessary to remove them, as they were a danger to the passers-by. Our worthy parish priest, and the good missionary priests, together with the personnel of the Bulgarian College, helped us like simple workmen.

And now, dearest sister, I imagine I hear you ask me, where we slept, during this most trying time. Why, in one of the wards of the hospital which, thanks to the Divine Providence of God, was nearly empty just then. We placed the sick in one room, and there we also remained for more than a month; but as the bad weather had begun, we had to give the ward wholly over to the sick, and have a small hut of only three rooms built for dispensary, parlor, and dormitory. The former dispensary had been taken for a chapel. As the rooms in this tiny hut were so small, we had to keep all the cupboards in the passages. You can readily imagine all the inconvenience and trouble of our situation packed thus into three small rooms. We pray that the dear Lord may come to our aid by inspiring some generous souls to help us in this great distress.

I think, my dear sister, that I have not told you of our different works of charity here, and I am sure you wish to know something of them. We have a hospital where all the sick are received without any distinction of creed, schools for poor children, most of whom we are obliged to clothe and feed, as well as teaching them and providing their books. We have a few Jewish and Greek children who pay a small sum. There is also here an association of charitable ladies; they are not rich, but they do all they can to aid those worse off than themselves. We have, moreover, a foundling hospital for poor and abandoned children; for these we are obliged to pay nurses. As they are very numerous this causes great expense. When taken from the nurses we pay for their maintenance in a home until they reach the age of six years, after which we bring them up or provide suitable employment for them, until the age of twenty-one. The poor naturally are also relieved at the door, by food and clothing, and frequently by gifts of money, so many sad cases appeal to us for help. The sick come to the dispensary for medicine, sometimes as many as two hundred are helped gratis. The sisters are also called to visit a great number to the greatest spiritual benefit of the children. The Ladies' Charitable Association have had some small houses and homes built for poor families who pay no rent and are helped when unable to work. They are presided over by an English sister.

And now, my dear sister, let me wish you a very holy and Happy New Year. May our dear Lord and His Holy Mother bless and protect you. Say a little prayer for us at the Grotto.

Ever your loving sister,
SR. M. JOSEPHINE BOURKE.

MISSION NOTES.

The *Précis Historiques*, a monthly magazine devoted to the missions conducted by the Belgian Fathers of the Society of Jesus, appears this month in a new form. Its size has been increased, its title page is ornamental and elegant, its paper and print are greatly improved, it contains a map and numerous illustrations of the best quality.

The Belgian Province of the Society of Jesus has three great missions—one in Bengal, one in Ceylon and one in the Congo country. The Mission of Bengal was begun by Father Depelchin, S.J., in 1859. He found 10,000 Catholics. There are now over 51,000 Catholics and over 15,000 Catechumens. The bishop who presides over this diocese, seven times the size of Belgium, is

Mgr. Paul Goethals. He has to assist him in the work, 99 priests. 47 scholastics and 27 lay brothers, all Jesuits, besides Christian Brothers, and three congregations of religious women.

In Ceylon there is a bishop at Galle and a seminary for the education of native priests at Kandy. This seminary was founded by His Holiness Leo XIII., who confided it to the care of the Jesuits. At present there are 80 students.

The German Jesuits have missions at Bombay and Poonah, the French Jesuits, at Madura and Trincomaly, the Italian Jesuits at Mangalore, and the Portuguese Jesuits on the western coast.

India contains about 300,000,000 inhabitants, of these not quite 2,000,000 are Catholics.

The Congo Mission was begun in 1893. The Fathers are assisted by the Sisters of Notre Dame. Many Mission-stations and schools have been established. Conversions are numerous and the Mission is flourishing. The Redemptorists and the Premonstratensions are also laboring in the Congo region. In Central Africa, there are at the present time six bishops, 150 missionaries and sisters, 50,000 baptized Catholics and 10,000 catechumens.

The Mission of Uganda has undergone terrible trials, the last being the danger arising from the Soudanese mutiny. For months the whole country was in peril of being overrun by the rebellious Mohammedan soldiers, and the Mission-stations being entirely unprotected, were in continual fear of pillage and massacre. God, however, protected them, and very little harm came to them. The mutineers have been defeated and scattered and the Missions once more enjoy a period of peace. Bishop Hanlon, Vicar-Apostolic of the Upper Nile, has improved the opportunity to make an excursion into the Usoga country, where he hopes to make many conversions.

The natives of Uganda are little inclined to industry, and it is difficult to get them to learn trades. But they are eager to learn to read and write, and will sit all day poring over a book. They also show great eagerness to hear about religion. They learn the whole catechism by heart as well as all their prayers. The French fathers have translated St. Matthew's and St. Mark's gospels into the language of the natives. They have also got out a prayer-book and a hymn-book.

A war between England and France would probably prove a great calamity to the missions. It must be remembered that French missionaries are laboring in nearly all of the British colonies. And though they would keep themselves sternly aloof from politics, still in the event of war it would be only natural for the British government to regard with uneasiness so many subjects of a hostile power. Hence their activity would be very much restricted, if not entirely suspended.

A new Catholic church, which cost $25,000, the gift of a generous Catholic, has lately been completed at Dawson City, Alaska. It was blessed by Father Judge, S.J., and will be in charge of the Oblate Fathers. The congregation numbers 500. It is expected that the number of people in Dawson City will soon reach 15,000.

The *Messenger of the Sacred Heart* for February, 1898, publishes some remarkable statistics of the work done by the Augustinians in the Philippines from 1892 to 1897, and the March number will supplement this report by many very interesting proofs of their zeal. Some of the statistics in the February number are as follows:

Year	Pueblos	Parishes, Missions	Souls	Baptisms	Marriages	Deaths	Augustinians in the Philippines.
1892	203	188	2,082,131	98,731	20,355	83,051	310
1893	208	—	2,096,281	103,015	21,279	78,335	286
1894	219	—	2,136,103	104,049	25,005	73,696	317
1895	231	—	2,191,604	107,573	22,660	81,652	317
1896	—	—	2,324,968	112,130	19,421	71,295	344
1897	—	225	2,377,743	110,233	17,909	67,508	319

Acknowledgment is made of the following contributions:

FOR ST. ANTHONY'S BREAD.   MOST NEEDY MISSION.
Anon. . . $1.00   S. M. G., Irvington, N. Y. . . $1.00

THE PILGRIM
OF
OUR LADY OF MARTYRS

GOOD FRIDAY.

Vos nostis afflictionem in qua sumus,
quia Jerusalem deserta est. 2nd Esdras, 2-17.

BY J. F. X. BURNS, S.J.

WHEN rolled the noon-day sun of Parasceve,
    Began my sorrow at my Saviour's woe :
  Each hour succeeding made my grief to grow
More uncontrolled, till, anguish-wrought, I crave
The wonted solace which the altar gave.
But woe is me! that source whence comforts flow
Lies bare and vacant now, nor does the glow
Of sacred light tell aught but of the grave.
By my sad loss aroused, I cast me down,
Full conscious of the boon to me denied ;
And pond'ring long the love that erst was shown,
With heart renewed, I thank The Crucified.
His absence now to me sweet courage gives :
I cannot grieve ; I know my Saviour lives.

THE JESUITS AND NEW FRANCE

In the Seventeenth Century.

From the French of Rev. Camille de Rochemonteix, S.J.

BY K. A. HENNESSY.

(*Continued.*)

IT would be puerile indeed to always look upon a desired but unexpected occurrence as a miracle of Providence, and yet it must be admitted that a wonderful combination of circumstances was attendant upon the return of the Jesuits to Canada.

Usually the works of God do not progress as rapidly as we wish, and from the very beginning, this undertaking had met with obstacles. The associated merchants who were, for the greater part, Calvinists, were sorely displeased at the choice made by the Franciscans . . . always the old hatred of Calvin for the sons of Loyola! Moreover, the friendship with which the Duc de Ventadour honored these religious was not calculated to find favor with the Company of the Duc de Montmorency; and we must add that what was looked upon as Jesuit influence at Court was greatly, though we think unnecessarily, dreaded. For these and many other reasons their departure for Canada was opposed, though all to no purpose, as the Viceroy had approved it, and in order to prevent the arising of new difficulties, bore the travelling expenses of six Jesuits.

Baffled on this point, the enemies of the Society of Jesus determined to carry another, and they next endeavored to circumvent the Franciscans. "Our choice of the Jesuits," says Gabriel Sagard, "was strongly opposed by many of our friends who tried to dissuade us by declaring that eventually they would drive us out of the country, but there was no apparent reason to believe that these worthy Fathers would ever prove thus ungrateful. They are too good and virtuous to wish to do anything of the kind, and even should one or two of them have such a project in view, one or two religious do not constitute a community any more than one swallow makes a Spring."

Then the friends of the Franciscans took the trouble to magnify and publish an incident which, though insignificant in itself, nevertheless served as a basis for their criticisms. We have said that the Association of Merchants provided for the nutriment and support of the Franciscan Fathers, and it appears that some Jesuits induced the council of Associates to settle upon them two of these pensions. To say the least, this was wrong, and when the Franciscans thus deprived of their rights, justly reclaimed them, the Jesuits yielded without resistance. At length "charity dissipated all mists," said Father Le Clercq, " the more so as the reasons made known to us savored principally of interest and vain-glory."

Father Coton, Provincial of Paris, selected Fathers Charles Lalemant, Ennemond Massé, Jean de Brébeuf, and two lay brothers, François Charton and Gilbert Buret, as the first detachment of missionaries.

Our readers are already acquainted with Father Massé, who after an absence of eleven years, now returned to the beautiful land of New France whence he had been so violently ejected, but where he had left his apostolic heart. Father Jean de Brébeuf, though the youngest of the trio, was by reason of his many great virtues and heroic death, nevertheless destined to become the most illustrious.

Father Charles Lalemant was appointed superior. Born at Paris in 1587, he had consecrated himself to God at the age of twenty, and though first assigned to teach grammar and literature and later the mathematical sciences, he was acting as President of the Clermont College, when by dint of entreaty, he secured an appointment to the mission at Quebec.

The Jesuits, accompanied by Father Joseph de la Roche-Daillon, a Franciscan, and member of the illustrious family of the Comtes de Lude, sailed from Dieppe, April 24, 1625, on a ship owned by Guillaume de Caen, and reached Quebec on June 15. It was the second time that the sons of St. Ignatius had set foot upon Canadian soil, but never before had they appeared upon the waters of the picturesque St. Lawrence, along which they were afterwards often to paddle in the canoes of christianized savages.

But the unpropitious circumstances attending their arrival in Quebec would have had a disheartening effect upon less valiant souls. The pamphlets published in France against the Jesuits had been extensively circulated in the little Canadian settlement, and Catholics, as well as Protestants, had become so imbittered against the missionaries as to bluntly refuse to receive them. In the absence of Champlain, who had been detained at Paris in the interest of affairs connected with the Colony, Emery de Caen, his substitute, declared that there was no room for the Jesuits either at the *Habitation* or the Fort, and moreover, that he had received no orders from the Viceroy concerning them.

Indeed, there is no telling what would have become of the maligned priests had it not been for the exquisite charity of the Franciscans. In 1615, the latter had built a temporary chapel near the storehouse of the Company of Merchants, and used it as a parish church ; but, five years later, realizing the necessity of a larger structure, they erected a convent and church on the banks of the Saint Charles, about a mile and a quarter from Quebec, where the general hospital now stands. Here the Franciscans had lived for some time prior to the arrival of the Jesuits in 1625, and, upon hearing of the supreme contempt shown the religious whom they had invited to Canada, they boarded a long boat and, going hastily in search of them, conducted them to the convent on the river bank and placed half the building, garden and enclosure at the disposal of their guests. The sons of St. Francis and St. Ignatius lived beneath the same roof for many long months thereafter, and the Society of Jesus will ever gratefully remember the generous, brotherly hospitality then accorded its subjects.

As soon as they were installed, the Jesuits set out to select a piece of land on which to build a home and part of which they could cultivate, and, not far from the Franciscan Convent, between the St. Charles and the small river called the St. Michel situated to the west of the Lairet, they discovered a most desirable site. The place known as Jacques Cartier's Fort, was an ideal location for the missionaries' residence, and the property was gladly ceded to them by the Duc de Ventadour. Accordingly, on the first day of September, 1625, in presence of a concourse of friends, a cross was solemnly planted on the premises where the residence dedicated to Notre-Dame des Anges was so soon to be erected.

On the first of August, 1626, the superior of the mission wrote to his brother as follows: " The Franciscan Fathers attended the ceremony in company with the most prominent Frenchmen who, after dinner, all began to work, and, from that day forward, we five Jesuits continued to dig up trees and break ground till we were overtaken by the snow and obliged to forego the work until Spring."

The cultivation of the land had, up to then, been sadly neglected, scarcely twenty or twenty-five acres being cleared, and this having been accomplished only by the Franciscans and the Hébert family. Such were the beginnings of the Colony. Moreover, there was no security against famine, a scourge which was liable to attack the little settlement at any time. Quebec being somewhat remote from the sea, was never visited more than once a year by European ships and these, sent from France by the Associated Merchants, would carry only such provisions as were necessary for the sustenance of the employees of the commercial society and the people at the *Habitation* Therefore, if a vessel were to be lost at sea or captured by pirates, there was the awful probability of the inhabitants of Quebec dying of hunger, a calamity which threatened them more than once. Champlain often warned them of the gravity of the situation and proposed the one possible remedy, that of tilling the soil, but his suggestion did not find favor with the Associates who, seeing therein no financial gain, refused to act upon it.

The Jesuits, having nothing to expect from the Associates who were so unfavorably disposed towards them nor from the savages, who were reduced to hard lines, pursued, from the moment of their arrival, the only reasonable course. " Like vigilant, hard-working men," said Champlain, " they set about tilling the ground, in order thus to procure means of self-sustenance and be totally independent of the provisions sent from France." Twenty men, including mechanics, carpenters and farmers, brought from France by Fathers Noyrot and de Noué, lent their valuable assistance and, near the junction of the Lairet and Saint Charles, was erected the unpretentious building which, for several years, was to be the principal residence of the Jesuits in Quebec.

Father Massé, surnamed "the useful Father," drew the plans and superintended the work; Father de Brébeuf devoted himself chiefly to studying the language of the natives and even spent the severe winter season among the Algonquins in order the quicker to become familiar with their speech and customs; and Father Lalemant divided his time between working in the field and performing apostolic duties, and frequently accompanied the Franciscans to Quebec, thereby to put himself in touch with the French and, if possible, dispel the harsh feeling harbored by the Catholics against the religious of the Society of Jesus. And in this he soon succeeded. The people drew near and studied him, and, little by little, their aversion gave way to confidence and esteem and they consigned the libellous pamphlets to the flames. Moreover, the captain of the *Habitation* loaned Father Lalemant some carpenters for a few days during Lent; two interpreters, acceding to the missionary's request, agreed to give him lessons in the Huron and Algonquin languages—something they had always refused to do for the Franciscans; and the Catholics begged him to prepare them for their Easter duty.

On August 1, 1626, Father Lalemant wrote as follows to the Rev. Mutius Vitelleschi, Father General of the Society: "During the past year we have done nothing but acquire a knowledge of the settlements, people and idioms of the two nations, though we have not spared ourselves in serving the French who are here to the number of forty-three. We have heard their general confessions—having first impressed upon them the necessity of this sacrament—and besides, each month we give them two sermons. . . . Thank God we keep well, but all of us, with perhaps one exception, sleep in our day attire, and our time, outside of that given to spiritual exercises and apostolic work, is devoted to agricultural pursuits."

These beginnings, though modest, were quite consoling, but the future looked gloomy and, as every one realized, the Company of Merchants was the greatest obstacle in the way of success. While this organization would remain under Calvinistic guidance and could boast not only the monopoly of commerce but the authority and independence it then enjoyed in Canada, it was useless to look for the spread of the Catholic faith, the establishment of fortified posts or the progress of agriculture, which helps so effectually to strengthen and enrich a new country. Either some radical change must be made or the colony inevitably be reduced to a mere commercial warehouse, a market-place for the traffic of skins and furs.

Therefore, without giving Father Noyrot an opportunity to rest, Father Lalemant sent him back to France by the same vessel in which he had come to Canada, and bade him acquaint the Viceroy with the actual state of affairs, and procure, if possible, the removal of Calvinists from official positions in the Company of Merchants. "I am sending Father Philibert Noyrot back to France," Father Lalemant wrote to the General of his Order, "in the interest of our mission, and I trust that Your Reverence will lend him your assistance in his dealing with those from whom we may look for aid and protection. It will even be necessary to exert your influence over our own Fathers who do not seem to understand the needs of our mission."

The messenger could have not been better chosen, as he had witnessed the existing trouble, and his zeal and prudent energy were to be relied on implicitly.

At Paris he displayed most amazing activity, spending entire days in going about procuring the required interviews, and nights in making memoranda and writing letters. He called upon the King and his councillors, the Viceroy of Canada and the most influential persons at Court, in fact, overlooked nothing that would tend to advance the cause in which he worked. Nevertheless, though the reasonableness of his complaint and the efficacy of the proposed remedy were readily admitted, the replacing of Calvinists by Catholics, as directors and employees of the Commercial Society, was opposed on all sides, and Father Noyrot found himself confronted by such inquiries as these: "Where, in this Society, could you find Catholics so disinterested as to consider their own worldly and pecuniary advantage secondary to the glory of God and the honor of France? Are you sure that their appointment would produce the desired results? On the contrary, would it not occasion serious dissatisfaction and lead to the dissolution of the Society as also of the Colony?" However, all these objections which were the outcome of fear, timidity, or inability to act, did not discourage Father Noyrot. The plan which he had in view he was determined to realize and he therefore resorted to a supreme measure.

Cardinal Richelieu was then at the zenith of his power. Summoned to the ministry two years previously, the superiority of his genius had won him a place apart. He was consulted upon all momentous questions; nothing of account was undertaken without his knowledge; army, navy, financial, foreign and interior affairs were directed by him; in fine, he was a sort of universal minister. The three great schemes which occupied him during the period of his ministry are familiar to students of the French history of that epoch: the humiliation of the House of Austria, the abasement of the French aristocracy, and the ruin of the Calvinist party. Just at this time he was leisurely considering the best means by which to crush the Protestants, and meanwhile, he allowed the French courtiers to denounce him to Catholic France as the pope of the Huguenots, because he had granted peace to the latter and signed the Treaty of Monçon with Spain.

Father Noyrot went with Father Francois Ragueneau to see the Cardinal, having prevously invoked the aid of all the saints of heaven. He dreaded the interview, and his apprehension seemed to paralyze his speech, which, at best, was marred by a painful hesitancy. But, according to his companion's statement, once that Father Noyrot found himself in presence of the minister all embarrassment vanished, and, contrary to his wont, he spoke with ease and fluency, becoming even eloquent and winning the Cardinal's whole attention.

At the close of that interview Richelieu took a great resolution. When endeavoring to check the progress of Calvinism in France, he could not afford to have it take the lead of Catholicity in a French colony. Therefore, he determined to suppress the company of the Duc de Montmorency, on the ground that it had not filled its engagements; to allow none save Catholics to people Quebec and the French posts in Canada, and finally, to found a powerful society capable of giving zest and importance to the colony, and also of effecting the conversion of savage nations.

Being prompt to resolve upon a plan, the minister was also quick to act. On April 29, 1627, Richelieu and five assistants cheerfully and eagerly signed the act establishing the *Company of the Hundred Associates* or of *New France*. In order the better to exact fidelity on the part of the new associates, the Cardinal placed himself at the head of the enterprise—the Duc de Ventadour resigning in his favor—and, at the request of Father Noyrot, the Marquise de Guercheville ceded to the company all her Acadian claims and became an associate by contributing 1000 écus.

In the *Édits et ordonnances* may be read the various articles in the act of establishment, and they all reflect great credit upon Cardinal Richelieu, who, in compiling the Act, had kept the great object, French-Christian civilization, well in view. The King granted the company complete ownership of Canada and Florida, as also the entire monopoly of the fur trade, under the following conditions: that the company allow none save Frenchmen and Catholics to emigrate to Canada; that, in the year 1628, it transport thither from two to three hundred souls, and up to four thousand during the fifteen succeeding years; that it lodge and maintain these emigrants for three years, at the expiration of which time it should distribute amongst them tilled lands and a quantity of seeds, or else procure them other means of sustenance; and that, during fifteen years, it defray the expenses of religious worship and provide for the support of three priests in the posts that would be established. Moreover, special advantages were to be given the converted savages, "who were to be regarded as natural Frenchmen." Father Noyrot had succeeded beyond all expectations, having obtained more than he had asked for or had been requested to seek.

However, the negotiating of this important affair upon which depended the future success of the Christian civilization of Canada, did not prevent him from taking an active interest in the secondary object of his mission, the victualling of Notre-Dame des Anges. That house could expect no aid from the society under the direction of Guillaume de Caen; its cultivated grounds could not provide nourishment for more than twenty people and, until further orders, all provisions must come from France. Thanks to offerings of money and gifts of other descriptions, Father Noyrot had procured, and sent on to Honfleur, provisions sufficient to keep the missionaries and their workmen for a year. The vessel carrying the precious freight was to arrive at Quebec about the middle of the year 1627, but Guillaume de Caen and Captain de la Ralde, who had gone to France on the same ship with Father Noyrot, had kept a close watch upon the priest's movements and eventually destroyed his plans. Through some malicious breach of discretion, they had learned of the complaints lodged against them and the company of which they directed the commercial operations. This information exasperated them and they vented their spite by detaining at Honfleur the supplies that were being hurried over to the Jesuits in Quebec. The effect of this revengeful act was seriously felt at Notre-Dame des Anges. The provisions brought from France during the previous year were almost exhausted and all too soon was ushered in the long, severe Canadian Winter with its train of privations, responsibilities and threatenings of want and famine. Seeing no aid forthcoming, Father Lalemant left Father de Brébeuf with the Hurons, Fathers Massé and de Noüe and three lay brothers at Quebec, and, with 20 laborers, set sail for France, arriving in November, 1627.

AN IROQUOIS MAIDEN,

OR

Life of Catharine Tegakwitha

(*Continued.*)

CHAPTER IX.

The Hunt.—Life in the Woods.—Calumny.

IMMEDIATELY after the Christmas holidays the savages prepare, according to their custom, to set out on their Winter hunt. It is the most favorable season. The rivers are frozen; the vast St. Lawrence itself, everywhere that the rapidity of the waters permits, has become a solid plain, facilitating travel in every direction. Snow in abundance favors the skill of the hunter, for, while armed with his raquettes (1) or snow shoes, he can walk with firm step and without sinking into the deepest or softest banks or drifts. The animals he is in pursuit of are hindered by the snow, and cannot flee with sufficient swiftness, and inevitably fall beneath his stroke.

The hunt is the chief source of wealth to these Indian peoples. But they do not employ it to augment their own comfort or well-being. They draw from it only their clothing, their food for the time being, and the material for barter with the Europeans. They receive from them arms and ammunition, which advantageously replace their tomahawks and bows and arrows. The savage finds in the vast forest of this country abundance of elk (Canadian reindeer), bear, roebuck (roedeer), beaver, marten, weasel, wildcat (catamount), fox, porcupine, otter and seal. In spite of his fatigue, and often even of great privation, the hunt always offers great attraction to the savage. To this rude child of

---

(1) The "raquettes" or snow shoes used for walking on snow owe their name to the resemblance they bear to the instrument used in the game of volant or shuttlecock. They are fastened to the shoes, and enable the wearer to walk on the softest snow without sinking into it.

nature good cheer is the greatest of all pleasures. Thus all pain and care are forgotten as soon as he has found the means of satisfying his gluttonous appetite. He even forgets all thought of the morrow and, like a careless child in the abundance of to-day, thinks not of the famine of the morrow should the chase cease to be successful. These long journeys and this wandering life during three or four months greatly endangered the inconstant character and feeble virtue of the new converts. They were no longer under the eyes of the enlightened guide, who served as their tutelary angel. However, to recall them to their duties, the missionary had given them instruction before their departure, by tracing on birch bark a sort of calendar, whereon were inscribed the Sundays and holidays; the days of fasting and abstinence were also carefully marked. On other pieces of birch bark were traced, in hieroglyphics or allegorical signs, the prayers of each day. The skins of bark, carefully rolled and enclosed in cases of the same material, were confided to the Dogique or most skilful of the family. It was he who each day gave the signal for the exercises of prayer and presided over it as the missionary might have done. Their life was such during these long absences, says a missionary of that epoch, that often on their return we hardly found matter for absolution. But for a great number these absences were not without danger.

Catharine at once understood what she would have to fear in thus withdrawing from the village, and from privation of the ordinary succors of religion. But the respect she owed to her brother-in-law and his wife, did not permit her to separate herself from them. God wished to show, by her example, that real virtue is of all times and places, and when solid, can never be false to itself. That of Catharine was to find new lustre in this way of life, since she was to triumph once more, in the rude trial of injuries and calumnies.

In the depths of the woods, Catharine was what she had been in the village. Nothing could interrupt the usual exercises of piety that it was still in her power to perform. She made up for such as were impossible by such practices as her devotion inspired. The prayers recited morning and evening by the savages, were not enough for her fervor. Long before the prayer in the cabin she was already in communion with heaven, and in the evening she still prolonged her pious devotions far into the night.

Each day, about the time when, at the Mission, the savages were going to hear Mass, Catharine withdrew to a little oratory that she had chosen for herself in the forest. A thick curtain of green trees formed the enclosure and isolated her from the whole world. Above her head the tall pines spread their tufted branches, forming a sort of gigantic dome. On the bark of one of the trees, she had traced with her knife, a large cross. It was the only ornament of the sylvan temple, but it was sufficient for her faith. She sought this spot to unite in spirit and in heart with those who, in the village, had the happiness of being present at the dread mysteries of our altars. She sent her guardian angel there to gather up for her the graces that the celestial victim was causing to flow in abundance. Often, even in the course of the day, she loved to slip away from the family for a moment, and shut herself up in this solitude to converse more freely with God.

Catharine's life, however, did not pass wholly in the practice of sweet and quiet contemplation. Piety, which is useful in everything, did not cause her to neglect her work. She was always counted upon for a certain amount of household labor, and was faithful in discharging it. Embroidery, the making of collars, preparation of skins for clothing or commerce, the care of birch bark for the construction of cabins or canoes, together with prayer, filled all her time.

Work was for her a real pleasure, and she possessed the skill of inspiring her companions with the same sentiments. How often did she know how to entice them to chant with her some pious canticle, or to edify by the story of the life of some saint, or a tale told them by the missionaries.

By this Catharine obtained two important results ; one was to banish evil discourse and frivolous conversation, the other to nourish her own fervor, and her union with God. Thus, zeal and piety, those two characteristics of real virtue, were constantly in practice. But the works she preferred were those which favored her taste for solitude and mortification. And this is why she willingly took upon herself the charge of domestic cares, while the family was scouring the woods, or went to the forest to gather provision of fuel for the hearth-fire. She thus found herself happy in being the servant of others, and at the same time having nothing to disturb her intercourse with heaven.

Although there was nothing not praiseworthy in this life led by Catharine in the depths of the woods, but much that was meritorious for herself, still her heart was not wholly there. It was evident that she found no pleasure in it, and that she was out of her element. The humble chapel of the Mission, our Lord in the Tabernacle, the Holy Sacrifice of the Mass, Benediction of the Blessed Sacrament, the Instructions of the missionary, all the practices of piety to which she had become accustomed, but especially the frequentation of the Sacraments, were like a powerful magnet, drawing her thoughts to the village and there fixing her heart, so that if her body was in the woods, her soul at least was wholly at the Mission of the Saut. In the designs of Providence this mission was to serve as a trial to this fervent soul, and for the second time she was to feel the force of the storm, the hardest for virtue to bear : calumny. But already familiar with all sorts of combats, this generous Christian was to gain still another glorious victory, and to remain humble, patient, and resigned, under the blow about to be dealt her.

Savages are naturally suspicious, and as we have seen, the least pretext often suffices to suddenly change their opinions. A woman of Catharine's cabin suspected her of having a guilty affection for her husband, and hardly had they returned to the village when she hastened to denounce her to the missionary. She misinterpreted even her most innocent actions, citing amongst other like charges, her frequent retreats to the solitude of the woods, her goings and comings always in the same direction, and always enveloped in mystery.

The husband of this jealous woman had unconsciously given new weight to her suspicions. One day in speaking of the canoe which he had prepared for their approaching return from the hunt, he added that he would need some help in finishing it, and transporting it from the forest. "It is Catharine who will do me this favor," he added with simplicity. He knew enough of the charity of this good girl to count upon her, but the wife saw in this only a proof of complicity. The missionary lent an attentive ear to this prejudiced tongue. He had no difficulty in discovering the truth, but he desired to hear Catharine's testimony also. Strong in her innocence she listened unmoved to the accusation, and contented herself with protesting against it with such candor, as could leave no doubt in the mind of the missionary.

Still, this trial was very painful to Catharine, but God permitted it, for the perfecting of her virtue. After having sacrificed for love of God, her relations, her country, the advantages she might have reaped by a suitable marriage, it would seem as if nothing remained for this admirable maiden, but to offer up that of honor and reputation. This she did generously, and, far from divulging the names of the authors of the calumny, never spoke of them, but let the matter die out of itself. One might have said that it was no affair of hers. All her revenge consisted in praying to God more fervently for the authors of it.

The poor savage who first gave rise to the sad report, understood, later, the injustice of her suspicions, and of her conduct. For three whole years, she bewailed her fault, and the missionary had to use all his authority to moderate the excess of her regret, and restore confidence to her heart.

All those who had thus spoken evil of Catharine, ended by acknowledging their error, and became, afterwards, the most ardent in exalting her virtues.

Chapter X.

Feast of Easter.—Conversion of Mary Theresa.

After her return from the hunt, Catharine only thought of making reparation, by her fervor, for what she called the losses her soul might have sustained in the midst of the woods. Of her own accord, she resolved to avoid distant journeys in the future, and never again to withdraw from the Mission.

The Easter holidays were approaching and all the savages engaged in the hunt within a short distance of the Saut, gathered there from all directions, to honor this great solemnity. It had a powerful attraction for Catharine. She saw, for the first time, the grand solemnities of Holy Week and the Easter holidays. It would be difficult to tell the salutary impression they made upon her. How greatly she appreciated them, and enjoyed the happiness of living in the midst of a wholly Christian population! And what abundant tears she shed on Good Friday, while listening to the recital of the Passion and death of our Saviour! On Easter Sunday the missionary granted her a favor which she had long desired, and which may, with reason, be regarded as a shining testimony to her virtues. In spite of her youth she was admitted into the Confraternity of the Holy Family, a pious association which had, not long before, been established at the Saut, and which had already produced there the happiest fruits; few persons were received into it, and those few were chosen from among the most fervent Christians of both sexes. This Confraternity was the real support or prop of piety in the Mission. It excited a pious emulation for good works, and a holy rivalry in virtue.

This favor was ordinarily reserved for Christians of a certain age, but, although Catharine only counted seven or eight months of sojourn at the Mission, an exception was made in her favor, and all fervent hearts applauded it. Her conduct fully justified the choice.

Catharine already knew, and zealously employed, the means of sanctification generally used by virtuous souls, to unite themselves more closely to God. The lightest faults of her earliest years, appeared to her as sovereign ingratitude towards the goodness of God. She armed herself, then, with holy severity against herself, and caused her innocent body to expiate inexorably, what she called, her crimes. In the pious exercises of penance which she practised with Anastasie, her faithful companion, and the confidant of her secrets, she had often on her lips burning words, to excite her fervor, "O my Jesus!" she would cry, "can I do too much for Thee! I love Thee, but I have offended Thee, and it is to satisfy Thy justice that I am here. Chastise me, O my God, chastise me." Or again: "O my Saviour, I cannot think, without sighing, on the three nails that attached Thee to the Cross. They are figures of my sins." Then her companion and herself would weep bitterly and give themselves up to rigorous penance. The remembrance of her faults, and the thought of our Saviour's suffering, kept alive in her that thirst for mortification and suffering, the pious excess of which it was more than once necessary to moderate. She understood, as if by instinct, or rather thanks to the grace of God that directed her, that this was, together with prayer, the way to union with God, and the promptest, and at the same time the most powerful weapon, against the worst enemies of her soul.

Her pious companion, whose wise counsels she always hearkened to submissively, greatly contributed to nourish these sentiments, by the recital of the lives of saints, the combats of martyrs, and the penance of solitaries of the desert.

An accident of which Catharine came near being the victim, justified in her eyes, her self-imposed penance, and incited to others still more severe.

While she was at work in the forest, helping to fell a tree, without having taken all the measures counselled by prudence, the tree suddenly fell before she expected it. Hardly had she time to spring aside, to avoid being crushed by its fall. But one of the branches struck her on the head with such force as to render her unconscious. They thought her dead, when after a short space of time she recovered consciousness, and spoke from her heart these pious words: "O Jesus, I thank Thee for having succored me in danger." She arose penetrated with the thought that God had only spared her life to give her time to do penance. She confessed this in confidence, to a new companion whom heaven had just sent her.

This was Mary (1) Theresa Tegaïgenta. Her relations with

---

(1) In the autograph MSS. of Father Chauchetière, we read *Tegaiaguenta* and *Te-aia-enta*.

this chosen soul were too intimate, and she herself too virtuous, not to merit being made known. It was about this time that she became the faithful friend of Catharine, and the worthy emulator of her virtues. She soon shared in all her pious practices of tender devotion.

Up to this time Catharine's only intimate companion had been the good Anastasie, who was to her as a mother, but who could no longer follow save at a distance, the child she had formed; her strength no longer permitted her to imitate her in everything. It was therefore, an advantage to Catharine to find a companion less advanced in age; endowed not only with the same good will, but with the same courage, and who in the desire to give herself wholly to God, was ready to walk with her in the path of suffering, in which the Lord seemed to conduct her.

If evil friendships spoil and corrupt by their contact even the most virtuous hearts, as rotten fruit that which is sound, friendship founded on religion becomes the prop and food of virtue.

But Theresa had not always been what she then was. Baptized while very young by Father Brujas at Oneida, her birthplace, she had not long preserved the fruits of her baptism. The license which reigned in her nation, and the bad example continually before her eyes soon caused her to lose sight of her holy promises. Even the emigration of her family to the Saut St. Louis, produced but a slight change in her conduct, and only partially arrested the shameful excesses of intemperance, to which she abandoned herself.

The Lord waited for her in the form of a terrible trial, the last resource perhaps, offered by Divine mercy to repentance. She had the happiness to profit by it.

It was in the winter of 1675. Having set off for the hunt with her husband, who was not yet a Christian, and one of her nephews, they halted on the banks of the great river of the Ontaonaks (1). Other Iroquois hunters joined them on the road, thus forming a band of eleven persons, four men, four women, and three children.

---

(1) It has also borne the name of Great River of the Algonquins.

Unfortunately the snow had fallen very late that year, which made the chase bad. Provisions, never plentiful with the savages, as they imprudently count upon the success of the hunt, were soon exhausted. An elk killed by the husband of Theresa, sustained them for some days longer, but no other game presenting itself, the horrors of famine were soon felt. To diminish them, skins of animals and even foot gear were thrown into the cauldron. After that, moss from the rocks, or lichen from the trees was the only aliment that could be procured. This frightful hunger, which could only increase, since they were far from all succor, could not fail to place before their eyes, the inevitable prospect of a horrible death. While things were in this state, Theresa's husband fell sick, and as he was unable to keep up with the others they were obliged to stop.

Two of the hunters, a Mohawk and a Seneca, set off to scour the country to try to discover some game. They were to return in ten days at the latest. The Mohawk, in fact, returned at the appointed time, but alone, and he announced that his companion had died of hunger and misery on the road. He was suspected, and with reason, of having taken his life, in order to feast on his flesh; he admitted not having captured anything, and yet he appeared robust and full of strength and health.

Hopeless of getting anything from the hunt, the unfortunate beings tried to persuade the Christian woman to abandon her husband in the woods, as there was no possibility of saving his life. They gave her to understand that unless she did so, there was no other way for herself of escaping death, and her nephew's life was also at stake, with that of the whole band. This proposition chilled her with terror, but she generously rejected it.

The other savages, finding her inflexible, decided to abandon her with her husband and nephew, and they departed in search of food. Two days later, the poor invalid died with the desire to receive baptism, which his spouse, in her ignorance, thought not of administering to him; and she buried his body in the snow. Then taking her young nephew on her shoulders she courageously took the road to the Mission once more.

Some days later she fell in with her former companions, who also decided to go in the direction of the French habitations, with the hope of obtaining succor. They were so weak and emaciated that, after twenty days of march, they could no longer continue their journey and stopped to await death.

Despair inspired them with a horrible thought. Of what excess is not unhappy man capable, when religion does not teach him how to bear his misfortunes! They formed the project of taking the life of one of the party, that he might serve as food for the others.

The wife of Tsonnontouan and her two children were already designated as victims. They desired to learn from Theresa, beforehand, as the best informed amongst them (she was the only Christian in the band), what *the Prayer* taught on the subject.

Terrified by so criminal a project, more terrified perhaps, lest she might be called upon to share the fate of her companions, she dared not reply.

An old man of the troop, seeing her hesitation, offered himself as the first victim, believing he had the right to give them power over his life. "What use can I be now? What trouble I would give you, were you obliged to drag me along over long and difficult roads! Let my flesh serve in preserving your life. It is the best way!" And he was put to death.

Theresa, witness of this horrible butchery, which the barbarians repeated a few days later on another of the band, was frozen with terror, and she opened her eyes to the state of her conscience, which was much more to be pitied than that of her body. The remembrance of her past disorders arose before her mind, and, penetrated with the liveliest sorrow, she began to lament bitterly before God. In her grief, she besought His pardon for undertaking such a long and hazardous journey through forests, without having purified her heart by the Sacrament of Penance. Her promises of conversion came from a sincere heart, and God gave her time to realize them.

ANNALS OF THE SHRINE.

The excellent number of the *Historical Records and Studies*, published by the United States Catholic Historical Society, contains a letter written by Father Isaac Jogues, dated April 6, and written, presumably, in the year 1636. The letter was first published by R. P. F. Martin, S.J., in his "Life of P. Isaac Jogues," and it appears in full in Dr. Gilmary Shea's translation of the same biography. It is difficult, therefore, to see what the editors of the *Historical Records and Studies* mean by calling it "an unpublished letter of Father Jogues." Père Martin's copy of the letter seems to be more accurate than the one given in the *Records*. Thus the spelling of 'sepmaine,' 'Tauzeau' is more in accordance with the MSS. copy than 'septmaine' and 'Taurau.' Both the *Records* and P. Martin vary in transcribing some letters of Father Jogues, as, for instance, the letter "s," one making "succes" instead of "succez," and the other "fils" instead of "filz." These are mere minutiæ, but they show the importance of a copyist's task, especially when MSS. may be used for the purpose for which we trust Father Jogues' letters will soon be employed, viz.: for making out the account of his life needed for presenting the cause of his beatification.

The gold and precious stones donated for the crown are in the hands of the jewellers, who are preparing it and completing the design of the crown according to the material in hand. It is more correct to speak of designs than of design, because, as we have already announced in the PILGRIM, besides the crown of thorns in gold, there will be two halos, to be used instead of crowns for the statues of our Lord and our Lady grouped in the Pietà.

A new hall is to be opened soon in Montclair, New Jersey, and the pastor, Rev. J. F. Mendle, has decided to call it the Tegakwitha Hall. A lecture on the "Lily of the Mohawks" was given by the Editor of the PILGRIM, in the basement of the handsome church Father Mendle is building near by, on Sunday evening, January 29th, to a large and appreciative audience. An illustrated lecture on Father Jogues, the pioneer missionary of the State of New York, was given in St. Peter's Church, Richmond, Staten Island, Sunday, February 26th.

CONTRIBUTIONS TO THE SHRINE.

J. S., St. Paul, Minn. . . . $1 00   M. L. S. H., Buffalo, N. Y. . 5 00

FOR THE CROWN.

E. W. C., Hoboken, N. J., an opal and gold ring.   J. A., a gold cross.
M. N., a gold ring.

MATER DOLOROSA.

BY JOHN J. BRANIN.

ALAS! the hour hath come,
   Which Simeon forespake,
When Mary's sinless heart
   Should of its sorrows break.

Oh, with what anguish deep
   She sees her Jesus dear
Nailed to the shameful cross,
   'Mid ribald shout and jeer.

To sympathy unmoved,
   Who could such anguish view,
While thus the sword of grief
   Her pure heart pierces through.

What seas of bitter pain
   Engulf that mother's soul,
As from His riven side
   The living torrents roll.

Oh, with what woe she hears
   Those agonizing cries,
As, helpless and alone,
   He bows His head and dies.

"Mother, behold thy son,"
   This word thy Jesus said,
Ere yet His soul had from
   His sacred body fled.

Then let that "son" be me,
   To comfort thee and bless,
In this thy direful hour
   Of sorrow and distress.

SISTER STEPHANIE.

BY D. S. BÉNI.

(*Continued.*)

"ON December 8th, the whole city of Lyons was magnificently decorated and illuminated for the Feast of the Immaculate Conception. It was a spontaneous pageant, for neither Church nor State had ordered or suggested it. The genuine piety of the people, the perfect silence and order that prevailed in the procession in which thousands of enthusiastic Frenchmen took part, made a deep impression upon my heart, and I often said to myself, these cannot be bad people, nor can a religion be bad, which exerts such an influence for good; but conscientiously, I banished the thought, lest I, too, might fall into the fatal snare in which my sister had been caught. It was decided that we should go to Rome, and to perfect myself in Italian, I sought a teacher, and was directed to the Monastery of the Visitation, so picturesquely perched upon the summit of Fourvière. I almost shuddered at the name of monastery, which I had heard only in connection with Protestant prejudices. But once within the walls of the house, I was introduced to an Italian nun, who, like myself, bore the name of the Proto-martyr, St. Stephen. Was she as good and holy as she was beautiful? At least I would have an opportunity to judge for myself.

"She knew my sister, Mrs. M. and her family, whom she admired exceedingly, always speaking of them as *la Santa Famiglia*. But the instant she touched on religion, I changed the subject; I would not allow myself to be led into temptation. I spoke of the magnificent scenery which surrounded us, the luxuriant vineyards, the beautiful view on every side. Sister Etienne said sweetly in her Italian, which was music itself: 'Shall I tell you the history of this lovely spot?' To this I readily assented; no harm could come from conversing of nature and nature's God. She then told me of the many difficulties the sisters had in procuring this place, which was supposed to be the ancient Pretorium, where a countless multitude of martyrs had the honor of being condemned to death for the name of Jesus Christ. She said: 'I will give you the Catechism of Grenada to read, in which you will find a letter written by the faithful of Lyons and Vienna, to the churches of Asia and Phrygia. This letter describes a cave, where a number of Christians died.' The name of Catechism startled me, so I said: 'Dear Sister, I would rather hear the story from your own lips.' Then she continued: 'This cave is within our enclosure. It contains three caverns which are deeper than the cave itself, and from which water is continually dripping. One of these caverns is closed by a heavy iron door, and among the many martyrs mentioned in the letter, who were thrown into these caverns, St. Pothinus, the first Archbishop of Lyons, is especially named. In digging the foundation for this monastery a mosaic pavement was discovered, and many large stones with epitaphs and devices engraved upon them, which proved the antiquity of the place sanctified by the blood of so many martyrs, whose number, according to the general opinion, is about nineteen thousand; so you see that we have catacombs here as well as in Rome.'

"This conversation was very interesting, but, lest it should drift into something of the Catholic religion, for, of course, I knew that all those martyrs were Catholics, I changed the subject, and remarked the luxuriant vineyards which covered the hillsides, and as I turned towards the window and looked down upon the city and the country which lay between, peace seemed to reign upon the earth. It was November, that season which we call Indian Summer, but the French piously call it the Summer of All Saints. The silvery clouds and hazy atmosphere softened the rays of the sun and gave mellow tints to the variegated foliage of purple, crimson and gold that still covered the slope of the mountain, which seemed to repose in that peace, promised, even here on earth, to men of good will.

"Would that peace ever come to my tempest-tossed soul? My dear child, no one but a convert can understand the agony of doubt, of fear, and the darkness which precedes conversion.

"The opening of the New Year, 1869, found us on our way to Rome. We had letters of introduction to Dr. C., then Rector of the American College, and to other persons, some of whom were American tourists. We had relatives in Marseilles, Spezzia and Genoa, whom we visited, and whenever our going to Rome was mentioned, everybody exclaimed, with unfeigned delight: '*You will see the Holy Father*,' as if that was the greatest happiness that could be bestowed upon mortal man. This impressed me very much, that one man should have such a hold on the affections of the people—for Rome was to them the Holy Father; they neither thought nor spoke of the city and its historic memories—only the Holy Father, the Vicar of Christ. I cannot tell you of my first impressions of St. Peter's, for the sensation I felt was indescribable. I looked at it in silent awe, and as the words of Childe Harold recurred to me, I saw in them a meaning I had not known before.

"Nor will I attempt to describe the magnificence of the Holy Week ceremonies in the Sistine Chapel, although the plaintive *Miserere* still sounds within my ears. It is impossible to convey any idea of the impression which it must produce upon the minds of all who hear it; first because of the solemnity of the entire service, the richness of its simple harmonies, and the exquisite art with which it is sung. The chapel was so dark, that it was barely possible to distinguish the Holy Father as he knelt before the altar, while a perfect soprano voice sang the antiphon: '*Christus factus est pro nobis obediens usque ad mortem*.' There followed an awful silence, then 'the first sad wail of the *Miserere* swelled forth from the softest *pianissimo*, into a bitter cry for mercy.' I hear it still: *Miserere mei Deus, secundum magnam misericordiam tuam*. Yes, according to *the multitude of Thy great mercies* blot out my iniquities, *according to Thy great mercies*, how those words swept over the chords of my aching heart, which still echo and re-echo that plaintive wail—*Miserere mei Deus—Miserere mei*.

"The first day I attended the ceremonies, I watched intently the door through which the Pope would enter, determined to study his face, and judge for myself. His Holiness appeared, accompanied by a brilliant procession of Princes of the Church. I gazed upon his benevolent face, which magnetized me, and I realized that pictures did not, and could not do justice to the gentleness and sweetness of his countenance, and every time I saw him I was more attracted to him. I told you that my sister had two little boys; now three others had been added to the little circle. No children are allowed to attend the great ceremonies, but as I wanted my nephews to see all they could in Rome, I took the two youngest boys with me. The guards invariably answered my appeal for their admission, with the words '*Non Io*,' but at the same time they graciously turned their backs to allow us to pass in. I was elated with my success, and when the procession passed down the chapel, I whispered to little John to step out and kneel before the Holy Father. He understood me perfectly and at the right moment fell on his knees. The Holy Father looked at him tenderly as he exclaimed '*Piccolo Americano!*' John seized the Pope's hand and kissed it eagerly, and then knelt with his little hands joined, looking up into the Pope's face, and after the Holy Father had patted him on the head, and given him his blessing, John stepped aside, a happy little boy, for although he was only four years old, he was very precocious and understood the favor he had received.

"Dr. C—— was the most courteous of friends. He escorted us to the Catacombs, to many of the churches, and made the arrangements for our audience with the Holy Father. He had heard of the conversion of Mr. M. and his family, and I think he was interested in us on that account. Never can I forget, or describe the sensation which passed through my heart and soul when I stood face to face with the Vicar of Jesus Christ. A sense of my own unworthiness swept over me, and as I knelt before him, he graciously extended his hand to raise me from the floor, and I said to him: 'Holy Father I am a Catholic, but not a *Roman* Catholic, I am not one of your children.' Looking at me with tenderness, he said: 'But you *will be* my child, I will pray for you,' and in my heart for the first time, I wished I was a Catholic, for the truth dawned upon my soul with the blessing of Pius IX.

"In the second audience, when His Holiness extended his hand to bless me, I seized it and pressed it to my lips, then I asked him to pray for me. He smiled, and looked upon me with such inexpressible benevolence, that I rose from my knees a Catholic, converted, as I will always believe, by the prayers of Pius IX. Mr. M. had for some time been suffering from partial paralysis of the right hand, and my sister Mrs. M. asked the Holy Father if he would deign to bless it. His Holiness complied with her request, and it was a beautiful sight to see the five little boys on their knees, their eyes fixed on that benevolent face, their hands joined, praying for their father, who recovered the use of his hand sufficiently to write.

"On Easter Sunday we had the happiness of witnessing the great ceremony known as the Benediction of the City and the World. It is said that more than 100,000 strangers had that year witnessed the magnificent ceremonies of Holy Week. Easter Sunday dawned bright and beautiful, and at an early hour the streets were filled with people in their holiday attire, and as the crowds kept increasing, detachments of infantry and cavalry hastened by, superb equipages were mingled in the throng, and here and there a Cardinal's coach, with its coal black horses, scarlet trappings, liveried coachman and footmen, rolled along to participate in the grand ceremony. The Italian troops and the French army of occupation, numbering thousands of cavalry and infantry, had been drawn up in long lines across the plaza, and the space back of them was filled with a sea of expectant humanity.

"After the services within were concluded, a picturesque procession filed out upon the lofty 'loggia' under the large canvas that had been stretched to shield it from the sun. Priests and Monks, Bishops and Abbots, Primates and Patriarchs, Cardinals, Chamberlains, Swiss Guards and Noble Guards, in all their gorgeous robes and brilliant uniforms, ranged themselves in order, and then came the great Pius IX., seated in the '*Sedia gestatoria*,' borne upon the shoulders of twelve men in scarlet uniforms. Two Cardinals advanced to the railing and read the benediction in Latin and Italian;

then dropped the papers from their hands. As they slowly floated down like white-winged messengers from heaven to earth, the crowd made an effort to secure them. One was torn into shreds by many hands; a long arm reached up from the crowd and seized the other as a precious memento of that thrice happy day.

"Then Pius IX. rose to his feet, the picture of majesty in his flowing white robes. The effect upon the crowd below was magical. The vast concourse of people fell upon their knees, while the Pope lifting up his arms towards heaven, and turning to the north, south, east and west, sang the Benediction in that rich, clear, powerful voice for which he was so remarkable. Every syllable could be distinctly heard, and as the last " Amen " died away; there followed a silence which was broken only by heart throbbings of emotion—then suddenly there was a roar of artillery from the Castle of San Angelo, twenty military bands burst forth in harmonious strains, the great bells of the city pealed, and the climax was reached when 150,000 voices gave vent to their feelings in prolonged shouts of ' *Viva Pio Nono*,' that made the earth tremble, and pierced the sky as if they would burst through the gates of heaven itself. Every nation, and clime, and tongue, was represented in that vast assemblage.

"As soon as I returned to Lyons, I sought dear Sister Étienne to rejoice her heart by my conversion, and to beg her to prepare me for baptism. L'Abbé Bouguet, the confessor at the convent, took upon himself my instruction, and May 21st was appointed for my baptism. Never will I forget that morning; the whole earth seemed to smile upon me as I turned my steps to the monastery on the hill.

'Clear were the heavens and blue, and May with her cap crowned
    with roses,
Stood in her holiday dress in the fields, and the wind and the
    brooklet
Murmured gladness and peace, God's peace. With lips rosy-tinted
Whispered the race of the flowers, and merry on balancing branches
Birds were singing their carol, a jubilant hymn to the Highest,
And adorned like a leaf-woven arbor, stood the old-fashioned gate'
    of the convent. 'And within, upon each cross
A fragrant garland was hung, new-twined by the hand of affection.'

"Never until that moment did I imagine how much dear Sister Étienne and her holy sisters had interested themselves in my conversion, and never will my heart cease to be grateful to them for reclaiming a wandering sheep.

"The sisters were assembled in the choir and the pupils in their tribune, to witness my baptism. The oldest of my nephews had been chosen for my godfather, and my sister was my godmother. After the exorcisms, l'Abbé Bouguet conducted me into the Sanctuary, where kneeling upon a *prie dieu*, I pronounced the long formula of abjuration from the Roman ritual. When the holy water was poured upon my head and the priest had given me the name of Mary, the pupils from their tribune intoned a beautiful *Magnificat*. As I returned home, one of my little nephews, having learned from his nurse that I had gone to be baptized, ran through the streets to meet me, and pulled me down on my knees in the mud to say some prayers with him to thank God that I was a Catholic.

"But still my trials were not all over, for perfect peace belongs only to heaven. I had to pay for the great happiness of belonging to the household of Faith. Mr. M. and my sister had suffered much, but our Lord seemed to fill my cup to overflowing. Upon my return to Philadelphia, I found I had few friends. My relatives looked upon me as a dupe, and they constantly plied me with questions which were most irritating and humiliating, and I, afraid to trust myself in argument, was forced to keep silent. I endured the contempt and opprobrium of those who had been most dear to me, suffering keenly, but supported interiorly with the unwavering conviction that I had the true faith, which gave me an inward peace, believing that in God's own good time He would quell the tempest. From the time I was four years old I had within my heart a constant yearning or craving for something which I had never found, a desire to belong wholly and entirely to God. How to accomplish this I knew not. I had frequently thought of the Protestant sisterhoods, and now that I was a Catholic, my heart turned instinctively to the cloister. 'One thing I had asked of the Lord, that I might dwell in His House all the days of my life.' My prayer was answered, and God led me into this House, where I have found the pearl of great price, and now my heart whispers to me unceasingly: 'Bless the Lord, O my soul; and never forget all He has done for thee.'"

(*To be continued.*)

MISSION NOTES.

In the province of Quang-Binh, Annam, more than 10,000 pagans have recently been received into the Church. Some of the new Christians have been thrown into prison where they had to endure hunger, sickness and horrible tortures. One of them received 120 blows from the cane.

Blessed Father Perboyre, a Lazarist, was martyred in China in 1840. A Chinese priest who saw him in his dungeon shortly before his death thus describes his appearance: "His whole body is one sore, and his emaciation shocking to behold. He has hardly strength to utter a few words. He can neither sit nor stand. Many of his bones are bare, his flesh hangs in pieces, and his clothes are soaked in blood." He was beatified in 1889. His sister—a Sister of Charity—and his brother, a missionary like himself, had the consolation of being present at the ceremony. His youngest sister—also a Sister of Charity—the last survivor of the family, died lately in China. She was eighty-three years of age, sixty-five of which she had spent in China.

When the Germans occupied Kia-tcheou, and the English Wei-Hai-Wei, they found the Catholic missionaries there ahead of them. These ports belong to the vicariate of Eastern Chantong, which was confided to the Franciscans in 1894. This district contains millions of idolaters. They are poor, hard working, of a peaceful character, and it is thought, well disposed for the reception of the Gospel. Everything has to be begun here. Schools and chapels have yet to be built. But the courage of the missionaries does not fail. Though their poverty is very great they rely on Providence and the prayers and alms of the faithful.

The Lazarists have re-entered Abyssinia. They have been well received by the people and enjoy the protection of the Emperor Menelik This mission holds out the brightest hopes of success.

The Marist Fathers who have gone to the Solomon Islands are living in tents until they can erect wooden buildings for a house and chapel. They have much to suffer from the heavy tropical rains, but at last accounts had escaped the fever so prevalent in these parts. The climate is damp and malarial. The natives are cannibals. The Fathers have already witnessed many of the horrors of cannibalism and on one occasion came upon a feast at which ten human victims were served up. They have enthroned a statue of our Lady under the title of "Queen of the Solomon Islands."

The province of Amazonia, Brazil, which was lately formed into a new diocese, is four times the size of France, yet when the bishop arrived, it contained but fifteen priests, but three of whom were present to take part in the installation ceremonies. Missionaries are now beginning to evangelize this immense district. The population consists of Brazilians who have been long deprived of the consolations of their religion and Indians still in a state of complete savagery. A small steamer was bought in Philadelphia. It is called the *Christopher* and is in reality a floating Church. On this the missionaries sail up and down the Amazon and its numerous affluents, stopping here and there to say Mass and administer the sacraments. The results of the first voyage were 521 baptisms, 830 confirmations, 101 marriages and a great number of confessions and communions. The missionaries are praying that they may soon have not one but many *Christophers*.

FROM THE MISSIONS.

JUNEAU, ALASKA, Feb. 2, 1899.

REV. DEAR FATHER :

May I ask your Reverence to recommend in a special manner the Intentions of our mission of Alaska, to the prayers of the League. Our best title to those prayers on the part of all the members of the League is our pressing need. Everybody has heard of Alaska and knows how distant, hard and wide a mission it is. Besides we are only at the beginning, and everything is to be done for organization and solid foundations. We have to contend against many obstacles of all kinds. Above all, we are in need of apostolic laborers. If you have read the letter lately addressed to President McKinley by Bishop Nicholas on his leaving for Holy Russia, you may have understood what it means, viz., the declining influence of the Russian Church in Alaska, which such a spiteful letter can only make more rapid and certain. Now is the time for the messengers of the Vicar of Christ to make ready for bringing all those poor natives of Alaska into the true fold. This is a great and consoling prospect which is open to us, but will Providence find in ourselves the suitable instruments of the divine mercy towards those people? That is the question.

There are signs equally evident in this southeastern part of Alaska, that poor Indians, scattered all over the Archipelago of Alexander, are only waiting for a call by apostolic men to solicit admission into the Catholic Church. Up to this day, little or nothing was done for their instruction. As our churches for the white population are too small, and the mixture of natives and white men has great inconveniences and would be detrimental to both, we are compelled, as it were, to let those poor natives almost alone, until we are able to attend to them separately and in a proper way. But who will enable us to start new Indian missions? Who will give us apostolic laborers in sufficient number and suitable for such a work of patience and self-denying without human reward? This is another reason for me to recommend our mission to the prayers of the members of the League.

As we go to press, news reaches us of the death from pneumonia of Rev. William H. Judge, S.J., so well known in connection with his apostolic and charitable labors at Dawson City, Alaska. He had just completed the building of a new church and hospital, and was preparing to abandon the comparative comfort and consolation which had grown up around him in this Gold Centre, to go back to evangelize the more uncivilized portions of Alaska, when he was overtaken by death. Father Judge was born in Baltimore, Md., on April 28, 1850, and entered the novitiate of the Society of Jesus on August 23, 1875. After fifteen years spent in different colleges of the Maryland-New York Province, he was transferred at his own urgent and repeated request to the Rocky Mountain Mission, and at once assigned to duty in Alaska. In our next issue we hope to give a detailed account of his labors in this distant field, and the circumstances attending his untimely death. R. I. P.

Acknowledgment is made of the following contribution:
For the most Needy Mission.
G. C., St. Louis, Mo. . . . $1 00

THE PILGRIM
OF
OUR LADY OF MARTYRS

XV. Year.   April, 1899.   No. 4.

RESURREXIT SICUT DIXIT.

BY E. M. SMITH.

FAR in the East 'ere yet the dawn is breaking
    Rings through the winter air
An Angel's voice, the drowsy shepherds waking
    With music rare.

Leaving their gentle flocks all calmly grazing,
    The Shepherds hasten on
And in a manger find—O love amazing !
    God's only Son !

High in the jewelled sky, the blue mists cleaving,
    Gleameth a wondrous star.
The Magi follow, doubting, fearing, believing—
    Journeying far.

Until they reach Judea's lowly stable
    And find on Mary's breast
A dimpled Babe, more fair than poets fable,
    Lying at rest.

Lo, at His feet the wise men humbly kneeling
  In holy reverence fall.
Hail Him their King in words of awesome feeling—
  Lord, God of all!

The years pass on and now thorn-crowned and bleeding,
  Up Calvary's rugged side,
Bearing His Cross with all our sins upon it,
  He comes, the Crucified!

O Lord of Hosts, sin-weary and grief-stricken
  To Thee alone we fly.
Hear us and save. The shadows 'round us thicken;
  Save us, we die!

On Easter morn amid the lilies' glory
  Radiant He rose again!
And seraph choirs proclaim the wondrous story
  Of hope to men.

Rejoice, sad hearts, lo, Easter's glad dawn bringeth
  To each soul peace and aid.
My faltering lip this message softly singeth,
  " Be not afraid."

What matter if thy cross of earthly sorrow
  Weighs thee with anguish down—
Arise, stand firm, and on some blest to-morrow
  Receive thy crown!

THE JESUITS AND NEW FRANCE

In the Seventeenth Century.

From the French of Rev. Camille de Rochemonteix, S.J.

BY K. A. HENNESSY.

(*Continued.*)

JUST at that time the French Goverment was more engrossed with its own home troubles than with transAtlantic affairs. After the treaty of Monçon, Richelieu had established law and order in all quarters over which he had jurisdiction, and, being now prepared to fight the ever-rebellious Protestants, led the King and the nobility forward to the siege of La Rochelle. This city was the stronghold of Calvinism. Soldiers, generals, the grandees of the kingdom, all had eagerly espoused this popular undertaking, and the royal army would soon have mastered the situation had its only antagonists been the Protestants of France. But Soubise and Rohan, chiefs of the Huguenot party, had appealed to the Duke of Buckingham, and this favorite of the King of England prevailed upon his sovereign to help defend La Rochelle.

This unexpected interference produced dire results in New France. David Kertk, born at Dieppe, and his brothers, Louis and Thomas, had gone over to the service of the English king, and these three French Calvinists gained the authorization of Charles I. to wage war against the French Colony in Canada. Accordingly, armed with a royal commission and accompanied by Captain Jacques Michel and other Frenchmen, Protestants like themselves, they sailed from London in 1698 with a numerous fleet, took possession of Port Royal, established themselves at Tadousac, burned the farm and took prisoners several colonists at Cap Tourmente.

Champlain was at Quebec when couriers brought him this distressing information and told him of the threatening approach of the English fleet.

Less than a year previously he had demolished the small fort of St. Louis, which crowned a rocky eminence, and, notwithstanding lively opposition from the company of the Duc de Montmorency, had replaced it by a larger and more solid structure, surrounded by barricades of tree-trunks, etc.

But this military post was in a most lamentable condition, lacking not only food supplies, but ammunition. Each man's rations had been reduced to seven ounces of peas a day, and the de Caens, far from trying to procure the necessary provisions for the settlement, had taken the trouble to withdraw the boats which might have been utilized in bringing food from a distance. The ground, being uncultivated, offered no resource, and the savages, themselves reduced to meagre fare, could certainly not be looked to for aid. The Jesuits, the Franciscans and the Hébert family put their crops at the commandant's disposal, but unfortunately their generous donation amounted to little when there was question of feeding so many, there being, as Sagard says, "eighty mouths in which the teeth grew like weeds, because of having no work to do."

But at this critical juncture, what was the Company of the Hundred Associates doing? Why could it not come to the rescue of threatened Quebec?

By an edict dated in camp at La Rochelle, 1628, Louis XIII. had confirmed the founding of this society, and, conformably to the dispositions of the edict, Claude de Roquemont, Commander of the Company's ships, had organized the first transport of colonists. On May 18, he left Dieppe, accompanied by Fathers Charles Lalemant, François Ragueneau and three Franciscans, and, two months later, reached the mouth of the St. Lawrence, where he was attacked by Admiral Kertk, and, being obliged to lower his flag, yielded upon the following conditions: "That the lives of the religious be spared, women be respected and liberty given to all." Kertk sent Roquemont and his colonists back to France, put the Franciscans on board an unsafe ship, which, after drifting about, finally put in at Bayonne, and, holding the Jesuits prisoners, brought them to England and sent them thence to Belgium at the request of Marie de Medici and the command of her daughter, Henrietta, Queen of England.

Father Noyrot, who had closely followed Claude de Roquemont in a vessel laden with provisions for Notre-Dame des Anges, heard the cannonading and dropped anchor near Anticosti. In the evening, learning that the English had been victorious, he took refuge in a solitary little inlet, anxiously awaiting a propitious moment to effect an entrance to the St. Lawrence, but, next day, July 31, feast of St. Ignatius of Loyola, upon issuing from his retreat he saw the necessity of steering immediately for France, and did so amid countless dangers, being hotly pursued by the enemy's ships.

But this first disastrous venture did not discourage the Company of the Hundred Associates and, on June 16, of the following year, 1629, Captain Daniel, accompanied by Father Barthélemy Vimont, set sail with four well-equipped vessels. Driven by a storm to Cap-Breton Island, he took possession of the fort built by James Stuart at the Port aux Baleines, demolished it and built another at the entrance to the Grand-Cybou River, where he left the Jesuit Father and forty men, and returned to France with sixty English prisoners. Captain Joubert, who had embarked at the same time as Captain Daniel, was no more fortunate than the latter, and, being obliged to retrace his course, suffered shipwreck off the coast of Brittany.

The intrepid Father Noyrot, together with Fathers Lalemant and Alexandre de Vieuxpont and Brother Malot, formed part of this expedition. The vessel which he and his companions boarded was one that he himself had freighted and it was tempest driven against the rocks of Canseau and split in twain. Father Noyrot sank to a watery grave pronouncing the words of his dying Redeemer: *In manus tuas, Domine, commendo spiritum meum,* and Brother Malot, who had accomplished a great act of Christian charity by converting the pilot—a Calvinist of the most pronounced type—was also drowned, but Fathers Lalemant and Alexandre de Vieuxpont were washed ashore on a desert island, the latter safe and sound, the former bruised and mangled and scarcely able to move. A few days afterwards Father de Vieuxpont went to join Father Vimont at Grand-Cybou and aided in converting the savages, while Father Lalemant was picked up by some

Basque fishermen and brought to Saint-Sébastien, which place he reached only after suffering a second shipwreck.

In truth, Quebec was most unfortunate. Of all the vessels sent from France to its assistance, not one had been able to reach it, and Champlain, thus reduced to relying on the dictates of his genius, hourly expected the arrival of the enemy. And what fierce struggles must not have agitated his dauntless soul! How should he proceed? What was his duty? Should he oppose violence to violence? But how make any show of resistance with only a few men, women and children, about sixty in all, in a fort where food and ammunition were lacking, against an enemy vastly superior in point of numbers and amply armed and provisioned? Had he any right to thus uselessly sacrifice the lives of his soldiers and workmen and also of their families? Or, would it be best to get rid of those who were only a burden and lead to the fight a mere handful of braves? He then wondered if it would not be best to surrender on favorable conditions—though such a course was naturally repugnant to his pride and valor. Whilst these ideas cruelly harrassed his wavering mind, he kept diligently at work trying to fortify his post till at length he received a letter from Admiral Kertk, sent from Tadousac, and calling upon him to surrender the fort and habitation. But the Admiral's threat came from too great a distance to terrorize Champlain, who replied: "Were we to yield them in our present condition we would not be worthy to be considered men by our King." This proud response disconcerted Kertk, who imagined that, by surrendering, his adversary would be relinquishing vast resources.

But a sort of fatality seemed to pursue this unfortunate colony. Champlain was obliged to construct a miserable boat of from ten to twelve tons capacity, and he commissioned Boullé to go first to Gaspé and thence to France, and inform Richelieu of how matters stood. A few days later some English ships were sighted back of Pointe Lévis, but in advance, came a small boat floating a white flag, and its commanding officer requested parley with Champlain, handed him a letter containing the information that Boullé's vessel had been captured and that his companions had told of the misery and destitution existing at the fort. The effect produced by such news can be readily imagined. Champlain consulted the Jesuits, Franciscans and most prominent colonists, all of whom seeing that resistance would be useless, agreed to capitulate on the following conditions: That the Frenchmen wishing to leave the colony would be transported to France; that the officers be permitted to retain their arms and baggage; the soldiers their arms, uniforms and a beaver robe apiece, and the religious their books and habits.

The act of capitulation was signed July 19, 1629, and on the following day Louis Kertk took possession of the fort, magazines, the Franciscan convent and Notre Dame des Anges, and thus all the church ornaments, sacred vessels, linens and papers belonging to the religious, passed into the hands of the English.

Several days later Champlain, the Franciscans and Fathers Massé, DeNoué and De Brébeuf appeared at Tadousac, where Admiral Kertk and Vice-Admiral Jacques Michel awaited them.

Michel was a Calvinist from Dieppe, who, when still very young, had come to Canada, where he had commanded one of Guillaume de Caen's ships, and later, either because of discontentment or to gratify his ambition, sold himself to the English. He was a skillful mariner and brave soldier, and lacked neither energy nor quickness of perception, and he conducted the English to Tadousac, Cap Tourmente, in fact to all the French posts, and led the attack against Roquemont and decided the victory. Kertk turned Michel's military qualifications and knowledge of the country to practical account, but he could not respect the deserter, nor could the English, who despised though they feared him.

The Calvinist traitor hated the Jesuits, and when the missionaries of the Society of Jesus arrived at Tadousac he accused them of coming to Canada to "convert beavers." But such an injury could not fail to elicit a rebuke, and, in presence of the Admiral, Champlain and the French prisoners, Father de Brébeuf charged him with having lied. This exasperated the turncoat, who, beside himself with rage, stood up and thus threatened the Jesuit: "It is only respect for the Admiral's presence that deters me from striking you for uttering this falsehood;" and his wrath took the form of such vile imprecations against God and St. Ignatius that Champlain could not refrain from exclaiming: "Good God! For a reformer, how you do swear!" "I know it," replied Michel, "and I'd rather be hanged than let to-morrow go by without boxing that Jesuit as he deserves." However, the next day did not bring forth what Michel wished or intended. According to his habit, he invited his friends to drink. "Come," he said, "let us drown in wine the anger which these sycophants have so justly aroused." The invitation was accepted, and Michel himself imbibed to such excess that he lost consciousness, and two days later he died miserably.

They buried him with all the pomp due to his rank, the straits of the Saguenay resounding with the funeral salutes of the cannon, and the remains were interred beneath the rocks of Tadousac. Three years afterwards when Father Le Jeune came from France, he remained a few days in the neighborhood of the renegade's tomb, and the Indians told him what they had done with the corpse. "They exhumed it," he writes, "hung it, according to the traitor's imprecation, and then flung it to the dogs." To his recital Father Le Jeune adds these serious reflections: "It is not well to blaspheme God or His Saints, nor to oppose one's king, betraying one's country."

The French prisoners left Tadousac in September, 1629, reaching Plymouth towards the end of October and, eight days later, they sailed from Dover to France.

The Quebec colony established by Champlain amid so many hardships, ceased to exist, although, thanks to the persevering efforts of its founders, it had survived for over twenty years, despite difficulties innumerable, and French Calvinists—traitors to their country—were required to effect its ruin. In this event historians have recognized, and justly, what Bossuet calls an avenging visitation of Providence. Louis

XIII. had decreed that all French Huguenots be sent back from Canada and God made their own co-religionists the instruments of their banishment.

The Jesuits, expelled from New France for the second time, were distributed among the different houses of their Order. Father Lalemant was named Rector of the College at Eu; Father Massé returned to La Flèche, where the memory of his zealous and pious instructions ever lived; Father de Nouë was sent to Amiens, and Father de Brébeuf to Rouen. During the following year Fathers de Vieuxpont and Barthélemy Vimont were recalled from Cap-Breton, the first becoming missionary in Rouen, and the second Prefect of Studies at Vannes.

One and all nurtured in their zealous hearts the ardent and unquenchable hope of soon revisiting the deeply regretted land of New France.

AN IROQUOIS MAIDEN;

OR

Life of Catharine Tegakwitha.

(*Continued.*)

Chapter XI.

Christian Friendship.

IT would seem as if the Lord had waited for the return of Theresa to better sentiments, that He might bestow graces upon her. After incredible fatigue and suffering, in company with four others, the only ones who had been able to survive so much misery and pain, she arrived at the Saut.

The hunger they had endured had been so cruel that, a few days before reaching the Saut, having come upon the carcass of a wolf half decayed, they had thrown themselves upon it with avidity, and devoured it. The flesh of their friends had sustained them till then.

On her return, Theresa threw herself at the feet of the missionary, to humiliate herself, and to become reconciled to

God. Her life then became a truly Christian one, and her relations with Catharine, opened up to her a new career.

In the Spring of 1678, the Missionaries had their chapel of the Saut St. Louis rebuilt of wood, and enlarged. The portal was to be surmounted by an elegant steeple.

Catharine was one day walking about the holy edifice, examining it, when Theresa was drawn thither with the same intention. This unexpected meeting seemed brought about by the Lord, in the interests of His glory, and for the spiritual good of these two privileged hearts. The two Christians were scarcely known to each other, they had never exchanged a word. However, by a secret inspiration, Catharine approached Theresa, to enter into conversation with her, and she soon understood that the impulse came from heaven. There exists, between the spirit of God and pure souls, a mysterious commerce, the secret of which is known only to themselves. Under an apparently frivolous pretext, Catharine voluntarily made the first advance : "On which side," said she to Theresa, "think you, will the women be placed in this new chapel?" "On this side, doubtless," answered Theresa, pointing to the Epistle side, where the women are generally placed. "It matters little, in point of fact," continued Catharine, "since this chapel of wood is not the place in which the Lord takes most pleasure, and where He desires to be especially honored by us. It is in our hearts that He wishes a habitation, that may serve Him as a Temple. But, alas! as for myself, I am unworthy even to penetrate into this material sanctuary. After so often forcing my God to leave my heart, I deserve that for my ingratitude He shut the entrance to it forever."

These words of profound humility, that tears of regret and piety rendered still more touching, penetrated like a fiery dart, to the depths of Theresa's heart. To her they were words of salvation, and completed what the fear of death had, till then, but imperfectly begun. There are moments, when the conquests of grace are assured, and its triumphs certain. They are, when the heart it wishes to gain, lends itself submissively to its action.

Theresa was one of those ardent natures, that, when once decided on any subject, embrace it with ardor. Vicious, they go to any excess. Virtuous, they are capable of the most heroic acts.

She listened to the words of Catharine, as to a lesson from heaven. God seemed to show her this pious girl, of whom so much good was said, as the guardian angel, charged to aid her in the reform she proposed to herself to undertake, and before which, like another Augustine, she seemed, however, still to hesitate.

Catharine's frankness and uprightness of soul won the affection and confidence of Theresa from the beginning, and induced her to hide from her nothing of what was passing within her. These two hearts understood each other perfectly. The conformity of their sentiments and desires formed a strong bond of friendship between them from that hour, all the more durable from being wholly spiritual. To converse more at their ease, they withdrew to a short distance, and seated themselves at the foot of a cross (1) placed on the banks of the St. Lawrence. There the river widens and takes the

---

(1) This cross, restored from age to age, was renewed in 1844. Three zealous inhabitants of the place bore the cost. Some ornaments of the pious Catharine are buried at its base.

Sunday, July 23, 1844, the Jesuit Fathers, who then administered the parish of La Prairie, to which this shore belongs, visited the spot with a great number of their parishioners. The Iroquois Mission of the Saut was invited to the celebration. The invitation was accepted, and led by its missionary, and accompanied by its interpreters and chiefs, came in a body. Its warriors, bearing arms, marched at its head with banners unfurled, and with their cannon, a recompense formerly accorded to their valor. A picture of *the good Catharine* was exhibited. The ceremony began by the firing of cannon. The *Vexilla Regis* was intoned by the clergy, and the procession, starting from a neighboring house, formed on the plain, and then ranged itself on the ground reserved for it. From an elevated platform, Father Martin explained in French, the object of this ceremony and recalled the memories that it awakened in all hearts. M. Marcoux, missionary to the Iroquois, then addressed his neophytes in their own language; they were justly proud of the honors rendered to a Christian of their village. Finally M. Hudson, Vicar-General, who presided over the ceremony, made an address in English to part of his audience. He then solemnly blessed the Cross and it was seen to rise majestically on the banks of the St. Lawrence, amid the chanting of hymns, the discharge of cannon, and the acclamations of the multitude.

name of Lake St. Paul, from the great island of that name, which lies to the north.

Catharine and Theresa then imparted to each other the different phases of their past life, even to the most intimate secrets of their hearts. Catharine, though much younger than her companion (Theresa was about twenty-eight or thirty years of age), put her to the blush, by her fervor and generosity in the service of the Lord, while Theresa, by the abundance of her tears, her bitter regret, her ardent desires, aroused fresh emulation of virtue in Catharine. They resolved to form a holy alliance between themselves, and to lead a life wholly consecrated to penance and prayer. However, already aware of the cunning of the tempter, who often transformed himself into an angel of light, in order to tempt souls, they went together to Father Frémin, Superior of the mission at that time, and submitted to him their pious project. He could only praise a friendship based on such holy motives, and which could only be salutary to one and the other.

From that time they may be said to have formed, in reality, one heart and one mind. They confided to each other their joys and their sorrows, their consolations and their trials. They took counsel together in their doubts, and mutually strengthened each other in the attacks which hell and the world more than once made upon them. They were regarded as being so intimately united, that, after the death of Catharine, her name was given to her faithful companion, as her most precious inheritance. (1)

History has preserved to us one of the confessions which Theresa in the fulness of her heart, made to Catharine on the subject of her past life. Before her misconduct she had had days of fervor, and she could not recall their memory without thinking of the joy and peace with which her soul had then been inundated, and without feeling more keenly regretful for not having always been faithful. She imparted to Catharine with simplicity, the hatred she then felt for sin, and her desire never more to commit a sin. "One day in the midst of the woods," she said to her companion, "while thinking over my

---

(1) Mss. of Father Cholenec.

sins, I felt such great indignation against myself and such hatred for sin, that I was drawn to punish myself severely, and I then chastised my body with all my strength. Another time having climbed into a birch tree whose bark I wished to strip off for my work, I glanced down to the foot of the tree, and beheld there a great heap of stones. Fright seized me, for were I to fall I should inevitably crush my head to pieces. God then gave me this good thought: 'What! you fear to fall on that pile of stones and be killed, and you are not afraid of falling into hell!' I then descended, my eyes full of tears, and prostrating myself on the ground, began to sigh for having had the misfortune to offend God, and to feel so little regret."

Catharine listened eagerly to these touching confidences. They aroused in her new ardor. God thus strengthened virtue in her heart, and prepared her for the trials she would yet be called upon to suffer.

One of the most painful was a new assault on the part of her relatives, on the subject of marriage.

The attack was all the more formidable and perfidious, for being conducted with more skill, and veiled under motives that appeared most lawful.

Chapter XII.

New Proposal of Marriage—Resistance.

In her character of elder and benefactress, Catharine's adopted sister, who was mistress of her "fire," that is to say of her cabin or *home*, believed she had the power of disposing of her person. She therefore formed the project of an establishment for her, in keeping with Catharine's precious qualities. But, unhappily, as it too often happens in such cases, purely human views, and the consideration of temporal interests alone, were consulted. It is so easy to deceive oneself, when acting solely under the influence of personal advantage.

It is true, that the wisdom of Catharine, her piety and her activity, had won for her general esteem, and there was not a young man in the Mission, who would not have deemed himself highly honored in obtaining her hand. Her sister was well aware of this, and she rejoiced in the thought of having as brother, some skillful hunter who would bring abundance to their cabin.

However, Catharine's repugnance for marriage was known. Even in her family one was not ignorant of the attacks she formerly sustained on the subject, nor the energy of her resistance. In spite of the little success of former attempts, this imprudent woman desired herself to make a new one. She counted on the influence which she naturally possessed over Catharine, and the skill with which she intended to negotiate the affair. She meditated long on the motives most likely to influence the mind and heart of the young girl in order to represent them in all their force. The upright judgment of Catharine led her to believe that she would appreciate them. For that matter, she was resolved not to be discouraged, even were she to meet with resistance, constancy in pursuing a design being oftimes one of the surest guarantees of success.

One day, when alone with Catharine, she had had occasion to give her a proof of very lively affection. She said to her in a tone full of sweetness and goodness: "It must be confessed, my dear sister, that you are under great obligations to our Lord for having drawn you, as well as ourselves, away from our unhappy country, and leading us here to the Saut, where you can work out your salvation so easily, and where nothing can trouble or hinder your devotions. If you are happy in being here, be assured that I am no less happy in having you with me. You increase this satisfaction by your good conduct, which brings you the esteem and approbation of the whole village. There remains only one thing for you to do, to crown your own happiness, and mine. Think of settling yourself, by choosing a virtuous husband. It is the habit of all wise maidens amongst us. You are of age to do the same, and you doubtless think of it, like the others, in order to avoid the many occasions of sin to be met with everywhere, and to provide against all solicitude for the future. Do not think that I speak in this way, my dear sister, in order not to have any more care for you, or to cease to provide for your needs. We will always take pleasure, your brother-in-law and myself, in not letting you want for anything, but, you know, he is growing old, and we have a numerous family. If we had the misfortune to die, what would become of you? Believe me, Catharine, take refuge as speedily as possible from the dangers that almost always accompany poverty, and threaten the soul as well as the body. It is the desire of all who love you."

This discourse, which Catharine was far from expecting, caused her as much sorrow as surprise. Nevertheless, full of deference and respect for her sister, she hid her feelings, and, after thanking her for this new proof of interest, told her that this was a matter of such grave importance that she would need to reflect upon it at her leisure, before giving a reply. Far from being wounded by the delay, her sister understood the justice of it. She even believed that she saw in this apparent hesitation the beginning of success.

But Catharine, to whom the Spirit of God had suggested how to elude a first attack, soon saw that she would be forced to defend herself from others. She therefore hastened to the missionary, guide of her conscience, and told him all that had taken place. "You are free," he replied, not wishing in any way to influence her decision. "The solution of this question depends entirely upon yourself, but you are right in giving it profound thought, for it is a step that once taken, there is no withdrawing from." "Ah, my Father," replied Catharine at once, and without hesitation, "never will I consent to what my sister demands. I do not love the world, and I have a positive aversion to marriage. It is impossible for me to think of it."

However, the missionary to sound and try her further, dwelt upon the reasons submitted to Catharine by her sister with so much force: "Poverty does not frighten me, my Father," responded Catharine firmly; "my work will procure me the means of livelihood, and I will always find some old rags for covering."

This missionary soon saw that there was in this energetic opposition, something more than natural repugnance, and without seeking to shake it more, he advised her to recommend the matter to God.

For a long time Catharine had felt herself drawn, to seek what she believed to be most perfect and most agreeable to our Lord. But in spite of all she could do, a secret voice told her that she could lead a holier life than that generally led at the Saut. She had even learned, though in a vague manner, that there were chosen souls who consecrated themselves to God in a special manner, by making to Him a generous gift of themselves, and by separating themselves completely from the world. She pondered on this sacrifice, though in a vague and confused manner.

Catharine had already complained one day to her faithful companion, Theresa, that the missionary did not tell her all that it was possible to do to walk in the way of the saints. Theresa then recalled the beautiful examples she had had before her eyes at Montreal, in the Sisters of Charity, *religieuses hospitalières* (1), and in the Sisters of the Congregation. Their retired life, their withdrawal from the world, from its joys and pleasures, their renunciation of marriage, their frequent practices of penance, their charity, had impressed her mind and remained graven in her memory. "I have not forgotten," she added, "what was also told me of the self-devotion and fervor of the religious of the Hotel Dieu (2) who live at Quebec. A good Christian, who had been the object of their care, related to me with deep emotion, the impression left on her by their beautiful example."

Catharine and Theresa in communicating these thoughts to each other, naturally encouraged each other in the resolution never to marry, but they kept it a great secret, and would only speak of it, at the last extremity.

---

(1) The Hotel Dieu, of Montreal, served from the beginning by the Religious of St. Joseph de la Flèche, was founded in 1659. A few years ago, it was transferred to the entrance of the city and rebuilt with splendor, to correspond better with the growing needs of this great city, and the zeal of these fervent souls.

(2) The Hotel Dieu, of Quebec, founded by the Duchess d'Aiguillon, mother of Richelieu, is kept by the religious *hospitalières de la Miséricorde de Jesus*, originally of Dieppe. They came to take possession of it in 1639, and still continue, till our own day, their work of charity and sacrifice.

A conversation that Catharine held one day with Father Frémin, Superior of the Saut Mission, powerfully contributed to ripening in her heart the thought of consecrating herself to God by the vow of virginity. From time to time, she went to give him an account of what was passing in her mind, and to obtain some wise counsel. One day she demanded, with simplicity, if, to be a good Christian, like Theresa, it was necessary to marry. "No," replied the missionary, and taking advantage of this opening, he explained to her the different states of life in the order of Providence. "God calls some to marriage," said he, "and they are the greater number, but there is a more perfect state, which He reserves for privileged souls. For love of Him, they do not follow the common way, and renounce entering into the marriage state. They will have no other spouse but Jesus Christ." Catharine carefully preserved these words. They were like a ray of light, enabling her to see more clearly what the Lord demanded of her.

However, Catharine's sister was impatient to learn the result of her first attempt to induce her to marry. When she thought that she had given her sufficient time for reflection, she returned to the charge, and again urged her, and with greater persistency, to resolve to settle herself in life.

In order to avoid all future attacks, Catharine then decided to make known her resolution. She therefore armed herself with courage, and, after recommending herself to God, said to the indiscreet woman, in a tone of holy firmness, "Permit me to speak freely to you, my sister. Your entreaties are useless. I have already renounced marriage, so I conjure you, to speak no more of it. I will not change my condition. I have sufficient clothing for a long time to come, and I need little. Fear not that I shall be a burden to you, or any one else. I have two hands; I will work and find food without difficulty."

"Do you think so?" replied her sister, moved by such a declaration. "Whence comes this strange resolution? Who can have inspired you with such a singular idea? Will you then expose yourself to become an object of derision, for all the nation? And give a hold to the enemy of your salvation!

How can you be so bold as to attempt what no other girl among us has ever done? Give up, Catharine, give up those dangerous thoughts; mistrust your own strength and walk in the ordinary way with other virtuous girls."

At these words, inspired, doubtless, by the vexation and bitterness of a wounded heart, Catharine replied calmly: "I do not fear the raillery of men as long as I do what is right. As to the temptations, I have confidence in God, and I hope that He will give me strength to surmount them, as He has hitherto done. You see that my resolution is well taken. All your efforts cannot change it. It will be better never to speak of this again."

Catharine's sister dared not break out for the moment; she was satisfied to let the matter drop, but she decided to put other springs in motion. She complained to Anastasie of Catharine's resistance. The adroit turn she gave to her cause and the novelty of such an example soon won Anastasie to her way of thinking.

But the latter, from prudence, wished to take time to weigh all the reasons. They appeared to her plausible. Persuaded, therefore, that Catharine had too precipitately taken a resolution of such importance, and that she might one day regret it, she decided to use the influence age and friendship had given her over the young girl's mind to turn her from her project. But Anastasie had no greater success than her friend, and, wounded inwardly by this opposition, which contrasted so greatly with the deference she had hitherto found in Catharine, she ended by reproaching her with bitterness.

At the moment when she was urging her most warmly, Catharine, without permitting herself to be gained over, cleverly turned the argument against her by saying, in a respectful, but decided tone: "If you have so much esteem for the married state, why did you not yourself marry? As for me, the matter is ended, and you will please me greatly by never referring to it again, for no man shall ever obtain my hand."

After this encounter they separated, mutually dissatisfied, and both resolved to seek the missionary and lay the matter before him.

SHRINE NOTES.

The Holy Father makes the following grateful allusion in his late Apostolical Letter to His Eminence Cardinal Gibbons. Speaking of the services of the Religious Orders, he meets the silly complaint that they do not help the cause of the Church in these terms: "What they add to this [*i.e.* to their objections to the vows of religious], namely that religious life helps the Church not at all or very little, besides being injurious to religious orders, will be admitted by no one who has gone over the annals of the Church. Did not your own United States receive from the members of religious orders the beginning of its faith and civilization? For one of them recently, and it redounds to your credit, you have decreed that a statue should be publicly erected."

Our readers will remember that the State of Wisconsin has chosen Father Marquette as one of the two men who in the annals of her territory are most deserving of the honor of representing her origin and civilization. In spite of opposition of the meanest sort, her legislators succeeded in having his statue accepted by the Congress of the United States and placed in the rotunda among the images of the greatest men of the nation. It was not necessary to mention that the Federal Government had lately honored his exploration of the Mississippi by issuing a postage stamp illustrating that event. The States of Michigan, Illinois, and Missouri, have also duly commemorated the splendid achievements of this humble missionary, and we are glad to learn that an effort is being made to erect a memorial church on the site of his burial.

What Father Marquette finally succeeded in accomplishing, had long been the dream of his predecessors. Readers of the life of Father Jogues, will recall how he closed his mission among the Ottawa Indians at Sault Ste-Marie in 1641. They had gone over there from the Huron Country, a distance of 250 miles in a birch canoe over the Great Lake Huron, coasting the northern shores, through a forest of islets which border it. Upwards of 2,000 Indians gave them a flattering reception, and the Fathers reciprocated as usual with presents and feasts. The chief wanted something more and begged the missionaries to remain with them; but it was unfortunately impossible to grant his request. The missionaries, however, did not depart from this hospitable land without leaving behind a token of their presence—a mark as it were, that they had taken possession in the name of the Gospel.

They raised a tall cross on the banks of the river, to show the limits reached by the preaching of its Apostles. They made it face the immense Valley of the Mississippi, to which their attention had been called in a vague manner, but which they were told was inhabited by numerous tribes of nations still unknown.

The statue of Father Marquette is not the only memorial or monument erected by a grateful people to men who devoted themselves to the establishment of the Faith in this country. And strange to say Protestants have done more to keep alive their memory than Catholics. Witness the splendid testimonies of Sparks, Bancroft and Parkman, who almost equal the national Catholic historian in their admiration for our pioneer missionaries.

The Spring has brought with it the usual number of suggestions about the Shrine and the pilgrimages for the coming Summer. Some of them are excellent; some of them are so impracticable, and so likely to hinder rather than further the progress of the work there, that we may some day print a list of them, so as to warn our readers to let them rest in oblivion. It seems that a number of people, we know of three at most, want to purchase land at Auriesville or to start new hotels there; and some are still bent on having the Fathers in charge of the Shrine attempt to manage or share in the management of a hotel. Better no pilgrimage at all. On this point the following extract from "Shrine Notes," in the PILGRIM for October, 1898, is final :

"More ample accommodations are surely needed for pilgrims who wish to spend some time at Auriesville. By extending the season for the pilgrimages, so that all need not try to find room there at one time, the lack of accommodations did not cause too much inconvenience this year. We say too much inconvenience, because pilgrims cannot reasonably hope to be entirely free from every inconvenience. Even when the exodus from the Putman House was made, as told in the September PILGRIM, room was found in other places, and no one had to leave Auriesville for lack of shelter. We trust that the experience of the past summer may open more doors to our pilgrims next year, because we can imagine no more satisfactory way of solving the problem of accommodations than by having our neighbors consent to harbor them. It is always wiser to build upon foundations already laid than to be devising new plans and starting costly projects, which in the end may not be satisfactory, even if they should not be a failure. After a canvass of those who are best acquainted with Auriesville and its needs, a new hotel there seems to be unnecessary and even undesirable, if the accommodations now available there be used to the utmost; but all agree that those who wish to build anything there should begin with cottages, and not venture to build a hotel until there is a general demand for one."

"Hotel life is not the most desirable mode of living either in city or country; indeed, it is much less desirable in the country than anywhere else. It surely does not help the spirit of pilgrims in the neighborhood of certain Shrines which are known to us. It would become doubly objectionable at Auriesville if it should necessitate the formation of a syndicate for purchasing land and building thereon, because the business and traffic thus introduced would mar the quiet and pious temper of the pilgrims. After all is said, we must never forget that the primary object we should have in view, is the advancement of the process of beatification of Father Jogues and his companions, and that even the pilgrimages, helpful as they are to this end, must not be extended or multiplied to the detriment of it."

Now that we learn that as usual at this season, every day brings offers to the Auriesville land owners for their property, we repeat this paragraph from the same number of the PILGRIM.

"Naturally, the owners of land near the Shrine look for fancy prices for their property; but when land worth $50 or $60 an acre (and no large tract of land near the place is worth more than that an acre) is offered for $200 or $300 an acre, purchase is out of the question, and we are fortunate that even for the cottage accommodations mentioned in the circular we have ample land of our own south of the Ravine."

Since we wrote the above, several sales of land near Auriesville, but more advantageously situated and also more improved, show that prices per acre range from $20 to $35.

In our next issue we hope to have more definite information on several points, as also on the better passenger service promised by the West Shore R. R., and the lecture on Father Isaac Jogues. Meantime we recommend to our readers a special intention connected with his cause.

CONTRIBUTIONS TO THE SHRINE:

K. T. K., Pittsburg, Pa.	$1.00	M. L. S. H., Buffalo, N. Y.	5.00
M. H., New York	.40	Anon, In Thanksgiving	5.00
"Anon"	25.00	C. H., New York	1.00
"Anon"	3.00		
A. R. H., Wheeling, W. Va.	50	FOR THE CROWN.	
"Anon"	10.00	"Anon," two gold Medals.	

SISTER STEPHANIE.

BY D. S. BÉNI.

(*Continued.*)

ONE day after I had finished my singing lesson I said to Mother B. that my father had known Sister Stephanie in the world, and that he had told me many interesting things about her, but that I had had the greatest difficulty in persuading Sister Stephanie to speak of herself, and to tell me of her conversion. For a long time she evaded my questions, by saying that she could not remember anything that happened in the world, but that at length she had yielded to my entreaties and told me the story of her conversion.

"All that your father has told you of Sister Stephanie has been related to us many times by persons who knew her in the world. There is an Episcopal minister in this city, who accidentally heard of her through one of our Protestant pupils, and he called at once to know if it could be his old friend, Miss Emily Clarkson. Since then he has called frequently, he often makes offerings of beautiful flowers for the altar, especially on the Feast of Corpus Christi; and on the anniversaries of his deceased relatives, he sends an offering for each, asking prayers for his dear dead. When he comes here, he always goes to the chapel and prays for a long time, and the pupils tell us that he always raises his hat whenever he passes our house. One day Sister Stephanie asked him if he believed in the Real Presence. His answer was: 'If I did, Sister, I would never leave that chapel or rise from my knees.' Once he sent us a beautiful, life size bust of the Blessed Virgin, which he said was a fac-simile of one which he had in his own room. He called one day during the Easter holidays and told Sister Stephanie, that on Easter Sunday he read to his congregation a sermon which had been delivered by Archbishop R——because he knew it was so far superior to anything he could say to them! We had some curiosity to know how it was received by the congregation, but we refrained from questions, contenting ourselves with praying that he might be gathered into the true fold. He has made us many donations and he seems to have a real affection for our community." I said: " Mother, would there be any impropriety in my bringing my father to call on Sister Stephanie? I have a reason for asking this. My father is not a Catholic and while he never opposed my mother in the practice of her religion, her conversion was a great trial to him, because it estranged him from his own relatives. He was so positive that my Sister Stephanie was not his conscientious Protestant friend, Miss Clarkson, that he said : 'If *Miss Emily Clarkson* is a Catholic, then I'll be a Catholic myself !' You know, Mother, that an old Protestant friend could say with impunity what we would not dare to say to my father about religion, but I will tell you what makes me hesitate. When I asked Sister Stephanie if she remembered Dr. Ben Millard, she answered : 'Yes, I remember him well. I always liked him,' but when I told her I was his daughter she did not express any desire to see him, which made me feel a delicacy in suggesting his visit."

"I assure you, Sister Stephanie would be glad to see him, but she would not ask him to call on her; bring him whenever you please ; Sister will be delighted to see him if she can be of any service to him, for she has learned well the maxim of St. Francis de Sales : ' We must do everything for our neighbor, except lose our own soul.' "

"If our reverses would lead my father into the Church, then indeed we would look upon them as blessings, for to be candid with you, dear mother, his present position is most humiliating to him, for he views it only from a worldly standpoint. He had an established reputation and a large medical practice in Philadelphia, but believing that he had a competency for our support, he retired in favor of my two brothers, who have not met with his professional success, and by unfortunate investments he lost nearly all we had. He is too old now to take up his profession, for he says he has fallen behind in the race, and would not succeed as formerly. My sister, though well educated, does not feel competent to teach. But if all these trials purchase the conversion of my father, we will be happy indeed."

When I went home, I told my father that I had an invitation for him to call to see Sister Stephanie. He seemed pleased, and said he would go with me to the convent the next day, which he did. The meeting between the old friends was very cordial, and after recalling some pleasant memories of the past, my father said: "But Miss Emily, how did *you* ever become a *Catholic?*"

In a few minutes I rose and asked to be excused under the pretext of speaking to Mother B., but I flew to the chapel, and not near enough to the Lord there, I went inside the sanctuary and knelt where I could touch the altar, while my heart was inside the Tabernacle pleading as I had never prayed before, for the conversion of that precious soul so dear to me. I begged our Lord to put on Sister Stephanie's lips the words that would carry conviction and conversion to the heart of my father, with the grace to correspond to the light given him.

In the meantime, as I learned afterwards from Mother B., my father opened his heart to his old friend, and admitted frankly that he had lost faith in Protestantism, but there were dogmas in the Catholic Church which perplexed him. First: "If the Church had fallen into error—" here Sister Stephanie interrupted him and said: "Now, let me tell you, my dear friend, I am not a controversialist, I will not argue with you, but I will speak to your heart. Our Lord promised that the gates of hell should not prevail against His Church, and He has kept his promise. Individuals have fallen and may still fall, but the Church purchased by His precious blood, is the same yesterday, to-day and forever, One, Holy, Catholic and Apostolic, for He promised to be with her till the consummation of the world. Do you think such men as Cardinal Manning, Cardinal Newman, Father Faber or our own American converts, Archbishop Bayley, Dr. Ives, Bishop Becker, Bishop Curtis, Father Kent Stone, Mgr. Doane and hundreds of others who made this one point the study of their life—could be mistaken? They were all, I think without exception, Episcopalians. They acted in good faith, and God repaid them by the true light, which they followed joyfully, despite all sacrifices. They knew there was but *one* Church, for Christ spoke of it always in the singular, and He says that the unity of His Church must be like that which exists between Him and His Heavenly Father."

"I admit all you have said, but I cannot subscribe to all the doctrines of the Church. I cannot believe in the Real Presence, or that Christ really gives us His flesh to eat and His blood to drink."

"My dear Doctor, if you admit that the Church is the one true Church, you must also admit that 'she cannot err in matters of faith, for Christ has promised that the Holy Ghost shall teach her all truth, and that He Himself will abide with her forever.' It is useless to say more on these points, but I ask you, for the sake of our old friendship, to promise me one thing. Before you close your eyes to-night, humble yourself before God and read, kneeling, the sixth chapter of St. John, and ask our Lord to give you the light to know and understand the meaning of those words which fell from the lips of Him who is Himself the Way, the Truth and the Life. Open your heart to receive the answer which He will give you, for 'an humble and contrite heart He will not despise.' It is prayer you need. 'Ask, and you shall receive;' ask for faith, and you will receive it. No one knows better than I the anguish of doubt, of fear and uncertainty—that darkness which our dear Lord allows to overshadow us before conversion that we may better appreciate the light of faith when it dawns upon us and all things are made clear to our wondering eyes. Believe me, you will find no rest for your troubled heart until it rests within the true Church. As to your dear wife, for whom you grieve, I do not for one moment doubt that you owe everything you have, or shall ever have of real goodness, to her; yet, when we think of our dear departed ones, we must not forget the permanence of their influence nor the fact that they are much more really engaged in our behalf now than when they were with us visibly."

My father listened in silence, and then said: "God bless you, dear Miss Emily, for your assuring and comforting words. I will do all you say, but I rely upon your prayers; of myself I can do nothing."

Two hours had passed and I still knelt alone before the Tabernacle, praying as I had never prayed before, when I heard my father's step in the chapel. I slipped behind the altar unperceived by him, but I felt that his heart was touched. I passed through another door into the Academy and met him when he came out of the chapel. He was very silent that evening and retired early, but I noticed that the gas in his room was burning all night, and at the breakfast table he looked worn and pale—and again he accompanied me to the convent.

Before the close of the year he was baptized conditionally, and through the condescension of the good bishop he received his first Communion and Confirmation in the convent chapel, and we felt that under God we owed this happiness to Sister Stephanie. She taught me how to spiritualize "the accidents of life" and to make of them stepping stones across "the running flood to reach the firm land beyond." In this new found happiness our trials disappeared, and as I look back upon the dark and shadowy days of my life, the hours I spent with Sister Stephanie are interwoven like gold and silver threads upon a sombre tapestry, and whenever I pronounce her name my grateful heart re-echoes the thanksgiving which so often fell from her dear lips: "Bless the Lord, O my soul: and never forget all that He has done for thee."

THROUGH THE PIETÀ.

BY T. M. JOYCE.

FROM within a deep window niche of an old Colonial house two ladies looked out upon the winding road leading over the western hills in the distance.

On either side the pine trees stood in rows like sentinels against the edge of soft gold sky. Clumps of leafless hawthorne waved their branches bare and gaunt above the river darkly glistening between broad fields of snow.

A well appointed carriage became visible on its journey over the stone parapet away in the west and soon disappeared over the brow of the hill.

"There is so much feigned stupidity about these Americans," exclaimed Madam Mabie in a well modulated voice, dropping languidly upon a low divan, piled high with scented cushions, and turning away from the window. "I told her my grandmother married a coronet, she said her sister had studied music in Germany. I am ostensibly entertained while really, Esther, I am bored to death by them. Their lack of deference to people of quality is positively beyond my understanding. Were it not that I longed for a sight of you and dear little Florence, I would never have left my fair sunny Italy. However, it appears my coming is opportune, since the present exigency requires the counsel which I alone am left to give you."

Her niece looked inquiringly, "I must have been dreaming, Aunt Mary, the fire makes one drowsy. The exigency?"

With a slight show of impatience the elder lady exclaimed: "Why, this latest presumption, this young man whose aspirations have blinded him so far as to seek your hand in marriage."

Esther's lids slowly drooped and a deep tinge of color darkened her features.

"It is too humiliating," continued her aunt, "for so contrary are things arranged in this world that I believe you regard him with favor, although he is the most undesirable suitor who has presented himself."

"Undesirable?"

The sweet seriousness of the girl's beautiful face raised in inquiry brought the memory of a dead sister back to Aunt Mary and she answered gently, "My dear, he is unworthy of you, of poor parentage most likely. His income is certainly small."

"Now, Aunt," interrupted Esther earnestly, "would you really judge whether a man were worthy by the amount of his wealth?"

"He also professes the Catholic belief," persisted the lady.

"But I can cure him of that," responded Esther smiling. "Nay, my pretty innocence, they are not so easily cured. Believe me, my dear, you have set yourself a difficult task. That faith is chronic in men's souls and no cure however effective is complete."

Her niece looked incredulous. "Why, Aunt Mary," she exclaimed, "his cousin Emily became a staunch Presbyterian when she married my brother three years ago. She is so thoroughly of our belief that it is really painful to her to mention the subject of her former religion in her presence." She leaned forward and her dark eyes were filled with grave earnestness as she continued, "Such is my confidence in Emily's sincerity that I will never believe the progressive step she has taken will prove unequal to fill the place of the old faith in her heart."

"I confess I would be happier if I might share your views," responded madame, "but I have grave fears of her constancy. However, as a member of our family she should be strongly advised upon no consideration to return to the fold she has left. She should think of the humiliation and serious disappointment such an imprudent proceeding would cause John and the rest of us. Why, I believe I could never read Dr. Channing with ease if such a thing were to occur," and the good lady reflected upon the Doctor's eloquent intolerance of Catholics.

"I should think, Esther," she suggested, "it would be well for you to invite her to attend the Theosophist meetings occasionally. They are very interesting and have become quite fashionable. I must advise her in regard to these matters," and she leaned back upon the violet cushions and reached for her novel. While turning over the pages she continued, "A church among whose followers are those who exile themselves from the world and wear sack-cloth, or who tend in hospitals to the sick and the dying, or care in asylums for unfortunate outcasts from society, is not the one suitable for people of culture or refinement."

"The sermon on the mountain however was preached to all notwithstanding the degree," interposed a tall dark man whose shadow fell across the polished floor.

She was about to respond in her quick imperious manner when, turning slightly, her glance met a pair of dark earnest eyes bent so pleasantly upon her, that she became infected at once by his smile and frank earnestness, and in that moment could almost have forgiven her niece for regarding Edmund O'Connell with favor.

"I must confess," explained the young man, dropping easily into an arm chair, "it was not my intention to intrude upon your conversation or to resume the topic of yesterday, as it is one upon which our ideas must necessarily conflict." "When one of us shall have arrived at a happier conclusion," interrupted Esther cheerfully, "there will be no unpleasantness about it," but the flush faded from her cheek when she saw how seriously her lover regarded her.

The sound of carriage wheels outside aroused Madam Mabie who arose and addressing Edmund, said graciously, "You may continue the subject with Miss Lee. For myself I admit the choice of a religion has been a very bewildering one. The various teachings are so intricate. With my niece it is different, she accepted her mother's faith long ago, and I believe is well read in these matters, and," she continued, "the gravity of the subject is such, that I beg you will pardon me for being but a poor listener, and for having an appointment this evening."

When she was gone the young man turned to Esther. "I received your letter this morning," he said in rather an unsteady voice. Finding it difficult to proceed without betraying some sign of the emotion he felt, he arose and crossed the room where he stood leaning his elbow upon the mantelpiece. "And you have come to tell me you will make the sacrifice?" questioned Esther with a ring of pleading in her tone. He saw her face illumined in its clear beauty, as she advanced from the background of the dim room, toward the fire, and he trembled at her words. "Aye, Esther," he answered huskily, "I am ready to make a great sacrifice." Then after a moment's silence he continued in a firmer tone: "In anything else you might move me. Your sweetness is exquisitely pure, and your eyes have a light in them that is almost divine, and I love you better than anything on earth except my religion. And now you have put it this way that I have to choose between you and it. Without you I will spend my life miserably. Without my religion my soul would be lost for eternity."

"But you would have religion," exclaimed Esther eagerly, "you would have mine."

With a slight wave of his hand, he replied in a low tone, "Once one has been a Catholic there is no other religion for him. Baptism in the Catholic Church means to be a Catholic forever. O, I wish I could take you into my heart that you might see the sublimity and the beauty of the Catholic religion as I see it. There could then be no barrier like this that rises between us broad and high and is fast dividing us forever." She was standing by the grate and the firelight shed a rosy glow about her, her eyes were downcast, and the meaning of his words sent a chill to her heart. "Then you do not care for me enough to exchange your religion for mine?" she exclaimed in a faltering voice.

He looked at her in astonishment. "Esther," he said, "I know one who has made that mistake. Religion is too holy, too sincere and sublime to be bartered or dealt with for any human consideration. I would not have you even if you would become a Catholic for my sake, pardon the vanity of the expression, and you could not if you would."

"There is no need of further words between us," said Esther, wearily moving away from the fire; and her dark eyes saddened visibly. "God knows which of us is right. There seems to be no way out of the darkness. If we have not our highest thoughts in common like Emily and my brother, we can know no happiness."

"Ah, my dear Esther," he replied, "the gaiety of the society in which my cousin moves tends to crowd out the consciousness of the old faith which I am sure lies deep-rooted within her heart. Emily is loyal to her husband in the extreme, for she accepted John's religion and ideals when she accepted him, but the old faith is still there. Some day I know you will believe me." A few moments later Edmund O'Connell turned his dark face toward the snow-clad hills in the west.

MISSION NOTES.

The Chinese missions which have borne such consoling fruit during recent years, are now passing through a severe trial. Ever since the Tartar dynasty of Tsing ascended the throne in the seventeenth century the partisans of the deposed dynasty of Ming have been striving for its restoration. This they do by means of secret societies whose business it is to excite insurrection. In order the more surely to win the people to their cause they have proclaimed their intention of driving out foreigners and destroying the Christian religion. The Empress, it seems, is doing all she can to protect the Christians, but her orders are not always obeyed. The secret societies, or brigands as they are called, have ravaged the country in many places, committing all sorts of outrages, and the local mandarins, anxious to be on the winning side, often show a lamentable indifference and sometimes even favor the rebels. From the last accounts we have received it does not appear probable that the revolution will succeed. One hundred thousand Chinese troops were gathered about Pekin, and the Empress, if supported by the European Powers, will act vigorously. In the meantime, the Christians have suffered much and are likely to suffer more.

At Pak-tong, one hundred and five miles from Canton, early on the morning of the 15th of October last, a mob of four thousand pagans surrounded the chapel in which Father Chanès had just finished Mass. About twenty Christians were present. After vainly trying to break in the doors with hatchets the pagans set fire to them, using petroleum to help on the conflagration. The flames arose on all sides, forming a wall of fire behind which the Christians were imprisoned. Four jumped from a window, two of whom were instantly killed by the mob, while two others escaped.

In the meantime within the building Father Chanès baptized seven catechumens, gave absolution to those who were already baptized, and divided the remaining time between exhortation and prayer. Thus they passed eight hours awaiting death. At 4 P.M. the front wall fell in, and the mob beheld the missionary standing calmly near the altar, surrounded by his little flock, all engaged in prayer. The pagans were about to rush upon their victims when the military mandarin of the town suddenly appeared and commanded them to desist. If the Christians conceived any hopes of deliverance from his arrival, they were soon undeceived. The mandarin merely took away one of their number who was a relative of his, and then departed, leaving the rest to their fate.

The pagans at once aimed and fired. Father Chanès fell without a cry, pierced by three balls. The mob then rushed in, stabbed, hacked, and even decapitated their prostrate victims, and split open the priest's head with an axe. During the confusion a few of the Christians who had not been wounded by the firing managed to mingle with the crowd, and so escaped. To them we are indebted for the account of this fearful scene.

The murderers then stripped the dead bodies of their clothing, and dragged them to the river side, which was not far off. Here they noticed that Father Chanès' hands were still moving, and to make sure of their work they crushed his head with a stone. They then returned to the chapel, stripped it of everything that they could carry away, tore down what remained of the walls, and left it a heap of ruins.

The number of those slaughtered was fourteen. Their bodies remained all night on the river bank, but the next day the Christians were able to secure all except that of Father Chanès, which had disappeared and was not found for some time.

The most significant feature of this massacre is that a large body of soldiers were posted at a short distance, yet neither they nor the mandarins made any attempt to save the Christians.

In the province of Hou-pé Father Victurin, a Franciscan, with a few Christians took refuge in a cave. They were discovered, and with their hands bound behind their backs led away as prisoners. Father Victurin was at first thrown into a well, but was afterwards taken out and hanged to a tree. The brigands amused themselves by cutting pieces of flesh from his dead body. The other Christians were to be put to death the next morning. During the night one of them managed to get away. As he was trying to find his way in the dark he fell down a steep precipice, but on reaching the bottom found himself on his feet entirely unhurt. He reached a place of safety and to him we owe the account of Father Victurin's death. At Y-tchang all were in trepidation at last accounts. The residence of the fathers had been converted into a fort, and the Christians were preparing to defend themselves.

THE PILGRIM

OF

OUR LADY OF MARTYRS

XV. YEAR.   MAY, 1899.   No. 5.

ALTAR FLOWERS.

BY H. M.

IN the breath from flowers ascending
   That watch by the altar side,
There's a murmur of prayer ablending
   Like incense streaming wide,—
   Like incense of the vesper-tide.

And their breath with prayer for a leaven,
   Love-sped, hath favor now;
For one to-day in heaven
   Crowned Queen will hear thy vow,—
   Will hear and bless each holy vow.

So blessed may that last firm binding
   Win for thee golden hours;
We keep, all glad for the finding,
   The memory of altar-flowers,—
   The breath, prayer-laden, of altar-flowers.

AN IROQUOIS MAIDEN;

OR

Life of Catharine Tegakwitha.

Chapter XII.

New Proposal of Marriage.—Resistance.

(*Continued.*)

AFTER deciding to make Father Cholenec the judge in the dispute over her refusal to marry, Catharine went to him and related the moral violence her adopted mother and sister wished to do her. She besought the missionary to allow her to accomplish the sacrifice she wished to present to Jesus Christ. She desired that an end might be put to the contradictions she endured in her cabin.

Father Cholenec advised her to take three days for reflection and to offer fervent prayers to heaven to know the will of God. "You know, for that matter," he added, "that you are mistress of yourself. You do not depend upon any one on earth in this matter, so, if you persist in your resolution, I promise to put an end to the importunities of your family."

Catharine willingly adopted an advice so wise, but the Holy Spirit urged her so strongly to declare her decision, and not defer her offering, that she could not deliberate, even for a quarter of a hour, on a choice that had been already so long made.

She soon returned, to the great surprise of the missionary, and said to him with holy firmness, "My father, it is finished. I cannot remain in this state of irresolution. There is no longer question of deliberation. My resolve is taken. I will have no other spouse but Jesus Christ, and I wish to make the vow."

"I confess," adds Father Cholenec, "that I dared not say anything to Catharine to influence her determination, in a thing till then unheard of among savages, and the practice of which seemed beset with so many difficulties. I preferred to let God act directly with His servant, not doubting that He would find her heart docile, if this thought came from Him. But the last words of the young girl showed me in a visible manner, that God spoke strongly in her heart, and that it was He Himself who had inspired a desire so heroic. I therefore took her part, and praised her resolution, and bade her carry it out with the same firmness with which it had been formed."

These few words delivered Catharine from all her perplexities. They restored her former tranquillity, and a holy joy was reflected in her face. This happy state endured till her last breath. Nothing could change it, as if God thereby wished to sanction and render visible to all His evident guidance of this privileged soul.

"Catharine thanked me," says Father Cholenec, "in affectionate terms. If she withdrew the happiest being on earth, I remained for my part, ravished with admiration for the young girl's courage, and in extraordinary joy to see how divine goodness was preparing for the Mission such a beautiful model of sanctity on earth, and such a powerful advocate one day in heaven."

Hardly had Catharine retired when Anastasie made her appearance, to complain to the missionary that the young girl would not listen to her advice, and only followed her own fancy. "I am astonished," said the missionary interrupting her, "that you torment Catharine for a thing which is, on the contrary, worthy of all praise. An aged Christian like you not to understand the generosity and merit of such a holy action! Far from blaming her you should esteem her the more, and find yourself happy in the honor the Lord shows you, by choosing from your cabin a young girl to raise the standard of virginity among the savages, and to teach them a state so sublime, which renders fragile man like to the angels themselves."

At these words Anastasie, who was full of faith and piety, awoke as from a profound slumber, and she at once reproached herself for her conduct. And this was not enough. From that moment she was the first to encourage Catharine, and to highly approve her pious resolution. She inspired the same sentiments in the heart of Catharine's sister, and thenceforward both regarded her with respect and a sort of veneration, giving her full liberty to do all that her piety inspired her.

Coming forth victorious from this painful combat, Catharine hastened to thank God, and thought only of preparing to consummate the sacrifice as soon as her confessor permitted. It was on March 25, 1679, Feast of the Annunciation, that this faithful maiden, after Holy Communion, made to God this complete offering of herself, by the vow of perpetual chastity.

During the struggle that Catharine sustained against her family she more than once had recourse to the advice and prayers of the good Theresa, who did not fail her. Theresa, on her part, a witness of the fervor and courage of her young friend, could not weary of admiring her, and made use of the example to excite her own fervor.

"What! a young girl so innocent, makes so generously to God, so many sacrifices! What then should not a sinner like me, do!"

CHAPTER XIII.

Virtues.—Devotion to the Blessed Sacrament.—Mortification.—Zeal.

At the approach of autumn, when the savages were preparing for the winter hunt, Catharine's relatives urged her to accompany them. "I myself," writes Father Cholenec, "wished to persuade her to do so, knowing that her health would be benefited there, sooner than in the village. You will find there," I added, "more substantial nourishment, and you need it. You will suffer greatly here during our long winter." Catharine began to smile, and, after a little pause, with that pious air habitual to her when speaking of her soul she made me this beautiful reply: "It is true, my Father, that the body is sometimes well fed in the woods, but the soul there languishes, and dies of hunger; while in the village, if the body suffers a little from lack of food, the soul finds satisfaction in being nearer to our Saviour; so I abandon this miserable body to hunger, and all that may happen to it, in consequence, provided that my soul be content and receive its accustomed food."

Catharine, therefore, remained in the village, during the winter of 1678. She was not mistaken in her anticipations. She had to suffer, but she found, at the same time, what she desired above all, to live near the altar, amidst the aids that sustain, and develop all the virtues.

This is the place to study, more in detail, some of Catharine's virtues. We will give in the first place, and as one great mark of her virtue, her devotion to the Holy Eucharist and her spirit of mortification. This two-fold sentiment, was, in her ardent heart, the result of that love for God, with which she never ceased to burn, and which, by its nature always tends to develop and nourish itself by sacrifices. The Altar, and Calvary, have ever been the common rendezvous of holy souls, and generous hearts.

Catharine never felt more at her ease, and the hours never passed more swiftly for her, than when she found herself at the foot of the altar. Then were revealed the sentiments of faith, respect and love, with which she was penetrated. In the rude season of winter, so long and so cold in Canada, she never missed going to church, as in summer, at four o'clock in the morning. After a long prayer, she assisted at two Masses that were generally said in the chapel, one at the break of day, the other immediately after sunrise. It was to the latter that the neophytes generally came. She loved to place herself near the altar railing, and, to have less cause of distraction she would remain motionless, her head buried in her blanket, her eyes closed, or fixed on the altar. Especially from the moment she was admitted to the participation of the Holy Eucharist, till her death, one may say, that she made of this August Sacrament, her dearest delight. She was seen assiduous in paying homage to our Lord in the Tabernacle, as often as five times a day, and in the celestial overflowings of her heart, she there shed abundant tears.

She one day told her faithful companion, in what manner she employed the long hours she passed in church. "In the first place," she said, "I make an act of faith, in the real presence of our Saviour, in the Holy Eucharist. Then I repeat some acts of contrition, of resignation or humility, according to the inspiration I feel most deeply, asking of God light and strength to practise that virtue. Finally I finish my devotions by the beads, which I recite with all my heart."

"Several times again," writes Father Cholenec, "I was constrained through compassion for her, to interrupt her pious contemplation, in order to force her, in the season of most rigorous cold, to approach the fire for a short time. But she would only consent to remain a few seconds, and as if with regret. The fervor of her piety soon took her back to the presence of her God. She would make her escape with an amiable smile, saying, "she did not suffer from the cold." Humiliating contrast, between the pious ardor of this humble servant of the Lord, so recently come forth from the midst of heathenism, and the indifference of so many Christians, who seem to disown the treasure they possess in our tabernacles, and always find too long the moments they are obliged to pass at the foot of the altar.

If Catharine loved to find herself so often, near our Lord in the Holy Eucharist, it may also be said that she never quitted Calvary. Her life was really a life of continual sacrifice, and when she saw that God seemed to spare her, on account of her wickedness, she was thus industrious in laying burdens on herself. Her thirst for suffering could not be satisfied. It was enough for her to hear of some act of penance, in the life of a Saint, to feel herself urged to imitate it, no matter how heroic it appeared to be. She wore around her neck the image of our Saviour on the Cross, kissed it frequently, and with lively sentiments of compassion and love, and always with a renewed desire to share His sufferings. She desired that her body, like that of St. Paul, should bear the marks of Jesus Christ.

When the love of God is developed in a heart, He inspires it, in the same proportion, with a lively sense of hatred against itself, and induces it to make the sacrifice of all that it possesses to God. Catharine, still young and inexperienced, did not always know how to discern the wise rules of prudence, or to avoid the pious excesses of indiscreet fervor.

In her illusion, she fancied she had the right to practise on herself all the severities of which she had heard speak, or with which her own heart inspired her. There were, therefore, few kinds of mortification that she did not put into practice. She employed, by turns, and according to circumstance, or season, hard and painful labor, long watching, fastting, iron, fire, discipline, the cincture studded with sharp points. When she went to the woods in winter, she often walked barefoot on the snow and ice, when not in company, or if not fearful of being perceived, for real virtue seeks to be seen only of God.

One day she asked her friend, always her confidant and rival in virtue: "What think you, my sister, is the pain to which the body is most sensible, and which can best show our love for God?"

The latter, not suspecting the design of Catharine, replied innocently: "I know nothing in the world so terrible as fire." "I think so, too," answered Catharine, without further comment. The reply that she had provoked, perfectly agreed, in fact, with her desires, and induced her to carry out a strange project of mortification, which the simplicity and purity of intention of the pious maiden, alone can excuse.

The evening of that same day, when all the inmates of the cabin were plunged in profound sleep, Catharine wished to make a trial of voluntary martyrdom. She recalled the horrible treatment to which her country people subjected their innocent prisoners before putting them to death. She knew they employed iron and fire, that they burned their flesh with flaming brands, or hot coals. The remembrance suggested the thought of treating herself in the same manner, since she was the slave of the Saviour, and, because she desired to bear in her body the marks of her servitude. With a courage beyond her age and sex, she applied burning coals to her legs, thus covering them, so to speak, with holy stigmatas.

In this state, in the silence and darkness of the night she went to prostrate herself before the church door, to renew to our Lord the offering she had already made of herself, but which she had now consecrated in so heroic a manner.

On another occasion, Catharine and Theresa, mutually exciting each other to crucify their flesh for love of God, agreed to place a burning coal between their great and second toe, and to let it burn the flesh for the space of a Hail Mary. Catharine suffered the torture without shrinking. Though more robust, Theresa was overcome by the pain, and fell fainting to the floor in the midst of the trial. What was her surprise, on coming to herself, to behold the wound Catharine had made, and supported with so much courage. She could only attribute such a miracle to strength of soul, and what confirmed her in this thought, was, that the morning following the torture, she found her companion entirely cured.

One of the strangest, as well as the most imprudent of Catharine's penances, was that she imposed upon herself shortly before her death. A trait in the life of St. Louis de Gonzague, of which she had heard the recital, gave birth to a thought which she took for heavenly light, and obeyed all too promptly. She was returning from the forest with a heavy load of wood on her shoulders, preoccupied with thoughts of the passion and suffering of the Son of God; she sighed that she was doing so little for Him, especially at this season of the year. They were then in Lent. By chance her eyes fell on some briers and thorns by the wayside. She at once gathered a quantity of them, and, binding them together, bore them home to her cabin. At night, when all were in bed, she strewed them on her mat, and stretched herself intrepidly on that bed of pain. During three consecutive days, she had the courage to renew the same martyrdom. It was too much for a body already so weak and attenuated. One soon saw that she was in a rapid decline. This was at first attributed to her ordinary infirmities, which visibly increased day by day, without possibility of remedying them. But the real cause of the malady remained still a mystery. Anastasie discovered it. She suspected that something was passing that Catharine did not confide to her, and she finally obtained the avowal of her excessive rigor. The fervent young girl even confessed that it was her intention to continue the torture till her death, which she felt was very near. "Take care not to do so," cried Anastasie; "know that such an action cannot be agreeable to God unless authorized by your director."

There needed no more to prevent Catharine, whom the idea of sin terrified. She reproached herself for her imprudence, and hastened in confusion to the missionary. On meeting him she exclaimed, "My Father, I have sinned!" She then accused herself, with candor and humility, of her pious excesses as one accuses herself of a fault.

"In spite of my admiration for such heroism, I did not fail," says Father Cholenec, "to appear displeased, and to blame her for such imprudence. I bade her throw the thorns at once into the fire, and to give up all thought of ever again using such rigor."

This circumstance gave a new lustre to the perfection of Catharine's virtue. She possessed in fact, and in a high degree the characteristics of really virtuous souls, and the most infallible marks of the spirit of God, that is to say, the most perfect submission to her superiors. She at once renounced her own ideas and hastened to obey the missionary, showing more eagerness to follow the directions of him who held in her eyes, the place of God, than she had done in listening to the impulses of her own devotion.

Let us sight a few more traits of Catharine's spirit of penance. On the Feast of the Purification, she was seen walking in the field, as if following a procession, with naked feet, the snow up to her knees. During this time she was reciting her beads with devotion, wishing to imitate in some manner, the holy ceremonies of the Church, in the processions of this day.

Wednesdays and Saturdays were her days of strict fasting, and, the better to hide the self-imposed privation, she would set off early on these days to seek provisions or wood in the forest. She would even remain there sometimes the the entire day, to render her abstinence more complete, and contented herself with taking a little food on her return in the evening. If anyone offered to spare her this fatigue, her charity was ingenious in finding motives to second her mortification. She would say, for example, to the woman who shared with her the cares of housekeeping, "Stay you, rather; you have a child to care for and feed ; it would be hard for you; as to me there is nothing to prevent me." This love of mortification, was, for that matter, a characteristic of the savages of the Saut St. Louis. Catharine had before her eyes numerous striking examples, quite capable of arousing in her heart holy emulation. It will not be going beyond our subject to cite some names and traits worthy of preservation in the history of this mission. The great Agnié (Mohawk) Joseph Togouirout, so famous for his courage, Paul Horïagnennhoy, former dogique and first Christian of the Saut Stephen Tégananokoa (1) were chiefs of their people, by their example as well as by their rank and title. Their hatred of and holy indignation against themselves, urged them to take revenge on their own bodies, for the injuries offered to God by sinners and they were seen to practise pious rigors of which the missionaries did not always possess the secret.

The women, and especially those who belonged to the pious association of the Holy Family, followed in the same path. One, still young, exposed herself three nights in succession to all the rigors of a severe winter. Another, at the same season, chose the moment when a violent and impetuous wind made the snow fly like light frozen dust, making it difficult to keep one's feet, to seek the banks of the great river, and at the most exposed point there half clad recite her beads. And it must be remarked that the Hail Mary in the Iroquois language is twice as long as in French, owing to the periphrase used in translating.

There were others who went still further in their imprudent penances. Some broke the ice with their hatchets, plunged into the icy water, and in this strange position recited several prayers. One came near paying dear for her temerity. She wished to bear this rude trial for three nights in succession without being betrayed. She took care, on her return,

---

(1) He was burned by the idolatrous Iroquois. For the story of his torture see Charlevoix I. 888.

not to approach the fire. But the third day, no longer able to resist, she was seized with a violent fever, which brought her to the brink of the grave.

The wife of the fervent Stephen, Anne by name, acted with still greater imprudence. Not satisfied with imposing these strange severities upon herself, she forced a young child of three years of age to share them. When the missionary was informed of this he sent for her, that he might reproach her. The simple soul innocently confessed that in the fear that her child might one day relapse from the faith and fall into sin, she wished to exact from her some acts of penance in advance.

Unhappily, the savages had not their mentor and guide always with them, and this was the case especially during their long hunting and fishing excursions. At these times it was that they committed these extravagances. Such actions are far from being in themselves infallible proofs of holiness, since vanity and self-love, as well as ignorance, might become the motive on certain occasions, and the demon, an ever skilful seducer, always seeks to lead men astray by a false exaggeration of good, when he cannot openly urge them to evil; but it may be truly said that heroic virtue is never to be met unaccompanied by mortification, which serves as its sustenance and preservative.

The edifying conduct of the neophytes of the Saut St. Louis is the best justification of what we may call their pious excesses, as Father Cholenec remarks in his account of Catharine. On arriving at the Saut, Catharine had set to work to study carefully the example of the most fervent Christians of the mission. This was not for sterile admiration; she wished to walk in their footsteps, and so great was her ardor that she succeeded not only in imitating but she could soon serve them as model. Father Cholenec avows, that he was more than once forced to yield to Catharine's reiterated entreaties, to be permitted to practise corporal austerities, his only difficulty being in moderating them. "Had I left her to herself," he says, "she would soon have exceeded the others, and her strength was far from being equal to her courage." Such a disposition generally betrays great purity of heart, for mortification is its safeguard.

"I do not think," says the missionary just quoted, and who knew her best, "that she had ever mortally offended God, her horror for sin was such, and her vigilance over herself so great, that, during the two years and a half that I passed at the Saut, one could not reproach her for anything ever so little serious; her excessive mortification was, above all, inspired by the fear of offending God. She fled from even the shadow of sin."

Then, with what sentiments of confusion and fear, did she each week approach the tribunal of penance! How many tears she shed, in accusing herself of even the slightest faults. In her own eyes she was the greatest sinner in the village, and this thought always nourished in her heart a profound contempt of herself. She suffered when she heard any words that sounded like praise, and would withdraw immediately, or, if she could not do this, would hide her face in her blanket to conceal her confusion.

Zeal, the characteristic virtue of real piety, had formed in this mission, and from the first day of its existence, as many apostles as neophytes. They knew so well how to appreciate the happiness they owed to the faith, that they would fain have had all their people participate in it. This it is, that inspired those apostolic journeys, of which we have spoken, in the course of which they themselves carried the *Good News* of the Gospel into their country, and strove to rescue their relatives and friends from the yoke of idolatry. Catharine did not remain a stranger to this generous apostleship; it inspired her with many wishes, many ardent prayers, and sacrifices for its success.

We have related, how, at certain epochs, the Iroquois in their journeys, came in great numbers, to ask hospitality from the inhabitants of the Saut St. Louis. Among these strangers, were sometimes found Christians, but more frequently pagans. For the good neophytes of the Saut it was a time of zealous rivalry. They anticipated the least wishes of the strange travellers. They encompassed them with all the forethought of Christian charity, to win their hearts, and inspire them with a high idea of the Faith. Catharine took an active part in the work, in such proportion as her age and sex admitted. To some she taught *the Prayer*, and the elements of Christian doctrine; she conducted others to the house of La Prairie, she explained to them the pious exercises that took place there, or the tableaux and statues that ornamented the holy place.

Another circumstance opened a field still more vast to the zeal of the good Christians of the Saut, and though Catharine could take no part in it, save by prayer, it is edifying to make known what love of the faith can inspire, even in savage natures.

At certain seasons of the year, the savages of the entire country, but especially the Iroquois, came in very great numbers to Montreal, to trade, that is to say, to exchange their furs, and the small articles of their fabrication for arms, ammunition, and utensils of all kinds, which they afterwards carried home to their village. Unhappily, this epoch of very legitimate commerce, became the occasion of horrible disorders.

French merchants, sordidly greedy, feared not, to the shame of humanity and religion be it said, to speculate on the passion of these savages for intoxicating liquors, and they thus obtained their merchandise at a low price, or by robbing them of their reason, they arrogated to themselves the right to commit the most flagrant injustice towards them.

But this hideous traffic had a still more deplorable result. Drunkenness always awakes in the heart of the savage the most brutal instincts, and makes him capable of every excess. Scenes of anger, of murder, of hideous license, are daily renewed. The peaceable inhabitants are so seized with fright, that they barricade themselves in their houses, to prevent the entrance of the savages. In the evening, the palisaded enclosure of the town is closed, and the savages abandoned to themselves, in the space alloted to them, in which to pitch their tents.

It was at this moment, that the fervent Christians of the

Saut visited them, hoping to bring a remedy for the evil; they put in motion every means that their charity could suggest. They arrested furious men, separated combatants, gave good advice, addressed reproaches, and above all, prevented, when they could, the sale of intoxicating drink, the cause of so much misfortune. They were seen to watch the entire night, in order to prevent the renewal of these disorders. How often was not their charitable presence among these tents, the safeguard of weakness and innocence, as well as a curb to the audacity of evil-doers.

MAY.

BY J. G.

THE month of buds and blossoms bright,
 The fairest time of all the year,
Sweet May, mild child of winter's might
 Now thrills us with its glad'ning cheer.

With joy we greet thy happy birth,
 But not alone for flowers rare,
Nor this green dew-bespangled earth,
 Nor liquid songs, blue skies so fair.

But dearer far than skies so blue,
 Than woodland songs, than meadows green,
Than buds and blossoms lovely hue,
 'Tis Mary's month, the May's fair Queen.

SHRINE NOTES.

Our readers will be pleased to learn that the Reverend Arthur E. Jones, S.J., for many years past Archivist of St. Mary's College, Montreal, Canada, has been named one of the historians of the Society of Jesus. In this capacity his chief duty will be to collect and contribute data about the early and present Jesuit Canadian Missions for the general history of his Order. This task will soon necessitate a journey to Rome, and much research in various libraries of Europe. It will give Father Jones an opportunity for using the valuable historical knowledge already in his possession, and incidentally it will enable him to gather important material for the process of the beatification of the missionaries, Brebeuf, Lalemant, Daniel and Garnier, of whose cause he is vice-postulator, and to further also the cause of Father Jogues, Rene Goupil, and Catharine Tegakwitha, whose lives and deaths are so closely connected in many ways with the heroes who gave their blood for the faith on Canadian soil.

* * *

According to the *Mohawk Valley Democrat*, Fonda's weekly newspaper, Mr. Stokes has retired from the Putman House to take up his residence in Gloversville. Mr. Thomas Glenn, formerly in charge of Glenn Hotel, in Fonda, has already leased the Putman House, and intends to make it as comfortable as possible for pilgrims visiting Auriesville, whether in summer or any other season of the year. We hope to visit him before long, and announce his arrangements in our June number.

* * *

An Appeal.

As the season for pilgrimages to Auriesville approaches, we must beg of our readers to assist us in meeting the expense of reopening and maintaining the Shrine. In proportion to the generosity with which our petitions have usually been answered, we have endeavored to improve the grounds and structures at Auriesville, and this we shall do again this year. The new road to the Ravine, and the damage done by the severe storms of the past year make our expenses greater this year, and our petition, therefore, more urgent than in former years.

Every patron of Auriesville and every reader of THE PILGRIM can answer this appeal. Help the Shrine by obtaining a new subscriber for the PILGRIM. Not all may be able to contribute generously, but all can either induce some friend or friends to subscribe for the PILGRIM, or even by subscribing for them, arouse their interest in the Shrine and in the pilgrimages. This is a simple and practical way of contributing in answer to our appeal, and we suggest it all the more confidently because with a larger subscription list we shall be able to improve the PILGRIM, and by making it more attractive, make it also a more effective organ of the Shrine.

* * *

CONTRIBUTIONS TO THE SHRINE.

C. H., New York	$1 00	Miss S	$4.80
M. H., New York	1.00	Anon.	10.00
M. L. S. H., Buffalo, N. Y.	5.00		

THROUGH THE PIETÀ.

BY T. M. JOYCE.

(Continued.)

DURING the year that followed they saw no more of Edmund O'Connell. Madame Mabie continued to talk of her ancestry, her gardens and her sea-side Italian villa, however, without thought or inclination of returning to them. She felt it to be her duty to remain on this side of the water until she could see Esther fairly settled, she told John and Emily, since by her interference Edmund's visits had been discontinued.

The summer months were spent among the mountains where Florence's rather delicate health became robust. A tour of the great lakes completed the year's travel, and they returned home in time to join a merry round of society's winter gaiety. It was during this time Madame met, and introduced in the household, a young Florentine artist, the son of an old time friend. John Leonardo's bright personality, cheerful humor and easy grace, won for him hosts of friends and made him a welcome guest at their firesides. Madame took delight in chaperoning the young people through the various art galleries, all of which were open at any time to Leonardo or his friends.

These excursions were a source of great pleasure to Esther, who admired the work of the masters with all the enthusiasm of an artist. Particularly she liked the Venetian Studio. It was there she first saw the picture of the Pietà.

On that day from the top of the staircase, she had observed Madame in conversation with a gentleman who stood with uncovered head in her presence. Looking absently after his retreating figure, she had recognized Edmund O'Connell. The old sense of loneliness returned and weighed heavily upon her. Slowly descending the broad steps, she began to entertain strange doubts of ever being able to entirely forget him.

Madame was standing beneath the mansion's high arch at the doorway, and met her with a smiling countenance. "He looks splendid!" she exclaimed, turning to look after him with pride. "He inquired particularly for you."

Here a shade of annoyance passed over her features and she added in a changed tone: "How red your complexion is sometimes, Esther! Your mother was never so, always pale and serene, but I was speaking of Edmund. He is going to be married to-morrow, and is starting for Baltimore to be present at his brother's ordination. It is very remarkable, for when I asked him concerning the bride, he answered hurriedly that his acquaintance with her had been very brief, but he believed her to be an estimable young woman. A romance in a nutshell, and the ceremony is to be performed by the young priest."

Had Madame but glanced at the colorless face of the girl beside her at that moment, she would surely have withdrawn her complaint in regard to her niece's complexion. "I have frequently congratulated myself, however," she resumed, "for appearing on the scene in time to proffer you the advice upon which you acted so wisely." They were joined by the rest of their number at this juncture and the subject was not again resumed.

The following morning Esther resolved to visit the "Pietà"

alone, where she would be at ease to dwell upon the thoughts suggested by the picture. She had always objected to the homage paid to the Mother of God by Catholics, but somehow she felt herself to be strangely attracted by the sadness in the painted story. Then her own heart was sorely wounded, more than she wished to acknowledge, by the news of Edmund's marriage.

As she walked briskly along the wide avenue in the keen air, she upbraided herself for seeking comfort or sympathy from the thought suggested in the studio. She had sacrificed the love and protection of one who had tendered her the highest compliment a man can offer a woman for her religion. To that religion then she must turn to fill the void left in her life. She sighed as she questioned herself as to whether a visit to the church she attended would be likely to soothe her aching heart, and slowly ascended the stairs which led into the studio. Although it was yet early, a number of students had assembled and were diligently at work. She passed them heedlessly and stood before the painting, gazing in sudden awe upon the depths of woe visible in the eyes of the grief-stricken mother.

"You are too near, Miss Lee, you will obtain a better view at this distance," exclaimed the cheery voice of John Leonardo. Turning in surprise she beheld the young artist seated before a half-painted canvas deftly plying his brush. "We are two minds with but a single thought," he resumed lightly, "with the difference that while you are clever enough to carry the memory of this picture away with you wherever you go, I am obliged to submit to canvas any choice bit of art I choose to remember. But what I am endeavoring to fathom, Miss Lee, is your motive for visiting this picture."

"I cannot answer that inquiry myself," she responded slowly.

"I would have remained here longer yesterday," he went on, "but feared you might think I was worshipping the picture, as it is said Catholics do."

Esther, now seated opposite him, quietly listened as he seemed inclined to continue.

"You know, perhaps, that I have very peculiar ideas in regard to religion?"

To her smiling reply in the negative, he proceeded: "I believe in living up to one of those easy going creeds, where you may attend the church nearest your lodgings, but when my American heiress appears upon the scene, I shall marry her in the Catholic Church or the ceremony will be performed by a priest if it can be satisfactorily arranged. I shall demand a bond which can be broken only by death, so that I may not be troubled with bad dreams of reckoning whom my wife's second husband may be."

Esther's lip curled slightly. She had not looked at the picture before which she was seated since she had been interrupted. "And you will continue to live up to the church in your neighborhood?"

"O, yes," he responded readily as he painted a shadow over the brow of an angel, "but I am not entirely done with the Catholic clergyman. I shall trouble him once more when I am dying."

"O, indeed!" interposed his listener with sarcasm.

"Yes," he added frankly, "just as I would wish to say to my own father if I had offended him and caused him much sorrow, that I repented my evil deeds and desired to make a confession of them, I would appear before the throne of God with the seal of repentance upon my soul."

Esther watched him as he painted the scars left by the wounds in the hands of our Saviour, and he continued: "I have in my mind the memory of a college friend, who died in Florence; he had lived a wild life, never troubling himself about affairs of the soul, and the minister said a prayer about 'They who believe in the Lord shall be saved.' Now, honestly, Miss Lee, do you think that man was admitted to heaven? Don't you believe if he had thought of the sins in his life by which he had offended the Saviour whose death is portrayed to us here, he would have been better prepared to appear in his presence?" Without waiting for a reply he added hastily: "Now, Miss Lee, I see I have wearied you," for she had risen, "I am conscious of having talked a great

Esther responded pleasantly as she took her leave, that she would come when there were fewer visitors, for a number of persons had assembled to view a new work by a popular artist.

One evening, some weeks afterward, seated before the fire in the drawing-room, Esther's reverie was interrupted by the appearance of Madame Mabie enveloped in a long, gray satin cloak, at the door.

"What!" she exclaimed in surprise, "not dressed for the dinner?"

"Why, no, aunt, did I not tell you I sent my regrets?"

"I had really forgotten. Well, my dear, as you will. I begin to believe you are a cunning diplomat, so conspicuous is your absence among these gatherings. Ah, Florence," she added, as the young girl tripped gaily into the hall, her round cheeks glowing, and at once proceeded to divest herself of her snowy ridinghood and cloak. "You may give your excuses to Esther, I have been waiting for the horses," and drawing her furs closely about her jewelled throat, Madame Mabie took her departure.

When the tingle of the sleigh-bells became indistinct, Florence seated herself on a low stool near her sister, and held her pink palms out towards the blaze, exclaiming: "I have been to the beautiful church, Esther, with Mary, all garlands of ivy and flowers, and a sweet white dove just ready to fly, perched high over the—the Queen's altar—"

"The Queen, Florence, what Queen?"

"Why, the Mother of God, and Mary taught me the prayer—"

"Florence," said her sister almost severely, "you must never say that prayer. Our church does not sanction it."

"Mary Keane says an angel first told it."

Esther heard this with some misgiving. A vague sense of terror crept into her heart and she drew the child lovingly to her. "Florence," she cried almost severely, "I will never allow you to enter that church again. There is something so real and awful about it. People who embrace that religion are bound in it body and soul. It seems to encircle them round and round with bands of steel that nothing in this world, love, affection, even death, is strong enough to loosen, and there are thousands of them, of these churches all over the world and they are all the same the one cruel unflinching creed." She was speaking louder and with grave earnestness and her voice trembled as she added, "Ah, Flossie, that church is my enemy. I am jealous of it. It has destroyed my life and embittered my heart."

"It is all very tender and sweet about the Queen mother," she added softly after a pause, recalling the sorrowful eyes of the Blessed Virgin as represented in the Pietà with the body of the dead Christ in her lap. The picture was vividly impressed upon her memory, and again she saw the angels hovering about to comfort the Mother of God and hiding their faces from the awful solemnity of the presence of His death.

The sound of bells approaching interrupted her thoughts and she arose suddenly and began to make preparations for going out.

"I think I will ask Abraham to drive me to Emily's while the horses are here. You may come if you wish, dear," she added, noticing a droop in the curves of Florence's lips. A few moments later, clad in their soft warm furs they were riding through the flying snowstorm beneath long glittering avenues of ice covered branches and gay flashing globules of light.

By the time they reached the wide square and the horses drew up before the home of John Lee, Florence declared they were both veritable snow images.

At the door a maid evidently much distressed, came hurrying to meet them.

"Oh, it is only you," she cried, "we thought it was Mr. Lee. The baby is dying. Took sick only an hour ago. Oh, Miss Esther, go up and comfort her," entreated the girl tearfully.

When Esther silently entered the room she beheld her brother's wife evidently attired for the dinner, in a beautiful evening gown flashing with diamonds, and the jewels glittering on her throat and in her hair, prostrate beside the bed of the still little child.

"Spare my boy, O Mother of holy love," cried Emily in

despair, "O Mother whose child I was, have pity on me in this my misery, who have turned from out the path into which you guided me. Look upon me and my sorrow, and stay the hand of retribution about to part my child from me. O I am most unworthy and it is thus that the enormity of my sins is revealed to me. I have bartered my faith for this. O God in heaven have mercy upon my poor soul. My child is dying and without baptism. O, Esther pray with me. I have forgotten my prayers!"

The last words ended in a heart-breaking cry of remorse. Then, Florence, who until now stood with wide eyes at the door, moved over to the bedside and kneeling there in sweet simplicity prayed fondly to the Queen of heaven in the words forbidden by her sister.

Esther, deeply moved and with tears of sympathy and disappointment in her eyes, went out of the room and down to the sleigh. "To the Church of the Pietà," she said, and as Abraham turned the horses in that direction, he silently mused upon the odd whims of young women.

Esther felt herself to be in a state of utter bewilderment. She had taught Emily to become a Presbyterian, and had brought Florence up in the religion, and she had looked upon the result of her efforts to-night. And even now she herself was hastening to summon a priest for the baptism of her brother's child. This, however, she felt to be a duty from which she dared not shrink.

In the church a mission was being held, and Esther was obliged to remain until the sermon was ended. She was not a little surprised to find herself a willing listener to a discourse by a Catholic priest. The speaker dwelt upon the subject of Christ's love for the souls of men, and the consummation of His sacrifice. He described the scene of the crucifixion and appealed to the hearts of the congregation by a vivid picture of the Blessed Virgin standing beside her suffering Son, knowing He endured most awful agony, the wounds gaping and bleeding from His majestic head, pierced by the cruel crown, to where the nails mercilessly stabbed His sacred feet, her mother's yearning heart going out to Him in His suffering, yet helpless to caress or soothe him with her loving willing hands; knowing of His extreme thirst, yet unable to give Him a drop of water, realizing how the prophetic sword had pierced down into the depths of her tender mother's heart enduring agony with her Son for whom she had cared so lovingly since His childhood, guarding Him against the slightest pain or wound, the dreadful death before her.

Then followed a vivid word picture of the Pietà, and Esther's tears flowed freely. She was listening to the truths of Emily's religion and thought of her still unshaken faith with a feeling akin to pride. He concluded the sermon by dwelling at length upon the final sacrifice of Christ giving Himself to us over again in the Blessed Sacrament.

Esther was filled with a wonderful peace. Her repentant heart went out in loving gratitude to the great heart of the dying Saviour. Her rebellious soul had conquered itself, and she found herself repeating these lines:

> "O holy mother, stand thou there
> Pleading 'twixt Him and me."

When Benediction was over, many persons remained kneeling about the confessionals. Esther alone in a pew was aroused from her silent meditation by a hand upon her arm. The sight of her brother's pale anxious face brought the object of her errand in the church before her mind.

The unexpected meeting with Esther seemed not to surprise him. He was passive to all feeling except the critical illness of his little son.

"Emily is waiting. She wants the priest to come," he said quietly. "Our little boy—" His faltering voice refused the words, but in his drawn features Esther read the pain of dark, despairing grief.

The good priest accompanied them to the bedside of the sick child and performed the baptism, while Emily's perturbed spirit broke forth in sobs of anguish. The minister of God, however, soothed her aching heart with words of comfort and assured her of that pardon which is never withheld from a repentant soul.

The father kneeling beside the bed with the tiny feverish hand clasped in his own, hopelessly watched the wistful upturned face of his little son. The best physicians were in attendance, and all the comfort and luxury which wealth affords or that loving hands could administer were heaped upon him.

Yet these were of no avail to withhold the soul of the little child from yielding to the voice of a Father's love whispering ever—"for of such is the kingdom of heaven." And into the hearts of the grief stricken parents descended the light of God's grace as involuntarily they turned to Him for strength in their sorrow.

* * * * * * *

The breath of Spring was in the air when Esther stood one bright morning, beneath the broad low porch where vines of budding ivy waved lazily in the sunlight. Apple blossoms were strewn about in such profusion as to give the orchard the appearance of having been deluged by a fall of pink tinted snow flakes during the night. The wide lane leading up to the entrance glistened beneath its covering of shining moist petals. The mad rush of the gleaming river eager to be away over its rocky bed, together with the sweet trilling of robins in the tree tops filled the air with melodious sounds.

A carriage rolled up to the curb and Madame Mabie waved to her niece from the window. As she slowly proceeded down the long gravel walk, clad in a close fitting gown of dark blue, her hat fairly nodding with bright colored roses, Esther Lee presented a fair picture upon the landscape on that beautiful Spring morning.

"You returned earlier than I expected," she said as she took her seat and finished buttoning her glove. "Well, my dear, I received a card 'from Madeline Leonardo last night, as you know," explained Madame, "requesting me to call at the Imperial Hotel where she had joined her son who was ill. Well, imagine my surprise this morning when I arrived there to find the whole place under quarantine. The doctors have pronounced it to be yellow fever, and poor John, our gay young friend, is the unhappy victim. A messenger boy had just arrived from the minister, who being a man of family declined to attend."

"Then there is no hope of his recovery," asked Esther, a world of sympathy in her large dark eyes. "None whatever," declared Madame decisively, adding after a pause, "My confidential messenger, who had the most delicious brogue, further informed me that the dying man had been imploring them to allow him to see a Catholic priest, but how Madeline, his mother, insisted before them all that her poor boy was raving, although to the doctor she admitted he had been baptized in the old faith."

Esther listened silently while thoughts of the conversation in the studio recurred to her, and she remembered how diligently he had sketched the famous "Pietà." "I am sure, Aunt Mary," she said thoughtfully, "if any priest were to know of such a wish of a dying man, he would consider it his duty, the duty of his calling, to visit him and administer the last sacraments of the Church, that he might be prepared to stand before the judgment seat of God with the seal of absolution upon his soul."

"I declare, Esther, since you have joined this church you are absolutely gloomy. It is so startling, the thought of one day standing alone before the judgment throne of an angry God," and Madame shrank perceptibly.

"Just, not angry," said Esther smiling, "but we are at the rectory, and I think if John Leonardo is dying and is anxious to see a priest, it is our duty to make known his desire." "But his mother, we might incur her lasting displeasure," objected Madame warmly.

"It will not be necessary for Father Stewart to state from whom the information came," answered her niece, as the carriage stopped before the tall white brick residence.

A few moments later they were seated in the plainly furnished parlor where Father Stewart, who also had just come in, joined them.

When Esther made known the purport of their visit, Madame explained and stated how much she deplored the fact that the minister had failed to respond to the call. "We could not conscientiously blame him though, could we, Madame?" said the priest. To her inquiring glance he replied.

"Why should he place himself in imminent danger in order to pray with a man who is dying? With a Catholic priest it is different. He is in duty bound to administer the sacraments of the Church to the dying and his life given over to the service of Christ, is of no consequence when compared with this duty."

At this juncture a messenger whose brogue Madame recognized at once, was heard in the hall inquiring for Father O'Connell.

"He is away on a sick call," answered the housekeeper.

"To the Imperial Hotel, is it?" asked the boy, eagerly.

"The same, child," responded the woman. "To a man low with the fever."

When Father Stewart returned to the parlor from which he had withdrawn for a moment, he said: "Our young priest was summoned while I was saying Mass. He is very likely with your friend even now. Father O'Connell is an exemplary priest"——

"Why," interrupted Madame, addressing Esther with surprise in her tone, "he must be Mr. O'Connell's brother. I remember having met Edmund when he was leaving for Baltimore to attend to his brother's ordination and his own wedding."

Father Stewart smiled as he arose, for the ladies were standing. "There is a mistake somewhere," he said, "Edmund is not married. However," he added, "Father O'Connell celebrated a nuptial mass for a relative on the day following his ordination. Being in Baltimore on the occasion, I assisted at the ceremony, and if I remember rightly Edmund was the groomsman. Father O'Connell and I have long been friends, although he was appointed to this parish only last week, having until then assisted the Bishop."

"It is strange," said Madame, turning to Esther, "and quite unaccountable how I misunderstood him that day. But," she added, addressing Father Stewart, "I cannot conceive how any one, even your loyal young priest, could actually court that dread disease." With a sigh she concluded, "He certainly must have perfect faith in the teachings of his Church."

"Your conclusion is entirely correct, Madame," said Father Stewart, as he accompanied them into the hall.

"When you have another mission, Father, or series of sermons, Aunt Mary has promised to attend," said Esther, at the door. "Out of curiosity, my dear, mere curiosity," said Madame as they were taking their leave.

As they reached the church, Esther decided to enter and offer up a prayer for the spiritual comfort of John Leonardo, Madame arranging to meet her when she had completed some purchases at a near-by shop.

Long, slanting bars of soft-tinted light streamed through the colored windows and shed a roseate hue upon the marble altar.

Esther knelt beneath the quivering glow of the sanctuary lamp, where shortly before she and Florence had received the grace of baptism. Long and earnestly she prayed, her eyes raised to the shining door of the tabernacle, the dwelling of the patient, loving Christ, imploring Him to grant peace to the soul of the dying artist. This favor she entreated through the death shown in "the Pietà" painted high over the altar. And before leaving, silently up from her heart arose a prayer of thanksgiving that Madame's mistake was made manifest.

At the door of the carriage she heard hasty strides descending the steps of the rectory, and turning, to her surprise beheld Edmund O'Connell advancing toward her. A quick pallor spread over his features when he took her hand in his and looked into her eyes which were smiling a responsive greeting to his own. "Father Stewart has just told me about you—about your conversion," he said.

"Indeed," she replied, "he has been very good to me," adding quickly, "I have been waiting for Aunt Mary. She is coming now across the street."

"I have been so miserable and lonely, Esther," he went on, without heeding her words, "for even a sight of you, it required all my strength to remain away. The last time I saw you, there was one great barrier dividing us. That is now removed. I have waited so long," he added, a great wistfulness settling in his eyes. "I hardly dare hope that some other may not have arisen to still keep you from me."

Overhead the birds chirped a sweet interlude, and down the long avenue, shadows of branches and fluttering leaves were waving on the broad sunlit pavement.

Madame was very near them, but Edmund's dark searching eyes were silently demanding an answer. "There is no other," said Esther so softly as to be almost a whisper as she stepped into the carriage.

"God bless you, Esther," he exclaimed in a low tone as Madame approached him.

She was mentally congratulating herself for having joined them in time to prevent any serious conversation.

"You are looking very well, Mr. O'Connell," she said, and glancing at his handsome flushed face, she added, "and happy." "I am both," he answered. "I have been quite well and Miss Lee has just made me very happy."

And away at the Imperial Hotel, Madame Leonardo was loud in lamentation over the death of her son.

THE JESUITS AND NEW FRANCE.

From the French of Rev. Camille de Rochemonteix, S.J.

(Continued.)

QUEBEC had surrendered on the 19th of July, 1629, three month after the peace concluded at Suze (April 24, 1629) between France and England. Champlain was ignorant at the time of the conclusion of peace; the English admiral however had been informed of it at Tadoussac. But Kertk pretended that he did not believe it, in order to get possession of the French colony of Quebec and to make good by pillage the great expense occasioned by the equipment of his fleet. His plans succeeded. He returned to England with ships loaded with furs and other merchandise taken from the French.

If the capture of Quebec was not an act of piracy, its restitution was an obligation of justice. Upon the earnest remonstrances of Champlain, Louis XIII. demanded that the fort and the *habitation* should be given back and Charles I. ordered that they should be evacuated and restored to the representative of France.

This order was not to be executed immediately for reasons recorded by some Canadians historians. According to them there were at this time at the court and even in the Council of Louis XIII. men who inquired whether this country was worth demanding back. What had it produced thus far, they asked, and what could be hoped for from a frozen region which could not support its inhabitants? They thought that enough sacrifices had been made without any profit. They saw but little gain and much loss in a colonial policy. They argued that France could not undertake to people the banks of the Saint Lawrence without weakening herself. In a word they proposed not to retire, since they were no longer in Canada, but not to go back and recommence the colonization of these distant lands.

Richelieu did not share this policy of abandonment based on narrow and utilitarian views. Taking a lofty view of things, he put before every other consideration the glory of the French name, the triumph of the royal armies and the spread of the Catholic religion. His patriotism and his faith refused to leave Protestant England to enjoy in peace upon the Saint Lawrence, conquests unjustly acquired. Nevertheless, being occupied in the Alps by the war of the Mantuan succession, he did not judge it proper to force Admiral Kertk to retire at once, for it did not enter into his plans to have two great enterprises on his hands at the same time. But the peace of Cherasco having secured French influence in Italy, he armed ten ships, and making no account of the objections raised by short-sighted and timid courtiers, he charged the brave Commander de Razilly to conduct the fleet to Quebec. The cabinet of London understood this demonstration, and, fearing a conflict, they hastened to sign the treaty of Saint-Germain-en-Laye (March 29, 1632) which gave back to France all the ports occupied by the English in Acadia and Canada.

In the month of July of the same year, the temporary commander of the colony, Emery de Caen and his lieutenant, du Plessis-Bochard, resumed control of the French possessions after three years of British rule.

They were accompanied by three religious of the Company of Jesus, Father Paul le Jeune, Father Anne de Noüe and a lay-brother. At the same time Father Anthony Daniel took up his abode with Father Davost, at Cape Breton, where his brother, Captain Charles Daniel, was in command, and where the return of the missionaries was ardently desired.

It is well known that Cardinal Richelieu had a particular liking for the Capucins. He proposed to them the mission of New France immediately after the peace of Saint Germain. He was, however, fully resolved to send but one religious order to Canada, for "he judged," says Abbé Faillon, "that it would be better for the new colonies to have in each religious of the same institute that there might be more union, agreement and dependence among the missionaries."

With a refined delicacy of sentiment the Capucins declined to accept the mission which they thought should rightly return to the two orders expelled from Quebec by the English. Richelieu had to choose between the Jesuits and the Recollects. His choice fell upon the former because according to their Institute they can possess goods and revenues and they would thus put the colony to less expense and be better able to attract the Indians. John de Lauson, superintendent of affairs in Canada and president of the Company of One Hundred, shared on this point, the views of the Cardinal.

The Jesuits being chosen, letters patent were provided empowering them to resume their posts. M. du Pont, nephew of the Cardinal, sent these letters himself to Father le Jeune, then superior of the residence of Dieppe. In them we read: "Armand Cardinal, Duke de Richelieu, Peer of France, Grand Master, Chief and Superintendent-General of the commerce of the realm, to all those unto whom these presents shall come, greeting. Having by contract of the twentieth of January last, charged M. William de Caen, formerly general of the fleet of New France, to give passage to Quebec, country of New France, to three Capucins with forty men . . . ; and having learned since from the Capucin Fathers, who have represented it to us in good faith, that the Jesuit Fathers have already been employed in the places to which it was proposed to send them, and that therefore it would be more proper and more reasonable to reestablish them in possession of the place from which they had been expelled, than to send thither the Capucins who have begged to be excused for the same reasons—for these causes desiring to satisfy both parties and that what belongs to the Jesuit Fathers should be restored to them to the end that they may labor there for the glory of God; we order that Fathers Paul le Jeune, Anne de Nouë and Gilbert Buret, who have been nominated by Father Bartholomew Jacquinot, Provincial of France, of the Company of Jesus, shall go to resume possession of the houses and places which they have already possessed in the aforesaid Quebec, to fulfill there the duties conformable to their institute."

The Jesuits eagerly desired to resume at Quebec the interrupted course of their apostolic labors. To this end they gained over heaven to their side. From the day of their expulsion the Province of Paris had a Mass celebrated every day to obtain the return of its sons to this mission. For the same object the Ursulines and the Carmelites of Paris organized a service of adoration and prayer continued night and day in their chapels without interruption. Every day fifteen religious approached the Holy Table for this intention. This was the only intrigue of the Jesuits. This was the means by which they got the Recollects excluded and themselves called to the mission of Canada. Is this proceeding in reality so very culpable?

Still, like men of wisdom and forethought, they took their precautions so as to be ready to set out for Canada should it be restored to France and should the Company of One

Hundred make an appeal to their devotedness. On the 6th of December, 1631, Father Charles Lalemant, then Rector of the College of Rouen, wrote to Father Charlet, assistant of the Province of France at Rome.

"The Canadian affair promises well. The English have given security for the execution of the agreement which has been entered into, by which they promise to restore Quebec, whereupon M. de Lauson is making preparations to return thither this Spring. The savages desire us very much, and sigh for the return of the Frenchmen, from whom they receive very different treatment from what they get from the English. I believe that we shall return in the Spring to the *habitation* of Captain Daniel, for the French desire our Fathers, and Captain Daniel is more attached to us than ever. He will be very glad to take Father Vimont, whom he regards as a saint, and Father Daniel, his brother. May it please our Rev. Father General to write to Rev. Father Provincial not to fail to give some of our Fathers if they are asked for."

Notified, towards the end of March, by the Provincial of Paris of their speedy departure for Quebec, Fathers Le Jeune and de Noüe were able to embark on the 18th of April at Honfleur on the vessels of Emery de Caen. The Recollects did not present themselves for embarkation, says Abbé Faillon, hence passage was not refused to them this year. Later on they were not permitted to resume on the banks of the St. Lawrence the post of combat where they had so valiantly struggled for fifteen years in the cause of God. This refusal was very painful to them, especially as it came from M. de Lauson, who owed to them in some measure his appointment to the presidency of Richelieu's Company. They were told at first that one religious order was enough for the present in Canada, considering the small number of the faithful. Then they were reminded of the difficulties which might arise between the Jesuits and the Recollects. Finally they were informed that the country was not yet prepared to support a mendicant order.

THE PILGRIM

OF

OUR LADY OF MARTYRS

XV. Year.　　　　June, 1899.　　　　No. 6.

RESIGNATION.
BY C. M. GIRARDEAU.

FORGET thy pain awhile, my heart,
　　And so forgetting muse awhile.
　　Come from the garish day apart
And seek with me this solemn aisle.
Here sit where thou canst see the smile
Of the dear Saviour, and the dart
Of sun that like a spear that heart
Doth pierce, transfixing thro' and thro'—
That quivering anguish—and the blue
And crimson of the altar-light.
Here sit with me, and with the night,
And hold communion with that bright
And awful sorrow. . . .
　　　　　　　　　Ah, the days
Of pain are endless, and the ways
Of grief so winding, and the tears
So slow . . . they seem to blot the years
With blood.　Oh, unavailing pain.
Oh, futile longing.　Dear refrain
Of woe—*to see His face again.*
To see Him, yes, my God, to see
Him once again.　Just once to be
Beside Him.　Not to hear Him speak,
If 'tis Thy will, nor press His cheek,
Nor hold His hand in mine, nor seek
Return of love.　But just to see
His face. . . . I know it cannot be.

Forgive the cry of love's extremest pain,
Hold Thou Thy hand upon my throbbing brain.
Speak to me, Lord, as to Thine own of eld,
And tell me that the life Thou hast withheld
Is all mine still, for being Thine alone.
Bless me, my Mother, as I make my moan
To thee—for thou didst lose thine only One,
Let me thy pierced bosom rest upon.
The air of day is fresh upon my brow,
Peace cometh to my soul, for even now
I know that He foresaw the end and cried:
" I will go home to-morrow," ere He died,
Meaning the mansion of our Father, God.

My life is with Him there; beneath the sod
His body lies. And tho' I walk this way
With grief's great angel, I will lift mine eyes
And see the radiant jasper walls arise;
And just beyond—the Light of Paradise.

AN IROQUOIS MAIDEN;
OR
Life of Catharine Tegakwitha.
(*Continued.*)
CHAPTER XIV.
Catharine's Chastity.

WHAT gives to the virtue of our fervent Christian, a splendor never before seen amongst the Iroquois, is the glory of virginity, which, as we have said, she had vowed to the Lord. She was first among her people to raise the sacred standard, and her example has had imitators. One may say, that she was prepared for it from the tenderest age, by her fidelity in corresponding to the special graces by which it had pleased the Lord to prevent her. Her modesty was ever angelic, and her face bore its impress. "I say it, and I cannot weary of saying it," here adds Father Cholenec, " that it is an ineffable miracle of grace that Catharine should have passed more than twenty years of her life amidst the corruption of her country, and two and a half years at the Saut St. Louis, in perfect integrity of body and soul, without ever suffering the least movement contrary to that virtue. But she also never deviated from the severe rule she had imposed upon herself, in order to shield her purity from all danger. She preferred to bear the mockery of the wicked and suffer them to turn into ridicule the wise precautions with which she surrounded herself, rather than compromise, in the least, this most delicate virtue.

A young man one day passed close to her, at a moment, when with her head almost entirely enveloped in her blanket, according to custom, she was listening with pious attention, to the wise counsel of good Anastasie. He stopped and cried out in a mocking tone, "This one has sore eyes, they say ; let us see a little!" and thereupon he lifted the blanket to look at her. The poor girl, speechless before such a piece of rudeness, only blushed, and, without showing the least impatience, quietly drew her blanket around her, and renewed her resolution of flying all company that could be dangerous to her. She understood better than ever before, how serviceable was the modest covering in use at the mission which replaced the veil of Christian women. The custom was to wear it only at church; she decided never to leave it off. She wore it, even during the greatest heat of Summer, at work in the fields, and in the woods.

What greatly contributed to preserve and develop in Catharine's heart this love of chastity, was a tender devotion to the Queen of Heaven. She had felt it from infancy, and owed it, without doubt, to her pious mother, who like a Christian mother, had made her form pious habits even before her reason was developed, or before she could understand their importance. This sentiment of confidence in the Blessed Virgin only grew with age. We have seen how she chose one of the beautiful feasts of the Blessed Virgin on which to offer to God her virginity. She loved to sing the praises of Mary, and to speak of her virtues. She did not let a day pass without offering to her a tribute of homage. The beads had become her favorite, one may say, her constant prayer. She habitually held them in her hand, as a salutary and easy means of conversing with God. On Saturdays, and the days that recalled any feast of the Mother of God, she added something to the mortifications, and to the practices of each day, as an evidence of her devotion and a title to new favors. Be not surprised that under this powerful safeguard Catharine preserved, pure and intact, the beautiful virtue that characterizes the angels of this earth, and permits them to follow in the suite of the Lamb.

The retired life led by Catharine, and her ardent desire to withdraw from everything that could in the very least expose this beautiful virtue, led her to dream of a new manner of life in which she saw greater security for herself, and a situation more in harmony with her tastes. Touching illusion of a fervent soul which the tempter strives to lead astray by the deceitful appearance of good!

One day Catharine and Theresa were bemoaning together their doing so little for God. In their pious ardor they sought the means of leading a more perfect life, farther from dangers of the world, and in consequence more agreeable to God. At first they thought of joining with another Indian woman of tried virtue, who would act towards them as a mother and counsellor, and with whom they might live as one family.

Theresa immediately cast her eyes upon Mary Skarichion, who had lived for some time at the Huron mission near Quebec, and in whom were united all the qualities necessary for the success of their project. This woman, whose zeal equalled her virtue, easily yielded to the invitation of the fervent neophytes, and all three went together to the foot of the cross on the banks of the river, to there form their plan of life.

Mary, who was the oldest, had had occasion to make the acquaintance of the religious of the Hotel Dieu, of Quebec, during an illness she had had at that mission. She suggested to her companions the design of a mutual agreement not to separate, to dress in the same manner and inhabit the same cabin; it was like a new-born community. Their taste for solitude, and their desire of breaking altogether with the world, whose dangers they feared, urged them on still further. They dreamed of living like hermits, of whose solitary lives they had heard. The tableau spread by nature before their eyes seemed to favor their bold project. They had the vast sheet of water formed in that place by the St. Lawrence, before them. On the same shore to their right, arose the thinly scattered dwellings of the first French settlers of the prairie. Far from wishing to approach, they desired rather to withdraw from them. They knew that by such contact, they had for the most part, far more to lose than to gain.

They then turned to the left, in the direction of the Saut St. Louis, whose abundant waters they saw falling in spray at their feet. Catharine, who only thought of realizing her dreams of solitude, and by what means she could compass them, was struck by the sight of a little isle named *l'Isle aux Hérons* (Herons Isle), in the midst of the rapids of the Saut.

It was, in fact, difficult to imagine an isolation more complete. This isle was only accessible from its farthest extremity, and, to land even demanded the utmost caution, by reason of the agitation and ebullition of the water falling from the rapids. We see, in the account of Champlain's voyage, that in the year 1611, some of his sailors wished to hunt on this isle, at that time full of herons. They killed, in fact, a great number, but, in departing, their boat, too heavily laden with game, capsized, and a Frenchman lost his life.

Thus our three fervent novices formed the most beautiful plans which suited singularly their exalted imagination. It seemed to them that they were going to make this desert soil, till then uninhabited, produce all the marvels of the Thebaïd. In fancy, their little hermitage was already raised, in the most retired spot. The unapproachable shores were to be their cloister, the thick woods their screen from mortal eyes; a tiny cabin of bark was to be, at the same time, their abode, and their house of prayer. Everything seemed to respond to their pious desires, and they already longed to put their plan in execution. Happily for themselves, they understood that they could not do this without consulting enlightened guides, and following the counsel of those God had placed over them, to direct them.

One of their number was chosen to submit the pious project to the missionary, and obtain his approbation. They seemed to have no suspicion that he would raise any objection, or put any obstacle in its way.

Father Frémin was, at that time, Superior of the Mission. While admiring the heroic thoughts of these fervent hearts, he readily discovered what dangers and illusions such ideas would entail. In order not to discourage them by absolute condemnation of their project, he contented himself with remarking that such a manner of life would appear strange, and unnatural. "You are still too young in the faith," he added, "to live thus alone, and without a guide. And who will undertake to provide you with food? You would do better to sanctify yourself in your present state, without seeking extraordinary ways, until you known the will of God better."

This was sufficient for these upright and docile hearts, and the projected hermitage on the Isle of Herons was at once abandoned. It merits a place in this history, however, as a beautiful proof of the sacrifices that fervor can inspire, and a testimony, at the same time, of the victory obtained by obedience.

The good Christians, then, contented themselves with their ordinary life, carefully avoiding, as had been recommended by their director, all that might appear singular. It was for this reason that Catharine forbore to cut off her hair closely, as she had several times wished to do, that she might offer to God one of the objects of vanity dearest to the heart of a young Indian girl. She thus preferred not to make parade of her sacrifices, but to lead a simple life, yet it was a life distinguished by the practice of uncommon virtues. She combatted, none the less, luxury and vanity. She would not choose for herself one of the bright red blankets so flattering to young girls, blue seeming to her more modest. On days of Communion, she also put aside collars and ear-rings, and refused to ornament her hair, dress, or leggings with the ornaments usually worn by young savage girls.

The French living at the Prairie de la Maddeleine, and who came from time to time to visit the Saut mission, were in admiration of so much virtue, as well as the Christians of the Saut. They considered it a happiness to converse for some minutes with the young girl, and to gather from her own lips some of her holy words. It seemed impossible to approach her without feeling more zeal for prayer, more love for chastity, more devotion towards the Blessed Virgin.

We may cite as fruit of the example and counsel of Catharine, the admirable progress made by two newly married young savages who had a most sincere desire to serve God well. These were Francis Tsonnatouan, surnamed the *grosse buche* (Big Log), and Margaret, his wife. They one day called Catharine into their cabin to question her on the life that good Christians should lead in the world, but fearing that her humility might prevent her from speaking freely, they invited Anastasie to accompany her. The conversation turned only on subjects of piety. With touching simplicity these two good Christians confided to Catharine and Anastasie their holy disposition and generous desire to please God with all possible fervor. Catharine and Theresa spoke with the same candor and God blessed this pious conversation. Francis, especially, lived with a great reputation for sanctity till an advanced age.

After Catharine's death he had the happiness to obtain one of her portraits, and he loved to contemplate it and recall her counsels and example. He even carried about him one of her relics. His confidence in the power of the pious girl induced him to invoke her often. He did so especially and with great success in the trials that it pleased the Lord to send him. Stricken with paralysis during the last fourteen years of his life, he was obliged to relinquish the life of a hunter and warrior, which had been, till then, his glory. The will of God appeared to him still more precious, and he submitted to it with perfect resignation.

One loved to visit him in his infirmity, for he had a great talent for exhorting to virtue. The missionary had given him a book containing figures from the Old and New Testaments, representations of the virtues and vices, as well as the principal mysteries. He employed it with much skill in instructing those who came to visit him. He made his children pray and himself taught them the catechism. Whenever he could, he was seen to drag himself painfully to church, and as he had learned all the sacred chants he was of great service to the missionaries. Towards the close of his life one of his greatest privations was not to be able to participate, like the others, at Holy Communion on feast days, but he knew how to resign himself by reflecting that our Lord knew the ardent desires of his heart. The souvenir of Catharine, which he always preserved, even to his last moments, constantly served to sustain his courage.

(*To be continued.*)

THE JESUITS AND NEW FRANCE
In the Seventeenth Century.
From the French of Rev. Camille de Rochemonteix, S.J.
BY K. A. HENNESSY.
(*Continued.*)

BUT these reasons were not convincing and therefore did not satisfy the Franciscans. The latter left no stone unturned in order to maintain their rights, but the Company of One Hundred could not be moved, although in Rome, the Propaganda renewed the Franciscans' privileges, and the Jesuits of Quebec sent them word that they wished to see them again.

Nevertheless, the Jesuits embarked alone. On December 6, 1631, Father Charles Lalemant wrote as follows to Father Charlet, assistant of the Province of France, residing in Rome: "Here I am, ready as ever and, God willing, I am to sail to-morrow! Any way, I do not see to what advantage I could be employed in France. To be Rector is not in my line, and as far as other occupations are concerned, I leave Your Reverence to imagine what could be successfully undertaken by one who has lost all his writings, some being confiscated by the English and the rest lost in two different shipwrecks." On May 1, 1632, Father Lalemant wrote again to Father Charlet from Rouen: "May I not accompany Fathers Brébeuf and Massé, next year? After all, I am merely languishing here, and I shall have been three years in charge between here and Eu."

In making these statements Father Lalemant did not do himself justice, for the memory of his gentle and successful administration in the colleges of Eu and Rouen was long and tenderly cherished. However, his superiors finally acceded to his request, and in April, 1634, he left France with Father Jacques Buteux. Father André Richard and Julien Perrault had embarked in February, and Fathers Massé and Brébeuf during the previous year. Charles Turgis, Claude Quentin, François Le Mercier, Jean de Quen, Pierre Pijart, Charles du Marché, Nicolas Adam, Pierre Chastellain, Charles Garnier, Paul Ragueneau, Isaac Jogues, Georges d'Eudemare, Jacques de la Place and Nicolas Gondoin soon joined them and, in 1637, the missionary band consisted of twenty-three priests and six lay brothers. In 1638 Charles Raymbault, Jérôme Lalemant, Simon Le Moyne and François du Peron swelled the number. Nicolas Gondoin, being quite out of his element, soon retired from the new field and sailed for France by the first vessel.

Father Paul Le Jeune, to whom we have already alluded, was named superior of the mission. He was born at Chalons-sur-Marne and his parents were Calvinists. While still a child he was favored with the light of the true faith which enabled him to discover divine truth in the bosom of the Church of Rome. He grew up under the influence of this supernatural attraction and when he attained manhood, despite the opposition of his parents, he abjured the religion in which he had been reared and, going to Rouen, became enrolled among the disciples of St. Ignatius. His ardor amounted almost to a passion and his firmness of soul bordered on obstinacy; in truth, he had a heart of fire and a will of steel. But virtue, aided by grace, had so far overcome the exuberant impetuosity of his nature that, combined with a wonderfully calm exterior, he had the charm of a warm and kindly manner; all within him was directed by a latent though ever vigilant power which deviated neither to right nor left. By a most singular contrast this man of broad, unprejudiced views was endowed with a geometrical mind, ever accurate and methodical and most keenly observing. The smallest detail never escaped him. At a glance, he could take in all the minutiæ and, in order to keep his superiors thoroughly informed of the exact condition of the persons and things under his charge, he obliged them to wade through a correspondence overloaded with scrupulously detailed accounts. The nine volumes of his *Relations* are a perfect reflection of his complex nature, which was at once great and small, bold and methodical, enthusiastic and moderate. "In him," says M. Casgrain, "virtue and apostolic zeal were balanced by science . . . . . in his Relations he has left traces of his brilliant intellect." Dr. O'Callaghan adds: He may be looked upon as the Father of the Jesuit missions in Canada. The solidity of his knowledge and the integrity of his character had won him such consideration on the part of the Government that the Queen-Mother, Anne of Austria, expressed a strong desire to see him chosen first bishop of the country in which he had been a missionary for seventeen years, but this, the rules of his Order forbade." Benjamin Sulte, who is not over lavish in his praise of the Jesuits, nevertheless recognized in Father Paul Le Jeune "a man of the greatest merit, a facile writer, an observer, a religious filled with an excellent initiative spirit."

Upon reaching Quebec, Father Paul Le Jeune found Notre-Dame des Anges in a most dilapidated condition. Of the two buildings erected by Father Lalemant within the enclosure, the one used as a bakeshop, storehouse and stable had been partially burned by the English, while the other, inhabited by the community previously to the taking of the fort, was in ruins. It had neither doors nor windows, the roof had almost disappeared and the only furniture found inside were two miserable wooden tables. The house that stood within two hundred feet of the river's edge was not large. "It has," relates Father Le

Jeune, "four low ceiled apartments, the first of which serves as a chapel, and the second as a refectory, and within this refectory are our cells. There are two small rooms as square as the average man is tall, and two others each of which is eight feet square, but in every room there are two beds. The third large apartment is used as a kitchen, and the fourth is occupied by our workmen."

Such then, was the residence of Notre-Dame des Anges, the humble cradle of the important missions of New France.

The superior gave his companion, Father de Noué, charge of the workmen. Father de Noué's early career had not been such as to fit him for an overseer of laborers or a successful mechanic, but circumstances often develop latent qualifications, and the willing worker soon becomes equal to his task. This religious, the son of a French gentleman known as the Seigneur de Villers and of other places in the vicinity of Rheims, had lived at Court, first in the capacity of page and later as an officer of the King's household, and, though witnessing much of the deplorable licentiousness existing in high life, he always held aloof from it, keeping his heart free and his soul pure notwithstanding that he was of a sanguine temperament and lively disposition. At the age of twenty-five he became a Jesuit and from that time forth there remained no trace of his early education save, indeed, his exquisite courtesy. In the religious life he made for himself a place apart, devoting himself to the humblest and most menial of duties. Benjamin Sulte has summed up his character in two lines: "He is the type of a fervent, devoted misssionary," says the historian, "seeking only to be directed in the way of sacrifice." Like Claver in Carthaginia Father de Noué wished to make himself the slave of the Indians in Canada, and thereby win them to Jesus Christ. He could not master their language despite the fact that he earnestly applied himself to do so and, to further this end, he even went so far as to accompany a band of Montagnais who started in the depth of winter on an elk hunt. But this plan succeeded no better than others and, after a few weeks, the zealous priest was brought back to Notre-Dame des Anges sick, starving and almost dead from exhaustion. Despairing of ever being able to understand and speak the language of the savages, he took a resolution entirely in keeping with his generous nature and became, in the mission, the humble servant of all.

To his lot it fell to build the new residence and to clear and sow the fields of Notre-Dame des Anges. He was placed at the head of all the workmen who had come from France with the Jesuits and were paid, lodged and fed by them, and to all he gave an example of industry, going about, as occasion required, with axe, hammer or spade in hand. The French colonists admired and imitated him, and soon a promising structure rose from the ruins and the surroundings took on a favorable aspect.

On the other hand Father Le Jeune ardently devoted himself to the study of the Indian language, taught the Catechism to some little savages whom he called aside, first to two, then to ten and later to fifteen and twenty, and cheerfully afforded spiritual comfort and assistance to the colonists of Quebec. There too the English had set fire to the *Habitation*, and the chapel built in the lower town and the fort also suffered. But, little by little, the situation improved, the colonists established themselves, and Quebec appeared once more as it had in 1629. In 1633 Champlain returned from France with three vessels laden with provisions and fire-arms and de Caen handed over to him the command of the Colony and left Canada, "his hands bound in golden fetters," and with him disappeared the Calvinist element.

The Company of One Hundred congratulated themselves upon de Caen's departure and wrote: "No one can now claim any right over New France and we may consecrate it entirely to God." These men had the correct idea about the necessity and influence of religion in a state, and they said to Father Le Jeune: "Religion is essential to forming the body of a colony, because it is to the State what the heart is to the human body—the first, the vivifying part." Moreover, the members of the Company showed great zeal for the conversion of the savages and Father Le Jeune, filled with gratitude to them, gives them unstinted praise.

Jean de Lauson, the Intendant in Canada, was strong in his support of all the missionaries' undertakings, the colonists were all Catholics, if not all fervent, and Champlain and his lieutenant, du Plessis, gave most edifying example, both being faithful to their Christian duties. Besides, there was a decided stir in the maritime provinces of the west of France, especially in Normandy, and Christian families from Perche, Beauce and l'Ile-de-France started for the solitudes of the New World in search of peace. Then too, Louis XIII. watched with marked attention the progress of the Mission, and Cardinal Richelieu, says Father Le Jeune, "sustained and animated the great enterprise, to disturb which would have been to attack the apple of his eye."

All seemed to augur well for the future of the colonists and it behooved them to turn to practical account, and that without delay, all the good will manifested, and thereby lay in New France the solid foundation of a truly Christian work. This task was reserved to the founder of Quebec and to Father Le Jeune, both of whom entertained the same holy ambitions, and they conferred together regarding the introduction of divine service in all the most important French posts: Quebec, Miscou and Three-Rivers. This blessed privilege was already enjoyed at Cap-Breton, a post occupied, like Miscou, by a small number of Frenchmen, and, though there might be only scant hope of making many Christians among the nomadic tribes of these two islands, the colonists there could not be left without the aids of their religion.

Miscou, later Saint-Louis, was an island situated at the entrance to Chaleurs Bay, and commonly frequented by fishermen in the beginning of the seventeenth century. After the departure of the English from New France, some Frenchmen built there for themselves modest little homes in the shape of fishermen's cabins, and Father Le Jeune sent them Fathers Turgis and du Marché. Scarcely had they reached the island when scurvy broke out amongst the colonists and Father du Marché, who was one of the first to be attacked by the baneful disease, was obliged to return to France while Father Turgis remained alone " consoling his little flock, hearing the confessions of some, fortifying others with the sacraments of Holy Eucharist and Extreme Unction and burying those whom death had slaughtered." He interred the captain, clerk, surgeon, all the officers and several employees, in fact more than half the colony. At length, he himself succumbed to the fearful scourge, and being no longer able to keep on his feet, had himself carried from one to another of the plague-stricken victims in order to console and fortify them, and when he died he left but one seriously sick man after him, and this one he had carefully prepared for the last great journey.

Other apostles replaced these first two missionaries in this fated land, and among them we note the names of Fathers de la Place, Gondoin, Claude Quentin, Richard, d'Olbeau, d'Eudemare, Martin de Lyonne and Jacques Fremin. Of these the most illustrious were Fathers Richard and Lyonne, the former of whom worked twenty-four years in this mission and the latter over fifteen. From Miscou, their zeal extended to the continent, to Richibouctou, Miramichi, Nipisiguit, to the south of Chaleurs Bay, to Chedabouctou and Acadia, and all along the coast from Cap-Breton to Gaspé Bay, their advent was marked by the baptism of a number of children in danger of death and the conversion of a few adults. Father Lyonne died a victim of his devotedness while attending scurvy-stricken patients, and when, in 1664, the Franciscans undertook the direction of the missions of Gaspésie and Acadia, Father Richard, although broken down after almost thirty years of painful journeying and apostolic labor, wished to devote the remainder of his life to the savages of Sillery, Three Rivers and the Cap de la Madeleine.

The Quebec Colony was the most important of all. Religious services were there inaugurated with the greatest care. After the capitulation of the fort, the Governor had made a vow to erect a chapel dedicated to Notre-Dame de Recouvrance, provided the French would be successful in recovering New France. Therefore, the very year of his return, he erected the promised chapel near the Fort St. Louis, and above the main altar he placed a picture of the Blessed Virgin, which had formerly belonged to Father Noyrot, and had been found intact in the debris of the shipwreck.

A few steps from the chapel Father Le Jeune had a small parochial residence built, and he confided the care of the parish to Fathers Charles Lalemant, Massé and de Noue. The letters of those days abound in minute accounts of the introduction and organization of public services and of the fervor of the colonists. On week days several low Masses were said, and on Sundays and feast days High Mass and vespers were always sung. Each parishioner in turn made an offering of blessed bread, and a sermon was preached at High Mass and Catechism taught after vespers. The most prominent colonists belonged to the congregation of the Immaculate Conception, and approached the Sacraments regularly. Family prayers were instituted, the observance of Sunday was all that could be desired, the Lenten and Ember Day fasts were faithfully kept, and, whilst all communicated on great feast days, many did so once a month. Some even practised austere penance, and abundant alms were contributed for the missions. Though all the colonists did not come to Canada with peaceful consciences and the best of dispositions, "in changing climate they changed their life."

The colony grew larger year by year, and as its recruits came from different provinces of France, bringing with them a variety of customs and characteristics, it was but natural to fear a sort of social clash, but, on the contrary, the greatest harmony prevailed, and the *Relation* of 1636 says "the increase of parishioners is the augmentation of God's praises." Historians confirm this statement made by Father Le Jeune, and in his *Histoire de la Nouvelle France* Father Charlevoix writes: "In this part of America was the beginning of a generation of true Christians, in whose midst reigned the simplicity of primitive times, and whose posterity has not yet lost sight of the grand example given them by their ancestors." "New France," adds the author of the Private Life of Louis XV., "owed its vigor to its first colonists, whose families multiplied and formed a strong and healthy people, full of honor and devoted to their principles." Protestants joined their tribute of praise to the sincere testimony of Catholic writers, and Canadians, descended from this first source, may be found with the same strong faith and pure morals as those of their ancestors. Out of 674 children baptized up to 1660 inclusively, the register of Quebec records but one illegitimate birth, and yet these children came into the world in the midst of a promiscuous population, composed, as it was, of soldiers, sailors, travellers and colonists.

It is true that the example set by those in authority excited in the souls of others sentiments of emulation, honor and a just pride in the practice of faith. The fort where the Governor resided was a veritable school of religion and virtue. During the noon meal some historical book was read and in the evening, during supper, the Lives of the Saints. The Angelus was rung three times a day and prayers were said in common and, in the privacy of his own room, each one made his examination of conscience. Du Plessis-Brochard, Admiral of the fleet, and la Rochejaquelin, Commandant of Saint-Jacques, were perfect models of faith. The feast of Corpus Christi was celebrated on shipboard by a solemn procession and indeed few parishes in France could boast more sincerely Christian lives among the members of their congregation, than could Quebec.

(*To be continued.*)

A Thanksgiving.

"I wish to record a thanksgiving I promised for a great favor obtained through the intercession of Our Lady of Martyrs and Father Isaac Jogues. It is that of taking the habit in a Trappist novitiate. Some time ago I began invoking Father Jogues's aid through Our Lady of Martyrs for light as to my vocation to the contemplative life. Shortly after, at the suggestion of my confessor and acting under obedience to him, I made application to this Order and was accepted. Of course, I claim no miracle of grace, but this public acknowledgment may serve to encourage others to ask for spiritual favors through his intercession."

SHRINE NOTES.

Our readers remember that the storms of last Autumn played sad havoc with the Ravine. As early as October last the course of the stream there was changed, and the entire surface of the place was covered with large cobble-stones, which had been washed from the neighboring fields by a sudden and violent freshet. It was hoped that the work of destruction would cease with the winter, but, unfortunately, the spring has renewed it. The stream which had begun to flow, without deflection, straight towards the bank underneath the Grotto of Our Lady, gradually undermined it, and carried away a portion of it fully forty feet in length, varying from eight to twelve feet high and one to five feet deep. It was thought that the stream would return to its original course after the heavy rains of last year, but its new course seems permanent, and, in fact, it is the natural one, since the streamlet flowing into the Ravine from the east must gradually, in rainy seasons, have found its level near the large stone and close to the bank under the Grotto.

*   *   *

The Ravine proper is not the only place that suffered from the freshets of the past year. The side hill south of the road leading down to the Ravine, which had already been sliding the past three years, has continued falling, and although at least ten feet of it were removed last year in order to give space for a broader road, the sudden thaw of April has loosened still more of it. The widening of the old road from nine to eighteen feet was begun none too soon: before the pilgrimages begin, there will be a broad way leading from the county road to the Ravine, eighteen feet wide, well graded and drained, and gracefully turning to follow the winding of the streamlet from the east, and a substantial bridge spanning a rectangular bend of the same. At the entrance to the Ravine, the road broadens, so as to make room for the processions entering and returning from the place. The surface has been sown with grass, so as to have smoother walking, less dust, and firmer resistance to the frost, thaws and rains. To obtain this fine broad path, nothing has been sacrificed, nor has any landmark been removed which would not have been removed eventually by the natural changes of a place like the Ravine. Young trees have already been planted on either side of this road, and when they will be large enough to give shade it will be the most pleasant place about Auriesville.

* * *

The improvements made at Auriesville during the past year, and the repairs made necessary by the damage just referred to, are ample reason for the appeal for donations which we were obliged to make last month, and which we respectfully urge upon the charity of friends of the Shrine. In proportion to the generosity with which this appeal is met, will be the arrangements for pilgrims and pilgrimages during the coming season. For those who cannot contribute something to the Shrine, there is still a way in which they can help it, viz.: by obtaining subscriptions for the PILGRIM. These subscriptions besides supporting the PILGRIM itself, would, if numerous enough, produce some slight revenue for the Shrine; and what is of greater importance still, they would make known to so many people the interests of Auriesville, and lead them to practise devotion to Our Lady of Martyrs, and derive the many benefits of this devotion. For this reason we have lately addressed to every PILGRIM subscriber an invitation to increase our subscription lists, by getting new subscribers for the balance of the year, and as a reward for the interest which we anticipate on their part, we have presented them with a Shrine pin or medal.

* * *

The Shrine will be opened again this year in July, not so early as last year, but not later than July 15th. This means that from that date, if not sooner, a priest will be at the Shrine to say Mass daily and to receive those who go there to make pilgrimages. This will make Sunday, July 16th, the first available day for a large pilgrimage. With the usual places for guests, and especially with the new hotel-keeper, Mr. Thomas Glenn, in charge of the Putman House, we are confident that every one visiting the Shrine can be provided with suitable accommodation, and we look forward to the usual pious and happy sojourn that pilgrims to Auriesville always make there, and we ask all the friends of the Shrine to pray that the pilgrimage season this year may be blessed.

For more definite information which we cannot publish before the issue of the July PILGRIM, subscribers will please apply to the Editor of the PILGRIM, 27 and 29 West 16th Street, New York.

TÉRÈSE AND PIERRE.

BY

K. A. HENNESSY.

CHAPTER I.

A Trip to Beverwyck.

IN the middle of the seventeenth century the Mohawk Valley was, as it is to-day, a locality endowed by nature with myriad charms. But, where are now thickly populated towns and cities, veritable hives of human industry, were then only the scattered settlements of the Iroquois Indians; and where now huge locomotives dash puffing and smoking through the country bearing great loads of precious human freight, over two hundred years ago were to be seen no other means of transportation than the frail bark canoe, in which the wary Indian would paddle along the waterways to parts near or remote, or the rough sled, drawn by deer or dogs, in which, during the winter, he would drive overland.

The Mohawks, who inhabited the valley bearing their name, were the most warlike and formidable of the five tribes constituting the great Iroquois nation, and they never wearied of attacking their enemies and especially of laying snares for the capture or murder of the Hurons and Algonquins, the objects of their implacable hatred. They were also antagonistic to the French Colonists in Canada, but on quite friendly terms with the Dutch who had a settlement at Beverwyck, where now stands the city of Albany. Being decidedly migratory in their habits, the Mohawks frequently changed their place of residence, and when one of their villages had been visited by a plague, or the onslaught of an enemy was expected or even when the soil failed to yield abundant crops, they hesitated not to pull up stakes, move their cattle and pitch their tents in a more desirable quarter. Their settlements usually consisted of a number of Long Houses, as they were called, many of which could accommodate twenty families, and the villages were generally fortified by a sort of palisade, erected to withstand the attacks of the foe.

Three times the intrepid and saintly Father Isaac Jogues had come among the Mohawks, first, as their captive, when they tortured him almost to death; later as an ambassador, bringing them a message of peace from the Frenchmen in Canada; and finally as a missionary, eager to clear from their benighted minds the mists of paganism and to point the way to Heaven. But, at his third and last appearance among them, they still thirsted for his precious life, and though some voted to give him his liberty, others clamored for his death and while the elders sat in council at Teonnontogen (1) debating the all absorbing question, a stealthy Indian lay in wait for the innocent victim and, with one stroke of his tomahawk inflicted the blow that gave Father Isaac Jogues a martyr's crown.

It was early one bright October morning in 1651, three years after Father Jogues' shocking assassination, and the inhabitants of Ossernenon (2) were not yet astir, but down by the waters' edge a canoe was moored and a stalwart, middle-aged Indian was busy lading it with skins and furs. Occasionally he would pause in his work and, shading his eyes with his brawny hand, take a look up the hill and then, as though disappointed, turn away again and resume his task. When at last it was completed, he strolled along the shore, reaching the foot of the hill just as a tall, slight Indian maiden emerged from the thicket surrounding the palisade, and tripped gaily down the hillside. She carried a bundle which seemed more precious than heavy and, at her approach, the man went eagerly forward to meet her.

"Canst thou find room for this, Father?" she smilingly inquired, as she placed the parcel in his extended hands.

"And what may it contain?" he asked in evident surprise.

"Oh!" she cheerfully replied, "a few trinkets I have

---

(1) The most important of the Mohawk villages or "Castles."
(2) A Mohawk village which was located very near the present site of Auriesville.

wrought in the hope of making a bargain with some Dutch trader at the Fort."

"So my little one has had a thought to business," he said, smiling. "I knew her hands had not been idle, but I dreamed not that besides her daily work at the lodge she could accomplish all this," and he looked admiringly at the package he held, although its contents were hidden from his view. In a few moments they had reached the river bank, and were comfortably established in their canoe, which Gonaterezon pushed from shore and began to paddle to eastward. This trip to the Fort was something that he had contemplated for many weeks, but, for various reasons, had been obliged to postpone.

Gonaterezon was one of the first captains of Ossernenon, and belonged to the Turtle family, and, moreover, he had been one of those selected to represent his clan at the council in Teonnontogen when Father Jogues' liberation was voted for. Gonaterezon's wife was a Huron captive and a Christian, but, despite his abomination of it, the Mohawk allowed her to profess the religion of her choice, even agreeing that their child should do the same, and, therefore, the girl had been baptized by Father Jogues during his captivity with her people in 1642, she being eleven years of age at the time. But in 1645 Gonaterezon's wife died, and from that time forward religion had been a forbidden topic between father and daughter.

The girl then understood that it was only because her mother's happiness had been at stake that her father had been so liberal, and she realized that thenceforth it would be only by strength of will and perseverance that she, who had promised her dying mother ever to remain a faithful Christian, could live up to her word. Her father took every means to keep her aloof from those of her own faith, and her associates in Ossernenon were hardened pagans and slaves of the blackest superstition, all intercourse with the Christian Huron and Algonquin captives being positively denied her. Indeed, so fully did she realize her painful situation that she marvelled at being permitted to retain her baptismal name, but the sweet French appellation was grateful to her father's ear, being that borne by his dead wife, and because of the tender associations which it awakened, he loved the name Térèse.

Gonaterezon was a true Mohawk, fearless, warlike and cruel, but nevertheless possessed of a sense of honor rarely found in any of his race. Whence it came we know not, but it is our privilege to suppose that thirteen years of happy wedded life with a woman whose instincts had been elevated and refined by the influence of Christianity could not but have had an ennobling effect upon his savage nature.

The mother's gentleness of manner and disposition were inherited by her daughter, in whom could likewise be discerned a marked physical resemblance to her father, as well as much of his spirit of dauntlessness. In appearance she was tall and slender, and, though her features were distinctly of the Mohawk type, the charm of her face lay chiefly in its expression, and the large, dark eyes bespoke such gentleness and truth, the brow, though low, such candor, and the thin lips, so firmly set, attested to such gentle determination, that one could readily excuse the too great prominence of the cheek bones.

As Gonaterezon sat astern, paddling his canoe down the Mohawk on that beautiful October morning with Térèse as his companion, a strange silence seemed to have settled upon them both. Sometimes, assuming a listless attitude, the girl would gaze admiringly upon the luxuriant trees skirting the shore, their leaves clad in autumnal glory and tinted in amber, green and red, or, leaning to one side, observe her own face mirrored on the stream's placid bosom, or again watch the prismatic effect of the sunbeams upon the tiny spray raised by dabbling her hand in the clear, cool water. But most of the time the father's eyes were riveted on his daughter, and when their glances chanced to meet, a smile was interchanged, but no more. At length Gonaterezon broke the spell, exclaiming:

"Thou art so like thy mother, my Térèse, that the sight of thee seems to bring her back. Dost remember when we all went to the Fort together?" Térèse's lip quivered and a quiet nod in the affirmative was her only response.

"Then," continued the father, "we were three, now we are but two, and next trip, I shall be alone."

"How so, father?" cried the girl in utter dismay.

"Oh! think not to deceive me, little one. I blame not the gallant Aharihon for seeking thy heart and hand, nor do I censure thee for loving him."

"For loving him? Believe me father, I love him not, nor do I yet know the man to whom I could give my heart. Thou hast my love, and fear not that thy Térèse is about to leave thee."

"But, daughter, Aharihon is a brave fellow. Who, of all our youth, is more fearless on the war-path, who, more skilful at the hunt, who, more loyal to the traditions of our forefathers?"

"Ah, father mine, his good qualities I've noted, but they have not won my heart."

Just then the sound of a paddle caught their hearing and, as they rounded a bend in the stream, they sighted a canoe coming towards them. It had but one occupant, and over his swarthy face broke a radiant smile as, upon approaching, Gonaterezon graciously saluted him. The two men rested their paddles, allowing their skiffs to drift side by side, and when the eyes of Térèse met those of the young Mohawk, the blood mounted quickly to her cheek, but her father saw it not, so absorbed was he in contemplating the immense outlay of fish in the bottom of his neighbor's canoe.

"Hast had great luck, Aharihon," he forthwith exclaimed, "the streams have surely yielded thee their best."

"Yes," replied the young man, looking over his spoils and selecting two large salmon which he handed across to Gonaterezon, "and allow me to give thee of *my* best." Then, picking out a few shining eels, he presented them to Térèse saying: "And, beautiful one, wilt thou not accept these? Their lustrous coats will furnish brilliant strips with which to bind thy raven hair."

Térèse put forth her hand to receive the proffered gift. "I

thank thee," was all she said, and immediately the Indian's face clouded. Evidently he had looked for more than these few words, had expected a glance or gesture which he might interpret to his own satisfaction, but no, Térèse, the girl he loved, was indifferent.

Gonaterezon's suggestion that his young friend accompany them to the Fort was not acted upon, and in a few moments, they had resumed their respective journeys. It was then within a couple of hours of noon and Gonaterezon, turning his canoe into the historic Hudson, took a southerly course. The clear morning air was so invigorating, the scenery so panorama-like in its varying attractiveness and the Mohawk's skiff so heavily freighted, that he paddled along very leisurely. However, it took but a short time to cover the six remaining miles and soon the infantile Dutch settlement of Beverwyck came into view.

It consisted of a mere handful of houses, low frame structures with thatched roofs and wooden chimneys, and down near the river's edge stood the Fort, which was built of stout logs and fortified on all sides by primitive sort of guns used for throwing stones. In the immediate vicinity were rich pastures where cattle grazed and moved drowsily about, and when the Mohawk and his daughter had disembarked, Gonaterezon unhesitatingly led the way to the trading-house where he was not an unfamiliar figure.

Some children played about near the wharf and, at sight of the Indians, they paused and gazed at them in mute astonishment. Gonaterezon, with his pack upon his back, walked indifferently by, but Térèse's sweet smile quite won their hearts and a chubby-faced little fellow, with big blue eyes and flaxen hair, leaving his companions, toddled along after the Iroquois girl till, hearing his footstep behind her, she turned and impulsively put out her hand. Instantly the child grasped it and the two walked on in silence, he gazing intently at her brilliant attire, and she looking affectionately into his wide-open, wondering eyes. Arrived at the trading-house Gonaterezon at once laid down his pack, and, after exchanging greetings with several traders whom he knew, began to display his skins, but Térèse remained modestly in the background till a young Dutchman, who stood near, came up and offered her a stool. She accepted it and then, for the first time, relinquishing her hold of the little boy's hand, she opened her bundle and drew forth one after another the pretty, deftly made articles she had brought. The man and child looked on with keen interest, the little fellow clapping his dimpled hands and crowing with joy. His appreciation was not lost upon Térèse, and when she handed him a tiny birch canoe embroidered with birds and flowers, he gesticulated violently, rattled off a few words entirely incomprehensible to his benefactress, and then, in an ecstasy of wild delight, scampered away in the direction whence he had come.

Just then the trader with whom Gonaterezon was bargaining, called to the young man beside Térèse and together they conversed in Dutch, probably discussing the value of the skins offered by the Mohawk captain; but, as soon as he could, the young fellow returned and, having exchanged a pair of scissors, a silver wire bracelet, a string of glass beads and a pewter spoon and bowl for a couple of finely carved pipes, three birch baskets and several ornamental trinkets, all of which Térèse assured him were her own making, he suggested that they take a stroll while their fathers were concluding an important transaction. Readily Térèse acquiesced and Jan Backer strode out of the trading-house with as proud a mien as though he were escorting a Dutch princess.

According to the prevailing custom, he wore a pair of black cloth knickerbockers girt in at the knee with steel buckles, and a long-tailed coat, the front of which was adorned with large metal buttons, while a pair of hand-knitted black stockings displayed to perfection his shapely legs. Low shoes, the insteps of which were decorated with huge leather buckles, and a hat with a high sugar-loaf crown completed the costume which he always changed for one of better material on Sundays and festive occasions. In striking contrast to it was that of Térèse. She was taller, by an inch, than her companion, and a long chemise of brown holland, a material which her father had purchased at the Fort during the previous season, enveloped her slender figure from her neck to her knees. Outside of it she wore a loose doe-skin garment, profusely beaded, the flowing sleeves of which, being slit almost to the shoulder, revealed arms of singularly beautiful mould. Her petticoat, made of a scarlet blanket, was short enough to show to ample advantage a pair of fancifully embroidered leggings and moccasins, and her straight black hair was held in place by fillet-like bands of beaded skin. As she and her guide meandered up the path from the trading-house, many wondering eyes were turned upon them, not that the sight of an Indian was at all uncommon, but because an Indian woman of such rare beauty was a novelty indeed.

It was then about noon and the men were turning homeward whilst their good *vrouwen* were busy preparing the frugal, mid-day meal. Suddenly Jan paused before a trim little cottage and, bidding Térèse follow him, led the way round to the back of the house. There, in an enclosed grass-plat, hens and chickens strutted independently about and a couple of goats grazed leisurely, while off in one corner three cows lay under the shade of a spreading oak. Through the open kitchen door could be seen a sturdy, tidy-looking woman dutifully performing the functions of cook, and around the wall on shelves and hooks the bright tin and copper utensils shone forth in neat array, their polished surfaces reflecting the golden noon-day sun. Spying Jan outside, the thrifty housewife stepped to the door but, upon beholding his strange companion, drew back in sudden dismay. However, a few words from the young man fully explained the situation and, the good *vrouw*, learning the cause of her husband's delay at the trading-house, returned at once to the kitchen and quickly reappeared with two generous portions of buttermilk and bread, which usually constituted the Dutch colonist's noon-day rations. For the moment Térèse seemed embarrassed. Never had she received hospitality at the hands of white people, and the kindness thus suddenly thrust upon her was quite overwhelming; but a look from Jan reassured her and she proceeded to partake of the refreshment.

For one to whom *sagamite* had ever been the queen of

broths, this new treat was sumptuous indeed, and it was small wonder that the Iroquois girl eagerly accepted a second helping. How strange that she who, when squatting on a rush mat in a smoky cabin eating coarse Indian meal, thought herself fortunately comfortable and well provided for, should now find herself seated on a wooden settle outside the cottage of a prosperous Dutchman, dining in company with his only son and heir, and catered to by his worthy spouse. And yet, stranger still was the fact that Térèse seemed quite equal to the occasion, and where savage *gaucherie* might have been expected, there existed an astonishing ease of manner. However, at times, she betrayed a certain shyness, more becoming than otherwise, and this was when Jan would look at her with much the same expression as Aharihon's face was wont to assume whenever he would speak to her of love. This disturbed, rather than flattered the girl, and she felt relieved when having smiled and bowed her thanks to Vrouw Backer, she and her escort started for the trading-house.

Jan's knowledge of the Iroquois tongue was limited indeed, but, ere he had rejoined his father and Gonaterezon, he had entreated Térèse to soon repeat her visit to the Fort and had made her conscious of his sincere admiration. At his words she flushed and, in a tone of tremulous earnestness, said: "I thank thee for thy kindness but, I pray thee, think no more of this simple child of the forest." Her quiet dignity awed Jan and seemed to rob him of his courage to proceed, and in less than an hour the Mohawk and his daughter were paddling homeward, Gonaterezon listening with interest so the maiden's recital of her experience at Beverwyck.

But his interest was not unmingled with the keenest anxiety for, in Jan's attention to Térèse, Gonaterezon saw just cause for alarm. That his daughter was unusually attractive he well knew, and as the Dutch and Indians frequently intermarried, he feared that some foreigner would win the girl's heart and he determined that she should bestow her affection on one of her own race. Therefore, though outwardly calm, he was making a mighty resolve which in substance, amounted to this: that Térèse should seldom, if ever again, visit Fort

Orange and that he would urge her immediate acceptance of Aharihon's suit. However, lest she suspect his motives, it was only gradually that he drifted to the subject nearest his heart and began to reprove his daughter for her indifferent manner towards Aharihon who, he assured her, was, of all her admirers, the most worthy of her hand. The girl hung her head and made no effort at self-defence. The truth was that her father's words hurt her. How inconsistent he was! Only that morning he had seemed grieved at the possible prospect of her leaving him, and now, he appeared more than eager that she would at once become Aharihon's bride. What could it all mean?

That night, when Ossernenon lay hushed beneath the spell of sleep, Térèse tossed restlessly upon her rush mat. Her father's reproof kept ringing in her ears and the thought of causing him displeasure smote her to the heart. His desire for her marriage with Aharihon was, she had concluded, due to the young Captain's brilliant achievements and social prominence, but she could not marry a man whom she did not love, and she could not love one who scorned the religious belief that was dearer to her than life. Aharihon was handsome, brave and true, but he hated the principles in which her dead mother had reared her, and abhorred even what, in the least, savored of Christianity. "Ah! my Jesus," she whispered, clutching at a small wooden cross suspended from her neck, "Aharihon may go his way, but I'll keep close to Thee, and Thou wilt comfort me."

(To be continued.)

CONTRIBUTIONS TO THE SHRINE:

Anon,	$10.00
B. C. C., New York, per Rev. Joseph McMahon,	100.00
J. C., New York,	5.00
M. L., Phila., Pa.,	1.00
M. L. S. H., Buffalo, N. Y.,	5.00
J. F. B., Fort Wayne, Ind.,	$1.00
Anon,	20.00
M. E. M., South Acton, Mass.,	2.00
A. E. A. Baltimore, Md.,	1.00
E. G., St. Catharines, Ont., Canada,	2.00

MISSION LETTERS.

THE DEATH PLACE OF FATHERS BRÉBEUF AND LALEMANT.

The following interesting letter from one who has recently visited the scenes of the labors and death of the Canadian Martyrs, is an important contribution to our knowledge of the early Missions:

COLDWATER, Ontario, May 18, 1899.

REVEREND DEAR FATHER,
P. C.:

I have just returned from one of the reputed sites of the village of the Hurons, which from 1648 to 1649, when it was destroyed by the Iroquois, was known by the name St. Ignace II, famous as the death place of Fathers Brébeuf and Lalemant. I call it one of the reputed sites, because, as you know, no one has as yet claimed to have identified the scene of their martyrdom, beyond all question. The place we visited to-day is about four miles southwest of this village, on a farm known as the Fox estate, now tenanted by a Mr. Gleadall. In the surveyor's phraseology here, it is in the Township of Medonte, on Lot XX, Concession X.

It was curious to hear the present tenant's view of our exploration. He was at the plough when we drove up. I had not much time to lose. On hearing that we wanted to examine the site of an ancient Indian village, he said the village had been there and the field beyond the one he was ploughing, and that "there was money in it," mistaking us for a Captain Kidd party. We were not surprised at this, for on mentioning at the hotel, the "British Arms" of Coldwater, that we were in search of some old Indian sites, the proprietor assured us that there was a story among the villagers to the effect that many years ago a priest had come that way and had declared that the Fox estate was the site in question, and that by digging in a certain spot a trunk or chest would be found. The digging was done as directed, the chest was found and the priest took it away. The priest was no doubt Rev. Father Martin, who visited some of the Huron mission sites in 1855 or 1856, and who has left careful descriptions of his itinerary and discoveries, but no chest; at least Father Jones, S.J., who has fallen heir to Father Martin's work, and who keeps sacredly the venerable historian's papers, has not acquired the chest and the money it is presumed it contained, and if any one is both competent and zealous enough to hunt after such a treasure, it is the same Archivist of St. Mary's College, Montreal, who prizes money only second to his valuable archives, since he needs it so much to keep what he has properly and to acquire others which he should have in his possession.

Local traditions should be respected, and they are often, no doubt, a great help to the explorer for old sites; but they must be received with the nicest discrimination, not because those who hand them down are not reliable but because they fail to ascertain, or to hand down with exactness, the various circumstances of time, place, person that would help one to identify a site infallibly with what is known of the one sought for. Of course, many traditions help indirectly, some to reassure the explorer that the site suggested is not the one sought for, and others to amuse and afford him relaxation in a quest that is often trying and laborious. Thus, when a man tells you that he was present when an ossuary, or burial pit, was opened and that he saw an Indian sitting on an inverted kettle, with beads, etc., lying about him, showing how great he had been; and when he tells you that the man was of such giant stature that his skull could cover our faces like a mask and that his thigh bone was fully ten or twelve inches longer than that of the present white man, you must either venerate the tradition as prehistoric or inquire which is the greater spur to the imagination nowadays, the encyclopœdic newspaper or the cramming done in our common schools everywhere.

Whatever credence we give to local traditions, certain it is that the field we walked over to-day has yielded to ploughman and explorer its due share of Indian remains, beads, and pipes and other things in use among the Hurons 250 years ago, and it is also certain that near by this field, on the clearance of Mr. Brimacome, Lot 8, Concession X, there is an ossuary, in which human remains must be plentiful, to judge by the fact that on our way thither, we found an Indian skull and tibia, which some one had carefully mounted on one of the tree stumps by the roadside. What is more in favor of this site is that it answers to the description given in the Relation of 1649, being a level piece of land on a hill top, three sides of which ascend so steeply that the palisade or fort erected on the plateau had the advantage of this ravine or moat, being accessible only from the fourth side, a weakness which was soon perceived by the vigilant Iroquois, who entered it by that route when they came to destroy the Hurons villages of St. Louis and St. Ignace in 1649. What would confirm this conformation of land as the proper site would be the discovery of some traces of the palisades, if only the ridges in the land along the line of their erection, such as we trace so clearly at Auriesville. As yet no such traces have been found; but with the new interest developed in the story of the Huron nation in Ontario County, it is very probable that these and other indications will be found wherever they may exist.

I shall have more to write to you soon on this question as we hope to-morrow to examine another site reputed to have been the village of St. Ignace, and before we leave here we shall see, please God, the sites of the villages in which Father Jogues lived and labored, such as, Ihonatiria, Teanaustaye, Ossosane, and St. Mary, where traces of the old fort built there in 1636 still exist.

There is something inspiring in travelling through country hallowed as this was by the heroic lives and noble deaths of so many devoted missionaries, and it is remarkable that their names and deeds are known so well not only to Catholics, but to Protestants as well, who really seem to take more interest in reading about them, and who venerate them for their piety and heroism.

Begging a memento in your holy sacrifices, I am
Yours in Christ,
JOHN J. WYNNE, S.J.

* * *

From the *Mangalore Magazine* we learn many interesting and consoling details of the short life and premature death of a young American Missionary, Rev. Maurice D. Sullivan, S.J. To these we may be permitted to add a few traits of character that have fallen under our own observation. Born at Ann Arbor, Michigan, on October 22, 1860, his classical studies were made at St. Charles' College, Ellicott City, Md., whence he passed on graduation in 1881, to the Jesuit Novitiate of the Missouri Province at Florissant, Mo. His three years of Philosophy were made at the Scholasticate, Woodstock, Md., after which he taught the Natural Sciences, for which he had a special aptitude, for six years. On the completion of his theological studies at Innsbruck, he returned a priest to his Western Province, where he was again appointed

Professor of the Natural Sciences at the Jesuit College in Detroit, Michigan. But with the grace of ordination there had sprung up in Father Sullivan's heart a strong desire for the Foreign Missions, and he was ready and anxious to make any sacrifice to accomplish his holy design. Before sailing to Europe, on August 4, 1897, he stopped several days in New York, during which he visited the PILGRIM office. The missions were the one absorbing topic of all his conversations. We have read much of the touching scenes of religious piety and enthusiasm that mark the departure of the young missioners from the House of the Foreign Missions in Paris, but we feel free to say that not one of these future apostles set out for foreign lands with more burning zeal and higher hopes than did Father Sullivan—an exhibition of feeling all the more striking as coming from one whom all his friends regarded as the least emotional and most unsentimental of men. Arriving in Mangalore on September 26th, he taught for a short time, and was then sent to his Tertianship at Ranchi. It was while returning from here to Mangalore to enter upon his duties as professor, that Father Sullivan was stricken down with enteric fever, and after lingering for about a month passed to his reward on January 4, 1899. "He had been in Belgaum for scarcely a month," writes Father Gonçalves, S.J., "but everyone already knew and esteemed him. At his funeral, the church was filled with both European and native Catholics, and many non-Catholics, without mentioning the many heathens who were outside. The funeral was the most solemn I ever witnessed in Belgaum. A long line of soldiers (to whom he had recently preached a mission) followed the hearse; the commanding officer at my request sent twelve men to act as a guard of honor, and all the other soldiers attended freely and in a body. It was for me a great consolation to see so great a demonstration of sorrow and gratitude towards a father who had been here so short a time. They knew well that he had come to Belgaum for them, and that was enough. Even non-Catholics were very sorry to hear the news, and expressions of condolence are coming in from all sides." R. I. P.

Acknowledgment is made of the following contributions:

FOR ST. CLAVER'S GUILD, JAMAICA, WEST INDIES.

C. K., Philadelphia $6.25

FOR THE ROCKY MOUNTAIN MISSION.

M. E., Dayton, O $3.00

FOR ST. MARY'S MISSION, ALMA, WASH.

K. McD., New York $2.00

FOR MOST NEEDY MISSIONS.

D. McE., New York, for Masses, $10.00
S. M. G., New York 1.00
M. H.. New York 5.00
G. C., St. Louis, Mo 2.00

THE PILGRIM
OF
OUR LADY OF MARTYRS

XV. YEAR.   JULY, 1899.   No. 9.

MONSTRA TE ESSE MATREM.

BY A. E. SULLIVAN.

WHEN He seems not to us the Crucified,
   With human woes and anguish as our own,
   But is the God transcendent on a throne,
Where justice, power, and majesty abide,
Be near us Mother, for the night comes down
Upon our souls like darkness on the sea,
And drear and barren would this exile be,
Without thy solace when His light has flown.

Show then thyself a Mother, for through thee
We hope to hear again His voice of peace,
In tones as sweet as bade the tumult cease,
So long ago one night in Galilee.
For never do we go so far astray,
We cannot feel thy loving hand is laid
In ours in tender pity, though afraid
To lift our eyes to Him for grace to pray.

THE JESUITS AND NEW FRANCE
In the Seventeenth Century.

From the French of Rev. Camille de Rochemonteix, S.J.

BY K. A. HENNESSY.

(*Continued.*)

ON September 8, Fathers Paul Le Jeune and Jacques Buteux went thither and took up their abode. In 1634 the former wrote: "We are going to Three Rivers to help our Frenchmen. As new settlements are usually dangerous, I considered it wrong to expose Father Lalemant or others." In another letter he said: "As a general thing, a few die at the opening of these new foundations, but death is not an evil. . . . Besides, if there be any danger, I myself should meet it. After all, we should not seek to escape the cross when it is so close at hand, . . . and one suffers in a new habitation, especially when it is erected as rapidly as this has been, . . . and above all when obliged to live hand to hand with the workmen, to eat, drink and sleep with them."

And indeed he and his companion suffered, but it was what these men of sacrifice desired, because they knew that since the tragedy on Calvary it is by means of the cross that souls are converted and sanctified. In the very beginning the colonists were stricken with scurvy, and for three months the disease continued its ravages. "Almost all the Frenchmen were attacked, and so great was the infection that no one could approach them." Night and day the two missionaries were at their bedside, consoling them, hearing their confessions and administering the last sacraments, and among these afflicted men, all of whom were repentant and resigned, they found many whose hearts were rich in beautiful sentiments. "Father," said one, "I do not wish to ask for health. God is my Father, and He knows better than we what is good for us; let us leave all to Him. May His Holy Will be done." Another thus answered the priest, who had advised him to petition St. Joseph for his cure: "If you leave me free in this matter I shall only ask the saint to obtain of our Lord the grace that I may do His Holy Will." A third one, part of whose life had been spent in great debauchery, became converted and, before dying, said aloud to his companions: "Adieu, my friends, I must leave you. I ask your pardon. I am grieved, indeed, to have led such a life, but I trust that God will forgive me. Lord, have mercy on me!" Instances such as these constitute the richest reward and sweetest consolation of the sacred ministery.

The Vicomte de Meaux relates that one bright December morning, when walking through a little village built on the bank of the Niagara, he came upon a humble wooden structure, a church, in which a low Mass had just been said. Some good women came out and plodded their way homeward through roads piled high with snow, and in front of two or three religious a troop of children, books and copy-books under their arms, ran towards a neighboring house, over the door of which was a cross and, surmounting it, the inscription: *Spes messis in semine.* It was the parish school. "The hope of the harvest is in the sowing." Therefore it is that from one end of the world to the other Christians and patriots attach so much importance to schools, and therefore do rival parties so vigorously dispute their direction.

Nothing is truer than the words *Spes messis in semine*, which apply above all to a barren, uncultivated land.

Education is the vivifying principle of every colony that wishes to grow and perpetuate itself. Colleges are to a colony what the source is to a river. It is from college that the stream of human generations issues forth; there it is fed, and in its course it carries either the greatness or decline of new countries. We must go back to the colleges if we would account for the condition of society, as society is daily recruited by the youth emanating from the schools.

Wherever the Society of Jesus takes foothold in a foreign land it establishes a college as well as a residence, and the professor imparts to the children the science that makes them Christians as well as the knowledge that makes them men.

Then the missionary continues the good work of the master by taking the young man on his departure from college, directing him in the way of life, instructing him from the pulpit, absolving him in the confessional and strengthening him at the holy table. He moreover carries to the sick and the poor the divine and salutary consolations of faith.

In 1626 there were not more than sixty Frenchmen in Quebec, and yet the Jesuits had already resolved upon a scholastic establishment. René Rohault, a young man from Picardy, had offered the money required for such a project. He was the eldest son of the Marquis de Gamaches, had studied at the Jesuit College at Amiens, and in 1625, while taking his course in Humanities, most earnestly sought admission into the Society of Jesus. At this time Father Coton was paying his official visit to the College at Amiens, in his capacity of Provincial of France. This religious whose long career was about drawing to a close, saw the young postulant, conferred at considerable length with the Marquis de Gamaches, and it was finally decided that during the month of March, 1626, René would enter the novitiate founded almost fifteen years previously, by Madame de Sainte-Beuve at the Hotel de Mézières, Paris. The *Monumenta* of the mission in Canada refer to this as one of the last important acts of Father Coton's life, as he died eight days later on March 19, 1626, and before taking to his bed, went for the last time to the novitiate where he tenderly embraced his young novice.

A year had not elapsed since Canada had become the scene of the apostolic enterprises of the sons of St. Ignatius, and at the time of bidding his family adieu, René thought of the beautiful American mission, so dear to the heart of his Provincial and so promising too, and he begged his father to devote a part of the patrimony destined for him, to the founding of a college at Quebec. The Marquis was a man of faith as well as of honor and virtue, and he willingly entered into his son's pious plans by giving Father Coton the sum of 6,000 *écus* in gold, to which he added during his lifetime an annuity of 3,000 pounds.

The contentions between France and England and the capture of Quebec prevented the founders from immediately realizing their desire, but upon reaching the shores of the St. Lawrence, Father Le Jeune took up the cause and laid the foundation of a college on some ground near Fort Saint Louis, donated to the Jesuits by the Company of One Hundred for that purpose.

The beginnings of the new establishment were humble indeed, there being but a few pupils and one professor, the latter teaching Christian Doctrine. This was exacted by René Gamaches' endowment. In a letter preserved in the general archives of the society, Father Jérôme Lalemant thus addresses Father Paul Oliva concerning the matter: "The desire of the founders is entirely contained in these words: 'for the aid and spiritual instruction of the Canadians.' This we are in justice bound to hold." However, to the study of the Catechism were soon added lessons in reading and writing for the little French children, and at the request of their parents, the first elements of Latin. The principles of Latin grammar once taught, it was necessary to go still further and include the circle of classical studies, grammar, the humanities, and rhetoric. At first the colonists complained to the missionaries that there were no tutors in Quebec; and that they, the Jesuits, alone could teach the children to read and write and instruct them in elementary Latin. Through charity the priests tendered their services.

Thus far successful the parents kept urging the case. "Of what use is this bit of Latin?" they argued. "Do they not teach more of it in your colleges in France?" Again the Jesuits yielded, and several of their pupils had finished a course in literature before Mgr. de Laval reached Quebec in 1659. Being in search of parish priests he thought of forming an indigenous clergy, and very naturally his eye fell upon the young rhetoricians desirous to enter the priesthood, and aware of the impossibility of bringing professors from France, he begged the Fathers to teach these young aspirants philosophy and theology. In order to comply with the request of His Lordship, the Fathers opened a course in philosophy, and then one in ethics and scholastic theology.

In 1665 the corps of instructors consisted of a professor for the day-school, who taught the children catechism, reading and writing; a professor of grammar, a professor of rhetoric, and the humanities, one of mathematics, and one of philosophy and theology. The last taught these two branches alternately. Later M. de Beauharnais, Governor-General of Canada, and M. Hocquart, the Intendant, found serious inconvenience in this disposition of the matter and thus complained to the Comte de Maurepas, Minister of the Navy: "If the young men who have completed their course in the humanities, find that of theology open, they are obliged to wait two years to enter philosophy, and this delay so disgusts them, that they quit their studies." Elsewhere in the same letter the Governor and Intendant said: "The two professors of the lower classes cannot do justice to their work because of the difference in the ability of their pupils. These should be graded. Give us a professor of philosophy at a salary of £300, and at their own expense, the Jesuits will supply three professors for the lower classes. They deserve this privilege in return for the interest they take in the education of youth. They maintain a Brother who teaches the children of Quebec reading, writing, and arithmetic gratuitously, although there was no provision made for it."

This letter makes no allusion to the course in mathematics and hydrography taught with eminent success from 1695 by Fathers Antoine Silvi, François Le Brun, Pierre de Lauzon, Michel Guignas, Joseph Deslandes, and Charles Mésaiger.

This course had been established in 1671 at the solicitation of M. Talon the Intendant, by one Saint-Martin, who entered the service of the Jesuits as a *donné*. He was "clever enough in mathematics," says the Intendant, and therefore was he asked to teach them to the French youth of Quebec. These children manifested great eagerness to learn, and showed a natural aptitude for the positive sciences, geography, physics, astronomy, and the art of navigation. They gave particular attention to hydrography, which in those days formed a part of geography, and in Canada, a country abounding in lakes and rivers, this study awoke a special interest and could be readily applied. It was hoped that this branch of study to which M. Talon pompously refers as the "course of sciences," would develop many navigators and discoverers, and besides, at that time there was a natural leaning toward navigation and discovery, and the utility of a naval academy had already been discussed. In fact the merits of Latin were to a certain extent ignored, notwithstanding that it was indispensable to candidates for the priesthood and to many of those preparing for a civil career. At length the Brother began to teach the desired course and even in Paris much interest was shown, the King wishing to furnish the Quebec College with the most useful of mathematical instruments. After a while this special branch flourished to such an extent that it was confided to the care of a Jesuit, Father Silvi, the first to be given official charge of it.

As to the request made by the Governor and Intendant for a second professor of philosophy and theology, the Minister of the Navy utterly disregarded it. Though the government of the metropolis was greatly interested in all that concerned the colony, it was determined not to deviate from the line of conduct it had theretofore followed. It had never made any but the most necessary sacrifices for the development, welfare and protection of New France beyond the sea, and even the reverses and misfortunes of this infantile country, always struggling with the English and the savages, did not induce the home government to change its course. It had always been over-sparing of its men and money and had left the French Canadians and missionaries to their own resources. The courage of the former and devotedness of the latter deserved success and enjoyed it for a long time, but it was not therefore forever assured. In the meantime the Jesuits, because of their interest in the Quebec College, which institution benefited the whole country, appointed at their own expense, a third professor of literature, their missionary work preventing them from doing more.

These literary classes were originally only a shallow imitation of the classical teaching in Europe, but in 1661, according to the testimony of the Bishop of Pétrée, they were in a flourishing condition. "The boarding school and education," says Monseigneur, "are on a par with those of France. Music is taught and introduced into all solemnities both religious and profane, children are drilled in the art of declaiming and made to take part in pieces, and public literary entertainments are given by them." On July 28, 1658, Pierre de Voyer, the Vicomte d'Argenson and Governor of New France, assisted at a drama entitled "The Reception of Mgr. d'Argenson upon His Assuming the Governorship of New France." At length academies and a sodality were established, the latter being founded by Father Pijart. In the beginning of the seventeenth century the Quebec College was a reproduction—small, to be sure, but nevertheless complete—of the colleges of France. It had its classes in literature, sodality, academies, dramatic and literary representations and all. Fifty years later, in 1712, Father Germain, Superior at Quebec, wrote to Father Dauchez, the Paris Provincial, as follows: "All things are carried out in this college as in our European colleges, though perhaps with more regularity, exactitude and care than in several of our colleges in France. Here there are classes in grammar, the humanities, rhetoric and mathematics. The pupils, though fewer in number than in the large European cities, are physically and intellectually strong, very industrious and docile and capable of making rapid progress in the study of letters and of virtue. I here allude to the children born in Canada of French parents."

The teaching of philosophy and theology was given equal attention with that of literature. The course was of four years, two of philosophy and two of theology; the scholastic method was adopted, and the Angelic Doctor, St. Thomas, followed. According to the correspondence of the Superiors, preserved in the general archives of the Order, the principal exercises outside of the professor's lesson were the *Répétitions*, the *Sabatine* and the *Menstruales*. The repetitions occurred daily. On Saturday of every week and at the end of every month the students would argue, in presence of a professor, upon some subject chosen in advance. The defendant would state and defend the thesis and the arguer raise objections. The argumentation was in Latin and always strictly syllogistic. It was called a disputation (*disputatio*), and was a sort of dialectic tournament invested with all the interest of a struggle. The Saturday and monthly debates were private, but before the close of the scholastic year a grand public contest was held, and that was known as the *Menstruale*.

The first solemn debate in philosophy occurred in Quebec on July 2, 1666, in the sodality. All the city authorities were present—the Governor, Intendant, officers and other functionaries of the colony. Logic was the subject in hand, and Louis Jolliet, who later accompanied Father Marquette when he discovered the Mississippi, and Pierre de Francheville, who was then aspiring to the priesthood, were appointed to sustain the thesis. In order to better stimulate the ambition of these participants, M. Talon, the Intendant, taking the initiative, began to argue in Latin, and, according to the *Journal des Jésuites*, did so "very well." The education of the time, given entirely in Latin, and the serious philosophical studies prepared magistrates to meet the subtle difficulties of argument, and enabled them to express themselves with facility and precision in the austere language of the schools, which was intelligible only to the initiated.

The pupils of the little seminary founded by Mgr. de Laval followed the college lessons. In the beginning they resided in the Jesuit boarding-school where Mgr. de Laval paid their board either wholly or in part, but as mingling with the other scholars proved detrimental to their vocation, they were soon withdrawn to another house known as that of the Infant Jesus. Here were no classes in literature, nor courses in philosophy and theology. The priests of the Foreign Missions were content to imbue their protégés with piety and virtue, and they prepared them gradually for the exalted functions of the sacred ministry by teaching them the ceremonies of divine worship and the sacred chant. Their classic instruction was however confided to the Jesuits, who according to Mgr. de Saint-Vallier, were "chosen men, full of ability and zeal, who fulfilled their duties through a spirit of grace."

This testimony is the extract of a letter written in 1688 to a friend by His Lordship after his first visit to Canada. Further on in the same epistle he says: "The classes are not as strong in pupils as they will be some day." In no document of the time have we been able to determine what their number was just then, but twenty years earlier they had numbered over one hundred. In *L'Etat général du Canada*, (1669), the Intendant wrote to the home government: "The Jesuits teach here from about fifty to sixty boarders and as many day pupils and the Hurons." This in itself was not much, but it was a great deal if we consider that in 1664 there were but five hundred souls in Quebec, and about 2,500 Frenchmen in all Canada, spread over a territory of about 240 miles. In 1670 five or six French Canadians had already been ordained priests.

In another part of his letter Mgr. de Saint-Valliers says: "The Jesuits' house is well built; their church is beautiful."

The house thus referred to was not the wooden structure reared by Father Le Jeune, where under the shadow of the Fort St. Louis, the first school-masters of New France made their plans and regulations. That building, as also the church, was set on fire in the spring of 1640, and was replaced by a larger and more commodious one answering the requirements of both school and residence. "In constructing it," says M. Faucher de Saint-Maurice, " Brothers Liégeois, le Faulconnier, Pierre Feauté, Ambroise Cauvet, and Louis Boësme, had learned like Christ to wield the axe, the plane, and the saw, and had given the first lessons in carpentry and building to those who were later to become the head of all those skilful workmen whom the Province of Quebec still yields."

The missionaries fatigued by their apostolic labors, came from time to time to this residence to enjoy a bit of well earned rest, and others of them worn out with age went thither, before being called to their last home, to recollect themselves in prayer in the peace and calm of community life. But they could and did make themselves useful, some of them by teaching, and all by directing consciences.

As to the college, it served the young religious arriving from France as a preparatory school for their missions among the savages; they learned the language of the country, and with the aid of the old apostles of New France, enlightened themselves as to the habits and customs of the Indians, and became acquainted with all the industrious inventions of charity calculated to attract and convert the savages to God. They likewise either made or finished their theological course, and during that time taught or did duty as prefects.

AN IROQUOIS MAIDEN;
OR
Life of Catharine Tegakwitha.
(*Continued.*)

Chapter XV.
Death of Catharine.

"IF Catharine," says Father Cholenec, from whom we borrow the greater part of this account, "had died in the Iroquois Cantons, it might have been said of her, in the words of the Wise Man: that God had removed her from this world, by a special favor, in the flower of her age, lest her innocent soul should be touched by the corruption of her country; but, as she ended her life gloriously, at a mission wherein reigned, at that time, the greatest fervor, it is more exact to say, but still with the Wise Man, that Catharine only quitted the earth because she was ripe for Heaven. She had happily accomplished, in three years, what others achieve, only after many years, and still others with difficulty, even during the course of a long life.

Catharine's health had always been weak, but especially for a year her strength had visibly declined. After a very severe illness she remained subject to violent pains in the stomach, with frequent vomiting. A slow fever consumed her secretly. Her constant labor, her watching, her fasting, her austerities of all kinds, not always regulated by prudence, only developed these germs of dissolution. about the space of two months, she kept her bed. Nig day she was obliged to remain in the same position, unable to make hardly any movement. It needed all her courage to maintain her fervor under so many infirmities, but, far from diminishing, she seemed to draw new strength from it, in her sufferings. No one will be surprised at hearing, that the last moments of a life so precious in the sight of God, were, for the entire mission, a time of grace and sanctity. The cabin of the Iroquois Virgin became a real sanctuary, all embalmed with celestial perfume, and her mat a pulpit, from which her example still more than her words, gave eloquent lessons. It may be said, that this last combat was the most beautiful of her triumphs; her virtues never shone more brightly than on her bed of pain.

Neither complaint nor sigh escaped her lips; only holy aspirations, pious ejaculatory prayers, feeble expressions of the love with which her heart burned for God. At whatever moment one visited her, she was found with an expression of joy on her face, and a smile on her lips. It was like a reflection of the peace of her soul, and the happiness she felt in suffering for Jesus Christ. After a life passed on Calvary with her Divine Master, she seemed still to congratulate herself that she could die, like Him, on the Cross.

The care that could be given to her was very little, as the hunt had just opened for the savages, and nearly all the men, as well as a number of the women, were already far away in the forest seeking skins, their one only article of commerce. The small number of women remaining in the village were absorbed by family cares, and overburdened with work, being obliged to go to the woods each day, and sometimes even to a great distance in search of wood for fuel. It was a very unfavorable time for the sick. They often remained alone from morning till evening, with only a little sagamite and a pitcher of water for sustenance.

This enforced abandonment was not for Catharine, as for the others, a subject of pain and sadness, it was too much in harmony with her tastes and habits. Accustomed for a long time to converse alone with God, she passed the long hours in continual contemplation. As long as her strength permitted, she dragged herself to church, where, in spite of her weakness, she would remain prostrate at the feet of her Saviour; but, soon incapable of continuing these pious visits, she consoled herself for this privation by at least directing all her thoughts and affections towards this centre of love. She united in spirit, with the perpetual sacrifice of our altars, the sacrifices each day demanded of her by her Lord, and, at every instant, she found in His adorable Heart, wherewith to sustain and excite the generosity of her own.

Still the illness made fresh progress each day, and death seemed to be approaching with rapid strides. Hardly had Holy Week of 1680 begun, than Catharine's state made it evident that she had reached the end of her sufferings.

To die during the holy days that recalled the mysteries of the Cross, and of the Holy Eucharist, must have appeared very sweet to her who had professed so much love for these mysteries.

In spite of her extreme weakness, Catharine wished to offer some sacrifice to God during this great week. She therefore begged permission of her confessor to fast, but failing to obtain it, she made such compensation as was in her power. An Indian who was just then visiting her, ventured to blame her for this desire of suffering, at a time already so painful. "You wish then to kill yourself," said he? "No, no!" replied Catharine, smiling, " but on the cross was not our Saviour much more uncomfortable than I am, and what are my sufferings in comparison with His?"

Holy Tuesday her condition appeared so serious that it was decided to bring her the Holy Viaticum. Out of respect for her virtues, the missionaries made no objection, under the circumstances, to deviating from the customs of the Mission, " for it was an unheard of thing," says Father Cholenec, " to behold the Blessed Sacrament carried into the wigwam of a savage." Ordinarily the sick were carried to the church on a litter of bark, but Catharine appeared to be in such a weak state at this moment, that it seemed dangerous to expose her to this fatigue. Neither was it just that, after such a life, she should be exposed to the risk of dying without the supreme consolation of the Last Sacraments. It was then decided that the Holy Viaticum should be borne to her.

The village soon heard of the resolution; all the savages at the Mission hastened to witness the death of the saint, and to render their religious homage to the God who for the first time was about to enter beneath the humble roof of bark.

Our neophyte had not waited for this moment to prepare herself to receive her Divine Guest. Deprived, for several days, of this happiness by reason of her infirmities, she had asked, with admirable piety, when it would be again vouchsafed to her, and she indemnified herself as best she could for the privation by Spiritual Communions. Great was her joy when it was made known to her that her desires were to be gratified.

All the savages, ranged in double rows, preceded the Blessed Sacrament, reciting the beads, and chanting pious canticles. On arriving near the cabin they surrounded it, and fell on their knees. As to Catharine, at the sight of Him, who, in the excess of His love for her consented to visit her, even on the mat whereon her sufferings held her, she could not restrain the exultation of her heart, and desired that all the Christians of the Mission might be witnesses of it. Before receiving the Holy Eucharist, she summoned up all her remaining strength, to renew aloud, the offering she had already made to God, of her whole being. She expressed with sentiments of ineffable joy, her gratitude for having been withdrawn from the perils of infidelity, and for having found in this Mission of the Saut, a salutary shelter. She then received Holy Communion, with the saintly transports of a heart which was to live henceforth for heaven alone.

When Catharine had adored, in silence, Him whom she had received for the last time, the missionary, knowing the influence of the words spoken by the dying, and solicitous for the spiritual interests of his beloved neophytes, begged her to speak some words of encouragement and consolation to the Christians gathered around her. She did so with touching simplicity, urgently recommending to them love of prayer, submission to the missionary, and union and charity among themselves.

It was a pious custom established at the Mission that when any one fell dangerously ill two members of the Confraternity of the Holy Family should be appointed to watch over them and keep them company in their last moments. They sustained the devotion of the dying person with pious words. When it became a question of watching with Catharine, there was a holy rivalry of zeal and charity among the savages as to who would be selected for this privilege. On the last night the missionary chose two of the most fervent Christians of the Association to remain beside this earthly angel. One of them was Theresa, her ever-faithful companion.

Theresa came to seek the missionary after evening prayers to obtain his permission to practise some acts of penance before going to the patient, to draw down upon her the blessing of heaven. She then went to the edge of the wood and for a quarter of an hour inflicted cruel sufferings on her body.

God revealed to Catharine this heroic act of charity and mortification. Turning towards the woman who watched beside her, the dying girl begged her to go and seek her companion in a spot which she designated. The woman obeyed, and soon returned with Catharine's friend.

"Rest yourself now," said Catharine to her messenger, "and let Theresa watch with me in her turn. You will take turns, and thus be less fatigued." She had formed this plan in order to speak in secret with this pious and charitable friend. She caused her to draw near, and when their companion was asleep she ardently encouraged her to persevere in the service of God and the practice of good works. "Our Lord loves you very much," she added. "Remain always faithful to Him. When I reach heaven I promise to aid you with all my power."

The good squaw, as humble as she was fervent, promptly rejected these praises, and did not fear to say: "Alas, my sister! your friendship deceives you; you little know me; I am but a poor sinner." Then Catharine, taking her by the hand and caressing her tenderly, made answer: "My sister, I know what I say. I know the spot in the wood whither you retired this evening, and what you there did for me. I wish to show you my gratitude. Take courage; you are agreeable to God, be assured of that. I will still be useful to you near Him."

The good woman remained abashed, persuaded that God alone knew the sacrifice that friendship had inspired. The esteem that Theresa had for her friend could only increase on seeing that heaven accorded her such favors. The following morning she hastened to inform the missionary of this new proof of the sanctity of his neophyte.

This was not the only fact that revealed, during Catharine's last illness, the extraordinary graces she had received from heaven. There is reason to believe that she had foreknowledge of the moment of her death, for on Tuesday morning, when, after receiving the Blessed Sacrament, she saw that preparations were being made to administer Extreme Unction, she said to the missionary, with that confidence that certitude alone can give, "There is no hurry, my Father, you may, without anxiety, wait till to-morrow," which proved true."

On the following Wednesday she received the Sacraments of the dying, in the presence of several Christians. Every one being persuaded that she had only a few hours to live, no one would consent to leave her. Each one desired the happiness of being present at that solemn moment. One especially remarked her pious companion, and those other friends who had been so devoted to her during life. Assured that the sight of that terrestrial angel, at the moment of quitting the earth to mount to heaven, would leave in their hearts ineffable traces of grace and virtue, they would not withdraw, although the rigorous season they were then in, demanded their presence in their own cabins. It was, in fact, necessary to go to the woods to provide fuel for the day, and for the two succeeding days of devotion, which would be passed, for the most part, at the foot of the altar.

In their touching simplicity these pious women appealed to Catharine herself, and made known to her their desires. "If we must go," said they, "ask God not to let you die during our absence." She fully reassured them. "You have ample time," she added, "to make your provision. On your return you will find me still here." They then confidently set out, and God blessed their faith.

Their labors ended, they returned in all haste. Catherine was still in the same state in which they had left her, and, it would seem as if she had only awaited their presence to breathe her last sigh. "In fact," relates Father Cholenec, an eye-witness, "at the moment that the last of Catherine's companions entered the cabin, the agony began, as the servant of God had foretold."

However, before dying, Catherine wished to take a last adieu of Theresa, the one of all her companions whom she had best loved. She called her to her side, and spoke these words, which, with religious respect, Father Chauchetière preserved for us.

"I leave you, Theresa, I am going to die. O, always remember what we did together from the beginning of our acquaintance; if you change, I will accuse you at the tribunal of God; but, take courage, despise the discourse of those who have not the faith. Should one try to persuade you to take a husband, have no other opinion than that of the Fathers. If you cannot serve God here, as you would like, go to the Mission of Loretto. Never give up the practice of mortification. I will love you in heaven. I will pray for you." Again she repeated, "I will love you in heaven," and the words died on her lips.

The missionary stood by her side, repeating the prayers for the agonizing, and strengthening her by holy invocations.

Catherine, attentive to the least word she heard, found new strength to suffer, every time she felt herself incited to the love of God. She was seen to raise her eyes frequently to heaven, as if wishing to indicate to those present that there alone was the object and end of all her desires. Her hands clasped to her breast a crucifix, which she unceasingly covered with kisses and tears. Theresa, her faithful companion, sustained her in her arms, contemplating with admiration her celestial attitude, when Catharine cried out three times: "Jesus, I love you!" It was the last salutation her dying lips addressed to her God on this earth.

SHRINE NOTES.

——To make room for the usual announcements about the pilgrimage season, we must withhold from this number the second letter of the Editor about his investigations, in company with Rev. A. E. Jones, S.J., of the sites of the early Huron Missions, in Simcoe County, Canada.

——The Shrine will be opened for pilgrims Sunday, July 16th, and from that day until after September 1st, one or more priests will be in attendance on the pilgrims, saying Mass daily and leading the other devotions, such as the Way of the Cross, the morning and night prayers, the Holy Hour, and when permitted Benediction of the Blessed Sacrament.

——The accommodations this year will be still better than in previous years, and we shall be glad to give information about the various places where lodging or board can be obtained. The Putman House is now in charge of Mr. Thomas Glenn, and judging from the interest he takes in the Shrine, and from the activity and success with which he has repaired the serious damages in the Ravine, owing to the storms of last Autumn, we can promise his guests a pleasant place in his house.

——We are very grateful to our subscribers for the alacrity and generosity with which they have responded to our appeal for subscriptions to the PILGRIM, and for contributions to defray the usual expenses of repairing and improving the grounds and structures at Auriesville. Through this kindness, which is as encouraging as it is helpful, we hope to be able to enlarge the open chapel, removing from it the rooms now used by the priests in attendance at the Shrine, and giving all this space to the sanctuary, sacristy and side-chapels. The fathers will be provided with rooms by extending the structure which was erected last year for their kitchen and refectory. By thus adding to their convenience, the pilgrims may be assured they will in turn derive even more help and benefit from them than hitherto.

——We are much pleased with the new time-table of the West Shore Railroad, which restores the trains taken off last year, and enables pilgrims to come from East and West daily. The season promises to be one of much activity and piety at the Shrine.

Already pilgrims have begun visiting it, and we regret that our labors during the month of June and early in July, prevent us from being there to meet them.

——As four pastors have already bespoken Sundays in July or August for their pilgrimages, to avoid misunderstanding and confusion pastors wishing to conduct pilgrimages to Auriesville, will do well to communicate with us as soon as possible.

——We need not remind either those who are fortunate enough to visit Auriesville, or those who are prevented from doing so that the chief object of the pilgrimages is to honor our Lady at the Shrine erected to her as Queen of Martyrs, with a view to obtaining through her intercession not only what we need for ourselves, but the beatification of the missionaries who died for the faith at this hallowed spot, and of the saintly Indian maiden who was born there, Catharine Tegakwitha, to whose intercession we are happy to ascribe a remarkable cure. Besides invoking our Lady, we may also privately ask God to show forth the proof of the sanctity of these holy souls by granting the favors asked through their intercession.

AURIESVILLE, N. Y., June 19, 1899.

DEAR FATHER WYNNE:

We have been here just three weeks to-morrow. The time has, indeed, passed very quickly.

I wish you could have been with us, at least for a few days, to enjoy the beautiful country, which, notwithstanding the long continued dry spell, never looked more lovely.

Yesterday, piloted by our faithful servitor, "Tout," who drove the new horse, which combines all the cardinal virtues for a small amount of money, we drove to Amsterdam in time for High Mass. The church looked very nice and the ceremonies were carried out in a metropolitan way. Next week the new organ comes, which will then complete the interior of the church.

The pilgrimage from Cohoes last week Sunday was well conducted, and brought as orderly and as nice a congregation as I have ever seen at Auriesville. There were over two hundred men in the pilgrimage, who wore the Sacred Heart Badge, consisting of a wide collar of red and gold, and who sang at Mass and at Vespers. The day was perfect, and the people seemed to enjoy everything.

Yesterday I went to the Ravine with Mr. Glenn, and looked at the work which had been done there. The road into the Ravine, which had been washed by the heavy freshet, is now filled in nicely, and they have made a very good wall at the foot of the Grotto, protecting it from further damage.

We will be glad, indeed, to see you, and hope you will remain for a few days, or spend Sunday with us. Two of the Amsterdam Sisters, with a young lady friend, spent last Saturday here, and it looks as if the new convenient arrangement of the trains this Summer would bring a good many visitors from the east.

Everything in the village is about as usual, excepting that a new boarding place will be found in that handsome house of Mr. Abel's. The parties who have rented it, a Mr. and Mrs. Davis, seem to be very energetic and are desirous of entertaining all the pilgrims who may come their way.

Come early, dear Father, and get the choice selection. With kindest wishes. Ever sincerely yours,

E. A. BROOKS, JR.

THE PILGRIMAGES FOR 1899.

WHERE AURIESVILLE IS.

Auriesville is in Montgomery County, New York. It is a station of the West Shore Railroad, forty miles west of Albany, fifty miles east of Utica, 175 miles from New York City, and equi-distant some 265 miles from Philadelphia, Boston, Buffalo, and Montreal.

The New York Central Railroad, the most frequented line of travel, runs parallel with the West Shore, but on the opposite side of the river (the historic Mohawk). Two stations on the New York Central are convenient to Auriesville, Fonda and Tribes Hill, the former three miles west, and the latter one and one-half east. Public conveyances are procurable at a slight charge from either to the Shrine. The New York Central being such an important artery of travel, its greater frequency of trains and superior service make it to many the more desirable route.

SUMMER TOURISTS.

Summer tourists on their way to or from Niagara Falls, Thousand Islands, Watkins, Clifton Springs, the Adirondacks, Plattsburgh, and the Lake district of interior New York, who hold tickets calling for travel on the New York Central or West Shore road, have the privilege of stopping over upon notice to the conductor, enabling them to visit the Shrine at their leisure. Visitors at Lake George, Saratoga, or the Catskills can conveniently make the journey back and forth to Auriesville on the same day.

How to Reach Auriesville.

For the benefit of pilgrims who desire to visit the Shrine, we subjoin a schedule of convenient trains:

FROM NEW YORK BY WEST SHORE R. R.

LEAVE.	7†	5*
Franklin Street	11.15 A. M.	9.15 P. M.
West Forty-second Street.	11 35 "	9.30 "
Weehawken	11.50 "	9.45 "
Arrive Auriesville	5.18 P. M.	

* Daily. † Daily, except Sunday.

11.20 from Penna. Depot, Jersey City, connects with train No. 7.

NOTE.—Train No. 5 leaving Franklin Street, 9.15 P. M., West Forty-second Street, 9.30 P. M., Weehawken, 9.45 P. M., will stop at Auriesville, on notice to conductor, to let off passengers from New York City, or New England States. Reaches Auriesville 3.50 A. M.

FROM POINTS WEST BY WEST SHORE R. R.

LEAVE.	8†	6*	18*
Buffalo		7.10 P. M.	7.00 A. M.
Rochester		9.05 "	9.10 "
Syracuse		11.25 "	11.40 "
Utica	6.50 A. M.	12.54 A. M.	1.35 P. M.
Fultonville	8.33 "	2.26 "	4.00 "
Arrive Auriesville.	8.40 "		4.13 "

* Daily. † Daily, except Sunday.

NOTE.—Train 6 will stop at Auriesville, on notice to conductor to let off passengers from west of Buffalo.

FROM ALBANY BY WEST SHORE R. R.

LEAVE.	
Albany	2.40 †P. M.
South Schenectady	4.36 "
Amsterdam	5.05 "
Arrive Auriesville.	5.18 "

† Daily, except Sunday.

FROM NEW YORK OR ALBANY, BY N. Y. C. & H. R. R.

LEAVE.					
New York	. . . .	12.10‖A.M	8.00* A.M.	10.30 †A.M	11.30†A.M
Albany	7.15 †A. M.	8.15 "	1.30 P. M.	3.00 P.M.	5.00 P.M.
Schenectady	7.50 "	8.46 "	2.07 "	3.30 "	5.35 "
Amsterdam	8.24 "	9.13 "	2.40 "	3.57 "	6.04 "
Tribes Hill	8.36 "	. . . .	2.51 "	. . . .	6.18 "
Fonda	8.48 "	9.30 "	3.01 "	4.13 "	6.28 "

* Daily.   † Daily except Sunday.   ‖ Daily except Monday.

FROM TROY BY N. Y. C. & H. R. R.

LEAVE.				
Troy	7.35 *A. M.	8.50 †A.M	2.30 †P.M.	4.40 †P.M.
Schenectady	8.46 "	10.08 "	3.30 "	5.35 "
Amsterdam	9.13 "	10.41 "	3.57 "	6.04 "
Tribes Hill	. . . .	10.53 "	. . . .	6.18 "
Fonda	9.30 "	11.02 "	4.13 "	6.28 "

* Daily.   † Daily except Sunday.

FROM BUFFALO BY N. Y. C. & H. R. R.

LEAVE.	A. M.	A. M.	A. M.	A. M.	A. M.	A. M.
Buffalo	. . . .	. . . .	. . . .	4.55†	6.00†	8.05*
Rochester	. . . .	. . . .	. . . .	6.42	8.15	10.00
Syracuse	. . . .	. . . .	7.15*	9.25	11.10	12.05
Utica	5.50†	7.00*	9 20	11.10	1.20	1.45
Fonda	7.29	8.40	11.04	12.41	3.16	3.02
Tribes Hill	7.38	8.49	11.14	. . .	3.26	. . . .
	A. M.	A. M.	A. M.	M.	P. M.	P. M.

* Daily.   † Daily except Sunday.

HUDSON RIVER STEAMERS—DAY.

Leave New York, Desbrosses Street Pier, 8.40† A. M.; West 22d Street Pier, 9.00 A. M. Leaves Brooklyn, Fulton Street (by Annex), 8 A. M. Arrive Albany 6.10 P. M., connecting with West Shore or New York Central & Hudson River R. R.

† Daily except Sunday.

ALBANY BY PEOPLE'S LINE—NIGHT.

Leave New York, Pier 32, N. R., foot Canal Street, 6† P. M. Arrive Albany 6 A. M. Connects with N. Y. C. 7.15 A. M. train.

† Daily except Sunday.

FROM BOSTON BY BOSTON & ALBANY R. R.

	LEAVE.		
Boston	5.00† A. M.	10.30* A. M.	11.00* P. M.
Worcester	6.33 "	11.42 "	12.28 A. M.
Springfield	8.33 "	1.14 P. M.	4 15 "
Pittsfield	10.28 "	2. 52 "	6.11 "
Chatham	11.23 "	. . . .	7.07 "
Albany	12.10 M.	4.15 "	7.57 "

* Daily.   † Daily except Sunday.

PHILADELPHIA TO NEW YORK BY PENN'A. R. R.

LEAVE.	A. M.	A. M.	A. M.	A. M.	A. M.	A. M.	A. M.
Philadelphia	5.15*	6.50†	7.38†	8.25*	9.50*	10.21*	11.00†
Trenton	6.04	7.44	. . .	9.10	. . .	. . .	11.44
Newark	. . .	8.57	. . .	. . .	. . .	. . .	. . .
Jersey City	7.32	9.10	9.21	10.25	11.40	12.31	12.55
New York	7.43	9.23	9.38	10.38	11.53	12.43	1.08
	A. M.	A. M.	A. M.	A. M.	A. M.	M.	P. M.

LEAVE.	A. M.	M.	P. M.	P. M.	P. M.
Philadelphia	11.10 †	12.00 †	4.02*	4.22‡	5.00†
Trenton	12.12	12.45	4.47	. . .	5.47
Newark	. . .	. . .	. . .	. . .	6.57
Jersey City	1.47	1.55	6.10	6.20	7.11
New York	2.00	2.08	6.23	6.30	7.23
	P. M.	P. M.	P. M.	P. M.	P. M.

* Daily. † Daily except Sunday. ‡ Limited express, composed entirely of parlor coaches, on which extra fare is charged.

NOTE.—The 8.25 A. M. train from Philadelphia makes direct connection with the 11.20 A. M. West Shore, which leaves from Penn'a. Depot, Jersey City.

FROM MONTREAL BY DEL. & HUDSON R. R.

	LEAVE.		
Montreal	8.40* A. M.	7.00* P. M.
Plattsburg	11.00 "	9.35 "
Saratoga	3.05 P. M.	1.35 A. M.
Troy	4.15 "	2.40 "
Albany	4.10 "	3.10 "

* Daily. † Daily except Sunday.

NOTE.—Trains from Montreal, Plattsburg, Saratoga, and intermediate points make good connections at Albany with the West Shore or N. Y. Central R. R.

CONTRIBUTIONS TO THE SHRINE.

M. McG., Providence, R. I.,	$2.00	M. M., Phila.,	3.00
M. J. C., Lamine, La.,	6.00	Anon.,	15.00
J. O'B., Chester, Pa.,	.50	Anon.,	25.00
J. F., New York.,	5.00	M. McK.,	2.00
J. J. C., Cincinnati, O.,	1.00	M. M., Buckingham, Canada,	4.50
M. L. S. H., Buffalo, N. Y.,	5.00	D. R., Battle Creek, Mich,	$1.00
M. D., Portland.,	1.00	J. A. G., Phila.,	2.00
Anon,	10.00	T. R., Geneva, N. Y.,	3.00
Anon, in memory of a dear Mother,	440.77	**FOR THE CROWN.** A. N. M., a medallion.	
N. K., New York,	1.00	A wedding ring from Mrs. J. G. S., per I. S., Elizabeth, N. J.	
Anon,	5.00		
J. W. C., New York,	3.00		

TÉRÈSE AND PIERRE.

BY K. A. HENNESSY.

(*Continued.*)

CHAPTER II.

Through Many Perils.

THE 17th of May, 1656, was a clear warm sunny day and Quebec was well-nigh deserted, for the bulk of her residents thronged the water's edge at the foot of the hill and men, women, and children strained their eyes to obtain a last glimpse of the little flotilla that was fast receding from their view. Some among the crowd wore an anxious troubled look; others shook their heads in doubt and apprehension; many shed tears of bitter regret, and abundant and sincere was the sympathy that went out from hundreds of stout hearts on shore to the occupants of the canoes then gliding out of sight down the picturesque St. Lawrence.

And who in all the mass of humanity lining the river bank, could realize the perils of the mission undertaken by some of his brave fellow-beings and think of their possible, even probable fate, without a shudder or a sigh of genuine pity? Surely not the parent, whose child might become the victim of vile Indian treachery; nor the maid whose lover might prove a target for some fiendish Iroquois marksman; nor the Governor, whose intrepid military protégé might be struck lifeless by a single well-aimed hatchet blow; nor the Father Superior, whose spiritual sons might be tortured to death by the savages unto whom they sought to open the portals of eternal bliss. Ah! there was just cause for misgiving, ample ground for fear, good reason for the gloom that weighed upon the inhabitants of the town as they wended their way back to their comfortable homes on the hill. But that there was also hope in the hearts of these people was shown by the many fervent prayers that ascended that night to the merciful Father of all, beseeching Him to bless and protect the dauntless priests and valiant Frenchman who had so willingly acceded to the request of the Onondaga Indians, and courageously set out to establish a colony in the wilds of their country.

To be sure the successful efforts of Fathers d'Ablon and Chaumonot, who less than a year before had gone forth to evangelize these barbarians, were promising indeed; and when the Onondagas, who were one of the five tribes composing the Iroquois nation, and were then at peace with the French, begged that the latter would come and live among them, it seemed but fitting that their request should be granted; but who could give the assurance that dire results would not follow? Who could fathom the depths of Indian faithlessness? Father d'Ablon, who had returned from the scene of his labors, and laid the matter before the civil and religious authorities in Quebec, was accompanied by representatives of the savage tribes, who gave evidence of such perfect good will and sincerity that the Governor of the French colonists and the Superior of the missions, after careful deliberation, decided to yield the point. Therefore, M. Dupuy, Commandant of the Fort at Quebec, gladly offered his services and allowed himself to be placed at the head of the intrepid band of fifty-five Frenchmen, including Fathers Claude d'Ablon, Jaques Frémin, François Le Mercier, and others who started, with some Onondagas, Senecas, and a few Hurons, for the Onondaga country.

The hardships and terrors of the long journey were truly appalling, but the little band was worthy of the noble standard under which it had enlisted, and when the banner was unfurled, and the all-powerful name of Jesus emblazoned on a background of spotless white taffeta, met the gaze of the weary pilgrims, their courage was revived, their ardor increased, and their hope strengthened. On the 30th of June, the party entered the village of Montreal, and eight days later resumed the journey southward. The rapids in the St. Lawrence were crossed with much difficulty, their turbulent waters at times threatening to play sad havoc with the frail canoes, and the skill of the Indian pilots was taxed to the uttermost.

But it was about a month later that a still more serious obstacle presented itself. When the party was coasting along the beautiful Lake of the Iroquois, now known as Ontario, their provisions gave out, even the stock of "wild cows," as the Frenchmen called the elk and deer which they had shot down *en route*, becoming exhausted, and famine stared the colonists in the face. Then a desperate effort was made to reach Otiatannehengué, a place not far distant which the Onondagas were wont to frequent during the fishing season, and by way of announcing the approach of himself and party, M. Dupuy ordered two small cannon to be fired. The report echoed far and wide but the men listened in vain for a returning salute, and at length reached the little fishing settlement only to find it deserted, and its streams destitute of fish. What was then to be done? Starvation seemed the inevitable fate of all, and to increase the general anxiety, Father Le Mercier fell seriously ill.

Just at this critical juncture an old Onondaga was suddenly seized with an idea. He was seated in Dupuy's canoe and, when he had whispered something in the Commandant's ear, an order was given to immediately put to shore. This done, the old Indian sprang from the light bark and darted off across the prairie. Patiently was his return awaited and when, in the course of an hour, he reappeared laden with clusters of red berries he was hailed with delight. The wild fruit, though very insipid, was a veritable godsend, and it was only a matter of a few minutes till the other canoes drew up beside the bank and the most agile of their occupants disembarked and started in search of more of the fruit. The hope of finding something with which to appease their gnawing hunger seemed to give them new energy, and, ere long, their appetites were amply satisfied.

Meanwhile, poor Father Le Mercier lay helpless in one of the boats, the hot July sun beating down upon his prostrate form and its penetrating rays scorching his pallid cheek and sapping away what little remained of his fast ebbing strength. There was no shelter on shore so it was useless to take him thither and thereby deprive him of the slight breeze coming from the water, therefore, ever constantly onward plied the canoeists till, on the night of July 7th, they entered the mouth of the river leading to Lake Gannentaha. (1) And here a new difficulty confronted them in the form of a counter-current so swift and strong as to threaten to shatter their fragile barks, and once more they found themselves face to face with starvation, that gaunt spectre that strikes terror into the bravest hearts and lays low even those of mightiest brawn. Faint from hunger and fatigue, the fearless wayfarers were forced to lay down their paddles and yield to nature's demand for rest; but " whom God cares for are well cared indeed," and, just when all seemed darkest, a canoe was sighted in the distance. It approached with marvellous speed, being quickly followed by two others, and when the Indian captain of the little fleet came near, he saluted the Frenchmen in terms the most gracious, offering them the contents of the three boats with the good wishes of his people, the Onondagas, and of Father Chaumonot. The hearts of the famished colonists swelled with joy and eagerly indeed did the poor, exhausted fellows partake of the coarse fare distributed among them, and the corn meal and salmon were as grateful to their parched palates as would have been the daintest confection prepared by a French *chef*.

This display of good will on the part of the Onondagas and the news of Father Chaumonot's well-being, were highly encouraging, and when some hours later, the Frenchmen resumed their journey, it was with a zest born of reassurance.

---

(1) Now known as Lake Onondaga.

Three days later when the canoes were moored and their occupants went ashore to seek shelter for the night, to their astonishment, they found awaiting them a captain who had come all the way from Onondaga in order to bid them welcome to his country, extend the greetings of his people and escort the Europeans to their new home.

On the afternoon of July 11th, the little party entered Lake Gannentaha, a smooth, clear body of water, about five miles long by one wide, on the southern shore of which Fathers d'Ablon and Chaumonot had selected a site for the French habitation. The firing of five small cannon, the reverberations of which travelled far over water and hilltop and well on through the forest, was the first salute of the Frenchmen to their new friends, and indeed the thundering of the light artillery had the desired effect, for it delighted the expectant Indians who flocked from all directions to the southern extremity of the lake where the colonists had disembarked. Father d'Ablon was naturally the first to whom the savages did homage, but when he presented Father Le Mercier, who had outlived the perils of the journey, and the other reverend gentlemen to his old protégés, assuring them that the priests had come to continue among them the good work which he and Father Chaumonot had begun, the red men were profuse in their protestations of respect. M. Dupuy, they regarded with something akin to awe; and his soldiers, though worn and jaded after their trying experiences, presented an imposing picture as they were drawn up in line, the shabby remnants of their once brilliant uniforms calling forth exclamations of surprise and admiration from the barbarians, to whose fancy bright colors and gaudy attire invariably appealed.

The next morning the fathers intoned the *Te Deum*, in which all the colonists joined, and fervent indeed was the thanksgiving that arose from the grateful hearts of those whom God's all-powerful hand had protected throughout the long, hazardous journey which had at last come to such a happy issue. Then the Holy Sacrifice of the Mass was offered and the land solemnly taken possession of in the name of

Christ whose gospel was to be announced to its benighted natives.

The surrounding country was one of singular beauty, and the site upon which the colonists built their blockhouse was a rugged eminence overlooking the placid lake and commanding a fine, unobstructed view of a magnificent landscape. In the immediate vicinity were springs of fresh water while, at no great distance, salt springs bubbled forth their saline waters which, when they evaporated, left the ground besprinkled with sparkling crystals. The salt springs had been discovered by Father Le Moyne about two years previously, and their existence so far inland was a mystery which he could not solve, their source, one which he could not trace. Luxuriant shade trees bordered the edge of the lake; great chestnut, butternut and walnut trees grew throughout the land; wild grapevines trailed along the ground, often twining themselves about the trunks of trees, and thence climbing to lofty heights; wild leeks, onions, peas and artichokes appeared in profusion, and many plants of rare medicinal value thrived in the rich soil. The streams fairly swarmed with fish, eels and salmon being especially plentiful, and geese, swans and ducks lived in the water in as great numbers as did the snipe, quail, heron, pigeon and other winged animals in the air.

The natural resources of the country were great and many, and these, considered in connection with the genial reception accorded them by the aborigines, led the missionaries and colonists to hope that blessed results might be consequent upon the sacrifices they had made in coming among a people whose nature was so coarse, whose habits were so revolting, and with whom association was scarcely tolerable.

On the Monday following the arrival of the colonists, all was hurry and bustle in and around their temporary tents on the shore of Lake Gannentaha. Those of their number who were most skilled in the use of carpenter's tools, set earnestly to work to erect a habitation worthy the name of home, and the spirit of energetic willingness which prevailed, gave promise that the task so eagerly begun would be speedily and successfully accomplished.

(To be continued.)

MISSION NOTES.

On April 18th there was held at Rome a session of the special congregation summoned by the Pope to inquire into the process of the fifty-two martyrs, all either members or converts of the Paris Society for Foreign Missions. There seems to be little doubt that they will soon be beatified. Of these fifty-two, ten were priests of the Society, the rest, natives of Indo-China, priests, laymen, women and children. All these martyrs gave up their lives between 1815 and 1856. The total number of martyrs which the Society claims for the 19th century is: European priests and bishops, about seventy; native priests, about one hundred, native lay Christians, over ninety thousand! The number of adult conversions recorded by the Society for the past year alone is seventy-two thousand seven hundred.

The Right Rev. Dr. Gibney, Catholic Bishop of Perth, while on a visit to Bulong, West Australia, to raise funds for the rebuilding of the Catholic Church which had been blown down, received the following address from the Protestants of that place:

"We, the Protestant inhabitants of the loyal town of Bulong, desire to avail ourselves of the opportunity offered by your most reverend lordship's visit to express to yourself and your co-religionists throughout the colony our sympathy in connection with the trials you have experienced in your efforts to extend the benefits of religion and civilization to this remote corner of the Australian Confederacy. Though we are aware the utmost effort on our part in the way of prayer, sacrifice and labor may often be insufficient to protect us from the desolating effects of such natural agencies as that which laid low the edifice in which your lordship's spiritual flock in this district have been accustomed to meet (and seek such manumission from the thraldom of sin and unordered lives, as they, equally with ourselves, so earnestly desire) we no less appreciate your lordship's solicitude in the moral and physical welfare of all of us, whether Roman Catholic or Protestant, as evidenced by this Episcopal and very friendly visit. Though separated from you in some points of religious thought and ecclesiastical discipline, we are conscious that your venerable division of the Christian Church has still many claims on our gratitude and good will, and while we are glad to notice the expansion of science has not diminished the love and regard of our Catholic neighbors for their most militant, well-disciplined and self-sacrificing Church, we gladly join with them in welcoming their Bishop, and further venture on the liberty of offering you all our sincere and respectful congratulations on the now almost secured recovery of His Holiness the Pope from one of the trials incident to a laboriously beneficent life, at his great age."

The following letter has been addressed to Mr. T. M. Healy, M. P., by Earl Grey, late Administrator in Rhodesia, South Africa:

DEAR MR. HEALY:

"You will be pleased to know, as you take an interest in the Dominican Sisters at Buluwayo, that the government of Rhodesia has given them a site on which to build their new Nursing Home, and a grant of £1,000 and that, in addition, we have collected over £1,000 from the outside public. This will, I hope, be sufficient to give them a good start.

I enclose copy of a letter I sent to a few friends of mine, asking them to contribute to the Dominican Sisters' Fund.

ENCLOSURE.

I am asking some of my friends who have made profitable investments in South African securities, to help the two following objects in which I take a special interest: (1) The raising of money for the Dominican Sisters of Buluwayo. (2) The raising of money for the Church of England in Rhodesia.

The Dominican Sisters,—for eight or nine years these splendid women have devoted themselves to the service of the settlers and the natives as nurses in our Rhodesian hospitals. It is impossible to speak in too high terms of them.

Never has one case of scandal of any sort occurred to tarnish the bright record of their service. They have not attempted to use their position for proselytizing purposes. They have devoted themselves exclusively to the work of nursing, and in the execution of their duties have shown so much gentleness, compassion, and tender and untiring energy, that there is not a single prospector in Rhodesia who has been under their care who does not entertain for them all the feelings of reverence and gratitude of which his nature is capable.

So long as the hospital at Buluwayo was under the control of the administration, the reign of service of the Dominican Sisters as nurses was undisturbed, but now that the town of Buluwayo has become responsible for the management of its hospital, it has been found desirable to replace them by certificated nurses, with the result that the Dominican Sisters are thrown on their own resources. To enable the people of Buluwayo to retain the great advantage of their presence and continued service, a fund is being raised by the people of Buluwayo and by their friends and sympathizers in England. The administration of Rhodesia are warmly coöperating. They have resolved to give the Dominican Sisters £1,000 and a free grant of land on which to build a nursing institute. We wish to supplement this sum by at least another £1,000, and as the settlers in Buluwayo have only very limited funds at their disposal, and many local objects competing for their support, we are appealing to those to whom the opening out of Rhodesia has afforded the opportunities of profitable investment, to come to their assistance with a contribution. I would be greatly obliged if you would send any subscriptions or donation you may be willing to give, either to me, or to the Secretary of the British South African Company, 15 St. Swithin's Lane, London, E. C.

The unfortunate natives of Terra del Fuego are being rapidly exterminated by the whites. The slightest pretext or no pretext at all, suffices for the murder of a native, and £1 is paid for the head of every Fuegian. Shocking tales of white barbarity come to us from this unhappy island.

Acknowledgment is made of the following contributions:

FOR POOR COMMUNITIES IN ITALY.
M. L. R., Cincinnati., O., . $1.12
FOR NEEDY MISSIONS.
J. C., Osawatomie, Kansas. 2.00

FOR PROPAGATION OF THE FAITH.
Anon, ... $6.00
FOR NAOTOLI MISSION, EAST INDIA.
T. M., Roseton, N. Y., ...50

THE PILGRIM

OF

OUR LADY OF MARTYRS

XV. Year.   August, 1899.   No. 8.

JANUA COELI.

(From an old Latin Hymn.)

BY REV. C. W. BARRAUD, S.J.

SING we the Virgin's praise,
    The Mother of our God made man,
    Begotten of His word who can
    Call unseen harvests from the ground—
So wonderful His ways.
    This is that city girded round
    With rivers sevenfold that spring
    Beneath the Almighty Spirit's wing.

    O closed gate through which our King
      Came forth to save us from the foe,
    Wide, wide thy golden portal fling,
      That we may tell Him all our woe.

Hail flower of purity,
    From whence the fruit of mercy grew,
    So sweet of taste, so fair of hue,
    Whereon the hope of man shall feed,
Nor ever wearied be;
    For Jesus doth no sickness breed.
    In Him the balm of every sore,
    His Church's life for evermore.

To thee a messenger,
    With welcome tidings swiftly shod,
    From the eternal throne of God
    Came down with greeting marvellous,

Copyright, 1898, by Apostleship of Prayer.

That, falling on thine ear,
    Found passage to thy heart, and thus,
    Within thy womb becoming man,
    His work of love the Word began.

Sweet maid, thou knowest well
    That the great King will honor thee
    E'en as in thy humility
    Thou shalt abase thyself; and, oh !
Who may thy glory tell?
    For, while with voice so sweet and low
    Thou call'st thyself His handmaid, we
    As His true Mother worship thee.

Into thy sinless breast,
    A temple sacred to His name,
    The everlasting Godhead came.
    Lo ! from thy body's virgin earth
The Truth that giveth rest
    Unto the weary took its birth ;
    And the eternal God was born
    A little babe on Christmas morn.

Lo ! on this holy sod
    Mercy and Truth together meet.
    Here Peace and Justice kindly treat
    And sign their treaty with a kiss.
O daughter of our God
    And mother, in the halls of bliss
    Plead for our pardon, make us one
    With God the Father through His Son.

    O closed gate through which our King
        Came forth to save us from the foe,
    Wide, wide thy golden portal fling,
        That we may tell Him all our woe.

AN IROQUOIS MAIDEN;
OR
Life of Catharine Tegakwitha.
(*Continued.*)

CHAPTER XVI.
Funeral.—Graces Obtained.

ON the very day of good Catharine's death, Father Cholenec paid a just tribute of homage to her memory. When the savages were assembled, as usual, in church for evening prayer he spoke to them with a sentiment of profound conviction, of the precious treasure that the Mission had just lost. He no longer feared to wound the modesty of his neophyte, or give occasion to vanity. After exalting the heroism of her virtues, before the whole congregation, and the generous sacrifice she had secretly offered to God in acknowledgement of His love, he advised each savage to gather up these souvenirs, in order to preserve forever the memory of the words and actions of the holy maiden.

The funeral took place the following day, at three o'clock, but it was less a day of mourning, than one of triumph. The Christians of La Prairie of Montreal, where the news was soon spread, wished to join with those of the Mission of the Saut, to take part in the public homage rendered to so perfect a life.

Out of respect for the virtue of Catharine, the Indians desired Father Chauchetiére to permit her body to repose within the church, but Father Cholenec opposed their earnest prayers, and it was interred in the common cemetery.

Thus was accomplished, a prophecy made long before by the virtuous Iroquois maid. She had one day found herself, with several women, near a grave that was being dug for one of her little nephews. The conversation turned on this place of general rendezvous, and the spot that each would one day occupy. "And where will yours be, Catharine?" asked some one lightly. "Here," replied Catharine, pointing to an empty place. She was not deceived. The place fixed upon by Father Cholenec, was precisely that which Catharine had designated in advance.

All those who came to take part in Catharine's funeral, and to pay her their last homage, had the consolation of beholding, with their own eyes, a living testimony of her virtue. Her face, as we have said, had been, from the age of four years, disfigured by the small-pox. Since then, her infirmities and her excessive mortifications, far from effacing the traces of her first sickness, had only contributed to render them more apparent; but, no sooner had she breathed her last, than her face, so disfigured and so dark, suddenly changed. "It became," says Father Cholenec, her historian, "so white and so gracious, that I could not refrain from uttering a cry of astonishment, and all the spectators could verify the strange fact for themselves. God seemed to wish that a reflection of that glory which her soul had resumed in heaven should be reflected on her virginal body."

Two inhabitants of the Prairie had arrived at the Saut village the morning of the interment. They perceived, in passing, the body of Catharine stretched upon a mat. Struck by the color and expression of the countenance, one remarked to the other: "There lies a woman who sleeps peacefully!" But, on hearing that she was dead and that her state was a subject of admiration for all the people, they retraced their steps, and could, like the others, verify the marvel. After kneeling near the body to recommend themselves to the prayers of the departed, they desired, out of respect for her memory, to prepare her coffin themselves.

The sight of this inanimate body, far from exciting repugnance, inspired love of virtue and the desire of holiness. Every one endeavored to kiss her hand with respect or obtain some object that had belonged to her. That all might have the consolation of beholding her face, it remained uncovered, contrary to usage, till the moment of sepulchre.

The crucifix that Catharine had held in her hands until death, the mat on which she had breathed her last sigh, as well as the blanket with which she had enveloped her head, were all carefully gathered up and treasured as precious relics. From that time the Indians regarded her as the tutelary angel of the Mission, and the numerous graces obtained through her intercession soon bore witness of her power with God.

Her tomb became a place of pilgrimage whither all came to recommend to this good Christian their dearest interests.

Some time after the death of Catharine, Monseigneur St. Valier (1), second bishop of Quebec, visited the Mission of the Saut in company with the Marquis de Denonville, Governor of Canada. His first thought was to go and pray at the tomb of Catharine, to recommend himself to her protection. "Let us console ourselves," said he, rising. "Canada has also her Genevieve."

This holy death produced the most salutary effects on the Christians of the Saut. A redoubling of piety and fervor was visible among them. "It seems," says one of Catharine's first panegyrists, "as if she returned a hundred fold to the mission what she had herself there found." Her memory alone excited to that perfection of which she had given such a beautiful example.

Married persons voluntarily obliged themselves to continency, and widows, still young, consecrated themselves to God by a vow of perpetual chastity. Others subjected themselves to such rigorous penance that it may be affirmed, without exaggeration, that they rivalled those practised in monasteries by the most fervent. The following example may serve as proof: Two young girls of fifteen years of age, closely united by their natural attraction for virtue, were conversing together on the life and sanctity of Catharine. Urged by an inward desire to imitate her more perfectly, they asked themselves what they could do the most agreeable to God and their new patroness. Make a vow of virginity was the answer inspired by grace, but there seemed to be an invincible obstacle in the way of this—the consent of their parents. They therefore fervently demanded of Catharine that if they could not follow her example and pass their lives in virginity, they might rather die in possession of this treasure. Not long afterwards death surprised them both in

---

(1) Monseigneur de la Croix St. Valier, second Bishop of Quebec, succeeded to this see in 1688, and died December 26th, after an episcopate of thirty-nine years.

the flower of their age, to the great astonishment of the family, who had not discovered in them the germs of any disease. Their confidence and joy in their last moments left no doubt as to the accomplishment of their desires.

The signal favors obtained by Catharine's intercession, were soon multiplied, strengthening more and more the confidence placed in her intercession.

Before recounting any of them we would like to quote the following words of her biographer, Father Cholenec. "The graces in question," he says, "are so well substantiated that I do not see how anyone can reasonably dismiss them in doubt. For that matter, though the incredulous still remain incredulous, God will none the less be glorified in His servants, and the good will find therein new motives to love and bless Him, on seeing Him so liberal in recompensing even a poor savage, for the homage rendered to Him."

On the Easter Monday following the death of Catharine, Father Chauchetière, a religious of great virtue, and well worthy of credit, being at prayer about four o'clock in the morning, suddenly the young girl appeared before him, surrounded by glory, her face radiant with light and her eyes fixed on heaven, as if to proclaim the ravishment of her soul. On her right was seen a chapel, overthrown; on her left was a savage bound to a stake and being burned by his enemies. This vision, which lasted two hours, and which the Father could thus contemplate at leisure, appeared to be symbolic. Events soon revealed the whole mystery. During the night of August 20, 1683, a terrible tempest swept over that coast, such as, in the memory of man, had never been equalled. The wind was so violent that the Church of the Mission, in spite of its solidity, was overthrown, together with the steeple. The missionaries were in bed in their apartments above the church. (They were liable to have been crushed beneath it.) They *must have been crushed beneath it.* They attributed their preservation solely to the intervention of the servant of God, whom they had the habit of invoking frequently, and whom they then called to their aid.

As to the savage burnt alive, it was also a harbinger of

what was to happen later. Several Christians of the Mission were, in fact, burned on that spot a few years later, and to Catharine was attributed the constancy they manifested in their torments.

The following year, the same Father Chauchetière was again favored with two other visions of Catharine, during which he heard these words: "*Inspice et fuc secundum exemplar.*" "Look and copy this model." He seemed to infer from this that God desired him to make pictures or likenesses of Catharine, a thought which he resisted for a long time. Finally he set to work, and these images (or portraits) have been, to a great many persons, the occasion of signal graces.

Anastasie, that fervent Christian, who had showed herself so full of charity in regard to Catharine, and who had had for her all the tenderness of a mother, well deserved some special proof of gratitude. She received it, in fact, eight days after her death. It was in the evening, when all the occupants of the cabin were already taking their repose. Anastasie remaining alone, and in prayer, at length yielded to sleep, and stretched herself on her mat, but hardly had she closed her eyes when she was suddenly awakened by a voice saying to her: "Arise, my mother." It was the voice of Catharine. Far from being frightened, she raised herself on her mat, and perceived the young Iroquois girl near her. She was standing, and brilliant with light. A crown, still more brilliant, shone resplendent in her right hand. "She was so luminous," declared Anastasie, "that I do not believe that there can be anything more beautiful." Then Catharine spoke to her these words: "O my mother! Look at this Cross! Ah, how beautiful it is! It was all my happiness in life. I advise you also to place all yours in it." She then vanished, leaving in the heart of Anastasie, a joy so profound, that, for long years afterwards, the memory of this vision had still lost nothing, for her, of its reality.

It is in memory of this apparition, and by reason of the love that Catharine always professed for suffering, that she is generally represented with a cross in her hand.

(*To be continued.*)

THE JESUITS AND NEW FRANCE
In the Seventeenth Century.
From the French of Rev. Camille de Rochemonteix, S.J.
BY K. A. HENNESSY.
(Continued.)

THIS college of Quebec, founded before any in America, even that of Harvard in Massachusetts, was the cradle of religion and the arts and sciences in Canada, and from the day of its establishment until that of its confiscation by the English, who converted it into barracks, it was entwined with sweetest memories and tenderest associations. M. Faucher de Saint-Maurice alludes to these in a page vibrating with emotion, and we beg the privilege of quoting his words.

"It was there that were formed interpreters, diplomats and, better still, hostages who, more than once, saved New France from terrible danger: Father Bigot, who succeeded in calming the irritated Acadians; Father Bruyas, who gained such control over the Iroquois; Father Gravier, who dominated the Hurons by his eloquence; Father Enjalran, who did likewise in regard to the Ottawas and Algonquins, and Father de Lamberville, to whom the Governor alluded, in one of his despatches, as 'the saviour of Canada.' Beneath this roof also, Fathers Le Jeune, Jérôme Lalemant, Enemond Massé, Chaumonot, Labrosse, de Brébœuf, Vincent Bigot, de Crépieul, and de Carheil, became distinguished linguists. Father Albanel, the discoverer of Hudson's Bay, and Father Allouez, who 'penetrated far into the north on one of his evangelizing tours and traversed about eight hundred miles,' came thither after their perilous journeys to pray and meditate. In the seclusion of the cells Father de Bonécamp prepared his work on hydrography and pursued the study of scientific voyages; Father Bressani made important astronomical observations; Father Laure adjusted the measurements of his map of the country stretching between the Saguenay and the Lake of the Mistassins, and Father Aubery sketched a map of the land lying south of the St. Lawrence; Father Lafitau prepared his herbariums and discovered ginseng; Fathers Charles Lalemant, Le Jeune, Barthélemy Vimont, Jérôme Lalemant, Ragueneau, d'Ablon, Brèbœuf and de Quen, edited the *Jesuit Relations*, an imperishable monument to their labors and devotedness, and Father Charlevoix began to prepare matter for his magnificent work entitled *Histoire et description générale de la Nouvelle-France.* Here too Fathers Ménard and de Noué came to beg of God grace and fortitude to die an isolated death for the greater glory of His Name, the one expiring in the heart of the forest—*martyrem in umbrâ*—and the other on Lake St. Peter amid snow and ice." There also lived, worked and prayed, Jogues, Gabriel Lalemant, Garnier, Daniel, René Goupil, Garreau, Buteux, Rasle, Chabanel and Auneau—all those generous apostles who suffered for the faith and shed their blood in the cause of Christ.

"Side by side with those whose names history has transmitted to us," continues M. Faucher de Saint-Maurice, "others lived beneath the same blessed roof, sharing the joys and sorrows of the apostolate and destitute of worldly honors but at peace with God. Some died of pestilential diseases contracted while ministering unto the soldiers and the people; others led a life of retreat and self-denial, or left the college to disappear among their missions without being further mentioned. Each member of the Society of Jesus who came to Canada, took up his cross at Quebec and, heavy as the burden may have been, carried it like the Master without murmuring, become a barbarian, so to speak, with the barbarians in order to make them all children of God!"

We know the superiors who governed that house of piety: Fathers Charles Lalemant and Jérôme, his brother, Vimont, Paul Ragueneau, Lemercier, d'Ablon, Beschefer, Bruyas, Bouvart, Bigot, Joseph Germain, Julien Garnier de la Chasse, du Parc, de Lauzon, Marcol and de Vitry, nearly all of whom were illustrious because of their personal merit and their noble work. Father de Saint-Pé, though the last of the rectors, was neither the least lovable nor devoted. In the course of this history these names will recur, but it is nevertheless fitting that they be inscribed upon these pages dedicated to the scholastic establishment of Quebec, which was the most important in all New France up to the time of the final conquest of that country by the English.

However, this college, which in the seventeenth century had sheltered so many men of noble ideals and lofty aspirations, was reconstructed about the year 1725 upon a much larger and grander scale. The population, which in 1721 amounted to only 25,000, doubled itself within two or three years, and, as the number of pupils increased proportionately, the old college became much too small. The new building, which till about twenty years ago could still be seen, was opposite the cathedral, and consisted of an immense square built around an interior court, and its large, massive-looking walls seemed destined, in the mind of its founders, to last for centuries.

But alas! its existence was a short one. On September 18, 1759, Quebec fell into the hands of the English, who, having put the college to a variety of uses, at length converted it into barracks, and later into a poorhouse.

When in 1877 M. de Boucherville, then Prime Minister, obtaining the approbation of the ecclesiastical authorities, caused it to be demolished, one could readily see how solidly it had been built. Battering rams and gunpowder could scarcely overthrow the courses in which mortar had the consistency of granite. The most powerful explosives known were used to raze the walls, and yet it was but reluctantly that the masonry yielded, revealing at length human remains which, when considered in connection with certain facts and historical coincidences, seemed to be those of Brother Jean Liégeois, architect of the old college, to whom, during two hundred and fourteen years, his work had thus served as a tomb.

Beneath the flags of the chapel the workmen also found the bones of Fathers Jean de Quen and François du Peron. The former, having discovered the regions of Lake St John, became a victim of charity and died in Quebec of contagious fever, and the latter, chaplain of Fort St. Louis, breathed his last in the arms of his soldiers, who watched all night beside his earthly remains and transported them from Richelieu to Quebec, where they interred them next to those of his friend and brother, Jean de Quen.

In 1878 Father Saché, Superior of the Jesuit residence, claimed the bones of these three old religious of the Society, and the Government approved the request. But—must we admit it?—when, on behalf of the President of the Legislative Council, these relics were about to be placed in the hands of the representative of the Society of Jesus, it was stated that "the floor of the *Regimental Magazine*, where the bones had been deposited, was almost totally excavated, and that the boxes containing these bones had disappeared with their contents."

The history of a college is, at best, monotonous and replete with endless insignificant details and therefore, not to tire our readers, we have endeavored to bring to light at once the general aim of the college of Quebec, and the principal events connected with it.

In 1635, Father Le Jeune laid its foundation. Samuel Champlain, the illustrious founder of the French Colony, still lived, but the establishment of a place of learning upon the very ground where he had struggled so valiantly to maintain the honor and interests of France, was the last joy of his roving and comfortless life. Every one knows Champlain, one of the most lovable and respected figures in history, a character in which greatness and simplicity, strength and kindness, enterprising audacity and measured skill and an unaffected and intelligent religious belief were admirably combined and balanced. In the beginning of the 17th century he was the first to plant the flag of France upon the lonely rock of Quebec, and to undertake the colonization and evangelization of the vast regions of the St. Lawrence. And all his enterprises bore the impress of this double intention. With this end in view he organized commercial societies, appealed to the zeal and devotedness of the Franciscans and Jesuits; formed an alliance with the Hurons and Algonquins and, with their support, waged against the Iroquois a war, the length and bloody horrors of which he never foresaw. Champlain well understood the difficult rôle he had assumed and, despite all the vexations, misfortune and reverses which confronted him, continued, to the end of his career, to play his part with scrupulous exactitude. And how severely he suffered at the hands of the mercantile companies! Even after the capture of Quebec by the English, he did not despair of accomplishing the work for which he had sacrificed all—health, fortune, comfort and domestic happiness. We know with what indomitable energy he made his way to London and Paris, seeking the restoration of Canada to France. Returning to Quebec in 1633, he applied himself most assiduously to discharging the troublesome duties of governor, encouraged the cultivation of lands, established peace and order among the Frenchmen, built a post on the Isle of Richelieu in order to prevent the northern savages from trading with the English; erected a fort at Three Rivers whence the incursions of the Iroquois might be espied and suppressed, improved the Fort St. Louis by additional constructions, and as no new colony can prosper save under the purfying and strengthening influence of the Gospel, devoted himself most zealously to the establishment of religion and the progress of the missions. The missionaries never had a more ardent defender nor edifying Christian than Samuel Champlain.

Falling a victim to paralysis in October, 1635, he felt that his last hour was approaching and carefully prepared himself to meet it. When first stricken with the baneful disease he had Father Charles Lalemant, his friend and spiritual director, summoned to his side, and sought his priestly assistance in reviewing a life of almost sixty years. The pure heart of the dying man discovered iniquity where that of another would scarcely recognize the shadow of wrong, and before appearing face to face with the Supreme Judge of his soul, he longed to enshroud himself in "holiness, justice and truth." Father Lalemant remained with him till he expired on Christmas night, and his death cast a gloom over all. Missionaries, officers, soldiers, colonists, all accompanied his mortal remains to Notre Dame de Recouvrance, where Father Lalemant officiated at the obsequies and Father Le Jeune pronounced the funeral oration, and the founder of Quebec was laid to rest on the majestic promontory where later was to flourish the proud capital of New France.

ANNALS OF THE SHRINE.

——Since the issue of the July PILGRIM we have sent to the friends and patrons of Auriesville a circular, the first page of which reads as follows:

AURIESVILLE PILGRIMAGES.

1899.

ANNOUNCEMENT.

"In order to satisfy the pious demands of the many clients of our Lady of Martyrs and promoters of the cause of beatification of Father Isaac Jogues, René Goupil and Catharine Tegakwitha, it has been decided to keep open the shrine erected under the patronage of our Lady of Martyrs on the site of the heroic death of René Goupil, the torture and death of Father Jogues and of the birthplace of Catharine Tegakwitha, from July 15th to September 1st. Mass will be said daily, and, when the number of pilgrims warrants it, there will be morning prayers in common, the Stations of the Cross, sometimes the hour of adoration or Holy Hour, evening prayers with Benediction of the Blessed Sacrament on days when it is permitted.

"The usual novena in honor of our Lady of Martyrs will be begun at the Shrine on Sunday, August 6th, and close on the Feast of the Assumption, Tuesday, August 15th. Besides the particular intention to be recommended by each one who makes this novena, the general interests of the Shrine and the cause of the martyrs should also be an object of our prayers. Special prayers for this novena are given in the Shrine Manual, so that even those who cannot take part in the devotions at the Shrine may join in spirit with the pilgrims there for their own and for our common intention mentioned above."

The circular also contains in a brief space what is given here in greater detail. By an oversight some of the circulars have September 15 for the date of closing the Shrine instead of September 1. Usually one of the Fathers remains at Auriesville during the first week of September, but it is not likely that the Shrine can be kept open after September 8, the latest.

―――The first pilgrimage of the season will be made Sunday, July 30, from the towns and cities on the Hudson between Poughkeepsie and Hudson. The train will leave Highland at 6:06 A.M.; Kingston, 7:30; Saugerties, 7:48; Malden, 7:52; West Camp, 7:55; Catskill, 8:07; West Athens, 8:17; Coxsackie, 8:26, and Ravena, 8:40. Returning, the train will leave Auriesville at 5:30 P.M.

This is the second annual pilgrimage from these places, the first having been made June 26, 1898, and it is announced to take place, "rain or shine," in the true spirit of a pilgrimage. Besides the Fathers of the Shrine the following Rev. Fathers are mentioned as its patrons: Very Rev. Dean Sweeney, Rev. D. P. Ward, Rev. P. Maughan, Rev. F. Fagan, Rev. Thomas J. Walsh, Rev. P. F. Smith, Rev. P. F. Donnelly, Rev. J. J. O'Brien and Rev. M. J. Murray, its principal organizer.

―――August 13 is the date set for the pilgrimage from Albany, and August 20 for the pilgrimage from Troy. On this day also, by special permission kindly given us by the Rt. Rev. Bishop Burke, the pilgrims will be consecrated to the most Sacred Heart of Jesus. In preparation for this a triduum of services will be held on the evenings of August 18, 19 and 20. There will be a pilgrimage every Sunday in August.

―――As announced in the July PILGRIM, the response to our appeal for subscriptions to this periodical and contributions to the Shrine has encouraged us to repair the damage done in the ravine by the storms of last autumn, and make some important changes and improvements in the Shrine grounds proper. The chapel is now exclusively for chapel purposes, the dwelling rooms of the priests in charge having been removed from behind the sanctuary. Accommodations have been provided for them by erecting an extension to the structure which last year served them as kitchen and refectory. The old Shrine has been saved from the destruction which threatened it by putting round about it a strong shed, circular in form, and ample enough in size to shelter at least one hundred and fifty persons. A new and larger storeroom has been built, and also a new toilet room for women. These, with other improvements still in progress, will make the Shrine and its surroundings more attractive than ever before. We need not remind our readers that we count on their generosity for the means of defraying the expense of these various improvements.

——During the month of August one or more priests will be in attendance on the pilgrims, saying Mass daily and leading the other devotions, such as the Way of the Cross, the morning and night prayers, the Holy Hour, and when permitted, Benediction of the Blessed Sacrament. We need not remind either those who are fortunate enough to visit Auriesville, or those who are prevented from doing so, that the chief object of the pilgrimages is to honor our Lady at the Shrine erected to her as Queen of Martyrs, with a view to obtaining through her intercession not only what we need for ourselves, but the beatification of the missionaries who died for the faith at this hallowed spot, and of the saintly Indian maiden who was born there, Catharine Tegakwitha, to whose intercession we are happy to ascribe a remarkable cure. Besides invoking our Lady, we may also privately ask God to show forth the proof of the sanctity of these holy souls by granting the favors asked through their intercession.

——"An Iroquois Maiden, The Life of Catharine Tegakwitha," which was begun in the PILGRIM for July, 1898, will be concluded in the September issue. We hope soon to be able to publish in book form the various biographies already printed in the PILGRIM, of the early missionaries whose lives were connected with Auriesville.

CONTRIBUTIONS TO THE SHRINE.

M. C., Soldiers' Home, Cal.	$1 00	H., New York City	$1 00
D. W., Green Farms, Conn.	$5 00	M. B., New York City	1 00
E. McC., Philadelphia. Pa.	1 00	M. L. S. H., Buffalo, N. Y.	5 00
Anon	20 00	A Friend of the Sacred Heart,	3 00
Mr. G., New York City	5 00		

For the benefit of those who may not have seen the July PILGRIM, we publish again the following information about the Shrine for the season of the pilgrimages, 1899.

THE PILGRIMAGES FOR 1899.

WHERE AURIESVILLE IS.

Auriesville is in Montgomery County, New York. It is a station of the West Shore Railroad, forty miles West of Albany, fifty miles east of Utica, 175 miles from New York City, and equi-distant some 265 miles from Philadelphia, Boston, Buffalo, and Montreal.

The New York Central Railroad, the most frequented line of travel, runs parallel with the West Shore, but on the opposite side of the river (the historic Mohawk). Two stations on the New York Central are convenient to Auriesville, Fonda and Tribes Hill, the former three miles west, and the latter one and one-half east. Public conveyances are procurable at a slight charge from either to the Shrine. The New York Central being such an important artery of travel, its greater frequency of trains and superior service make it to many the more desirable route.

Summer Tourists.

Summer tourists on their way to or from Niagara Falls, Thousand Islands, Watkins, Clifton Springs, the Adirondacks, Plattsburgh, and the Lake district of interior New York, who hold tickets calling for travel on the New York Central or West Shore road, have the privilege of stopping over upon notice to the conductor, enabling them to visit the Shrine at their leisure. Visitors at Lake George, Saratoga, or the Catskills can conveniently make the journey back and forth to Auriesville on the same day.

How to Reach Auriesville.

For the benefit of pilgrims who desire to visit the Shrine, we subjoin a schedule of convenient trains:

FROM NEW YORK BY WEST SHORE R. R.

LEAVE.	7†	5*
Franklin Street	11.15 A. M.	9.15 P. M.
West Forty-second Street.	11.35 "	9.30 "
Weehawken.	11.50 "	9.45 "
Arrive Auriesville	5.18 P. M.	

*Daily. †Daily, except Sunday.

11.20 from Penna Depot, Jersey City, connects with train No. 7.

NOTE—Train No. 5 leaving Franklin Street, 9.15 P. M., West Forty-second Street, 9.30 P. M., Weehawken, 9.45 P. M., will stop at Auriesville, on notice to conductor, to let off passengers from New York City, or New England States. Reaches Auriesville 3.50 A. M.

FROM POINTS WEST BY WEST SHORE R. R.

LEAVE.	8†	6*	18*
Buffalo		7.10 P. M.	7.00 A. M.
Rochester		9.05 "	9.10 "
Syracuse		11.25 "	11.40 "
Utica	6.50 A. M.	12.54 A. M.	1.35 P. M.
Fultonville	8.33 "	2.26 "	4.00 "
Arrive Auriesville.	8.40 "		4.13 "

* Daily. † Daily. ‡ Daily, except Sunday.

NOTE.—Train 6 will stop at Auriesville, on notice to conductor to let off passengers from west of Buffalo.

ANNALS OF THE SHRINE. 241

FROM ALBANY BY WEST SHORE R. R.

LEAVE.		FROM N.Y.C.H.R.R. STATION.	
Albany	. . . .	7.30 *A. M.	2.40 †P. M. . . . . . .
South Schenectady	. . . .	8.36 "	4.36 " . . .
Amsterdam . . .	. . . .	9.05 "	5.05 " . . .
Arrive Auriesville.	. . . .	9.18 "	5.18 " . . .

* Daily.   †Daily, except Sunday.

FROM NEW YORK OR ALBANY, BY N. Y. C. & H. R. R.

LEAVE.					
New York	. . . . .	12.10‖A. M.	8.00 *A.M.	10.30†A.M	11.30†A. M
Albany	7.15 †A. M.	8.15 "	1.30 P. M.	3 00 P.M.	5.00 P. M.
Schenectady . . .	7.50 "	8.46 "	2.07 "	3.30 "	5.35 "
Amsterdam . .	8.24 "	9.13 "	2.40 "	3.57 "	6.04 "
Tribes Hill	8.36 "	. .	2.51 "	. . . . . .	6.18 "
Fonda	8.48 "	9.30 "	3.01 "	4.13 "	6.28 "

* Daily.   † Daily except Sunday.   ‖ Daily except Monday.

FROM TROY BY N. Y. C. & H. R. R.

LEAVE.				
Troy	7.35 *A. M.	8.50†A. M.	2.30 † P. M.	4.40 †P. M.
Schenectady	8.46 "	10.08 "	3.30 "	5.35 "
Amsterdam	9.13 "	10.41 "	3.57 "	5.04 "
Tribes Hill	. . . . . .	10.53 "	. . . . . .	5.18 "
Fonda	9.30 "	11.02 "	4.13 "	5.28 "

* Daily.   † Daily except Sunday.

FROM BUFFALO BY N. Y. C. & H. R. R.

LEAVE.	A. M.	A. M.	A. M.	A. M.	A. M.	A. M.
Buffalo . .	. . . . .	. . . . .	. . . . .	4.55†	6.00†	8.05*
Rochester	. . . . .	. . . . .	. . . . .	6.42	8.15	10.00
Syracuse	. . . . .	. . . . .	7.15*	9.25	11.10	12.05
Utica	5.50†	7.00*	9.20	11.10	1.20	1.45
Fonda	7.29	8.40	11.04	12.41	3.16	3.02
Tribes Hill	7.38	8.49	11.14		3.26	. . . .
	A. M.	A. M.	A. M.	M.	P. M.	P. M.

* Daily.   † Daily except Sunday.

HUDSON RIVER STEAMERS—DAY.

Leave New York, Desbrosses Street Pier, 8.40 †A. M., West 22d Street Pier 9.00 A. M.   Leave Brooklyn, Fulton Street (by Annex), 8 A. M. Arrive Albany 6.10 P. M., connecting with West Shore or New York Central & Hudson River R. R.

† Daily except Sunday.

ALBANY BY PEOPLE'S LINE—NIGHT.

Leave New York, Pier 32, N. R., foot Canal Street, 6† P. M. Arrive Albany 6 A. M. Connects with West Shore 7.30 A. M. train which leaves N. Y. C. station, Albany, and arrives at Auriesville 9.18 A. M., daily.

† Daily except Sunday.

FROM BOSTON BY BOSTON & ALBANY R. R.

LEAVE.						
Boston	5.00†	A. M.	10.30*	A. M.	11.00*	P. M.
Worcester	6.33	"	11.42	"	12.28	A. M.
Springfield	8.33	"	1.14	P. M.	4.15	"
Pittsfield	10.28	"	2.52	"	6.11	"
Chatham	11.23	"	. . .		7.07	"
Albany	12.10	M.	4.15	"	7.57	"

* Daily.   † Daily except Sunday.

PHILADELPHIA TO NEW YORK BY PENN'A. R. R.

LEAVE.	A. M.	A. M.	A. M.	A. M.	A. M.	A. M.	A. M.
Philadelphia	5.15*	6.50†	7.38†	8.25*	9.50*	10.21*	11.00†
Trenton	6.04	7.44	. . .	9.10	. . .	. . .	11.44
Newark	. . .	8.57	. . .	. . .	. . .	. . .	. . .
Jersey City	7.32	9.10	9.21	10.25	11.40	12.31	12.55
New York	7.43	9.23	9.38	10.38	11.53	12.43	1.08
	A. M.	A. M.	A. M.	A. M.	A. M.	M.	P. M.

LEAVE.	A. M.	M.	P. M.	P. M.	P. M.
Philadelphia	11.10†	12.00†	4.02*	4.22‡	5.00†
Trenton	12.12	12.45	4.47	. . .	5.47
Newark	. . .	. . .	. . .	. . .	6.57
Jersey City	1.47	1.55	6.10	6.20	7.11
New York	2.00	2.08	6.23	6.30	7.23
	P. M.	P. M.	P. M.	P. M.	P. M.

* Daily.   † Daily except Sunday.   ‡ Limited express, composed entirely of parlor coaches, on which extra fare is charged.

NOTE.—The 8.25 A. M. train from Philadelphia makes direct connection with the 11.20 A. M. West Shore, which leaves from Penn'a. Depot, Jersey City, arriving at Auriesville, 5.18 P.M.

FROM MONTREAL BY DEL. & HUDSON R. R.

LEAVE.		
Montreal	8.40 † A. M.	7.00* P. M.
Plattsburg	11.00 "	9.35 "
Saratoga	3.05 P. M.	1.35 A. M.
Troy	4.15 "	2.40 "
Albany	4.10 "	3.0 "

* Daily.   † Daily except Sunday.

NOTE.—Trains from Montreal, Plattsburg, Saratoga, and intermediate points make good connections at Albany with the West Shore or N. Y. Central R. R.

With the consent of the Right Rev. Thomas M. A. Burke, Bishop of Albany, in whose diocese Auriesville is situated, a Confraternity of Our Lady of Sorrows was established last year, with the altar of Our Lady of Martyrs in the old shrine as the central altar of its devotions. Hitherto the Fathers attending the Shrine have been empowered, by the kindness of the Servite Fathers, to bless the beads of the Seven Dolors and invest with the scapular of the same title. Now, by the faculties to be received from the Father-General of the Servites, the Father in charge of the Shrine will admit as members of the Confraternity of Our Lady of Sorrows all the pilgrims who wish to be received into it, and extend to them the right to gain the various Indulgences attached to its practices of devotion.

The origin, object and organization of the Confraternity of Our Lady of Sorrows are as follows :

In the middle of the thirteenth century, seven noblemen of Florence, who are now honored as saints, founded in their native city the Order of Servites, or Servants of Mary. Their chief object was to meditate on the sorrows of the Blessed Virgin, and to spread devotion to her as the Mother of Sorrows among the faithful. The Order adopted the rule of St. Augustine, and was approved by Alexander IV., in 1255. It grew and spread very rapidly, especially under St. Philip Beniti and St. Juliana Falconieri, in whose time it numbered fully ten thousand religious.

The founders of the Servites were accustomed to give to the faithful, who adopted their practices of devotion to the Mother of sorrows, a small scapular, the "Black Scapular," as it is called, as a sign of their special devotion to the sorrows of our Lady; and all who wore this scapular, constituted the Confraternity of Our Lady of Sorrows. This Confraternity increased very rapidly, and found favor everywhere in the Church, many Popes granting its members numerous indulgences and privileges.

To become a member of the Confraternity of Our Lady of the Seven Sorrows, one must be invested in the Black Scapular by a priest who has been empowered by the General of the Servites to receive members, or appointed by the same authority as Director of a branch of this Confraternity. When receiving members, he invests them with the Black Scapular, and enrolls their names in the Confraternity register ; and he may also bless for them the beads of the Seven Dolors, thus extending to them the right to gain all the indulgences attached to the various practices of the Confraternity, and to share in its privileges.

The indulgences are: Plenary.   1. On the day of the reception in the Confraternity.

2. On the day of the solemn Feast of Our Lady of Sorrows, the third Sunday in September, or, in case of impediment, on one of the seven following days.

3. At the point of death.

4. On one of the Sundays of the month, by joining the procession in honor of our Lady of Sorrows.

5. On Passion Sunday, by meditating in the church on the Sorrows of Mary and the Passion of Jesus.

To gain these Indulgences, confession and communion are required. When the visit to the church is enjoined, we must pray in it for the peace of Christian princes, the extirpation of heresy, and the welfare of Holy Church. This visit may be made, as a rule, from the first vespers of the Feast to the sunset of the feast day itself. The church spoken of here and hereafter is always the church or chapel where the Confraternity exists, or, in case of great distance, the parish church.

Indulgences granted for reciting the Rosary of the Seven Dolors.

1. An Indulgence of two hundred days for every Our Father and Hail Mary, said upon blessed Rosaries, to all the faithful, who, being contrite for their sins and having confessed them, or having a firm purpose of confessing them, shall recite the said Rosary in any church of the Order of the Servants of Mary.

2. The same Indulgence for reciting the Rosary in any place on Fridays, as well as on the Feast of the Seven Dolors, during its octave, and on all days in Lent.

3. An Indulgence of one hundred days, when recited on any day of the year.

4. An Indulgence of seven years and seven quarantines for reciting it entirely, either alone or with others.

5. An Indulgence of one hundred years for reciting it devoutly after confession, or having the intention to go to confession; provided, the Rosary has been received directly from one of the Religious of the Servants of Mary.

6. An Indulgence of one hundred and fifty years for reciting it devoutly on Mondays, Wednesdays and Fridays, and on all holidays of obligation, when one is contrite for his sins, confesses them, and has received the Rosary, as mentioned in the foregoing, and carries it.

7. An Indulgence of two hundred years for reciting the Rosary after confession, when one prays for the exaltation of our Holy Mother the Church, for the extirpation of heresy and for the welfare of the Church.

8. An Indulgence of ten years to those who wear the Rosary about themselves, whenever sorry for their sins, and having approached

confession and holy communion, they assist at Mass, hear a sermon, accompany the Blessed Sacrament when brought to the sick, act as peacemakers, bring sinners to their duties, devoutly recite seven Our Fathers and seven Hail Marys, or any work of mercy, spiritual or temporal, in honor of our Lord Jesus Christ, or of the Blessed Virgin Mary, or of their patron.

9. A plenary Indulgence once a year for reciting it four times a week, to be gained on any other day of the year, if recited again on that day after confession and communion.

10. A plenary Indulgence once a month for reciting it entirely every day, having gone to confession and communion, and prayed for the exaltation of our Holy Mother the Church, for peace and harmony between Christian princes, and for the extirpation of heresies.

The privileges of the Confraternity of Our Lady of Sorrows are:

1. All the associates who, on account of sickness or by any legitimate cause cannot visit the church of the Confraternity, may gain the Indulgences by having their confessor name some other good work for them to perform instead.

2. By a recent grant of His Holiness Pope Leo XIII., members who live in a place where there is no church of the Order, or of the Confraternity of Our Lady of Sorrows, can gain the Indulgence attached to visiting one of its sanctuaries by visiting their own parish church.

3. All the Indulgences given above are applicable to the souls in Purgatory.

4. All the members of the Confraternity have a share in the merits and good works of the Order of Servites.

The rules recommended to the members are:

1. To go to confession and communion on the day they are enrolled, in order to gain the plenary Indulgence.

2. To recite daily the *Our Father* and *Hail Mary* seven times, in honor of the Seven Dolors.

3. To recite at least once a week the Rosary of the Seven Dolors.

4. To fast, or to practise any other mortification on the vigils of our Lady's Feasts, and on all Fridays of the year.

5. To visit the altar of our Lady of Sorrows, and to go to confession and communion on the two principal Feasts of the Dolors, the third Sunday of September and Friday in Passion week, and on the third Sunday of every month.

6. To pray for the welfare of the Servite order.

N. B.—These rules are not binding. Those who omit them only lose the Indulgences attached to them.

Advantages to those who practise a tender devotion to Our Lady of Sorrows as revealed to St. Mathilda and St. Bridget.

1. Contrition at the hour of death.

2. Assistance in all their afflictions, and especially at the hour of death.

3. Jesus Christ will imprint on their hearts compassion for His sufferings and the sorrows of Mary, that He may hereafter reward them for it in heaven.

4. Jesus promised His mother, who had suffered so much on His account, that He would grant whatever grace may be to the advantage of those amongst her children who are devout to her Sorrows.

TÉRÈSE AND PIERRE.

BY K. A. HENNESSY.

(*Continued.*)

Chapter II.

Through Many Perils.

IN the meantime Father Le Mercier, whose strength had happily been restored, informed M. Dupuy of his intended visit to Onondaga, and the commandant at once placed fifteen of his best soldiers at the missionary's disposal. Together they all set out for the Indian village and the inhabitants, forewarned of their approach, came forth in numbers to greet them. Upon entering Onandaga, Father Le Mercier's military escort fired a salute, and this increased the delight of the savages who were all curiosity to see how matters would proceed, and all eagerness to show the Europeans every possible mark of hospitality and respect.

What a contrast was this triumphal entry to that of poor Father Jogues amongst the Mohawks, when he and his companions were forced to run the gauntlet of torture and submit to every torment which cruel, savage instinct could suggest.

To the Frenchman, too, the event was a decided novelty. To be received with open arms by these wild children of the forest, be assured of their good will and friendship, be welcomed into their cabins, dined by their chiefs, invited to smoke the calumet with their elders and be catered to by the wary, agile, young warriors to whom the scalping of a European would once have given the most sanguine satisfaction, was strange almost beyond realization. But it was nevertheless true. Here was this handful of Frenchmen, headed by a courageous priest, in the midst of hundreds of barbarians who were vieing one with another in heaping kindness and attention upon their pale-faced guests. Besides, delegates from the various tribes of the Iroquois nation came to tender their respects and worm their way into the good graces of the Frenchmen, and, for a week, the village of Onondaga was the scene of hilarious excitement.

Then, on July 24th, Achiendasé (1) was given fresh proof of the esteem in which he was held as, at a council convened on that date, he was chosen arbitrator between the Senecas and Mohawks. A Seneca captain had been slain by Mohawks somewhere in the vicinity of Three Rivers, but, great as was the feeling of animosity harbored by the murdered Indian's friends, against the tribe to which his assassins belonged, Father Le Mercier succeeded in making peace between the foes and, before the council closed, valuable presents were exchanged between the Frenchmen and Indians of the different tribes. Then Father Chaumonot, who was thoroughly conversant with the Iroquois language, harangued the savages in such ardent and eloquent terms that they were fairly aglow with zealous determination, and many of the Frenchmen present were moved to tears. Surely this auspicious event presaged a rich harvest of souls.

Chapter III.
Life at St. Mary's, Gannentaha.

Upon his return from Onondaga, Father Le Mercier found that the building of which he had dreamed had really begun to assume very fair proportions, and the soldiers who had formed his escort also lent willing hands to the accomplishment of what one and all had so much at heart. But many and severe were the experiences lived through while the Fort was in course of construction. The felling of trees, drawing of lumber, sawing of wood, besides the clearing of a site and

---

(1) Father Le Mercier's Iroquois name.

digging of a foundation, were far from being either an amusing or pleasant occupation; but the workers did not lose courage and their expectations were happily realized when, as the result of their labor, a fortress-like residence, its cupola surmounted by a large wooden cross, crowned the brow of a picturesque hill near the lake shore.

The Onondagas who came and went daily, gazed in wonderment at the "great house" as they called it, and manifested such eagerness to see its interior that many, indeed, were the visiting parties which, conducted by a missionary or soldier, examined its numerous conveniences. In fact, it seemed as though all Onondaga had turned out in small detachments to view the beauties of the white men's home. And the Indians had not been slighted, for during the month of August a chapel had been built in their very midst, and all augured well for peace and harmony between the dwellers by the lake and their dusky brethren a few miles inland.

But the reaction of the hardships borne during their rough journey from Quebec, coupled with the strain brought on by overwork and the ill-effects due to change of climate and diet, resulted as might have been expected, and about all of the fathers and Frenchmen fell ill. Then came a great test of their moral stamina. Far from home and friends, deprived of tender care and proper nourishment, it required the utmost strength of purpose to keep their courage from ebbing fast. How long seemed the days, how intolerable the nights, and how cheerless the surroundings! How the poor sufferers missed the affectionate ministrations of mother and sister and the comforts of their distant homes! But their deplorable condition aroused the sympathy of the Onondagas, both men and women, who came, dispensed their herb remedies and prepared food which, though cooked in savage fashion, did its part towards recuperating lost strength, and as a consequence, the patients recovered far more rapidly than they could have hoped.

Then began the routine of regular life. The Fort was a spacious building, including living apartments, a large refectory, which at times was converted into a council chamber; a chapel, granary, kitchen, lumber room, military store-room and great subterranean cellar. The fathers divided their duties, two usually residing at Onondaga, some going about through the cabins instructing and catechizing the Indians, and others remaining at the fort to receive any of their spiritual charges who might wish to consult them.

Nor could the Frenchmen afford to idle. There was ample work for all, and while some cultivated the fields and others fished in the lake and neighboring streams, others still penetrated the woods, bringing thence all the game that they could lay low. Moreover the household cares were not few. A large family was to be fed and lodged and several worthy individuals were required constantly on hand to play the roles of cook, housekeeper, etc.

One morning as Father Le Mercier came back from a stroll on the lake shore, where he had been reading his office, he met two young Frenchmen returning from an early fishing expedition. Upon observing the priest they respectfully doffed their caps and Father Le Mercier graciously returned the salute, greeting them with a hearty : " *Bon jour, mes enfants.*" Then, addressing the taller of the two, he said :

"Pierre, may I ask you to go to Onondaga for me? I wish to send Father Chaumonot a package and thought perhaps you would be kind enough to take it to him."

" I shall do so with pleasure, Father. Will it answer if I go this afternoon ? "

" To be sure, my son. I shall give you the parcel in the refectory after dinner." Then, turning to Pierre's companion, the priest continued :

"And will you also do me a favor, Jules? I told Guillaume Beauchamp that I would ask you to make a new paddle for his canoe. Will you have any leisure to-day?"

"Yes, Father," the young Frenchman cheerfully replied. The missionary smiled kindly.

"It is indeed a pleasure to have such obliging friends," he said, and then, before retiring, inquired affectionately for Pierre Boudreau's scalded hand. Pierre held up the afflicted member and assured the priest that it was healing nicely.

"In fact, Father," he continued, "I think that I shall soon be able to use it. Those Indian remedies are certainly very effective."

"They are indeed, and you may consider yourself fortunate when your arm escaped;" and so saying the priest withdrew.

"Say, Pierre," remarked his companion when the two were left alone, "you never told me how you met with that accident. It occurred at Onondaga, did it not?"

"Yes. When I was over there last week with Father Le Mercier, we spent an hour or so in Orrewati's cabin, and an Indian girl, when handing me a bowl of boiling sagamite, struck against my shoulder and away went the steaming stuff down my jacket sleeve and over my left hand. It was badly scalded, and I suppose I showed the intense pain I felt, because the look of mingled embarrassment and regret on that girl's face was really pitiful to see. She apologized and hastened to get some grease which she applied, and then, taking my handkerchief, bound up the poor hand as skillfully as though she had been trained in one of our French hospitals. Really, she's the most civilized savage I've ever met, and her eyes, Jules, are positively glorious."

"Is she Orrewati's daughter?" inquired Jules, evidently interested.

"Yes, but you'd never think it. She bears no resemblance whatever to the gruff old fellow. His wife must be dead, because the daughter was the only woman there except an old slave. Really, Jules, the girl mystified me. She's beautiful beyond doubt, and her manner is quite as refined as that of many a French girl reared in the heart of civilization."

"Now see here, old fellow," and Jules slapped his companion playfully on the back, "your head is just a wee bit turned. Because we've been roughing it to such an extent out in these wilds and have been awhile without meeting any of the choicer specimens of womankind, and you've chanced upon one Indian girl of somewhat finer fibre than the rest, you unconciously magnify her charms. It's not fair, I think, for you to compare an uncouth child of the American forest with the winsome maidens of our loved France. Come, come, my boy, no more such high treason."

Pierre took the reproof very good-naturedly, but it did not have any great weight, and when later in the day he set out for Onondaga the hope of meeting the object of his admiration was uppermost in his breast. Indeed, strange as it may seem, when he reached the outskirts of the village hers was the first familiar face he saw. She was picking berries from a bush near which he passed, and upon hearing his footsteps looked up to see who was coming her way. As soon as their eyes met she recognized Pierre, and stepping forward said: "How is thy hand?" The directness and simplicity of her inquiry pleased the young man, and meeting her on her own ground, he replied:

"Almost well, I thank you. I applied the remedy you gave me and it has worked wonders; you were very kind."

"Kind!" she exclaimed. "What less could I have done when I had caused thee so much pain? Is there aught else that I may do for thee?"

"Perhaps so," he answered promptly. "Achiendasé has sent me on a message to Father Chaumonot; can you tell me where to find him?"

"He is probably in his own lodge with the children. Each day at this time he instructs them. Knowest thou where is the blackgowns' cabin?"

"No, but will you be good enough to guide me there?" She looked steadily at him for a moment, then slowly but emphatically shaking her head replied:

"I may not go with thee, but I can point the way."

Pierre questioned her no further and together they started villageward. Many of the Indians whom they met paused and looked after them, but the girl seemed in no wise disconcerted, and talked to her companion without any apparent restraint. She said that she had no acquaintance with any of the blackgowns except Achiendasé, who had been at Orrewati's cabin during the previous week, and that she seldom went in the near neighborhood of the fathers' lodge, and then she proceeded to tell him how anxious she was to see the Fort at Gannentaha.

(*To be continued*)

FROM THE MISSIONS.

A BRIEF ACCOUNT OF THE INCIPIENT MISSION OF NELLIKUNJA.

This part of India, where the Mission of Nellikunja is situated, namely South Canara, is one of those parts where the Christians and, indeed, of high caste, are most numerous. In this, comparatively, small district of the Madras Presidency there are more than 70,000 Catholics, of whom many are Brahmins, converted "*en masse*" by the Jesuits and other religious orders, before their immigration into Canara from the territory of Goa more than three centuries ago. Notwithstanding this large number of Christians, the Pagans are far more numerous; for, the whole district numbers altogether not less than one million inhabitants, of whom all are non-Christians, with the exception of those 70,000 Catholics, of 4,000 to 5,000 Protestants and of about fifty more of other creeds.

This being the state of things, the Superiors of the Mangalore Missions have been anxious for several years to do something for so many people who sit in the darkness of death, but as the Venetian Province of the Society of Jesus took over charge of this mission from the Carmelite Fathers only in 1879 and as the mission consisted, in the beginning, only of seven fathers and two lay brothers, it was not possible to undertake the work of the missions among the Pagans, on a large scale, the more so that in the second year after our arrival here, we started a College, which required a large teaching staff of fathers. Notwithstanding these difficulties, in May, 1882, a father was sent to work among the Pagans; but, as soon after the monsoon rain set in and, after the subsidence of the monsoon, the missionary was recalled on urgent affairs, not much was concluded, and in April, 1883, the mission among the Pagans was given up with the hope of resuming it when the mission could dispose of more subjects. The interruption, however, lasted rather long; for, only last year (1898) it was decided to resume the work and the consequence was that I had the great fortune of being sent here towards the end of 1898 for the purpose of resuming the work I had interrupted, through unavoidable circumstances, in 1883. Before, however, settling here, in September and October, 1898, I went on an excursion in S. Canara to find out a proper place to begin with and having at last come to this place and having found it to be so, I came here definitely on the 31st of December, 1898, not indeed to remain here only, but to make Nellikunja so to say the centre of my excursions. I may state from the outset that the method I intend to follow is (according to the Provincial Council of Bombay held in 1893 but published only last year) not to go about and preach to the gathered multitudes, which here are not to be found out of town, except at the time of their fairs and feasts, but to choose some quiet place far from towns and from the influence of the materialistic civilization and of Protestantism, to start there a school, to give medicines and the like and thereby to come into friendly communication with the Pagans, who then may be gained to Jesus Christ.

This place where I am and keep my headquarters, is about forty miles to the southeast of Mangalore, the capital of the District of S. Canara. Physically, the place is most picturesque, as it consists of small and big hills like mountains, valleys thickly peopled, between the hills. To a great extent it is covered, in the villages, with arecanut trees in great abundance, and with palm trees; out of the villages with forests of wild trees, where wild animals as tigers, cheetas, porcupines, etc., are very frequent. Nay, two tigers, I am told, live constantly in a cave not a mile distant from my hut. If they are not there now, they were there not long ago, and make their howling heard by night when they go about for prey. Socially, not to mention their ethnological character, which would take too long, they are very ignorant, the great majority not knowing how to write their own name. In religion, if we except few Christians and some Maplas, interspersed among them, they are almost all followers of the Hindoo religion, though I doubt whether they know, theoretically, anything more than the name of Hindoo religion; they go, however, once a year, or even oftener, to their temples, and practise superstition, etc. In this place there are a few temples, but none or scarcely any person appointed to conduct the service. Some of these people *i. e.*, the Brahmins, are supposed to worship the so-called Hindoo god; the lower castes, however, worship expressly the devil as such, and have temples expressly dedicated to the devil. Philologically, one should think that the confusion of languages at Babel took place here, for there are not less than five languages spoken within three miles by a comparatively large number of people : these five languages are Marathi, Konkani, Tulu, Kanarese, Malsalam, spoken, mostly, in a corrupt form. This increases much the difficulty of the work, for, the missionary has to speak to them in their own language if he wants to make himself acceptable to them. The reasons of such multiplicity of language are these, that the inhabitants of this country are, to a large extent, immigrants from the North, as the Konkanies and the Marathas, and that this place is bordering on Malabar; hence Malsalam. Tulu seems to be one of the primitive languages of this place. Kanarese has been imported from the outlying Karnakaka.

When mentioning above "my house," one must not undersiand a regular house, as the name implies. It is a wretched hut with four walls of mud, which, in addition are full of cracks, through which one can see the sky, which hut, therefore, can scarcely afford shelter against sun and rain, and may fall at any moment if rain penetrates through the cracks of the walls. Since I am here, *i.e.*, the last twenty days, rain having fallen nearly every day, the hut was full of rain-water which penetrated through all sides and against. I do not know how to protect myself and find a shelter; for, it leaks, I may say, in every corner.

As to the mode of life here, one has to be satisfied with rice; for scarcely anything else can be found, even paying for it a high price. No meat, no bread, no eggs, no milk (except that of she-buffaloes) can be found here. When I came from Mangalore, I brought with me some toasted bread which was to last about two months. As to milk, I purchased some tins of condensed milk, which, however, after some time became very disgusting. But the salvation of souls deserves this and much more.

After these introductions, I may begin to speak of the work of the Mission. As the attempt to convert these people *en masse* *i.e.*, going in search of men purposely and appointing a father only for this work, is quite new here, and as there is a great probability that if these Pagans, in whom the fanaticism for Hindooism is not extinct, would know the real object of my coming to this place, they might create obstacles to my work, in the beginning I have only told them that having heard of their desire of having a school opened in their midst, I had come to satisfy this want of theirs. For various events, over which I had no proper control, I could not actually begin and open the school, and this on a small scale, but on the 20th of March, though I had tried from the very beginning to start it, so many were the difficulties thrown in my way, against such an apparently easy thing. God in His Providence deigned to send me from the very beginning several trials which give me hope of God's blessing over this work, *e.g.*, the person whom I had taken with me as catechist and schoolmaster, got sick repeatedly, and I had to send him back. This was one of the reasons of the delay in opening the school.

At present my plan is to try to gain over some landlords of the place, not so much Brahmins, as those of inferior caste, who are more amenable to reason and faith, first because their example may be of influence in the conversion of others; secondly, because it is to be expected that some at least of their tenants will embrace the Christian religion; thirdly, because the attempt to convert tenants or quasi-slaves without gaining their landlords and masters, may lead to very great difficulties, as they may be expelled by their masters at any moment and their support would devolve on the mission. Thereby it is not intended to put aside the tenants, some of whom offer bright hopes of conversion, but it is intended to attempt the conversion also of the landlords who have tenants under themselves. From this it appears that conversions at least *en masse* are not to be expected from the very beginning, according to ordinary providence, because first I must try to speak to them by actions rather than by words, to gain their friendship, esteem and confidence, and then attempt their conversion. Notwithstanding this sweetness of method, it is to be anticipated that many new Christians and catechumens will be in need of help, not indeed to become Christians, but because by becoming Christians they have lost everything and must be supported until they find their way to support themselves. Moreover in this work we must make use of catechists (and indeed more than one) who are to go to prepare the way to the missionary and lead the people to him, for if we Europeans enter directly their houses, without first preparing us the way through the native catechists, they, the Pagans, would not deal freely with us, whereas those Hindoos are far more free with the natives, and these in their turn, are more with them, and thus they understand each other. Now, if we want that our catechists do their work properly, they must be paid, and indeed well paid; for their work is not an easy one, but one of much fatigue. If God blesses this work, as I hope He will in His mercy, after the conversion of a certain number of Pagans they will have to be organized in a body, with chapels and many other things necessary to a new Christianity. These things will require a good deal of money, and although at present I am just beginning the work, I cannot wait to ask for some help till the actual moment comes when help will be required; for in that case, before I get anything from such a distant country months may elapse; meanwhile the works for which help is required may suffer much, or may even be entirely spoilt, or the help may come too late. Though not actually in urgent need of help while I am writing these lines, the time will come very soon I hope, when I shall be in need of help, perhaps before these lines are read by the benevolent supporters of the mission. For this reason I apply now, through you to those generous souls who are in a position to give some help and to promote thereby, the glory of God and the salvation of souls. May the Sacred Heart of Jesus who gave His life for each soul, inspire the readers of these lines to come to the relief of so many souls. I do not ask help for my sustenance, for in this wilderness I require very little; some rice and toasted bread are sufficient for me, and for this sustenance of mine my mission can afford to give me help; but it cannot afford to give me what is required for the wants of my mission (as mentioned above), as it has to satisfy many other more pressing and immediate wants of this place or diocese, to which it has first to attend. Any small amount will be received with gratitude. If any help comes to me from any country, as I hope it will, I shall not fail, *Deo volente*, to give to the supporters of my mission further information about the same, and about the wants which their timely help satisfied.

Acknowledgment is made of the following contributions:

FOR NEEDY MISSIONS.	FOR ZAMBESI MISSION.
J. G., Troy, N. Y. $1 35	Miss S., New York City . . . $5 00

THE PILGRIM

OF

OUR LADY OF MARTYRS

XV. YEAR. SEPTEMBER, 1899. No. 9.

MATER AMABILIS.

BY REV. C. W. BARRAUD, S.J.

THE people of two villages went out with sword and shield
    In deadly fight to prove their right to a disputed field.
Saint Stephen's Abbot saw them pass and seeing, shook his head;
Then, summoning his monks in haste, "For God's dear love," he said
"Take down the Virgin from her niche; for sore is now our need:
"There will be bloodshed an ye fail; so follow me with speed."
They took the Virgin from her niche upon the high clock-tower,
Adorned with many a wreathed band, with many a carved flower;
And, singing hymns, they all went forth where sounds of strife arose
And set their blessed burden down between those angry foes.
Then, in the sight of all there met with thoughts of vengeance deep,
The Virgin's image bent its head, and, lo! began to weep.
From mouth to mouth the marvel flew, while every quivering hand
Let go the weapon from its gripe, as 'twere a scorching brand;
And side by side those angry men knelt down upon the grass
And swore an oath that from that day all enmity should pass.
But the debated land they gave, with twelve good acres more,
In honor of our Lady's joys, to feed a hundred poor;
In honor of our Lady's joys; for, as they loved to tell,
A smile henceforth on that fair face was ever seen to dwell.

AN IROQUOIS MAIDEN;
OR
Life of Catharine Tegakwitha.
(*Concluded.*)
CHAPTER XVII.

A FEW months after Catharine's death, the French as well as the savages, began to frequent her tomb, to have recourse to her intercession. God was not slow in showing to them how agreeable to Him was this confidence.

At the same time, Father Cholenec felt himself strongly urged to publish all that he knew of the virtues of his neophyte, but he always resisted the thought. In the bottom of his heart, he even disapproved of the homage bestowed on her memory, although, in the midst of his doubts and combats he sometimes went himself to kneel by her tomb, and to pray to her with fervor.

While he thus hesitated, he was called to the village of La Prairie, to visit an inhabitant by the name of Claude Caron, who was in danger of death. This was in the month of January, 1681. He was filled with joy at this news, convinced that God had found for him this occasion in order that the glory of His servant might shine forth. He therefore went first to her tomb, and only set out after praying there with confidence. But when he arrived, his patient was in extremity. He heard his confession, gave him the Holy Viaticum, and then advised him to solicit his cure, through the intercession of the good Catharine. The dying man willingly consented, and made a vow, in case he was restored, to visit her tomb, there to return thanks to her for her intercession.

Before departing, the missionary placed in his hands the crucifix that Catharine was still kissing in her last moments. A few minutes later, while changing the sick man's position, he slipped from the hands of those who were supporting him, and it seemed as if this fearful fall must hasten his death. They succeeded in placing him upon his bed, however, and then awaited his last sigh. What was the surprise of those present, when the sufferer fell peacefully asleep, and on awaking, found himself cured. The doctor from Montreal could not believe his eyes when he saw him the following morning, eating and drinking beside the fire.

As to Father Cholenec, he could only visit him three days later, but it was only to share the joy of the sick man and all his family, and to thank, with them, their holy protectress.

A cure even more extraordinary, perhaps, was that of a poor woman of the Prairie, already a sexagenarian, named Roanez. Reduced to the last extremity, she received the Blessed Sacrament from the hands of Father Cholenec. On quitting her, he exhorted her to put all her confidence in the good Catharine, and left her the crucifix of which we have spoken. She begged her children to suspend it around her neck, and hardly had it been placed there, than she felt herself entirely cured. When the missionary returned to claim it, she would part with it only on receiving a little grain of dust from Catharine's tomb, which she also placed in her breast. But it twice happened, on imprudently putting aside this precious relic, that she was seized by the same illness, and with equal violence. Each time she recovered her health on having recourse to her precious treasure.

The spiritual graces obtained by Catharine's intercession were not less striking. We may cite, among others, the conversion of a poor Indian girl of the Saut Mission, passionately addicted to gambling. From the age of eight years, she had been subject to a cruel malady, whose painful attacks returned each spring time. She was then paralyzed in her members, and all remedies thus far employed had proved useless. The missionary gave her Catharine's crucifix, to hang around her neck, and then urged her to make a Novena in her honor, with the promise to renounce gambling, in case she should be cured. Her prayers were heard on the third day. During the fourteen years that she survived, she remained faithful to her engagement, and never felt a return of her sickness.

The husband of this woman was one day about to yield to despair, and to throw himself into the river to put an end to his life, when, in passing by the tomb of Catharine, it seemed to him as if an invisible hand held him back. After useless efforts to break away from this restraint, he recognized his fault, and recovered his liberty. This event was, for him, the occasion of a complete return to virtue.

All these prodigies confirmed and spread abroad the high reputation for sanctity left by the good Catharine. Recourse was had to her in necessities. Masses and Novenas were offered in her honor, and each day, new favors were the reward of this confidence. It was no longer only in the village of the Saut, or that of the Prairie, that these singular graces were obtained, but at La Chine, a village opposite the Mission of the Saut, and in all the neighboring parishes.

A venerable priest of the Seminary of St. Sulpice, Father Rémi, curate of the parish of La Chine, at first blamed, as rash and imprudent, these testimonials of honor and confidence; but, soon persuaded by his own convictions he was the first to record them. This is how he makes known to Father Cholenec the change in his sentiments.

"I confess to you, Reverend Father, that I was, for some years, incredulous, and for a long time could not persuade myself that God had accorded to the intercession of this poor girl, the innumerable prodigies related to me by my parishioners, and the singular graces they claimed to have received. Finally, I was one day inspired to make the trial on myself. About eight or nine years ago, I became very deaf in the right ear, and, a thing that had never happened to me before, I could not hear confessions on that side. For the space of three months, I tried several remedies, but in vain, when, one day, a virtuous woman who had been cured of the same trouble, by the intercession of Catharine Tegakwitha, asked me to offer a Mass of Thanksgiving for her.

As I was mounting the steps of the altar, it occurred to me that I ought also to solicit of this good girl the cure of my deafness. I then made a vow to celebrate the Holy Sacrifice three times. That same day after Holy Communion, I found myself all at once relieved, and by the end of Mass my deafness had completely disappeared. Since then, I have had such great confidence in that pious maiden, that I have recourse to her in all my needs, spiritual and temporal, and I have never yet been deceived in my expectations.

(Letter to Father Cholenec, March 12, 1696.)

Tuesday, April 13, 1696, anniversary of Catharine's death, this worthy priest, whose virtues and·merits are still known in Canada, came with his parishioners to chant solemn Mass at the Saut Mission, in honor of their common benefactress.

Several Jesuit missionaries also experienced the happy effects of Catharine's intercession. The first was Father John Morain (1), missionary to the Seneca Indians, when he was struck with paralysis, and forced to leave his mission. Taken to the Saut in 1683, he made a Novena in honor of the holy maid, and promised God, in case he was cured, to return to the Iroquois. He obtained the recovery of his health, but the misfortunes of war prevented him from realizing his project.

The second missionary cured by Catharine was Father Bruyas. For some time he found himself deprived of the use of his right arm, and, in consequence, of the consolation of saying Mass. He appealed to Catharine, and on the last day of the Novena, he found himself entirely cured. " The year *1695* must be signalized as the *beautiful year* of Catharine" (la belle année) says one of her historians. It is the one in which it seemed as if God wished to render her glory more brilliant by giving her for theatre, the cities of Quebec and Montreal, and for witnesses, the most distinguished persons of those places. Here are a few examples.

The governor of Canada, M. de Champigny, had lost his voice, in consequence of a stubborn malady of the throat, which lasted two years. After a Novena of prayer, made at the Saut St. Louis, he obtained a complete cure, and in gratitude, Mlle. de Champigny showed admirable zeal in spreading the devotion to the good Catharine.

She was the first to have her likenesses engraved, and to dis-

---

(1) Father John Morain was not a priest when he came to Canada in 1674. After professing two years in the College of Quebec, he was ordained priest, and was successively missionary at the Rivière du Loup, and to the Iroquois. He died at Quebec, February 24, 1688.

tribute them, not only in Canada, but also in France among the most distinguished families of the Court.

A grand vicar of Quebec, canon of the Cathedral Church, and afterwards member of the community of St. Sulpice of Montreal, M. de la Colombière (1) a man of rare talent and virtue still more eminent, suffered during six months from slow fever and a flux of blood, without finding any relief from remedies. He addressed himself to the holy Iroquois maid, and made a vow to return thanks at her tomb, if God restored his health. The same day the fever left him, and, while he was on his way to return thanks, in accomplishment of his promise, he was completely cured. To gratify his piety he passed several days at the Mission of the Saut, and after praying a long time in the chapel where her bones then reposed, he withdrew, after leaving abundant alms in the hands of the poor.

It was about this time that a very remarkable favor was obtained by the family of M. de Granville, a gentleman attaché of M. de Frontenac (2), Governor-General of Canada. He had passed the winter of 1695 at Montreal, and had often heard the illustrious Indian maiden spoken of with admiration. As his piety led him to Catharine's tomb, he gathered there a little of the earth that covered her remains and took it with him on his return to Quebec. The opportunity for testing its virtue presented itself immediately. On reaching home he found one of his daughters, who was still very young, reduced to the last extremity. "You come," said Mme. de Granville, "just in time to see your child expire." "No," responded the father, "she will not die. I bring her cure with me." The husband and wife began to pray together and recommend to the protection of Catharine their beloved child. The young sufferer was given some water mixed with the holy dust, and in a few minutes the child was restored to perfect health.

---

(1) He was a brother of the Jesuit of the same name, confessor to the Duchess of York, and a celebrated preacher.

(2) The Count de Frontenac succeded M. de Courcelle in 1674. Replaced in 1682 by M. de la Barre, he was again sent to Canada as Governor-General in 1689, and died there in 1698.

In the excess of his joy M. de Granville could not refrain from crying aloud, "Miracle! Miracle!" and all the city soon heard from his own mouth what had taken place.

It may be said, however, that it was over the Saut Mission that the Iroquois virgin exercised the greatest benevolence. She had loved it here below as the orphan loves those who lavish upon him a mother's tenderness, but she reserved for it till after her death her choicest benefits.

One loves to think that it is to her that are due the fervor that made the village a paradise, where all the virtues emulously grew, the intrepid courage of its warriors, under all circumstances where their inferior number did not prevent them from coping with numerous enemies, and finally that wholly celestial protection which had more than once warded off from the Mission all the horrors of war. This protection never appeared more visibly that in 1688, when the Isle of Montreal was invaded by 1,500 Iroquois, carrying everywhere carnage and death. A weak palisade protected the Mission of the Saut, but the good Catharine, whom the Christians called to their aid, arrested the enemy, even in the midst of his triumphs, and he did not approach the St. Louis Mission. It would be impossible to enumerate all the marvels due to her intercession. Father Cholenec himself says in the sketch he has left us that he ceased to write down the prodigies of which he was the daily witness, so greatly did they multiply. "Everywhere we go," he adds, "one speaks only of Catharine Tegakwitha and the miracles obtained by her pious patronage."

Why should it not be thus in our own day? Let it revive, then, in our midst and in all the brightness of its glory, this virginal figure, worthy emulator of Genevieve of Nanterre! Holy maiden of the Canadian woods, good Catharine, since it is thus that thou art saluted by the people of Canada, extend forever thy protecting hand over the land where the days of thy mortal life were passed, but remember France also. She gave thee thy Fathers in the faith. In return ask of God, for her children, a part in the glorious inheritance of thy virtues.

TÉRÈSE AND PIERRE.

BY K. A. HENNESSY.

(*Continued.*)

CHAPTER III.

Life at St. Mary's, Gannentaha.

"ORREWATI has been at Gannentaha," she said, "and has told me of how wonderful the Fort is; but I shall soon see for myself as he is to go over to-morrow and will take me with him."

"Your father has business there?"

"Didst think Orrewati my father?" she asked in evident surprise. "He is not, but he is very good to me." Her voice quivered a little as she uttered these last words, but in a moment she continued with perfect self-control: "Yes, he has business there, and when he goes any distance from home he always wishes me to accompany him, because . . . " she hesitated, and observing that she was not about to resume, Pierre made haste to ask:

"And when you come to Gannentaha to-morrow, I shall see you, shall I not?"

"Thou shouldst know that better than I," was her quick reply. "Surely I would be glad to meet thee. But—seest thou that long cabin yonder with a curl of black smoke issuing from its roof?" Pierre looked in the direction which she indicated and nodded assent. "That," she said, "is the blackgowns' home. I may go no further, so must leave thee here."

Impulsively Pierre held out his hand to her but either she did not notice his movement or else failed to realize its import, because, ignoring it, she hastily withdrew, saying, "Au revoir," as she moved away.

These words had almost a paralyzing effect upon the young man, who stood motionless, watching the graceful figure disappear among the trees. His side of the conversation had been quite labored, his knowledge of the Iroquois language being so slight as to preclude any fluent use of it, and now, just at parting, his charming companion had enunciated those two words with such ease and accuracy that he naturally supposed her to be familiar with his mother tongue. The discovery astonished, pleased, mystified him; but this was no time for dreaming so, rousing himself, he proceeded in the direction of the missionaries' cabin.

On his way thither he met a number of the dusky villagers, all of whom smiled blandly and saluted him most graciously but did not otherwise detain him. As he neared the tent, a dozen or more scantily clad small boys and girls bounded forth through the open doorway and scampered off shouting and hooting, evidently rejoicing at their release from the restraint under which they chafed. Father Chaumonot saw them out, stood for a moment looking after them and was about to return indoors when, chancing to see Pierre Boudreau approaching, he went forward to greet the young man, and together they passed into the lodge. After Pierre had made known the object of his errand and delivered the package, Father Chaumonot begged him to partake of some refreshment before starting homeward, and, whilst the young man regaled himself, he and his host exchanged various items of news and discussed the existing state of affairs.

"Of course," explained the missionary, "the present outlook is fair enough. We seem to have gained the good will of these people, but you see, superstition has so strong a hold upon them that our work will therefore be the harder. Moreover, though we are here at their request, the Indian nature is so treacherous that, even while smiling upon us, they may be concocting some diabolical plot for our ruin; therefore, we must be ever on the alert. But, with God's help, we'll accomplish much good."

"Well, Father, have you any avowed enemies here in Onondaga?"

"None of whom I know," replied the priest, "but there are many who, though they never molest us nor interfere with our work, are very dark and distant. However, I always meet them as if they were among my best friends, and, in return, they treat me with a sort of freezing courtesy—if you can imagine such a thing. But there is one old man here who is particularly sinister; Orrewati, they call him, and yet he was politic enough to entertain Father Le Mercier when he was here last week."

"Yes, I know that but too well, Father, because it was on that occasion that my hand was scalded. I was with Father Le Mercier."

"Oh! were you his companion? Then you probably know that Father d'Ablon and I were not in Onondaga that day. Indeed I wish Father d'Ablon were here now, he would be more than glad to see you, but I can not say just where he is at present. He went off to visit a sick catechumen and there is no telling how much else he may do before he returns. But, Pierre, tell me about your unfortunate accident; how did it occur?"

Pierre gave the missionary a detailed account of the affair, and finished by inquiring if he or Father d'Ablon knew the attractive looking maiden who had spilled the sagamite. Father Chaumonot said that they did not, and that she was probably a new-comer in the village, as they had not seen her till about a month previously.

"Some say," he continued, "that she is a captive, but if so, Orrewati does not treat her as such, for she seems to live on the best that the land affords."

"Well," admitted Pierre with perfect simplicity, "she interests me very much, and she is so far above all the other Indian women I've seen that I mean, if possible, to learn the reason of her superiority. Some refining influence has certainly left its impress upon her life."

It was quite late when Pierre Boudreau returned to the fort, but after he had reported to Father Le Mercier he found time to have a chat with his friend Jules and to relate what had transpired during the day.

At breakfast next morning M. Dupuy informed his men that at three o'clock that afternoon he wished them all to appear at headquarters in full uniform, as he intended drilling them on the open in front of the fort. The day was clear and beautiful, and at the appointed time a squad of soldiers paraded from headquarters around to the drilling ground, where at M. Dupuy's bidding they began maneuvering. A group of spectators stood at some little distance and heartily applauded, but the enthusiastic hand-clapping indulged in by the Fathers and Frenchmen who looked on was almost deadened by the hoarse shouts of the Indians who were present to witness the stately military exercise that bore so striking a contrast to their weird, grotesque war dance. The drill over, M. Dupuy paid his subordinates a glowing compliment and ordered them back to the fort, whence in a very short while they dispersed.

It had been announced that for the balance of the day work would be suspended, so that all hands might enjoy a few hours of complete relaxation, and the men sauntered off in different directions, some towards the woods and others lakeward, till the immediate vicinity of the fort was well nigh deserted. Pierre Boudreau was one of the last to leave the premises, and before doing so he made sure that Orrewati and his ward were not among the dusky-faced few who had witnessed the drill. "They'll not come now, because it's so late," he mused as he joined a jolly set of fellows who were starting on a nut-hunt, but there was a vague feeling of disappointment in his heart. A half hour later Father Frémin came out of the fort calling aloud for Pierre Boudreau, but that individual was well out of hearing, being then nearly a mile away. Unsuccessful in his quest, the priest returned to the house and undertook alone the task which he had intended Pierre should share with him, that of showing the interior of the building to an Onondaga who, with a young squaw, had just arrived and wished to interview Father Le Mercier on a matter of business.

The two visitors looked with wonder and admiration upon all they saw and the young woman evinced the greatest interest in her surroundings, listened eagerly to the priest's explanations and proved herself a keen observer by not failing to call his attention to whatever he had omitted pointing out; and when, at length, the chapel was reached, Father Frémin entered it with the utmost reverence and, genuflecting, remained for a moment in fervent prayer. Then rising, he turned only to behold Orrewati standing back against the wall, his arms folded across his breast and a fierce scowl upon his dark face, and as the girl, who had lingered in the hall, was about to enter the sacred enclosure, he thrust out his sinewy hand and, holding her back, exclaimed: "Away, away child, we must go hence; this is no place for us. Why insult Areskouë (1) by tarrying here?" At these words a look of disappointment clouded the girl's sweet face, but she offered no resistance and together they all retraced their steps. Once out of the chapel, Orrewati resumed his affable manner and when the starting-point was reached, Father LeMercier was there awaiting the party and Orrewati immediately proceeded to talk business. At this juncture the maiden asked if she might wait outside the building and, as the old Iroquois was willing, she went forth, leaving him in conference with the two priests.

Having gained the open air, she looked cautiously about and, seeing no one, gave a sigh of relief and sought the shelter of a spreading maple. Here she sat leaning her head against the trunk of the great tree, her wistful gaze travelling far over the bosom of the beautiful lake and her hands clasped loosely in her lap, her whole attitude bespeaking utter dejection. Her reverie was undoubtedly a sad one, for tears stood in her large, dark eyes, and a cloud of sadness overpread her sweet countenance, and so preoccupied was she that she noticed not an approaching footstep.

"What, here and alone?" exclaimed a voice that made her start. Looking up she beheld Pierre Boudreau, and surprised and somewhat disconcerted, she rose to her feet and, as she did so, the tears that trembled on her lids fell to her cheeks. Pierre saw this and for a moment stood irresolute, doubtful whether to speak or not, but as the silence threatened to become embarrassing, he said :

"Can I do anything for you, my friend ? "

"Thou art far too good," she replied, her voice quivering with emotion, "I deserve not such kindness." Then, with an

---

(1) The Indian god of war.

air of determination, she continued: "But this is childish and I am a woman now. Do not scorn me for this weakness; perhaps some day thou wilt know the reason of it. It ill becomes an Iroquois to thus yield to her feelings, but," she pointed to her heart, "there are other forces at work here than those which the ordinary Indian girl has to combat."

That she had intended paying herself a compliment Pierre could not believe, but he nevertheless felt the truth of her intimation—that she was no ordinary Indian girl.

"Fear not," he said reassuringly, "I scorn not those who merit only my sincere respect. Could I but help you I would be happy indeed, and if, at any time, you feel that I might be of service to you, do not hesitate to call on me. Will you promise me this?"

"Yes, I promise thee freely, gladly, for I need a friend." She then lapsed into a sad, dreamy mood, and it was some moments before either of them spoke. Then, suddenly looking up, she asked:

"Thou wilt have to work to-morrow?"

"Yes," he replied, "to-morrow we must once more face work. But I regret it not, I am happier when occupied. In the morning I start out to fish in a stream not far distant, mine being the duty to provide sufficient fish for our evening meal at the Fort. You see, each of us has his assigned task."

"Thou goest alone?" she inquired, her brow slightly knitted and her eyes fixed upon the ground as if seeking there the solution of the problem which seemed to perplex her. "Well," she continued, as though thinking aloud, "we do not return to Onondaga till the morrow. We will spend the night in Garistarsia's lodge, so, if Orrewati agree to my accompanying thee, would I, thinkest thou, prove too great a burden for thy canoe?"

"Assuredly not," Pierre cheerfully replied, "I would be glad to have you with me."

"Well, if Orrewati oppose me not, I shall meet thee at the fort as early as thou mayest wish to start. When will that be?"

"Just after the second roulade, which will be beat upon the drums a couple of hours after sunrise."

"Then I shall be at hand," declared the girl, "but if I appear not on time, delay not thy departure, as I shall be prompt unless Orrewati forbid me."

"And should he do this?" Pierre inquired anxiously.

"Then I know not when we shall meet again. It is because I dare not trust the future that I have determined to talk with thee on the morrow."

Scarcely had she uttered the last word when she perceived Orrewati beckoning to her, and in a trice Pierre found himself alone, the maiden having flown rather than run in the direction of the fort.

Chapter IV.
An Exchange of Confidences.

Through a dense wood, situated about a mile to the east of St. Mary's at Gannentaha, there flowed a broad stream, which, with innumerable and fitful curves, wound its way in and out among the tall umbrageous trees like some great serpent intent upon baffling pursuit. On this beautiful October morning its placid bosom was slightly ruffled by the drifting about of a canoe, the two occupants of which, though engaged in earnest conversation, were not neglectful of the task they had undertaken. The Indian maiden, seated in one end of the skiff, heaved a deep sigh, and, looking towards her companion, remarked:

"This scene brings to memory something that occurred full seven times twelve moons ago. It was when my father brought me from our home at Ossernenon to Fort Orange, where he went to trade with some Dutchmen of Beverwyck. We set out on just such a beautiful morn, and the river bank was carpeted with moss as green and soft as this, and the trees were decked with leaves of varied tints, just as are these great giants towering above our heads. Ah! those were happy days!" She paused, and Pierre Boudreau asked:

"Then you have not always lived at Onondaga?"

"No, my time there has been short, and I was brought thither without my knowledge. Mine is a strange, sad story, and I never speak of it, but in thy face I see that which gives me confidence, so may I tell thee all? 'Twill do my heart good to be relieved of its secret."

"Think not that your recital will bore me; on the contrary, I am sure that it cannot fail to interest me, so proceed, I pray you."

"Well, my name is Térèse, and my father was Goneterezon, a Mohawk captain, brave and true. My mother was a Huron princess, but her father was a Frenchman, and she was very unlike the Indian women among whom we lived. Her manner was so easy, her voice so soft, her speech so clear and sweet, her face so beautiful, that she seemed like a creature out of her proper sphere. She was a Christian, and my father, though a staunch pagan, always permitted her to live according to her belief, and, moreover, allowed her to rear me, their only child, in the faith which she professed. When Ondessonk (1) was led a captive to our village she brought me to him secretly, and he poured the saving water of baptism upon my head, but I thank the good God for taking my mother from me before that awful night, some years later, when the noble black-gown was slain and his venerable head stuck up on a post to be jeered and mocked at. Such a sight would, I fear, have broken my mother's heart. When she lay dying she called me to her side, and, grasping my hand in both her own, asked if I would make her a promise. It was this: that I would always remain true to what she had taught me, and that I would never marry a pagan. I made the promise, and so far I have kept it, and, come what may, I hope to keep it to the end. But it has been hard at times to do as she asked.

"After her death my father deprived me of all intercourse with Christians, and forbade me ever to speak to him of my religion. Then I had no one to whom to turn, no one but God and His Holy Mother. Morning and night I prayed to them as my mother had taught me, and often, when alone, I would sing the sweet French hymns I had learned from her. I never knew why the Mohawk braves admired me, it was

---

(1) Father Jogues' Iroquois name.

not because of any encouragement I gave, but many of them paid court to me, though none so persistently as Aharihon, a gallant young captain of Ossernenon. But I had no liking for him, and this deeply grieved my father who saw an advantage in my alliance with so promising a youth. One rival Aharihon feared above the rest, and when they would chance to meet, I could see the jealousy he would fain conceal crop out in many ways. So it was that the days wore on, my father often reminding me that I should not ignore Aharihon's suit, and warning me that I should be settled in life as, in case he should die, I would be alone and unprotected. But I always defended myself by telling him that I could not marry a man I did not love.

"When I heard that Father Le Moyne had come to the Onondagas and was about to visit the Mohawks, I rejoiced to think that I might manage to talk with him; but whether or not my father suspected this, I cannot say; however, under pretext of business, he took me from home and we remained at one of the distant Mohawk castles till the missionary had gone his way. Aharihon's attentions had, by this time, become so annoying that I began to feel a strong dislike for him, and though he must have noticed it, he continued to intrude upon me. But oh! the end of it all!"

She shuddered as she said the last words, and wringing her hands, looked skyward, an expression of anguish distorting her features. Then, after a moment's pause, she resumed her story, though this time her voice was lowered to a whisper, and leaning forward, she rested her clasped hands upon her knee and gazed eagerly into Pierre's face.

"One clear, cold morning, less than eight moons ago, my father said that he must go into the forest to bring home the carcass of a deer that he had slain the day before, and he asked if I would go with him. 'The exercise will do thee good, my little one,' he said, ''twill warm the blood within thy veins and deepen the glow of health upon thy cheek.' I at once made ready to accompany him, and when I brought out my snow-shoes, he stooped and fastened them and then tenderly wound and strapped my bear skin about me, and together we started forth to face the wintry blast.

"On, on we glided over the crusty snow chatting merrily, he sometimes outdoing me in speed, and then suddenly slackening his pace and waiting for me to overtake him. The wind whistled through the trees, their limbs swayed and creaked, and the snow-laden boughs shook off their feathery burden, thus filling the frosty air with clouds of tiny crystals. Suddenly an arrow whizzed by us and buried itself deep in the trunk of a tree close by, and, upon turning quickly to see whence it came, my father staggered and fell, his breast pierced by a second dart.

"It was Aharihon who took the fatal aim, it was he who slew my father, for I saw him fling away his bow and fly, as if for his life. Terrified, I sank to the ground, raised my dear one's head upon my knee, kissed his brow, stroked his hands and called to him to speak. But in vain I held my ear to his dear lips, and, to my horror, I saw that the snow beneath us was dyed with his life's blood. In an agony of grief and fear I cried aloud for help, but no answer came, nothing save the echo of my own terror-stricken voice.

"What happened next I know not, but when I awoke to consciousness I found myself in Orrewati's cabin, being cared for by an old squaw. Gradually the memory of the horror I had lived through came to me in awful vividness, and, as my strength returned, I ventured to question the old woman who watched me so tenderly. From her I heard the truth. She said that I had been brought there by Orrewati, who had found me almost frozen to death beside my father's corpse in the forest, and that I was now recovering from an illness of many weeks. She also assured me that, though I was not an Onondaga, she knew Orrewati meant to show me every kindness and treat me as a daughter. 'Heed me, my pretty one,' she went on, 'obey him in everything and all will be well; but rouse not his anger, for it is terrible indeed.' This and other advice the old creature gave me, and I learned that she was an old Huron captive and Orrewati's slave.

"One day when I was strong enough to walk about the cabin Orrewati spoke his mind to me. He said that out of the sheerest pity he had brought me to his lodge and ordered his old slave to care for me, and now that I was recovering, he wished to know my history. I related it, without, however, mentioning aught of my religious belief, and when I had finished my recital he said: 'Thou sayest that thou hast neither kith nor kin; well, henceforth I will be to thee as a father, and this shall be thy home; but, think not that I impose no conditions. First, none of our villagers must know how or why thou camest hither, and thou must hold no intercourse either with the blackgowns who are here now, or any that may come later. If I find thee playing false to me and having converse with these base intruders, whom I only tolerate for policy's sake, it will be bad alike for them and thee.' Now, my friend, thou seest my plight. Near as I am to these men of God, I dare not approach them unless in Orrewati's company. Were I alone concerned I would risk all and fly to them, but there is too much else at stake. Their lives are too precious to be put in peril by me. And so I must live on without ever gaining absolution for my faults; must pass for a heathen, when, with all my heart I love God and His Holy Mother."

Having thus unburdened her mind, the girl ceased speaking, and Pierre paused in the work of arranging his fish in the bottom of the canoe, for, though he had been a most attentive listener, he had not neglected hauling in a goodly share of spoil.

(*To be continued.*)

COURAGE!

BY S. T. SMITH.

THE stars are bright beyond the veiling mists;
    The blackest midnight pales to radiant morn;
The wind, wild blowing whereso'er it lists,
    In the far heaven of deep peace is born.

ANNALS OF THE SHRINE.

A small group of pilgrims is following the priest over the Way of the Cross. As I write they are just mounting the hill, and before they come into view I can hear them singing the *Stabat Mater*, the verse for the Eighth Station:

>Fount of love and holy sorrow,
>Mother, may my spirit borrow
>Somewhat of thy woe profound.

For some reason or other they sing it in Latin more frequently than in English, the words,

>Eia, Mater fons amoris
>Me sentire vim doloris
>Fac ut tecum lugeam,

being much sweeter in sound and more expressive than the translation. The Way of the Cross is fully one-third of a mile long, and the Stations are about eighty feet apart from one another, so that there is just time to chant one stanza for every Station. After prayers and blessing with the relic of the Holy Cross at the Calvary the devotion is continued, the priest leading the way to the old shrine, while the others chant the remaining verses of the *Stabat Mater*, and all join in the prayer to our Lady of Sorrows before the Pietà.

* * *

The Way of the Cross is the most frequent if not the favorite devotion here, and has been so since Father Loyzance first erected the Calvary with its circle of fourteen crosses, each the gift of some of his many friends. Even were this devotion not an indispensable one at every Catholic shrine, it would have suggested itself to one who, like Father Loyzance, had in view when purchasing this place the commemoration of Isaac Jogues, who consoled himself during his long captivity here with the reflection that he had been born under the shadow of the Cathedral of the Holy Cross in Orleans, France, and was only earning by his tortures the right to be called "Citizen of the Cross." The first memorial structure raised on these grounds was the large cross donated by the late Father Hourigan, inscribed with the title given to his mission by Father Jogues, The Mission of the Most Holy Trinity, which is brought back to our minds by the sign of the cross. It is now the starting point for the Way of the Cross, which winds about the hill along an avenue planted with young trees, which will soon shade the small, if not the large, groups of pilgrims on this penitential journey, though in time even the two thousand who went over this path last Sunday will be sheltered from the burning rays of the sun. To the credit of all who make the Way of the Cross here it should be said that no one seems to mind the sun, nor has any one ever been harmed by it, and it is a common thing on pilgrimage days to witness from one thousand to three thousand men, women and children at this devotion at midday in August, and the sight is inspiring and memorable. Last week it was very edifying to see some of the men who had gone over the Way during the day returning again to repeat the devotion in the clear moonlight with which we were favored. As the round is made the view is ever changing, the valley, the river at its most beautiful turn, the village, the hills, the Shrine grounds and, not the least, the Stations themselves succeeding one another, and all contributing some stimulus to recollection and piety. The new Stations are the gifts of pious pilgrims, whose intentions are not forgotten, even when they are absent. Some day the figures in these Stations must be life-size, and each group or Station must have its pedestal or grotto.

* * *

The relic of the Holy Cross is the only relic offered for public veneration here, and it is the only one applied to those who come to be relieved of mental or bodily ailments. It is not surprising that a relic of such virtue should be the means of obtaining many singular blessings in a place where everything disposes one to better faith and confidence. We have a relic of Catharine Tekagwitha, but, since she has not been beatified, it cannot be offered for public veneration. It has been used privately, however, and with success, nor is it strange, since her life was so saintly, and since the widespread and enduring veneration for her virtues merit in some way special graces and favors through her intercession.

* * *

The Most Blessed Trinity is honored here because this mission was founded under that august title ; and the Holy Name is also honored because Father Jogues used to honor it specially here and carve it on the trees ; but since it is a Shrine of Our Lady, pilgrims all seem to cultivate in a special manner her title under which she was first venerated in this valley, *Notre Dame de Foye,* which in those days expressed what we now mean by the title "Our Lady of Sorrows," or as we style it here "Our Lady Queen of Martyrs." Prayers are said before the Pietà after the Way of the Cross ; the Seven Dolor beads are in demand and are always recited on the way to the Ravine; the black scapular is also conferred here, and a Solemn Novena is made here yearly in preparation for the feast of the Assumption. In this Novena people join whether it be their good fortune to come to the Shrine or not, and the custom has grown of sending intentions to be placed on the altar. These intentions or petitions for prayers embrace every conceivable object spiritual or temporal, the former especially, and it is gratifying to observe that vocations and conversions figure most prominently as well among the thanksgivings for favors received as among the requests for prayers.

*   *   *

The influence of the League is plainly visible in the way in which these intentions are presented. Promises of prayers and other good works usually accompany them, promises to report favors when obtained to the Editor of THE PILGRIM, to keep candles burning before the altar of the Pietà, to contribute donations or to make a pilgrimage to the Shrine. The resignation manifested in so many of these written intentions show plainly the sweet force of the example of the Sorrowful Mother, and the simplicity with which the prayers are made either through her intercession merely, or through the prayers of the faithful who died here so heroically, proves that pilgrims to Auriesville appreciate the title under which this Shrine has been dedicated, and that they do not lack confidence in our Blessed Mother, or in the power of her servants who died here after honoring her so much.

*   *   *

The number of thanksgivings is quite remarkable this year, more so than in previous years, and the favors received are in many instances extraordinary, some spiritual, some temporal. Indeed, the character of many of them induces one to be more careful in keeping record of names and of data which, though they do not make the answers to prayer miraculous, or even marvellous, at least make them so clear and definite, that they increase the confidence and fervor of the clients of Our Lady of Martyrs and help to prove the power of the intercession of those who were put to death here for the faith. Thus one comes to report the solution of difficulties about a vocation ; another has won back a wandering father to his home and to the faith ; one has obtained patience under great trials; another relief from falling sickness ; a sufferer from violent headaches returns to the Shrine to thank our Lady for her cure ; a mother comes each year with a young son once crippled and helpless, who began to walk and grow strong after his first visit here ; a happy looking young man comes from a distant place the fourth time, this year with his bride, to report that at last he considers his cure from lung trouble and other internal disorders so certain that he wishes to make public thanksgiving for it. The Novena made here prior to the 15th of August was particularly favored by many blessings sought for both by the pilgrims stopping here, and by those whose intention they recommended.

* * *

It is strange to hear the notions which some people, Catholics as well as Protestants, have about a Shrine. They imagine there must necessarily be some famous relic, or a curative pool, and sensational miracles occurring daily. Some view it entirely from the business point of view, and, in true modern fashion, suggest a hundred ways of "booming" it, supplying hotels, increasing traffic, etc., as if everything depended on the concourse of people coming to it, whether they came as devout pilgrims or not. Very few can appreciate what it is to have a place of prayer. Those who come here, or who study the sacred association of the site, with the reverence for well founded traditions which is the mark of a Catholic instinct, soon view things with the proper spirit, and go away with the conviction that heaven has favored this spot naturally and supernaturally, and are not surprised to see the number and fervor of the pilgrimages increase from year to year, in spite of obstacles and of the failure, pardon the vulgarism, to " boom " Auriesville and its surroundings.

* * *

Naturally, those who spend some days at Auriesville appreciate the Shrine and the place at their true worth. " It appeals strongly to an intelligent piety," remarked a medical doctor, who spent a week devoutly in pilgrimage here lately, and he added that the place would force one to pray. " There is but one thing against the Shrine," is the parting reflection of many pilgrims, "and that is it is hard to leave it." With few exceptions all return, and every year, during most of the month of August, there are enough pilgrims stopping here to have in common other services besides the daily Mass, such as the Way of the Cross, Night Prayers, and sometimes the Holy Hour. The Shrine Manual contains all these devotions, as well as the others, which are made privately, and the only slight change to record this year was the addition of the *De Profundis* to the night prayers, the bell tolling while priest and people recited it. This year, for the first time, the prayers in honor of the Holy Name, given in the Shrine Manual were said in common after the last Mass, and at Night Prayers during a novena preparatory to the first Friday in September, for the special intentions of the fathers at the Shrine, and also of the visiting pilgrims. With the Ravine in good order next year, we shall be able occasionally to have the devotions there before the Grotto, or at the Oratory and Holy Sepulchre, which we hope to erect before next pilgrimage season.

* * *

——The season for pilgrimages grows longer from year to year, but until more accommodations can be provided at Auriesville, it would be wise to choose some day between July 1st and September 1st for visiting the Shrine, especially with an organized pilgrimage. This year pilgrims came as early as June 11th, as described in THE PILGRIM for August, and the last large pilgrimage will be made on September 3d. As usual, during the month of August, many came to spend a few days or longer in the neighborhood of the Shrine. What with dry weather and better accommodations than in previous years, they had every reason to be pleased with their visit. The number of these pilgrims was about the same as last year, though no special notifications had been given about the pilgrimages in the places whence they came. Next year, with more accommodations for receiving visitors, due notice will be given of the season and route of the pilgrimages early enough to enable all who wish to come here to choose their own time.

——For the first time since the Shrine was established, the fathers in charge of it have lived in their own dwelling this year, and plain and simple as it is, it is quite commodious. The space back of the open chapel, formerly used for their sleeping rooms, has been devoted entirely to chapel purposes, the sanctuary being deepened, the rooms on either side made side chapels for cool weather, and the other rooms turned into sacristy and offices. The old Shrine has been surrounded by a porch, octagonal in shape, and a sash, instead of the heavy blinds of which the sides were made formerly, lets worshippers see the statue and even hear Mass in stormy weather. The old store has been converted into a registry and pilgrim room, and a larger store stands near by. These and other improvements have taken much time, and it will be all we can do to have them finished before we leave here; but it is all-important that everything be done while we are on the spot to superintend the work, and to have the material structures ready so as to be free next year to give our attention to preparing for the greatest event as yet in the annals of the Shrine, the crowning of the statue.

——Before we close the Shrine, about September 8th, we hope to have the Ravine in good order and secure against damage similar to that of last year. All that could be done since the freshets of September and October, 1898, was to restore the road leading down the hill, and terrace with stones the hillside on which the grotto is built. With all this, the Ravine looked sadly changed to those who had been fond of visiting it in other years, and it is only now beginning to take a new and attractive appearance. A bed has been dug for the creek, running from the south, and another for the streamlet, running down the Ravine proper, where, when satisfactorily banked and sloped, some fine bridges will be thrown across these streams, and there will be an ample green sward for the audience during the sermon, which is usually preached below the grotto of our Lady. By having all this done now, we can exercise due supervision, and have the surface both of the road bed and the Ravine ready to sow in the Spring, or even this Autumn. In the glade beyond the creek there will be a grotto of the Holy Sepulchre.

——For all these repairs and changes the pilgrims and friends of the Shrine have been contributing quite generously, and, although we have not secured enough to defray all the expense incurred, we trust that the clients of the Shrine will enable us to keep it as it has always been, a worthy offering to our Lady, clear of debt and of every other obligation.

——Since the question is often asked how may the clients of the Shrine best further its interests, we answer: first, by their prayers, as well for the spiritual purposes for which it has been established, for increasing devotion to our Lady of Martyrs, for proving the intercessory power and virtue of the martyrs who died here, and for obtaining the grace to imitate their zeal and self-sacrifice; and secondly, by prayers for its temporal welfare, for the means to make the necessary purchases and improvements of land, to erect and keep the various structures needed for the pilgrims and ourselves, for the crown, for the new Pietà, for the grotto of the Holy Sepulchre, and at present especially for the improvements in the Ravine.

——Since the number of subscribers to THE PILGRIM has increased of late we should repeat for their benefit what its readers already know, but this we cannot do until our next issue, as the Annals are so long this month. Of all the ways of helping the Shrine, the circulation of THE PILGRIM is the most effective, and our new system of helping subscribers to bring it to the notice of their friends makes it easy for them to increase its subscription list.

THE PILGRIMAGES.

——The second annual pilgrimage from Saugerties and some of the cities on the Hudson above Poughkeepsie took place on July 30, about 150 pilgrims coming under the direction of Father Murray of Saugerties, accompanied by Father Ward, of Wilber, and Father O'Brien of Saugerties. On the arrival of the train at 10:45 Mass was said for the pilgrims, by Father Murray, and after lunch, about 1:15 the Way of the Cross was made. The usual procession to the Ravine, and devotions before the grotto of our Lady, were led by Father Lamb, and Father O'Brien preached the sermon. Benediction of the Blessed Sacrament was given at 4 o'clock and the pilgrims departed at 5. Besides the usual number of sightseers about 100 Catholics came from neighboring cities, and all together made an edifying pilgrimage. In fact, as a result of the edification given by the Saugerties pilgrims a year ago there was one conversion to the faith.

——On Sunday, August 13, about 400 pilgrims came from Albany to the Shrine, under the direction of Mr. Felix McCann, arriving in time for the Mass at 8:30, at which 250 received Holy Communion. On the arrival of 200 pilgrims from Fonda, coming by barge on the canal, under the direction of Father Dolan, pastor of St. Cecilia's, Fonda, Mass was said, at which about 300 others, who had come from Amsterdam, Johnstown and Gloversville, assisted, all in the most orderly manner, and all joined in making the Way of the Cross at 11:30. About 1 P. M.

nearly 1,000 people marched in procession to the Ravine, led by Father Brosnan, who recited the Beads of the Seven Dolors, the pilgrims answering. The Litany of Loreto was sung before the Grotto, and Father Wynne preached on the gospel of the day. In the procession of the Blessed Sacrament, Father Dolan officiating, the men led the way, followed by the choir, altar boys and clergy, the people kneeling on either side of the roads, or following the Blessed Sacrament. At about 4:30 all departed, leaving behind a fine impression of the piety of the Catholics who inhabit this valley.

——Although there was no special pilgrimage on August 15, about seventy-five or eighty persons assembled for the Mass at 7 o'clock, chiefly visitors from a distance, and fully 250 people came from the towns between Amsterdam and Canajoharie for the Mass at 9:30. The usual programme was carried out, the Way of the Cross, procession to the Ravine and Benediction of the Blessed Sacrament. The following day nearly 200 pilgrims came to the Shrine, most of them from Schenectady, arriving on the barge "Kitty West" about noon. After taking lunch, they marched in procession to the Ravine, where they sang most beautifully their hymns in German in honor of our Lady. After Benediction of the Blessed Sacrament, they returned by the same steamer, delighted with their pilgrimage.

——The largest pilgrimage of the season so far was on Sunday, August 20, when 1,200 came from Troy, under the direction of Rev. David B. Walker, S.J., of St. Joseph's Church in that city, and fully 800 other pilgrims from other towns near by, some 400 coming from Amsterdam; but we shall have to reserve our report of this and other pilgrimages for the October number.

CONTRIBUTIONS TO THE SHRINE.

T. M. Roseton, N. Y.	$ 50	M. L. S. H., Buffalo, N. Y.	$5 00
E. G., Villanova, Pa.	3 00	J. P., New York City	2 00
M. T., Newport, R. I.	1 00	R. F., Devon, Pa.	1 00
M. M., New York City	4 50	J. S. M., Albany, N. Y.	1 25
Anon	5 00	A Grateful Priest	5 00
	B. H., Jersey City, N. J.	2 00	

FROM THE MISSIONS.
CONSECRATION OF A BISHOP IN CHINA.

The Rt. Rev. John Baptist Simon, titular Bishop of Circesium and Vicar-Apostolic of Nanking, was consecrated in the Mission Cathedral at Shanghai, Sunday, June 25, 1899. Bishop Simon was born at Issé, a little town in the diocese of Nantes, in the year 1846. After a course of ecclesiastical studies in the Sulpician seminary of Nantes, he entered the Society of Jesus in 1868. After his novitiate and philosophical studies in the Society, he was employed as prefect and professor in various colleges, filling with credit, among other charges, that of Professor of Literature at the College of Vaugirard, Paris. His accomplishments in literary studies determined superiors to appoint him Professor of Literature for the young men of the Order, who were then living in England, and Father Simon had the opportunity of becoming familiar with the language of that country.

In 1886, he asked and obtained the favor of being sent to the Chinese Mission, little thinking that he was coming so far to find a mitre. From 1887 to 1897, Father Simon was in Nanking, a very important station, not so much for the missionary work and the number of Christians, as for the frequent relations the missionary has with the many mandarins in the old capital, Nanking, as the government seat of the most important viceroyalty of the imperial administration, is the second city of the empire. It is visited, too, by almost all foreign travellers in the interior, and as it has no foreign settlement, and nothing like a European hotel, Father Simon was the host of many a distinguished visitor. Among others, the present Czar of Russia, then Crown Prince, sought the hospitality of the Catholic Mission for the few days he spent at Nanking, upon his tour of the world in 1891. For those who know Bishop Simon, it is easy to believe that his guests at Nanking must have been as much captivated by their host, as was Robinson Crusoe, according to his veracious narrative, by the Father Simon he avers having met in China, not far from Nanking. For the real Father Simon was strangely enough a faithful reproduction, or rather realization of his fictitious prototype, with all his many accomplishments and winning manners.

The ceremony of the consecration was very imposing for such

a distant mission. Besides the consecrating prelate, Bishop Bulté, S.J., of another Chinese mission, there were two assistant prelates, Bishop Carlosare, O.S.F., Vicar-apostolic of Haw-how, in the interior, and Bishop Reynaud, C.M., of Ning-po, on the coast, not far from Shanghai. The consuls of the foreign powers were present in their respective uniforms, and the principal mandarins of the city assisted in their official robes. The Cathedral is situated in the Chinese suburbs, where there is a large Catholic congregation, and there were present, moreover, a number of Christians, who had come in from the country around to see the consecration of their chief pastor. The church is very large, and the court without had been covered with matting for the accommodation of those who could not find place within. It is estimated that within and without about four thousand assisted at the ceremony.

After the consecration the prelates and visiting missionaries, the home missionaries present for the occasion, the fathers and young ecclesiastics from the House of Studies, at Zi-ka-wei, the Marist Brothers, from the school of Shanghai, all sat down to a table of 130 covers, set on the long veranda of the residence. The presence of so many missionaries, following the imposing ceremonies in the church before such a numerous congregation, impressed one with the proportions of the Chinese missions at present, and in particular of the mission over which Bishop Simon has just been placed.

The new prelate has chosen as the device on his arms: *In Corde Jesu.* May his government of the mission be long and fruitful, bringing many souls to sweet service of Him, to whose Divine Heart the mission is especially dedicated by its chief pastor!

With the consoling news that comes from China of the Emperor's edict granting greater liberty and protection to the Catholics in the practice of their religion, there are not wanting facts which show that the era of persecution has not yet passed. The martyrdom of the Franciscan Father Victorin at Che-Keon-chau in the Vicariate Apostolic of Southern Hou-Pé on December 11, 1898, was attended by circumstances as cruel as any that have marked the blood-stained annals of the Chinese Mission. Captured with eight of his neophytes, who were tortured and beheaded before his eyes, he was first scourged with bamboo rods, after which he was hung for five days by his bound hands from a tree. During this time he was frequently tortured by the application of red hot irons. Finally, on December 11, he was beheaded, and as each of the seventeen chiefs desired to have a share in his execution, it was only after the last had struck his blow, that death came. His corpse was submitted to horrible indignities. Father Victorin was only twenty-eight years of age, and had been laboring little over a year on the Mission.

The first number of a new publication of great interest to all who follow the progress of the missions in distant lands has just made its appearance in Paris. *Les Missions Catholique Françaises, au XIXe. Siecle*, edited by the Rev. J. B. Piolet, S.J., has for its object a detailed account of the labors of the missionaries sent out by the "Eldest Daughter of the Church." We quote the brief resumé of their work given by the Rev. Editor as affording a fair insight into the character and extent of the good that is being effected. After pointing out how the other European countries are prevented from engaging to the same degree in the work of the foreign missions, he continues: "There then remains France. She has not been false to her mission. Already are the children of St. Vincent de Paul and the priests of the Foreign Missions making heroic efforts to save the work begun by the suppressed Jesuits. The restored Society of Jesus has again entered upon this field of labor, and with them the Fathers of the Holy Ghost, the Picpus Fathers, those of the Sacred Heart, the Marists, Cardinal Lavigerie's White Fathers, the Oblates of Mary Immaculate, the Oblates of St. Francis de Sales, the African Missions of Lyons, the Franciscans, the Capuchins, the Dominicans, and in the company of these various societies, the Christian Brothers, the Marist Brothers, the Sisters of Charity, the St. Joseph Sisters of Cluny, the Sisters of St. Paul from Chartres, the Missionary Helpers, the Religious of the Assumption, the Little Sisters of the Poor, etc., etc., all throwing themselves, with holy emulation, into the work before them, ready to face the unknown, dangers innumerable, and even martyrdom. And to aid and support them, in the absence of governmental appropriations, there has arisen at Lyons, under the marked guidance of the Holy Spirit, that wonderful institution, the Propagation of the Faith, which, and more especially in France, has been associated with the labors and success of the missionaries, has contributed to their support, has prayed and suffered to ensure their success. Since its foundation, in 1822, down to the end of the year 1897, the Propagation of the Faith has distributed among the missions 303,063,986 francs, and of this sum 192,704,378 francs were contributed by France alone, as against 110,359,607 francs collected by all the other nations of the world.

"As to the number of missionaries, out of 13,314 two-thirds are Frenchmen. Four-fifths of the teaching Brothers—4,500 in all—are likewise French, as are four-fifths of the 42,000 missionary Sisters. We have the care of the oldest, the largest, the most prosperous, and what is of more merit, the most savage and abandoned missions—all Japan, the greater part of China and Indo-China, in India and Oceanica, America and the Continent of Africa, all the ports of the Levant, Madagascar, etc. * * * * Is it, then, an exaggeration to say that the work of the Catholic missions in the Nineteenth Century is pre-eminently French, the glory and honor of those who devote themselves to it, and that to it may be applied with even greater force than of old to the crusades the words: '*Gesta Dei per Francos?*'"

The above details of the funds collected for the Missions through the Propagation of the Faith may be supplemented by the Annual Report of the Association for 1898. The total receipts amounted to $1,338,311.49 of which the Dioceses of France contributed $815,417.12. The contribution of the United States was $53,642.00, not a large sum, if we consider the number of our Catholics, although it is but fair to take into account the growing needs of many poor parishes where the priest has before him the task of building church and school house, and the generosity of his people is severely taxed to give their pastor needed material support.

Acknowledgment is made of the following contributions:

FOR THE PROPAGATION OF THE FAITH.　　FOR NEEDY MISSIONS.
M. D. . . . . $50 00　　A Promoter of the League . $1 00

AN INSTANCE OF GRATITUDE.

It was in 1887 that His Holiness, Leo XIII., who is ever ready to advance the interests of the flock committed to his charge, separated the Syro-Malabarese from the Verapoly mission, and placed them under the Vicars Apostolic of Tricshur and Kottayano. At the request of the Syrians of the Kottayano Vicariate, Right Rev. Charles Lavigne was sent hither, who brought with him as secretary, the Rev. Louis Ricard, S.J. It is difficult to describe in the space of a short article how the missionaries who came with them restored order out of chaos, with what unflagging zeal they worked for the good of the country, how they instilled a strong religious spirit into the minds of the Syrians, and with what stately edifices they beautified the town of Changanacherry, the place of their residence.

Of the several institutions with which the name of Monsignor Lavigne is associated in this country, none contributes more to the common weal than St. Berchmans's High School, at Changanacherry, which was founded in 1891, and which will ever be a standing monument of his work in the country. This institution was placed under the able management of Rev. Louis Ricard, S.J., whose amiable disposition and ready sympathy won the affections of students and teachers alike. This venerable clergyman bade farewell to the shores of Travancore September 2, 1896, and his sudden and unexpected death on February 4, following, threw the whole school into a consternation. There was one wail of woe throughout Changanacherry the day the news was received here. The present Bishop of Changanacherry, the Rev. Dr. Mathew Makeel, and the present director of the institution, Rev. A. Syriac Kandankaril, deserves all praise for their untiring efforts to perpetuate the memory of the man who labored hard for the cause of education in the country.

But what is more gratifying to note is that the above-named gentlemen have made arrangements to observe the anniversary of Father Ricard's death. Owing to some unavoidable circumstances the ceremony had this year to be put off to Thursday, February 17. With the permission of the Bishop, the manager of the school, who is also the Dean of the local cathedral, had arranged a special service for the occasion. On the evening of the 16th, all the Catholic boys and teachers went to confession

At 7 A.M., on the 17th, was chanted a solemn High Mass by the director, assisted by a deacon and a sub-deacon. The school was granted a half holiday in honor of the occasion. In the evening all the students, led and drilled by the teachers, went in procession to the church, where they were received by the directors. The stately procession added dignity to the occasion and recalled to the inhabitants the memory of that noble father, who had worked in their midst for well nigh seven years. The office for the dead was then celebrated and the services terminated with a sermon from the director, whose pathetic reference to the work of Father Ricard brought tears to the eyes of the audience. All this goes to show that the people here are not so ungrateful as they are painted to be, and that there are some at least among them, who are alive to a sense of duty.

In this connection it gives me much pleasure to state that the above-named institution, under the patronage of His Lordship, Rt. Rev. Dr. Mathew Makeel, and the able management of Rev. A. Syriac, Kandankaril, is progressing, and that seven out of the twenty-one students sent up last year for the matriculation examination came out successful, a result, which speaks for itself, when compared with that of other schools in Travancore.

MOVEMENT TOWARDS CONVERSION AMONG THE COPTS OF UPPER EGYPT.

From August, 1898, till February, 1899, some fourteen hundred conversions to the Catholic Church took place in eleven different villages. In seven others, the number of Catholics has considerably increased and even doubled. Moreover, the inhabitants of fourteen villages, all schismatical, have received the first impulse towards the Catholic Church, and there is every reason to hope that they will be converted in the course of this year. Seven new schools have been opened by the Jesuits; five more are earnestly asked for, but for want of means their opening must be delayed. At present the Jesuits have under their direction thirty schools. Chapels and schools are in process of construction in eight different stations. These results are so much the more remarkable, as the obduracy which not long ago characterized the Copts, is a fact noted by several Catholic writers.

THE PILGRIM

OF

OUR LADY OF MARTYRS

CAUSA NOSTRÆ LÆTITIÆ.

REV. C. W. BARRAUD, S.J.

SHALL we not rejoice to-day
    With the blessed Queen of Heaven
For whose love the Church is gay?
On this morn, O gentle maid,
    All our vows to thee are given,
At thy feet our homage laid.

Day by day the whole year through,
    Mary, are thy praises chanted;
But to-day the chant is new.
Lift the voice in song and prayer,
    All ye ask will now be granted.
Be not grudging of your care.

Lady, none is like to thee.
    Wherefore, if we hymn thy praises,
Tis but as it ought to be;
For the heart must needs confess,
    When upon thyself it gazes,
That it could not offer less.

Lo! to-day within thy breast
    He who all the world created
Laid Him down and took His rest.
Thou the inn that shelter lent
    To that traveller belated
When the day was well-nigh spent.

Wherefore all was made anew,
    All the wrongs of Nature mended,
While the babe within thee grew,
Grew in substance like our own ;
    That wherein we had offended
He, our Maker, might atone.

Blessed was that day of yore
    When our God from labor rested,
Blessed thence for evermore.
Yet more blessed far art thou,
    In thy maiden garment vested,
Heaven's own light upon thy brow.

For our Sabbath comes between
    Days of toil and days of sorrow,
Bringing back what aye hath been.
But whose sleep is on thy breast
    Needeth not to fear the morrow,
For it shall not break his rest.

Lo ! to-day Christ's little flock
    Safety and cool shelter findeth
'Neath the shadow of his rock.
Lo! to-day our Mother's ear
    With unwonted pity mindeth
Every grief and hope and fear.

Who then can to-day withhold,
    Or in service be more chary
Than our fathers were of old ?
Nay, with them we do entreat
    That thou wilt befriend us, Mary,
Guiding home our weary feet.

ANNALS OF THE SHRINE.

THE TROY PILGRIMAGE.

——Sunday, August 20, was a memorable day in the Annals of Auriesville. As the Right Reverend Bishop had permitted us to have the Consecration of the Shrine and its clients on any day of our choice, this Sunday was chosen, and a solemn triduum of preparation was begun on Thursday, August 17. On each day of the triduum the newly approved Litany of the Sacred Heart was recited after the seven o'clock Mass and at Benediction of the Blessed Sacrament; the Holy Hour was made every afternoon at four o'clock, and a short instruction was given each evening after the night prayers. On the day of Consecration itself the Blessed Sacrament was exposed from the first Mass at 6.30, until the departure of the pilgrims from Troy, and during all that time the chapel was filled with adorers.

——The Pilgrims from Troy came by the West Shore R. R. in a train of two sections, arriving at 8.40 and 9 o'clock. They walked in procession up the hill, the choir singing the Litany of the Blessed Virgin, and Masses were begun for them immediately at the chapel and old Shrine, by Fathers Walker and Frisbee, Fathers Brosnan and Wynne hearing confessions. At both these Masses, as well as at the one following by Father Brosnan, it was impossible to give Holy Communion to all who wished to receive it, and it was not until the last Mass that all could communicate, between 800 and 900 having come prepared. So many people wished to come from Amsterdam that the regular West Shore train arriving here at 9.18 A.M., could not accommodate them, and accordingly after some delay a special train was made up for more than 300 persons, and, as no word had been given to the Fathers at the Shrine, some of them who had not heard Mass in their own churches were too late for the last Mass here; but they strove to compensate themselves for this loss, which was no fault of theirs, by the fervor with which they entered into all the exercises of the pilgrimage.

——By the time the Stations were begun, about 11 o'clock, there were fully two thousand pilgrims on the Shrine grounds, all as orderly as if in church. The way was led by crossbearer, acolytes and priest, followed by the Italian society of men from Amsterdam in neat uniform, and the choir chanted the *Stabat Mater*. The same order was followed in the procession to the Ravine at 2 P.M., where a sermon was preached by Father Wynne on one of the leading texts quoted in the letter of our Holy Father on the consecration of the world to the Sacred Heart, "All power is given to me in heaven and on earth," to prove the title of Christ as King over all mankind. As the day was very warm, it was considered prudent to have merely the Benediction of the Blessed Sacrament instead of a procession. A copy of the Act of Consecration issued with the Pope's letter was given as a souvenir to every one on the grounds, and all read it aloud after the priest during the Benediction. At 4:30 P.M. the Troy pilgrims departed, arriving in Troy at 6:30 without mishap. The pilgrims from Amsterdam were not so fortunate. Owing to an oversight of the station master, who had taken no steps to provide them with trains, though he had sold them return tickets, they would have had to wait until after 12 P.M. had not a canal boat been ready to give them an evening sail home. It was the only drawback to the pleasure of an eventful day in the annals of Auriesville, but it happened fortunately to people who know and like the Shrine too well to consider even the delay caused as unpleasant.

THE UTICA PILGRIMAGE.

——The Utica Pilgrimage was organized under difficulties this year, but never were the pilgrims more fervent, and never did they return home more enthusiastic. Sunday, September 23, 600 arrived at the Shrine at 10.30 A. M., by the West Shore R. R., about 100 being from Little Falls, and the rest from Utica and cities nearby. Nearly 200 received Holy Communion at the Mass which was said immediately on their arrival. Soon after a small party arrived from Syracuse, and later still, about 11.30 A. M., came many from Albany, Schenectady and Amsterdam. All were in time for the Mass which was sung by the Rev. Dr. Lynch, of St. John's, Utica, N. Y., supported by his fine choir of thirty voices. This was something new at Auriesville, and we trust it will be repeated often. Ordinarily low Masses only are said, so as to leave the few priests in attendance there free to care for the many pilgrims who need their services in the confessional, at the communion rail or in other ways, and to have enough time to carry out the entire programme of a pilgrimage. With a Mass so well sung as this one was, we might well afford to dispense with one or the other of the ordinary services. It was observed that the choir attracted everyone to the chapel, even those who had heard Mass previously. The sermon was preached by the Rev. Owen Hill, S.J., who has lately been appointed to assist the Fathers in charge of the Shrine.

——The rain of the day before made walking to the Ravine unpleasant, especially as the work of levelling the road and raising an embankment for the creek had been under way some days, and the soil was too soft for walking. It was just as well. As the Mass had been begun only at 11.45 A. M., and as the sermon was preached in the chapel instead of the Ravine, where it is usually delivered, there would not have been time for a common ceremony before the grotto; but nearly all the pilgrims visited it privately. All took part in the Way of the Cross, in which devotion the choir from St. John's, Utica, sang the *Stabat Mater*. A storm which had been raging for some time above the valley, began to threaten Auriesville, and we were obliged to make the last Station and prayers in the chapel. Very soon the storm was over, so that we could have the procession of the Blessed Sacrament. This over, and the pious articles blessed, all proceeded to the train, leaving for Utica about 6 P. M., delighted with their pilgrimage, and delighting their friends at home, as we have since learned, by their account of all that had happened.

——This was the last organized pilgrimage to Auriesville this year. Until as late as September 18, Mass was said daily at the Shrine, and small parties visited it. The work in the Ravine necessitated the presence of one of the priests in charge. Mass was accordingly said at Auriesville on Sunday, September 17, feast of the Seven Dolors, the first time in the annals of the Shrine, and in the evening the few pilgrims who were still remaining at Auriesville attended the ceremony of the consecration to the Sacred Heart of Jesus in St. Cecilia's Church, Fonda, N. Y., the Rev. J. W. Dolan officiating, and Father Wynne preaching the sermon. The Shrine was closed for 1899, Monday, September 18, the improvements in the Ravine having been for the most part completed.

——These improvements required much labor and expense. They consisted in raising an embankment about 325 feet in length; about thirty feet in width, and varying from two to eight feet in height. To obtain material for this the road leading down to the Ravine was graded, and the hills on either side cut down and sloped. In all over 1,800 loads of dirt were drawn for this purpose. The embankment forms a channel for the creek, about twenty feet in width and eight in height, and the sides are faced with railroad ties and hemlock boards well set in the earth and fastened to the banks. To those who know the force of the water that accumulates in the Ravine in times of heavy storms and freshet, the strength of this embankment will not appear extravagant. Some of the effects of the freshet there our pilgrims had an opportunity of seeing this summer, for though part of the damage done by the rains of last September and October had been repaired this May, not all could be repaired before the pilgrimages, and, indeed, the desolate appearance of parts of the Ravine was the only drawback to the general satisfaction with everything at Auriesville this year. As the Rev. J. A. Brosnan, S.J., of Georgetown University, who planned and directed these improvements, could not visit the Shrine before the middle of August, it was decided not to begin the work there until his arrival. The friends of Auriesville owe him much gratitude for the devotion and success with which he has not only restored, if not increased, the former beauty of the Ravine, but also taken means to preserve it by raising a barrier against the water, which will be strong enough to resist the violence of storm and freshet for many years to come. For one month with the assistance of four teams and twenty-five men daily he labored for this end, and we have every reason to be pleased with his success.

———As our readers may imagine, all this work was very expensive, even though with Father Brosnan's aid we were enabled to do it with great economy. Still, all will agree that it was needed, even though we had to begin it without any other fund than the kind donations offered by some of the pilgrims who took special interest in it. The dry season was particularly favorable for these improvements. Father Brosnan's presence was an advantage we could not well have at any other season of the year, and unless all would have been completed before the frost, we could not without great difficulty hope to have the Ravine in proper order for the pilgrimages next summer. We are confident that the friends of Auriesville and readers of the PILGRIM will contribute speedily the amount expended on this work, so that we may be ready to prepare for the pilgrimage season of 1899 without debt. All who contribute for this purpose during the month of October, will be recommended in the Holy Mass to be said at the Shrine Wednesday, October 18, the anniversary of the death of Father Isaac Jogues.

———One of the recommendations in the letter of our Holy Father Leo XIII., on the celebration of the Jubilee Year, is that Catholics in every part of the world should join in making pilgrimages to shrines and holy places, so as to unite with more fervor in public worship and prayer. We hope to make Auriesville the scene of many devout pilgrimages next year. Indeed, it is with a view to being free to attend to the organization of these pilgrimages that we devoted so much time this year to the material improvements about the Shrine. We were not able, as we had hoped, to erect the grotto of the Holy Sepulchre in the Ravine this year, but with God's help, now that the Ravine is ready, it will be ready for next summer, and the figure of Christ in the tomb will be an additional incentive to devotion to the Sacred Passion, which is so piously practised at Auriesville.

———More than usual attention has been paid to the Shrine this year by the secular and religious press of the country. Ordinarily their reports were quite correct in every particular, though now and then the sensationalism of the day appeared in some of them. Thus, it sounds sensational to speak of Auriesville as an "American Lourdes," and it looks sensational to picture the blind and the halt walking or carried to the chapel for prayers and cures. One newspaper actually asked for a photograph of the Shrine and painted in a few such details. Now and then even a Catholic weekly had something to say about miraculous favors. The modern reporter cannot understand that a bishop's tribunal has rights prior to those of an editorial sanctum, and that miraculous favors should not be published before being submitted to a proper ecclesiastical examination. However, there is this much foundation for the exaggerations of the newspapers, that each year the number of remarkable answers to prayer at Auriesville keeps growing, that those whose prayers are answered recognize more clearly that it is through the intercession of the servants of God, in whose memory the Shrine has been erected. It speaks well for the pilgrims who come to Auriesville, that they appreciate the blessing of visiting this place of prayer, even were it merely to satisfy their piety, without obtaining any special or marvellous favor, and they are well aware that as people pray graces are granted, as they are granted so confidence increases, and with confidence grows the faith simple enough to ask, and strong enough to move mountains. From the nature of some of the favors obtained the past year through the intercession of Father Jogues and his companions, confidence in his sanctity and power has been greatly and widely increased, and the day is not far off, we trust, when Almighty God will deign to grant some miracles through the intercession of his servants to show to men that the belief of all who know their virtues is true, and that after heroic lives they reign with Him in blessedness.

——The *De Profundis* which was added to the Night Prayers at the Shrine this year was said for the relatives and friends of those who were present, and chiefly for the departed who in life had assisted the Shrine by their prayers, contributions or labors. To the number of those who, like Father Loyzance, S. J., and Father McIncrow, late of Amsterdam, N. Y., had advanced its interests, we have had to add during the past summer the name of Rev. John Farrell Galligan, S. J., who had so much endeared himself to pilgrims to Auriesville. R. I. P.

——On Friday, September 29, Rev. F. J. Lamb, S. J., will say Holy Mass at the Shrine, in memory of the death of René Goupil, a companion of Father Isaac Jogues, who was put to death at Auriesville on this date in 1642. In this Mass, Father Lamb will recommend the intentions of the benefactors and friends of the Shrine and of all the pilgrims to Auriesville the past season.

——On Wednesday, October 18, the anniversary of the death of Father Jogues in 1646, Mass will be said at Auriesville by Rev. J. Wynne, S. J., who on the Sunday night previous will lecture in Johnstown on "The Mohawk Valley in Iroquois Days." This Mass will be offered specially for all who contribute towards the work of improving and beautifying the Ravine, and especially for the Grotto of the Holy Sepulchre.

——The anniversary of the death of Catherine Tegakwitha is April 13, and, if possible, Mass will also be said at the Shrine on that day. In this way, though the Shrine be closed during the year, those who wish may keep uniting their intentions and recommending them from time to time through the intercession of those who died there for the faith, so as to obtain from Almighty God not only their own petitions, but also proof of the sanctity and blessedness of his servants. That our readers may have before them the circumstances of the deaths of Father Jogues and René Goupil, we reprint here from Father Martin's "Isaac Jogues," Father Jogues' own account of René's death, and the historian's narrative of Jogues' own last moments.

The Death of René Goupil.

"But I must hasten to his death, which wants nothing to be that of a martyr.

"After we had been six weeks in the country,* as confusion arose in the councils of the Iroquois, some of whom were for sending us back, we lost all hope, which in me had never been sanguine, of seeing Three Rivers that year. We consoled one another then at this disposal of Providence, and prepared for all He should ordain in our regard. He [René] did not see the danger we were in so clearly: I saw it better. This made me often tell him to hold himself in readiness. Accordingly, one day when in our mental pain we had gone out of the town to pray more becomingly and undisturbed by noise, two young men came after us and told us to return home. I had some presentiment of what was to happen, and told him, 'My dear brother, let us recommend ourselves to our Lord and to our good mother the Blessed Virgin: these men have some evil design, as I think.' We had a little before offered ourselves to our Lord with much devotion, beseeching Him to accept our lives and blood, and unite them to His life and blood for the salvation of these poor tribes. We were returning then towards the town, reciting our beads, of which we had already said four decades. Having stopped near the gate of the town to see what they would say, one of these two Iroquois drew an axe which he had hidden under his blanket, and dealt René a blow on the head as he stood before him; he fell stiff on his face on the ground, uttering the holy name of Jesus, for we had often reminded each other to close our voice and life with that holy name. I turned at the blow, and seeing the reeking hatchet, fell on my knees to receive the blow that was to unite me to my loved companion; but as they delayed I rose, ran to him, as he lay expiring near me. They gave him two more blows on the

---

* At Ossernenon, the Mohawk village where, after having been tortured, they were held as prisoners.

head and extinguished life, but not before I had given him absolution, which, since our captivity, I had given him regularly after his confession every other day.

"It was the [29th] day of September, the Feast of St Michael, that this angel in innocence and martyr of Christ gave his life for Him, who had given him His. They commanded me to return to my cabin, where I awaited during the rest of the day and the next the same treatment. It was the belief of all that I would not wait long, as they had begun it; and in fact for several days they came to kill me, but our Lord prevented it by ways which would take long to explain. Early the next morning I did not fail to start out to inquire where they had thrown that blessed body, for I wished to inter it, cost what it might. Some Iroquois who had a wish to save me said, 'Thou hast no sense; thou seest that they seek thee everywhere to kill thee, and thou goest out still—thou wilt go to seek a body already half putrefied, which has been dragged far from here. Seest thou not those young men going out who will kill thee when thou art past the palisade?' This did not stop me, and our Lord gave me courage enough to be willing to die in that office of charity. I go, I seek, and by the help of a captured Algonquin become a real Iroquois, I find it. After he had been killed the children had stripped him, and tying a cord around his neck dragged him to a torrent which runs at the foot of the town. The dogs had already gnawed a part of his thighs. At this spectacle I could not withhold my tears. I took the body, and, aided by the Algonquin, I sank it in the water and covered it with large stones to hide it, intending to return the next day with a spade, when there was no one near, and dig a grave and inter it. I thought the body well hidden, but perhaps some one saw us, especially of the youth, and took it up.

"The next day, as they sought to kill me, my aunt * sent me to her field to escape, as I think; this compelled me to defer it till the next day. It rained all night, so that the torrent was extremely swelled; I borrowed a hoe in another cabin, the better to conceal my design, but on approaching the place could not find the blessed deposit; I entered the water, already quite cold, I go and come, I sound with my feet to see whether the water had not raised and carried off the body, but I saw nothing. How many tears I shed, which fell in the torrent, while I sang as I could the

---

* The squaw whose slave he was.

psalms which the Church chants for the dead! After all I found nothing, and a woman known to me who passed by, seeing me in trouble, told me, when I asked her whether she did not know what had had been done with it, that it had been dragged to the river, which is a quarter of a league from there, and with which I was not acquainted. This was false, the young men had taken it up and dragged it to a neighboring wood, where during the fall and winter it was the food of the dog, the crow, and the fox. When I was told in the spring that he had been dragged there, I went several times without finding anything; at last, the fourth time, I found his head and some half-gnawed bones, which I interred, intending to carry them off, if taken back to Three Rivers, as was then talked of. Repeatedly did I kiss them as the bones of a martyr of Jesus Christ.

"I gave him this title, not only because he was killed by the enemies of God and His Church, in the exercise of an ardent love for his neighbor, putting himself in evident perils for the love of God, but particularly because he was killed for prayer and expressly for the Holy Cross. He was in a cabin where he prayed daily, which scarcely pleased a superstitious old man there. One day seeing a little child, three or four years old, in the cabin, from an excess of devotion and a love of the cross, and in a simplicity which we, who are more prudent according to the flesh, would not have had, he took off his cap, and putting it on the child's head made the sign of the cross on his body. The old man seeing it ordered a young man in his cabin, who was starting on a war party, to kill him; and he obeyed the order, as we have seen.

"The mother of the child herself, in a voyage which I made with her, told me that he had been killed for that sign of the cross; and the old man who had given the order to kill him invited me one day to his cabin to dinner, but when I made the sign of the cross before beginning, he said, 'There is what we hate; that is what we killed thy comrade for, and will kill thee too. Our neighbors, the Europeans, do not make it.' Sometimes, too, as I prayed on my knees in hunting time, they told me that they hated that way of doing, and had killed the other Frenchman for it, and would kill me too when I got back to the village.

"I beg pardon of your Reverence for the precipitation with which I write this, and my want of respect in so doing. Excuse me, if you please; I feared to miss this opportunity of discharging a debt I should long since have discharged."

THE DEATH OF FATHER JOGUES.

[Father Jogues had been chosen to found a mission among the Mohawks, the most savage of the Iroquois Nations, and had already started on his journey to their country.]

"Some well-founded presentiments of death at the hands of the savages, and the desertion of his companions almost at the very outset of the voyage, ought to have disheartened him completely. Far from it. The thought and sight of death will not make him falter ; he will march on as though he were going to fulfill his most ardent desires.

"Meanwhile the public calamities had acted violently on this people. They excited to madness and fury these fierce and credulous savages. In natural events they beheld only effects of duplicity and ill-will, and they forgot their recent promises of friendship. The agitation kept increasing. The most sensible and prudent wished the peace maintained, but the turbulent and irascible prevailed ; and it was decided to renew the war against the French, the Hurons, and the Algonquins, who were regarded as treacherous men, plotting the ruin of the Iroquois.

"A war-party immediately took the field, aiming at Montreal, and surprised two Frenchmen in the vicinity of that city. Another band marched against Fort Richelieu, and came upon Father Jogues two days' march from their village. They fell upon the missionary and his companion, stripped them of their garments, loaded them with insults, and led them off as prisoners. On the 17th of October, 1646, these warriors made their triumphal entry into the town where the servant of God had already passed a captivity of thirteen months.

"From all sides threats of death sounded in their ears. Blows from fists and clubs soon accompanied these gloomy heralds of their execution. 'You shall die to-morrow,' they were told ; 'do not fear—you shall not be burned ; your heads shall fall beneath our tomahawks, and we shall set them upon the palisades around our village to show them for many a day to your brethren whom we capture.'

"Father Jogues endeavored to show them how unworthily they were acting, reminding him of his confidence in placing himself in their hands, the invitations they had given him to come and live among them, the promises which they had solemnly made, the manner in which the French had acted towards them, their treaty, their plighted word, and finally the unhappy results that war would draw down upon them. All was vain; a gloomy silence told him that he was speaking to men who would not hear.

"This was not all; one furious savage sliced bits of flesh from his arms and back and devoured them, saying, 'Let us see whether this white flesh is the flesh of a Manitou!'

"The courage of the sufferer did not flinch. 'No,' he replied, 'I am only a man like you all, but I fear neither death nor torments. Why do you put me to death? I have come to your country to cement peace, make the earth solid and teach you the way to heaven, and you treat me like a wild beast! Fear the chastisement of the Master of life.'

"Meanwhile a division arose in the tribe. The families of the Wolf and Tortoise wished to save the lives of the prisoners, and made every effort to rescue them. 'Kill us,' they said to their opponents, 'rather than butcher in this way men who have done us no harm, and who came to us by faith of a treaty;' but the Bear family stubbornly insisted that they must die.

"It was a grave question, affecting the whole nation. It was referred to a great council of sachems and chiefs, which met at Tionnontogen, the largest of the Mohawk towns, situated several miles farther west. Here the peace party prevailed. It was decided that the prisoners should enjoy life and liberty, but the party who thirsted for their blood did not wait for the result of this resolution, and their crime was accomplished when the delegates to the council returned to prevent it.

"On the 18th of October some Mohawks of the Bear family had secretly formed a wicked plot to execute by themselves, and by their own private authority, this odious crime.

"On the evening of the 18th these Indians went to Father Jogues and perfidiously invited him to take a meal at their cabin. Accustomed to see in everything a mysterious disposition of Divine Providence, the servant of God followed them humbly. It was the hour of his last sacrifice. But sudden as was the blow which struck him, it was not unexpected by the faithful missionary. He kept himself always ready for any event. At the moment when Father Jogues crossed the threshold of the cabin they dealt him a blow with a tomahawk which laid him dead. His head was immediately cut off and set up on one of the palisades encircling the place, the face turned toward the road by which he had come.

Early the next morning his companion and the Huron who had guided them met the same fate, and their bodies were cast into the river.

CONTRIBUTIONS TO THE SHRINE.

K. W., Albany, N. Y. . . .	$1 00	A. F. C., New York City . . .	$5 00
M. D. B., Charlestown, Mass. .	2 00	For a departed soul	1 00
M. L. S. H., Buffalo, N. Y.	5 00	M. de P., New York City . . .	50

TÉRÈSE AND PIERRE.

BY K. A. HENNESSY.

(Continued.)

CHAPTER IV.

An Exchange of Confidences.

"MAY I ask you a question or so?" he inquired, looking straight into her honest eyes.

"Yes," she replied, "why should I deny thee this privilege?"

"Are you not fearful that some day this Aharihon may loom up and perhaps cause you serious annoyance?"

"At first I felt that way," she said, "but now I need have no fear, for they say that he was killed near Three Rivers by some Hurons whom he had attacked. At any rate, he must have lost all love for me when he could so basely deprive me of all that I held dearest on earth. It was Orrewati who told me of Aharihon's death, because, when the Mohawk ambassadors came to Onondaga to assure you Frenchmen of their good will, Orewati bade me remain in the cabin. He feared that some of our tribe might recognize and claim me. But I would not have wished to return to Ossernenon where once I was so happy, and besides I would be going far from the saintly men of God whose very presence is a blessing, even though I be deprived of speech with them."

"I thank you for the faith you have reposed in me," said Pierre, after some slight hesitation, "and promise that you shall never have reason to regret it. Your story is indeed a sad one, but I hope that brighter days will dawn for you; surely life cannot remain so dark."

A sigh was Térèse's only reply, but presently her face brightened as she exclaimed: "And now, may I not know why thou camest hither?"

"Because life in France seemed unbearable. I could not endure the awful loneliness I felt when, within a year, death snatched my fond father and mother and also my promised bride. At the time, I had finished my studies with the Jesuits and was taking a course in medicine, but, in the depth of my grief I fled to Father d'Ablon who had been my friend and instructor while I was at the college of la Flèche, and begged him to direct me, assuring him that life had lost its charm and that I could never again be happy. He reasoned with me and told me that, when most deeply wounded, the human heart is sometimes capable of its best and noblest sacrifices, and he bade me continue the study of medicine and consider myself free to consult him whenever I should feel so inclined. When he told me of his prospective departure for New France, I was seized with a desire to accompany him, and last year I came to Quebec. I longed to come with him and Father Chaumonot when they made their first excursion into this country of the Iroquois, but they would not allow me to do so; however when Father d'Ablon returned to Quebec looking for priests and laymen to help in the good work begun here, I presented myself and was gladly accepted. Here I am, ready to do all in my power to aid in enlightening the poor pagan Iroquois and to cement a friendship between them and the French in Canada, but, till now, it seems that I have been of little use."

"And now," asked the maiden, her sweet face betraying the eagerness she felt to know all, "now, what findest thou to do?"

"I find that I may be able to bring some consolation to a poor soul that requires it, and therefore, I am happy." Pierre smiled as he spoke and Térèse, yielding to the simplicity of her nature, bent forward and laid her hand upon his arm.

"I understand thee well," she said, "as well as though thou wert my brother. But," and she glanced at the cloudless sky, "the sun is almost at its height. Had we not best return to the fort? Orrewati may wish to leave for home any time past mid-day."

"Yes," replied Pierre, beginning to paddle vigorously down stream, "we will put to shore at once. I have fish enough here to serve us all generously at the evening meal and I feel that the morning has been well spent."

"And hast thou no advice to give thy newly-found friend? When are we to meet again? I know not when Orrewati will next visit Gannentaha, perhaps not for many moons," said Térèse as, taking her companion's proffered hand, she sprang lightly ashore.

"My advice is that you live on as you have lived through all these months past, and I shall see you as soon as I shall have talked with some of the Fathers. You should meet one of them and you will, never fear."

"The thought of it makes me shudder," exclaimed the girl, involuntarily trembling from head to foot, "not that I do not trust you, but if our plan were discovered——"

"It will not be discovered, I can promise you that;" and Pierre spoke with such determination that the girl felt reassured. "But," he continued, "there is something that I had almost forgotten to ask. Do you speak French?"

"Only to the good God and His Holy Mother," she smilingly replied. "I have said the *Je vous salue, Marie*, and the *Notre Père* daily since my mother died, and I remember a few little phrases, but I could not converse well. Since then I've never met any one to whom I could speak French, and still, when the tall blackgown talked with thee yesterday, I understood all that he said. But I love it dearly and hate the harsh Iroquois that I am obliged to speak."

"Well," Pierre gently remarked, "until to-day, I often marvelled at how unlike other Indian women you were, but now I can readily account for it."

As they walked towards the fort, Térèse stopped suddenly and turning upon Pierre a smiling yet searching glance, exclaimed:

"And thou who art practised in the use of medicine didst allow me to care for thy scalded hand. Didst not deem this a risk?"

"None whatever," was the prompt reply. "I approve the ointments used by the Indians, and indeed I could not regret having trusted my hand to the care of so charming and skilful a nurse." Térèse had always detested compliments, possibly because she had generally felt them to be insincere, but this one evoked within her a sensation of delight.

The rest of the road they traversed in silence and reached the fort just in time for the noon-day meal, of which Orrewati had been invited to partake in the large refectory, but having an abhorrence for food prepared either for or by the blackgowns, he freely announced that he would start at once for home, where old Gannendaris would have a pot of steaming sagamite ready upon his arrival.

Pierre's offering of some of the fish he had caught was eagerly accepted by the old Iroquois, who grabbed them as if they were his rightful property, and the young Frenchman could not but congratulate himself upon his own tactfulness. It disturbed him to see Térèse setting out upon her journey without having taken any refreshment, but, fearing the inadvisability of offering any further hospitality, he contented himself with assuring Orrewati that he and the maiden must soon again visit Gannentaha, where a hearty welcome would await them.

Chapter V.

Discord.

A long, dreary Winter succeeded the beautiful, mild Autumn of 1656, and the first heralds of Spring were welcomed with eager delight by the little colony of Europeans at Gannentaha. Their life during the bleak, cheerless months from November to April was by no means comfortless, but it was one of bitter hardship when compared to that led in their native land, or even in Quebec, although on the shores of the St. Lawrence the Winter season was more severe than in the Iroquois country.

The deep snows and frosty air did not prevent the Onondagas from frequenting the fort, but they did not travel thither in as great numbers as in milder weather, and most of the visiting was done by the men. Then, when Winter's backbone was broken, a number of Onondaga villagers came to pitch their tents in the vicinity of the great Gannentaha residence, and within a short time the neighborhood of the fort assumed the appearance of quite a promising Iroquois settlement. Indeed, to one unacquainted with the Indian nature, the serene aspect of affairs would seem a harbinger of great achievements for the Fathers and their worthy co-operators, but fortunately the good missionaries knew the fickle, superstitious bent of their dusky neighbors, and, therefore, did not place undue confidence in their flattering ways.

God had certainly rewarded the sacrifices made by His self-denying servants, by permitting their inspired words to bear fruit in many a savage heart, and this not alone among the Onondagas, as in the land of the Cayugas, Senecas, and Oneidas, were souls also won to God. Fathers Chaumonot and Mesnard were tireless in their journeyings from one place to another, announcing the Gospel to those who would hear it, and endeavoring by every possible means to court the favor of such as were hostile to it. But Onondaga was the scene of their richest harvest, and where at first were many who not only insulted and reviled the missionaries but openly threatened their lives, were now to be found men who listened willingly to their preaching, and even promised to abide by the lessons they taught.

Among these was Orrewati, the fierce, unrelenting old Iroquois who terrorized his enemies, awed his friends, and was feared even by the gentle young ward whom he so tenderly loved. Wonderful indeed it seemed to behold him in the Onondaga chapel listening to the blackgown's discourse, or bowing his proud old head in adoration when the priest would hold the Sacred Host aloft at the elevation of the Mass. As yet the old warrior had not received Baptism, and the fathers were in no haste to administer it. To be sure his demeanor was beyond reproach, but they could not vouch for the workings of his heart, and they resolved not to admit him within the true fold till his sincerity would have stood the required test.

In the meantime, happier days had dawned for Térèse, who who was now permitted the untrammelled practice of the religion in which Ondessonk and her mother had so well instructed her. The first ray of comfort had come to her when she had unburdened her heart to Pierre Boudreau, and through his tactful intervention, had been brought into contact with one of the Fathers, who heard her confession and counselled her as to her future course. Cautiously she had felt her way, trusting with filial confidence in the Mother of God, till finally all had come about according to the dearest wishes of the girl's heart. At first it seemed strange that Orrewati had not frowned upon her acquaintance with the several Frenchmen she had met, but her surprise vanished when she reflected that the old Iroquois had strong reasons for wishing to stand in their good graces. He knew them to be personal friends of Onontio (1) and therefore, could ill afford to incur their disfavor lest they report any incivility on his part to the great official with whom he hoped one day to trade. The black gowns, however, he could scarcely tolerate and it was only after Father Le Mercier had concluded a satisfactory bargain with him for twenty-five bear skins to be used as cloaks by the soldiers at the fort, that the old fellow's heart began to soften. Gradually then he realized that the missionaries had no evil intent toward him, but, though they, too, were Onontio's friends, it was some time before Orrewati could so far shake off his old superstitions as to make much freedom with them, and it required repeated advances on their part to assure him of their sincerity.

As for Térèse, the peace of mind which she now enjoyed was reflected on her lovely countenance, adding immeasurably to its beauty, and contributing additional ease to the quiet, graceful manner which had always been hers. She was beloved by one and all. The children hailed her coming with delight; the grave elders looked with favor upon the sweet creature who had a helping hand for any one in need;

---

(1) Indian name for the Governor of Quebec.

the staunch Huron converts loved to talk with her of heavenly things, and the youth of the village, though dazzled by her unusual beauty, stood in awe of her calm dignity, while her modest demeanor commanded their utmost respect and held in check their passionate inclinations. The Fathers, too, admired not only her singular purity of soul, but her extraordinary intelligence and cheerful readiness to aid them in whatever she could.

She found untold enjoyment in the company of those young Huron women who, though captives in the Onondaga community, were unflinching in their adherence to the Christian faith, and whose happy privilege it had been to spend two and, in some in some instances, three years with the Ursulines in Quebec. These holy religious, who had come from France in 1639, succeeded in sowing in many a savage heart seeds of purity and zeal that later blossomed forth and helped, in no small degree, to disinfect the moral atmosphere of their forest home. With delight Térèse listened to the tales of convent life told by the Huron maidens, and she often found herself trying to picture the good black-robed nuns who were so kind and gentle, the lovely chapel with its pretty altar and soft lights, the pleasant games played between the hours of study, the quiet, peaceful life led within the convent walls, and she longed for even a glimpse of a place where it was so easy to be good and happy. At home she seldom alluded to religious matters, deeming it best, as Father Chaumonot had suggested, to influence Orrewati not so much by word as by example, and so indispensable had she become to the old man's happiness that he could not bear to be long separated from her. Besides, so great was his solicitude for her well-being, that the faintest shadow upon her sweet, grave face was sure to elicit an affectionate inquiry as to what was amiss.

During the winter of 1656-57 Térèse had made but one trip to the fort, that being when Orrewati had gone thither with the last of the dressed bear skins for which Father Le Mercier had negotiated and, on that occasion, she had not seen Pierre Boudreau. Of course, it was now no longer necessary that she depend on him to procure her an interview with the Fathers, or devise means for her to secretly attend divine service, but still she could not forget the help he had given her when she most required it, the spiritual consolation he had obtained for her when her soul was famishing, and, so sorely was she disappointed at not meeting him, that she at length ventured to ask Father Le Mercier where he was. "I regret to say," replied the priest, "that Pierre is confined to his bed. He caught a heavy cold and, though he is much better, we think it wise for him to remain in the dormitory for a few days."

"A winter in our forests is trying indeed," observed Térèse, endeavoring to conceal the anxiety she felt, "and M. Boudreau does well to be careful." However, for many days after her return to Onondaga, her mind continually reverted to the young Frenchman who had so gallantly befriended her and of whom she could not bear to think as being ill, and then, realizing the utter uselessness of worrying, she placed him under the protection of the Mother of God.

Balmy Spring, during which nature had appeared verdant and flower-decked, had given place to sultry Summer and scarcely a breath of air stirred the luxuriant forest foliage, or caused a ripple upon the tranquil bosom of the woodland streams. But, while nature was mild and almost listless, the Indians of Onondaga went about with a sinister look on their swarthy faces, a suspicious gleam in their dark eyes. There had been no open rupture between them and their pale-faced neighbors, but the constantly diminishing attendance at divine service and the ever growing indifference manifested towards the Fathers and their work, foreboded trouble, and a late summer episode caused the Frenchmen at the fort to enter into gloomy speculations regarding their future. On July 26th, Father Ragueneau left Quebec in company with fifteen or sixteen Senecas, thirty Onondagas and about fifty Christian Hurons, including men, women and children. The Iroquois had induced the Hurons to go with them to their country, promising to treat them as brothers and boon companions, and Father Ragueneau was *en route* to join his brethren at

Gannentaha, where he hoped to aid them in the glorious work in which they were engaged. But, on August 3d, a horrible tragedy was committed when an Iroquois captain slew a Huron woman who, despite him, upheld her honor, and thereafter seven Christians were put to death, and the women and children taken prisoners and stripped of all their possessions. (1) A like fate would probably have awaited the Europeans at Gannentaha, were it not that a number of Iroquois had taken up a temporary abode among the Frenchmen at Quebec, where they had remained in the hope of persuading more of the Hurons to accompany them to their fertile country. But an attack on the Frenchmen at Gannentaha could be readily avenged by one made upon the Iroquois then at Quebec, therefore, the wily savages waited. However, their perfidy became daily more apparent and though they did not openly revolt, there was an under-current of restlessness and dissatisfaction which, try as they would to conceal it, was nevertheless discernible and led the Frenchmen to mistrust them more and more.

The Christian Hurons, who constituted a large portion of the Onondaga community, were for the greater part sincere, but a change came over many of the Iroquois, who belonged to the thriving settlement. Some of them had begged the Frenchmen to come and live among them, because they thought to strengthen their own trading relations with the Europeans in Quebec, while others hoped to make use of the new-comers and their firearms in time of war, and to turn into a place of refuge for their squaws and children the fort which they knew the white men would surely build.

But now the Onondagas had so far quelled the troublesome tribes of the neighborhood as to feel quite independent of any aid from the white men at Gannentaha, and, moreover, they had begun to listen to the suggestions of the Mohawks, who urged that the Frenchmen be exterminated. The outlook grew constantly worse, and, though the Fathers and M. Dupuy's little garrison were in no way blind to the fact, they

---

(1) *Relations des Jesuites.* (Quebec Edition.) Year, 1657, Chap. XXII, pp. 54-55.

realized that the safest course for them to pursue was one of careful policy. Therefore, though ever alert, they feigned complete ignorance of the covert scheming that was continually carried on, and bided their time in prayerful patience.

Meanwhile Térèse had felt the influence of the change. At first Orrewati had ceased attending services at the chapel and then endeavored to dissuade her from so doing, but the girl, with a fearlessness which he could not understand, deliberately resisted him, and no argument that he used could wring from her the promise that he tried to exact.

"'Tis strange," she at length said, "that thou seekest to make me happy, and still wouldst deprive me of what has for me the greatest charm. Have I not been a good and faithful child? Do I deserve such treatment at thy hands?"

"No;" was the quick reply, "thou deservest not that I should render thee unhappy but, do I merit that thou shouldst hold out against my wishes? Have I not been a father to thee? What would have become of thee had I not rescued, sheltered and protected thee? Perhaps thou hadst frozen to death in the forest, or become the prey of ravening wolves, or the victim of some base fiend who would covet thee for thy beauty's sake but be heedless of thy delicate instincts. Have I not the right to demand of thee what I will?"

"Yes, Orrewati, a right which Térèse fully recognizes, but her first duty is to God."

"Ah! thou art glib, indeed. Verily the blackgown's words have turned thy pretty head, but such nonsense availeth naught when there is so much at stake. It was well for us to harbor these pale-faced creatures and their allies at the fort when we needed their friendship and firearms, but the good Arekouë has dispelled the war-cloud and we Onondagas no longer require assistance from these bold intruders who would abolish the customs of our fathers. Thou, child, hast ever done my bidding and I charge thee not to oppose me now. Thy intercourse with these men must end, thy visits to their chapel must cease; I'll have no more of it."

Orrewati spoke with calm determination and his words chilled Térèse's heart. However, she was silent for a moment only when, taking courage, she approached the old Indian and, in a voice which at first trembled slightly but grew steadier as she proceeded, said:

"Orrewati surely is aware that Térèse loves and venerates him, but she cannot do as he commands." There is no mistaking the girl's meaning, no doubting the sincerity of her words, and her straightforward manner for a moment quite disarmed the sturdy old Indian who was totally unprepared for such unfaltering opposition; but recovering from his surprise, he resumed:

"I see that thy will is fixed, but it is no stronger than mine, and yield thou shalt, or rue the consequences. Think on what I say. Have the teachings of these pale-faced deceivers so deluded thee that thou art blind to all reason?" Orrewati grew more and more vehement and his young ward, seeing that an angry outburst was sure to follow, thought it as well to hasten the crisis which she knew to be inevitable.

"Be the consequences what they may, my good friend, I shall continue to frequent the chapel at least on Sundays, and, whenever my soul requires their help, I shall apply to the blackgowns. They could not force me to do these things did I not know that all my happiness depends thereon. My life here in the forest, whether blissful or miserable, must sometime come to an end; whereas the life that is to follow will be eternal, and, if I prove true to the God of the palefaces, who is the God of the red men as well, when I die He will take me to His kingdom where all is peace and love, where no enemy can penetrate nor fury of the elements disturb. Is such a future not worth struggling for?"

"Thou talkest as one in a dream. In truth these men have woven a spell about thee, but break it I shall."

"But Orrewati," exclaimed the girl, "wilt tell me the reason for thy present action? For many moons past thou hast not only left me free to do as I would, but thou thyself hast gone to hear the blackgowns preach and to be instructed as a Christian. Wherefore this change in thee? Were not the Fathers good and kind to thee?"

"That is the trouble, child; their slick, polished ways are

deceiving, and, as I have told thee, we no longer need the aid of their friends at the fort, and even the Mohawks have warned us against them. . . . But such talk is not for thy ear; thy spirit must not be troubled. Thou hast merely to obey me and all will be well. I could not permit thee to openly defy me. What would our chiefs and captains think did I allow thee to pursue thy chosen course, I who cherish the memory of our forefathers and would give my life for the protection of our lands and cabins?"

"Orrewati, it were well for thee to know the truth at once; thy words are powerless to dissuade me."

The Indian's brow contracted in a fierce scowl, his eyes gleamed with rage, and doubling his fist, he stepped up to the girl and shook it in her face, exclaiming: "Then, away with thee, ungrateful creature! This cabin can no longer shelter one who thus proclaims herself the enemy of her race. Begone, I say, begone to those whose cause thou maintainest, nor dare to let thy shadow darken my abode." Increasing rage and excitement had carried the man's coarse voice to the screaming pitch, and he fairly yelled the last words while Térèse had gradually receded till she found herself at the entrance to the cabin. There, however, she paused, and choking down a sob which threatened to impede her utterance, she said:

"Remember, Orrewati, Térèse goes not hence in anger, and only for her God would she thus leave him of whose old age she should be the comfort and joy." The old Iroquois was looking away from the girl, but at these tender words he turned and faced her.

"Hold!" he cried as she was in the act of withdrawing. "Stay and hear me further." His rough voice trembled, his stout frame shook, and the fierceness of his expression softened, as after a pause he continued: "Accept these conditions and thou mayest remain. Go to the chapel if thou wilt, but only when sure that no eye save that of a Christian will be upon thee; say no word to a blackgown without first warning me of thy intent, and hold no intercourse with any of the soldiers from the fort, unless when in my presence

Dost agree?" Térèse slowly nodded assent, and her inquisitor continued: "Wilt promise on thy honor?"

"Yes;" was the simple rejoinder, and thus ended the first stormy interview that had ever taken place between Orrewati and his ward.

(*To be Continued.*)

FROM THE MISSIONS.

The following letter speaks for itself, and we print it with the hope that it may enlist the sympathy of our charitable and zealous readers.

ULTAL, MANGALORE, P. O.,
INDIA, May 23, 1899.

REV. AND DEAR FATHER:

Allow me to apologize for my slowness in acknowledging your kind letter of February 28. Since January 9, the beginning of missionary work, I have had very little time to spare. The heavy Lenten work over, I began on Easter Monday to prepare the children for First Communion. I am writing this at ten o'clock at night. After my last letter to you I spent a month in the interior, one-fourth of a mile beyond the miraculous fountain of Ven. Father Joseph Vaz. There, in an open veranda, I gathered together the children, taught them the sign of the cross, their prayers, the rudiments of faith, and admitted them to First Communion on Candlemas Day. During the week-days I catechised the children from 8.30 in the morning till 12 noon, and from 2 to 4.30 P. M. Parents here are possessed of a certain diabolical characteristic. They put every obstacle in the way and allow their children to attend church sparingly indeed. The cause is their complete ignorance of Christian doctrine and their bias for superstitious practices. They seem utterly unable to appreciate the things of God in their true light. The people of this parish are famous throughout the neighborhood for the obstinacy with which they cling to ancestral superstitions. Superstition, in fact, is their daily bread. And yet they never like to be reckoned guilty of the crime. When questioned on the subject they profess profound ignorance about the whole thing. Nevertheless, on a feast-day the first offering, the choicest morsel necessarily goes to their "dear god," hiding somewhere in a dark room. If anybody falls sick, they straightway consult some soothsayer or other minister of the devil. If disease attacks the cattle, they at once cut the neck of a chicken and offer its blood to the devil to satisfy his wrath. Every sickness, according to them, comes from the devil. Hence their eagerness in calamity to propitiate his offended majesty. As long as he reigns in their hearts, the growth of God's Kingdom must suffer a serious setback. They can have no love of God, no love for religion, Church or priest. I give you this brief account of my people to awake your sympathy and appeal to the assistance of your readers. To push God's interests in this remote corner of the world I have hit upon the following plan. I am going to stay three months in one place and catechise the people there from June next. From September to November I mean to occupy another station, the centre of four villages with at least seven hundred souls. I intend to then proceed to the far East and spend there a couple of months in the same work. A chapel at the second place, the centre of the four villages, is a much-felt want. But the people are poor. Their pastor is, comparatively speaking, even poorer. Besides, we are without a single school among a Catholic population of 2,890. Schools are sources of untold good; but they cannot be raised without money. I pray you, therefore, be pleased to advocate my cause; not mine, but that of 2,890 Catholics, having for their patroness our Lady of Mercy. In behalf of these many souls, speak through your pages to generous and charitable men and women who by their bounty may yet be instrumental in making these people Christians and good Christians. Their charity can be shown in whatever way zeal for souls and love of religion suggest. Briefly, my needs are these: A portable altar for my missionary journeys, together with rosaries, scapulars of Mt. Carmel, badges of the Sacred Heart, medals, crucifixes and other objects of devotion. Secondly, means to build a chapel. For this two hundred dollars would be quite enough. Thirdly, means to build at least two schools in two places where the German Lutherans have by their wealth and commodious buildings attracted the poor and uneducated people of the interior. If we could get fifty dollars a year, we could keep up the schools and the teachers. Besides, the whole sanctuary of our present church is in so dilapidated a condition, that, unless speedy measures are taken to set it right, it must necessarily fall in ruins. My needs, perhaps, are too many. My tale, perhaps, is annoying. But, Father, forgive me, please. I am writing as one in grief, to a dear friend, able and willing to relieve my needs.

Your humble servant,

R. M. LOBO.

To awaken interest in the work, we submit to the attention of our readers this graphic and interesting account of what is being done by our missionaries on the island of Syra in Greece: "In 1873 the diocese of Syra, called, from its devoted attachment to the Holy See, the "Island of the Popes," was solemnly consecrated to the Sacred Heart of Jesus by its pious Bishop, Monsignor Alberti, at that time Delegate Apostolic for the whole of Greece. The imposing ceremony had place in the Cathedral, June 29, in the presence of a large and enthusiastic multitude. On this occasion the Bishop made a vow in his own name and in that of his successors, promising to consecrate to the Sacred Heart the island's first church. This vow is perpetuated in a tablet of marble occupying a prominent position in the wall of the Cathedral. The vow itself was fulfilled some years after the Bishop's death by his successor, Monsignor Massimi. A town in the beautiful valley of Gallissas rapidly grew to proportions large enough for a church. Its inhabitants asked and easily obtained permission to build, on the one condition that they consecrate their new church to the Sacred Heart. The edifice is situated on a promontory commanding a view of the bay below. Though not yet quite finished, it is regularly attended, and during the first week in August was the scene of magnificent ceremonies in honor of the Sacred Heart. This public manifestation of piety was but another effect of the devotion planted in the souls of the faithful by a congregation of the Sacred Heart established in their church over a century ago by the Jesuit Fathers. After the suppression of the Society this congregation was transplanted to the Cathedral, where once every year solemn High Mass was sung in honor of the Sacred Heart. To renew fervor, grown cold with the lapse of time, we established the Apostleship of Prayer in our church in 1886. To-day it is in a most flourishing condition. The good people of Syra have unbounded confidence in the Sacred Heart of Jesus, and they display a fervor worthy of all praise. The first Friday of every month is kept with great splendor in our church. At six in the morning Mass is said for the Associates, all receive Holy Communion in a body, beads are said, and hymns, in keeping with the occasion, are sung. In the evening we have a sermon, exposition, the offering, act of reparation, all interspersed with most becoming music. These first Friday reunions are a continual renewal of spirit and piety for such as assist at them and for their families.

All the sodalities take part in this grand movement in honor of the Sacred Heart, and the devotion daily grows stronger and stronger in the midst of the Catholics of Syra. Foremost among the sodalities come the two of young men and young women, under the patronage of St. Aloysius Gonzaga. These two sodalities are veritable gardens of piety and modesty. The church is so small that we are obliged to separate them and hold meetings at different hours. This is the one great difficulty we experience in the matter of communions for the six Sundays of St. Aloysius, and for feasts of great solemnity. The narrow dimensions of the church detract from the splendor of the events, they necessarily lessen the number of such as should and would take part in the services and diminish the external grandeur proper to these beautiful and edifying ceremonies. The feast day of these two sodalities is beyond doubt, the most gladsome and splendid of any celebrated in Syra. It is youth's holiday. Preceded by the confessions and communions of the six Sundays, and by a fervent novena, it is encompassed round about by all the touching simplicity of youthful innocence. Music, hymns, decorations, banners, lilies, are everywhere. The statue of their angelic patron is borne in triumph through the village, accompanied by a long procession of devout clients, with the entire population abroad to view the moving scene. The enthusiasm of the day communicates itself to the Greeks of the town below. Out of curiosity they flock in crowds to the upper town, go away profoundly touched and return to their homes in the evening with an image of the lily-Saint imprinted in their hearts. At night Syra is all on fire, and this grand illumination marks the close of a day that ought to have no end. On the octave of the feast all the people assemble again in Sodality Park, a field outside the village, which serves every Sunday as a playground for the sodalists. The bishop with his clergy honors this meeting with his presence. The governor is there with the town council and a large concourse of spectators. In the middle of the field stands a raised platform. After the distribution of prizes a young member of the sodality mounts this platform and delivers the panegyric of the sodality's patron saint. The angels of Paradise then seem to join hands with earth's angels, and hearts capable of hearing their mystical voices are touched to their depths, and carry away from the event a sense of sweetness wholly absent from what joys this world knows. Within the last few years we added to the sodality a feature, bound to prove a decided help for faith and sure to win in spite of opposition. The enemy of souls puts every energy in motion to drag the young men of the sodality to destruction by clubs, formed with the avowed purpose of dethroning faith and morals, and piety. To offset this attack we organized a society, naming it "The Young Men's Club." We built a fine hall for receptions and public entertainments, and soon added apartments to serve as living-rooms for the members. In this corner of the world the good work of saving souls knows no greater enemy than the spirit of independence peculiar to the country. This inclination is wonderfully helped by the people's extreme poverty, paralyzing in its effects and furnishing a specious pretext for all the deplorable irregularities of weak nature. A Greek never submits with good will to rule or order, and if he sometimes promises to do so, his promise is unsteady and soon broken. A modern wit puts it in this terse language, "Greeks never carry burdens on their backs." For this reason and others of the same kind the club has not yet come up to our expectations. Many of our young men still prefer to frequent the saloons, the gambling houses, and the theatres. Nevertheless we are far from losing hope. Perseverance hath a perfect work. After all, we are most seriously handicapped in our work by one overwhelming difficulty. Our church is entirely too small to contain our people. We are therefore determined to enlarge its size at the earliest possible opportunity. Allow us then the freedom of your pages to make an earnest appeal to men of zeal, most of all to men devoted to the interests of the Sacred Heart, for funds needed to carry this good work to completion.

Your Reverence's servant in Christ.

G. M. ROMANO, S.J.

MISSION NOTES.

——It may be news to some of our readers to learn that Rev. Frederick Hopkins, S.J., has been lately named Vicar-Apostolic of British Honduras. Monsignor Salvator di Pietro, his predecessor in office and a Jesuit, died during his course of this year. The present Very Rev. Vicar was born in England, May 25, 1844, and for several years proved a laborious and successful missionary in the field now committed to his care.

——The Emperor of China has lately issued a decree regulating the intercourse of missionaries with the mandarins or Chinese local authorities. It is a set of five rules. The first of these fixes the rank of various church officials. Bishops are put on terms of equality with viceroys and governors of provinces; directors of districts, or rural deans, rank with Tao-tais, and the other priests with prefects and sub-prefects of cities. Hitherto justice as between Christians and the native Chinese has been next to impossible, owing, in great part, to the fact that personal communication with the State officials was, on account of differences in rank, either difficult or entirely out of the question. Now, however, the mandarin cannot refuse to see a priest of equal rank with himself, and affairs can be speedily expedited. In virtue of another ruling, a priest, when appointed to a district, must bring a letter of introduction from his bishop. His Lordship must likewise notify the viceroy and governor of the appointment. Official rank in China makes necessary a host of calls and visits of ceremony, entailing great loss of time and bound seriously to interfere with the duties of bishops and priests. A third article in the decree meets this difficulty, and allows bishops, even at New Year, to salute the viceroy and governor by card or letter. A fourth ruling prescribes that when matters of consequence connected with the Church arise the bishop or priest must apply to the consul or minister of the nation appointed by the Pope to protect the interests of the Church. Last of all, the local mandarins are advised to put forth proclamations exhorting the common people to live in harmony with the Catholics. The bishops and priests in turn must urge their Catholics to practise virtue, preserve the good name of their religion and provoke others to admiration by their edifying conduct.

——In spite of legislation in their favor, our missionaries in China are still exposed to grave danger. Witness the following letter copied from "Annals of the Propagation of the Faith:" "Mgr. Reynaud writes from Ning-Po, May 12, 1899: Our situation at Tai-tcheon, is getting worse and worse. Seven chapels have already been burned. We cannot count the number of Christian families plundered and burned out. The brigands sow ruin in their path. They have taken fifty neophytes whom they keep as hostages. Some have been tortured in the most horrible manner. One of them, the most influential in this region, has had both feet cut off and his eyes torn out. There have been no defections. Our Christians remain good, and are taking refuge at Hay-men. We hardly know how to shelter them. The bands rejoined by In-vain-te, number about four to five thousand brigands, all well-armed. Their garments bear inscriptions, such as: 'Protect the Kingdom; Exterminate Religion!' That is clear enough. All our stations have been visited; there has been no vigorous intervention. In expectation pray for this young Christian settlement of Tai-tcheon, which has received the baptism of fire and blood, and is still clothed in its white robe like the virgin-martyrs of the primitive Church. We weep, but what joy is our tears to see the courage of our neophytes and the promise of new conquests which the trials of to-day assure us for to-morrow."

——*L'Univers* of September 16, 1899, is authority for the following statistics: The Catholics in India, including Ceylon, now number 1,938,996 souls. There are 818 European priests, whilst the native priests count 1,580. In the archdiocese of Pondichery, 8,793 conversions have been made; in Mysore, 536; in Coïmbatore, 605. The Jesuits, without counting their other missions in India, have converted 2,000 in the diocese of Calcutta, and 2,159 at Madura.

Acknowledgment is made of the following contributions:

FOR NEEDY COMMUNITIES OF NUNS IN ITALY.
Anon $1 00

FOR THE SISTERS OF THE GOOD SHEPHERD IN HAVANA.
M. O'N., New York $5 00

FOR THE PROPAGATION OF THE FAITH.
M. A. B., Danville, Canada . . $ 50

FOR THE SUPPORT OF A PRIEST IN CUBA.
J. R., Dubuque, Ia $50 00

FOR THE CHINESE MISSIONS.
A child of Mary, Phila. . . $ 1 00

FOR ST. LABIS MISSION.
J. M. J., Edgerove, Pa . . . $ 5 00

THE PILGRIM

OF

OUR LADY OF MARTYRS

XV. YEAR. NOVEMBER, 1899. No. 11.

ANNALS OF THE SHRINE.

ANNIVERSARIES.

———On Friday, September 29, Mass was said at the altar of the old Shrine at Auriesville, on the occasion of the death of René Goupil, Rev. F. J. Lamb, S.J., being the celebrant. On Wednesday, October 18, Mass was again said at the same altar by Rev. Alan McDonell and J. Wynne to commemorate the death of Father Isaac Jogues. Father McDonell was the first to say one of these Anniversary Masses some seventeen years ago, using for this purpose the mission church at Tribes Hill near by, before the site of the captivity and death of Father Jogues and René Goupil, which the Shrine now occupies, had been accurately located. He was naturally well pleased with this opportunity of showing his veneration for the memory of these servants of God, and for recommending an intention for which we ask every friend of Auriesville to pray most earnestly.

* * *

———For some time after the purchase of the Shrine property, the Mass usually offered on the anniversary of Father Jogues' death was not said, the Feast of the Assumption, the first day he spent at Auriesville as a prisoner under torture, having been chosen to commemorate his life and death. Since 1896, the two hundred and fiftieth anniversary of his death, Mass has been said at Auriesville each eighteenth day of October, but owing to our apprehension lest the weather should be unsettled at that time we did not invite pilgrims, content with asking clients of our Lady of Sorrows to unite in spirit with us in the celebration of the august mysteries of the Sacrifice of Calvary. From our experience the past four years we may reasonably hope for both good weather and accommodations at Auriesville on one or other of the dates, September 29 or October 18, and we shall therefore encourage the many persons who have asked to attend these Masses to come to them next year.

* * *

——The next anniversary Mass will be in memory of Catherine Tegakwitha, but as the date of her death is April 13, and as, in 1900, Good Friday will fall on that day, it is likely that the Mass in her memory will be said on April 18, the Wednesday following, a day devoted to the honor of Blessed Mary of the Incarnation, foundress and first Superioress of the Ursulines of Quebec, in 1642, so deservedly celebrated for her zeal and fruitful work for young Indian girls like Catherine. Although Catherine never came under the influence of Blessed Mary or her Ursulines, readers of her life will remember how much she was attracted by all that she saw in the lives of the Hospital Sisters in Montreal, whom she visited when travelling to Caugnawaugha, the Indian Catholic settlement near that city. In coupling the memory of Catherine with that of Blessed Mary of the Incarnation, we shall be honoring a servant of God who helped the missionaries so much in the education of young Indian girls.

The Ravine.

——The fine weather of the past month has been of great benefit to the improvements made lately in the Ravine. The grass seed sown in September has already covered the newly built bank of the Ravine and the road bed with a velvet green growth, and the sods covering the hillsides have taken hold and flourished. The Ravine is now very beautiful, and the labor and expense it cost us are fully justified. Our appeal for funds to meet this expense has moved some of the clients of the Shrine to a generous response, but we are still far short of the sum required to cover the entire outlay, and we beg of our readers to help us to clear it speedily. By doing so they can manifest their piety to our Lady who is specially honored in the grotto there, and make it possible for us next summer to erect in the glade across the stream a grotto of the Holy Sepulchre, as a representation of the tomb in Gethsemane, with a figure of the dead Christ reposing in it.

A Shrine Lecture.

——Sunday, October 15, Father Wynne delivered a lecture in the opera house of Johnstown, N. Y., under the auspices of the Knights of Columbus of that city on the subject, "The Mohawk

Valley in Iroquois Days," dealing especially with the history of Father Jogues' captivity and of the Mission which he tried to establish at Auriesville. In the audience were many who are quite familiar with Auriesville as it is to-day, and also non-Catholics as well as Catholics for whom this was the first opportunity of hearing of the heroic work of the Missionaries among the Indians who inhabited the valley two centuries ago. The lecture, which was illustrated by eighty well-chosen lantern slides, was preceded by a fine sacred concert.

THE CROWN.

——Since our last issue we had the pleasure of seeing the crown of thorns which the jewellers, Messrs. J. W. Feeley & Co., of Providence, R. I., are making for the Shrine at Auriesville, and which they have well-nigh finished. As our readers are aware, clients of Our Lady of Martyrs at Auriesville began about six years ago to contribute gold and precious stones to make a crown for her statue. As at first it was thought proper not to crown her statue in the group known as the Pietà, in which she is represented as sitting at the foot of the Cross, and supporting on her knees the Body of the Christ just taken down from the Cross, a model was made for a statue representing the Mother of Sorrows as she stood at the Cross. It is this model which now occupies the grotto in the Ravine.

——For several reasons, however, it has been decided to use the gold and precious stones to adorn the Pietà, which naturally excites the piety of the faithful more than any other statue of our Lady in the Passion, since it connects her with her Divine Son. No crown could contain the abundant offering sent us, nor for that matter, can any crown of earthly pattern express the exalted dignity of the Queen of heaven and earth. Accordingly it has been decided to make from the beautiful and precious offerings of gold and precious stones, the crown which of all others the Mother of Sorrows prized, a crown of thorns in gold, similar in size and design to the one which the rude soldiers plaited for the head of Christ, when they saluted Him in mockery as their king. This will be held in the hands of the statue of our Lady or be at her feet. To adorn the heads of the statues of our Lord and our Lady, the usual halos representing their holiness will be made in gold set with precious stones, so that the figures will be properly crowned, and the gift of the faithful will be used to make the most proper adornment for the dead Christ and His sorrowing Mother.

———To help our readers form some image of the crown of thorns destined for the Pietà at Auriesville, we repeat here the following extract from the *Messenger of The Sacred Heart* for March, 1897, from an article on the "Instruments of the Passion," based on the researches of the eminent archæologist Rohault de Fleury:

"There is something very striking in the bald simplicity with which St. John relates the horrible insult and fearful torment inflicted on our Lord in His mock coronation. 'The soldiers platting a crown of thorns, put it on his head.'

"Not a word of comment does the Evangelist add. Perhaps he had not the heart to describe the awful agony this crowning caused—agony not only to the sacred head but above all to the Sacred Heart, indescribably wounded by such an insult.

"We are accustomed to think of the crown of thorns as a mere circlet resting on the temples, whereas it was, in all probability, a sort of cap, covering the whole top of the head, and inflicting intense pain at every point of the skull. Judging from the relics extant, it was composed of two sorts of plants. There was a large wreath of reeds, bound together by filaments of reed, which served as a frame, so large was it that of itself it would have slipped down from the head to the shoulders. The reason of its size was that the thorns were interwoven and inserted into the wreath of reeds thus diminishing its inner diameter. So horrible was the torment which this cruel cap of thorns inflicted that the early Christians could not bear to represent it in its awful reality, and so only expressed it by emblems. Thus in a bas-relief in the Lateran Museum a soldier is seen respectfully placing a crown of roses and laurel on the head of our Lord. Perhaps, too, this is the reason why, in Christian art, the crown of thorns is rather suggested than depicted as it really was—an instrument of fiendish torture.

"This explanation of the forming of the crown removes what was formerly considered a great difficulty—how to account for the reedy circlet preserved at Notre Dame in Paris and the numerous thorns treasured in various places. The combination solves the difficulty satisfactorily.

"The next question is the authenticity of the relics. Like the other instruments of the Passion it remained providentially hidden during the four first centuries. In 409 St. Paulinus, Bishop of Nola, in Italy, admits its existence as a well known fact. St.

Gregory of Tours seems to be the first to speak of it explicitly. About the year 800 the Patriarch of Jerusalem sent to Charlemagne a nail, some thorns, and a considerable piece of the Cross. King Charles the Bald presented these relics to the Abbey of St.

Denis, and an inscription of the twelfth century on his tomb records the gift.

"At the time of the First Crusade, the Emperor Alexis Comnenus wrote in 1100 to Count Robert of Flanders that many remarkable relics were kept in Constantinople, hoping thus to tempt the Latin princes to take possession of that city.

"A little more than a century later, Baldwin II., Emperor of Constantinople, involved himself hopelessly in debt to the Venetians. In 1248, he appealed to the King of France to come to his assistance. The debt amounted to 156,900 francs, an enormous sum in those days. What a pledge had the emperor given? The holy relics and especially the Crown of Thorns.

"In our cold, skeptical times it is hard for us to realize the esteem and veneration that kings and people felt for sacred things. It is worth while, therefore, to read the graphic account of the translation of the Holy Crown.

"'St. Louis, having obtained this grant, sent to Constantinople two Dominican friars, James and Andrew, one of whom having been prior of a convent in that city, had more than once seen the Holy Crown of Thorns, which formed part of the relics to be surrendered, and understood well all that concerned it. Baldwin, then at St. Germain, caused them to be accompanied by one of his officers with letters patent commanding his representatives to deliver over the holy relic to the envoys of the king. Before leaving Constantinople, they took all the necessary precautions to attest the authenticity and the preservation of this sacred object. The case which enclosed it was sealed with the seals of the French envoys. Having escaped the dangers of the sea, serious at that time of the year, for they had embarked about Christmas time, the Holy Crown reached Venice, where it was placed in the treasury of the Chapel of St. Mark, until all the conditions of the contract with the Venetians should be fulfilled. The ambassadors of the king, having taken cognizance of the seals, set out for France. St. Louis, accompanied by the queen, his mother, and by the princes, his brothers, and many prelates and lords, went to meet them, and received the Holy Crown at Villeneuve-l'Archevêque, about five leagues from Sens, on August 10, 1239. They first removed the wooden case which enclosed the relic, and then verified the seals with the acts establishing its authenticity. Next they opened the silver reliquary, then the golden vase containing the Holy Crown and showed it

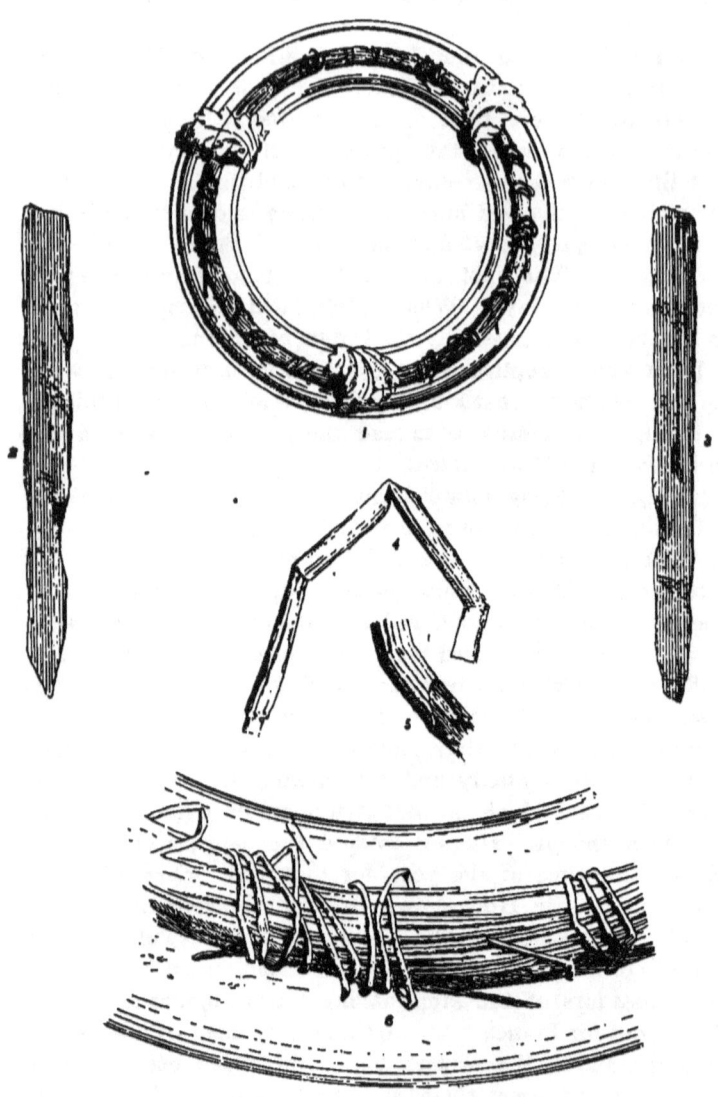

RELICS KEPT IN NOTRE DAME, PARIS.

1. The reliquary and crown.
2, 3. Two views of the holy nail.
4, 5. Fragments of the crown as seen through the microscope.
6. Fragment of the crown in its natural size.

to the king and all his suite. The next day the king left for Paris, where, eight days later, the solemn reception of the sacred relic took place.'

"We have given this long account because it conveys a great lesson to us—the wonderful reverence and devotion which Catholics of the thirteenth century had for our Lord and all that was connected in any way with His precious Passion and death.

"A few years later, the saintly monarch built, at immense cost, by way of reliquary, that gem of Gothic architecture the Sainte Chapelle, still standing in Paris, the chapel of the palace now called Palais de Justice.

"We may here fitly mention another reliquary of the same kind and for another portion of the same relic, the exquisite church of *Santa Maria della Spina* at Pisa.

"So highly were the Holy Crown of Thorns and other sacred relics preserved in the Sainte Chapelle prized by the Kings of France, that they either kept the keys of the chapel themselves, or confided them to a nobleman specially delegated, who could not lend them without the king's express order. This custom prevailed for over two hundred years. In 1791, by order of Louis XVI., the Holy Crown was transferred to the Abbey of St. Denis. Two years later it was taken back to Paris, despoiled at the mint of its rich casings, and placed in the National Library in 1794. It was restored to the Church authorities in 1804, and in 1806 it was solemnly translated to Notre Dame by the Cardinal de Belloy, Archbishop of Paris.

"The precious relic is now enclosed in a crystal ring in six pieces, held together by three clasps in gold bronze. Apart from the authenticity which its history assures, the very improbability of its genuineness which it presents at first sight, but which vanishes after a careful study, proves that it is really the true crown of our Lord. For if anyone would have made up a counterfeit they would have done so according to the common and natural idea which painters have followed, and would never have put a wreath of reeds instead of thorns, nor would they have made it too large for the head. Thus, what seems the hardest to understand about it is, in fact, the strongest proof of its genuineness. There are very many relics of thorns extant, but their number is not surprising when we consider what a quantity could have been massed together to form that horrible helmet. We must, however, notice that the crowns of thorns which we see in many

ANNALS OF THE SHRINE. 329

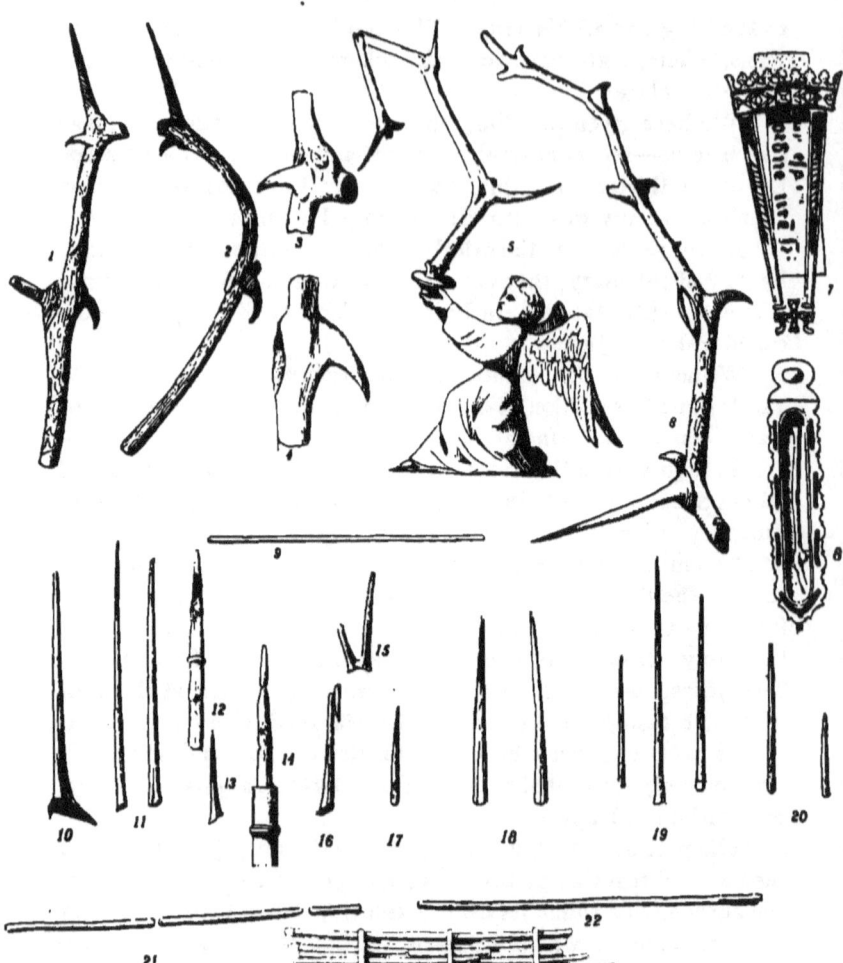

RELICS OF THE THORNS OF THE HOLY CROWN.

1, 2, 3, 4. The thorn at Pisa—two views and portions magnified.
5. Thorn at Wevelgheim, diocese of Bruges.
6. Thorn at Treves.
7, 8. Portions at Autun, cathedral and seminary.
9. Reed at Arras.
10. Thorn at Carpentras.
11. Turin, Chapel Royal.
12. At St. Acheul.
13. Pisa, cathedral.
14. Florence, Santa Croce.
15. At Nice.
16. Dome.
17. At Rome, St. Bernard.
18. Santa Croce.
19. Saint Praxedes.
20. St. John Lateran and Santa Maria in Campitelli.
21, 22. Jesuit Fathers at Vaugirard, Paris.
23. Reeds from the crown in Paris at Chablis.

places are merely pious mementos, which may, at most, have touched some genuine relic and consequently are honored. One thing must impress us, and that is the jealous care which the Church takes in authenticating relics and in honorably preserving them."

——We recommend to the prayers of our readers the soul of Rev. Arthur McAvoy, of the Society of Jesus, who was well known to some of the pilgrims at Auriesville, and who died at Frederick, Md., during the past month.

An Appeal.

——When in February of this year we were giving the offerings of gold and precious stones for the crown to the jeweller, we notified our readers not to send more gifts of jewelry. Now that the crown is well nigh complete and that the jeweller is about to proceed with the halos of gold for the heads of the figures of our Lord and our Lady, we shall be glad to receive donations of gold or of precious stones for these objects, and in view of the fact that the design for both is to be made soon, it will be well to send offerings as promptly as possible.

Should those who have jewelry to offer in this manner prefer to donate it for a chalice, paten or ciborium for the Shrine, let them kindly state this wish and we shall heed it.

Offerings of money will be gratefully received for any or for all of the needs of the Shrine, for the improvements in the Ravine, for the statue for which we are preparing the crown, or for the cost of the work on the crown itself.

CONTRIBUTIONS TO THE SHRINE.

M. R., Nashua, N. H.	$10 00	J. D. W., Philadelphia, Pa.	$1 00
N. N., New York	1 00	K. R. H. W., Roxbury, Mass.	1 00
M. L. S. H., Buffalo, N. Y.	5 00	Anon	1 00
F. L. McB., Philadelphia, Pa.	1 00	C. H. M.	1 00
J. F., Huefner, Pa.	5 00	D. J. M., New York	100 00
M. H., Utica, N. Y.	6 60	F. W. G., England	25 57
Mrs. G., Boston	5 00	Anon	20 00

FOR THE CROWN.

Miss O' C., Cleveland, Ohio, a gold ring.

Mrs. K., a brooch, a gold ring and three pair of earrings.

Anon, a gold ring, a brooch and a dollar in gold.

M. D., Dushore, Pa., three gold rings, two chains, a gold watch and a pair of gold spectacles.

TÉRÈSE AND PIERRE.

BY K. A. HENNESSY.

(*Continued.*)

CHAPTER VI.

"I Must Be Good to Him."

AS the year 1657 drew to a close the Gannentaha Frenchmen appeared less frequently in Onondaga, though they did not remain away altogether lest their absence cause too much suspicion on the part of the Indians. But, from time to time, some of the Huron converts living in the village would chance to hear a whispered rumor concerning the attitude of the red men, and these they always zealously reported to the Fathers.

Three months had passed since Térèse had met Pierre Boudreau; but, in the meantime, she had occasionally heard of him through the Fathers who came and went frequently between Onondaga and the Fort. Once every few weeks was as often as Orrewati would now agree to her interviewing a priest and, though she was eager to confess her sins more frequently, the Fathers bade her ask no further privilege, but keep in the favor of her old protector in the hope that, through association with her, he might some day change his ways.

One cold night in February in 1658, when the red men of Onondaga slumbered peacefully in their cosy wigwams, Térèse suddenly awoke and, raising herself upon her elbow, rested her head on her hand and listened intently. Presently she heard a faint moan which, after a few seconds, was followed by another and then, feeling sure that she was not mistaken, the girl arose, crept stealthily to the mat where Gannendaris lay and gently tapped the old woman on the shoulder. "Gannendaris," she whispered as the squaw sat up and began to vigorously rub her eyes, "there is some one outside who is in pain. Come, let us see what the trouble is." The woman acquiesced, as indeed she invariably did when called upon by her charming young mistress and, wrapping themselves in bear-skins that were close at hand, the two hastened to the cabin door and peered out into the night. The moon was shedding a soft radiance upon the snow-clad ground, whence myriads of crystals sparkled a silent tribute to the star-studded vault above, and the death-like stillness that prevailed was broken only by such deep groans as that which had awakened Térèse.

The women looked hurriedly from right to left, but discovering no one, paused a moment endeavoring to locate the sound, when suddenly Térèse led the way round to the back of the wigwam beckoning Gannendaris to follow, and, crouching beneath a large oak, they discovered an Indian. A huge branch of the tree cast a deep shadow across his face, thereby making recognition impossible, but Térèse quickly ascertained all that she required to know, which was that a fellow-being was in a state of most pitiable suffering.

"You remain here," she said to Gannendaris, "and I'll call Orrewati, for whether friend or foe the man must not be left here to perish," and, suiting her action to the word, the girl flew back to the tent, rapped lightly on the birch wall that partitioned the old Indian's apartment from her own, told him what had occured and begged him to come outside. He soon followed her and gently raising the sufferer in his strong arms, carried him into the tent, and laid him upon a mat. Then Térèse applied snow to the victim's face and hands and rubbed his benumbed limbs but, even after she had succeeded in restoring the circulation, he still remained apparently unconscious and she felt that he must be suffering from something more than severe exposure to the cold. Tenderly she raised him to a sitting posture, that Gannendaris might place a rolled blanket on which he could rest his head, when, to her dismay, she found blood oozing from a frightful gash over his right shoulder. The size and nature of the wound indicated that it had been inflicted by a tomahawk and the girl shuddered with horror as she proceeded to wash and anoint it.

The flickering pine blaze cast an unsatisfactory light upon

the stranger's face but Térèse could see that his features were distorted in consequence of pain and her sympathy was thoroughly aroused. Towards dawn Orrewati insisted that Térèse take some rest, assuring her that he would watch the patient, and the girl agreed to do as she was asked, and, by sunrise, was lost in a sweet, peaceful slumber. After a few hours the stranger gave signs of returning consciousness, his first words being a request for water, which Gannendaris promptly offered him, and the desired drink seemed greatly to refresh him. Then, in the course of a few moments, Orrewati ventured to question him a little, gleaning in return that his unknown guest was a Mohawk who, when returning to his country, had been mistaken for a Huron and attacked by a band of young Onondaga warriors. The wound in his shoulder was caused by the misaimed blow of a tomahawk, his antagonist's intention having been to strike his skull, and he had been left for dead, but when he could manage to drag himself along, he saw that he had lost the trail, and after much wandering about, he strayed into the village of Onondaga alone, unknown and weakened almost to death.

The tale interested Orrewati, who at length inquired if the young man had known Gonaterezon, a Mohawk from Ossernenon, who was slain in the forest. The question produced an unfavorable effect upon the sufferer, who replied with difficulty: "I've heard of him;" and, fearing to impose upon his guest's greatly impaired strength, Orrewati refrained from interrogating him any further, and after a while, the patient dozed off into a troubled sleep.

At noon Térèse awoke and hastened to his side, and the sun's bright rays penetrated the wigwam, falling full upon the face of the wounded man. As Térèse bent low over his prostrate form and gazed intently at his features that had now become relaxed, she gave a low, piercing cry, as she uttered the name: "Aharihon!"

This startled the slumberer, who instantly awoke and looked vacantly about him, but when his eyes lit upon the face of the trembling girl beside him, a sort of stifled scream escaped him, and he turned his face to the wall. Orrewati stood by in utter dismay and turned upon Térèse a look of mute appeal to which, between sobs, she replied:

" 'Tis Aharihon, my father's slayer, Aharihon whom I had thought dead: my God, my God!"

"Turn him out," shouted Orrewati, "my cabin shall not shelter thy father's murderer, fling him to the wolves;" and the irate old Indian vented his anger by giving the sick man two or three vigorous kicks.

"Don't, don't, Orrewati;" pleaded the girl, placing herself between Orrewati and the object of his wrath. The old Iroquois turned away, uttering blood-curdling oaths, and Térèse, once more bending over her enemy, observed that his cheek was aglow with fever whilst his whole frame trembled convulsively as he muttered and raved incoherently.

The girl was dazed. The discovery she had made, besides proving a rude shock, had awakened such heart-rending memories that she seemed to be living over again the horrors of that awful day when, by a foul, dastardly act, she had been deprived forever of her father's love and protection. And here lay his assassin, prostrate and helpless, and she had it in her power to avenge the cruel murder, to yield to the feeling that now swelled her bosom and grew momentarily stronger, demanding retaliation—revenge. But the words which her dead mother had so often quoted: "Do unto others as you would be done by," kept ringing in her ears till, at length, her nobler nature asserted itself, her Christian spirit triumphed and when Orrewati, once more giving way to his rage, lifted his tomahawk threatening to sever the slender thread of the sufferer's life, she raised her hand and parried the blow, crying beseechingly: "Nay, nay Orrewati, such would not be Christian; I must be good to him."

Instantly the Onondaga's arm dropped and he stood looking into the eyes of the girl whose simple words had bent his iron will and stemmed the tide of his wrath, and presently the sound of a faint moan fell upon his ear. Térèse heard it too, and turned quickly towards the wounded Mohawk.

"Térèse," the latter said.

"Yes, Aharihon," she softly replied, kneeling beside the prostrate form, "Térèse is here."

"Térèse!" This time the voice was weaker. "Wilt give thy hand into that of thy father's slayer?"

Gently and unhesitatingly she placed it in his outstretched palm, though at the moment a shudder went through her whole frame, and the flush upon her cheek mounted even to her brow.

"It grows so dark that I may not see thy face," feebly articulated the sick man, "but once more I hold thy hand—thy loved hand. . . . Wilt bend thy ear unto my lips?" She did as he asked, and then, in a labored, broken whisper, he continued:

"Think not I sought thy father's life; far from it; I mistook him for Chinaooich, my hated rival. Not a drop of Gonaterezon's blood had I ever wittingly spilled. I'd die happy could I look on thee once more, but it is so dark, so dark!" Then, after a pause, he gasped: "Forgive me!" and Aharihon's heart ceased to beat.

"O God be good to him!" Térèse exclaimed aloud, and Orrewati, who, awed and silent, had seen and heard all that had transpired, stepped out into the bright sunlight, his mind filled with wonderment at Térèse's spirit of forgiveness.

In the meantime much anxiety prevailed at St. Mary's, where the outlook grew daily more ominous, and the Fathers of the mission concluded that, as neither their death nor captivity could in any way benefit the poor Huron converts and the struggling Iroquois Christians whom they had instructed and baptized, it was their bounden duty to thwart, if possible, the fiendish designs of their enemies and to help, as effectually as they could, the Frenchmen who looked to them for advice and support and for whose lives they felt largely responsible.

One night, before the inmates of the fort repaired to the chapel for evening prayer, Father Le Mercier summoned one and all to the refectory, and when the roll was called not an individual of the vast household was missing. Of course all the missionaries were not present, Fathers Chaumonot and Mesnard being at the lodge at Onondaga, but it rarely occurred that all the Fathers met together at St. Mary's, as two or more were continually away on outside mission duty. On the night in question, when Father Le Mercier rose to address those assembled, an expression of mingled eagerness and apprehension could be detected on every face, and an almost breathless silence reigned.

"My children," said the priest, "you know, quite as well as I, the danger that confronts us. Turn where we will, the eye of the foe is upon us and he is but awaiting an opportune moment for the perpetration of his treacherous schemes. Our lives are constantly in peril and we cannot tell but that the sun, which rises bright and glorious in the morning, may set at evening upon our charred or mangled corpses. My purpose now is not to increase your anxiety, but to suggest means by which we may aid and comfort one another and thus prepare to meet the desperate crisis which seems inevitable. Our every movement is watched, and we must therefore proceed with the utmost caution, as even an ill-timed word might arouse the enemy's suspicion. How or when we can make our escape we know not, but, let us keep close together and work in unison. Many tasks will have to be imposed in addition to our usual daily occupations but, I beg of you, let there be no murmuring, no dissatisfaction: rather let each one do his alloted part, and as much more as he can, with ready hands and willing heart. M. Dupuy will appoint four sentinels to patrol our enclosure each night, and I urge that all of you, who can, take an active interest in the boat-building that is to be superintended by Jules Dupont. And now, my sons, dark though the outlook be, you must not become disheartened, but remember that when God is with us no one can be against us, and that if you implore His all-powerful aid, He will not refuse it. Keep ever in His holy friendship; live each day as if it were to be your last."

Father Le Mercier's words, though full of warning, carried with them abundant consolation, and his spiritual children felt much the better for having heard them. When on his way to the dormitory that night, Pierre Boudreau passed Father d'Ablon and the priest called him aside.

"M. Dupuy had selected you for sentinel duty to-night,"

he said, "but I begged you off on the plea that you are looking far from well. Does your head ache, Pierre?"

"No, Father, but my heart does. I suppose anxiety is telling upon me."

"Well, my boy, I can understand that it should, but, after all, have you any more to suffer than the rest of us?" Pierre hesitated a moment and then said:

"Father, may I see you to-morrow? I could answer you better then than now."

"Yes, come to me immediately after dinner;" replied the priest, and he walked away feeling much concerned about Pierre's altered appearance.

Next day, according to agreement, Pierre sought his worthy friend, and together they set out for a walk on the lake shore.

"As it is, Father," said Pierre, "you know every secret of my life, and I would feel disloyal were I to conceal my present trouble from you."

"Then, my child, speak out. In whom should you confide if not in him who has watched you from your tender youth and ever striven to guide you aright. What so disturbs you?"

"Well, Father," the young man replied, lowering his voice to a confidential whisper, "I'm in love."

"Tell me, my son, is Térèse of Onondaga the object of your affection?" Pierre vouchsafed a simple "Yes." "Ah!" resumed the priest, thoughtfully shaking his head. "I knew that you admired her, but I was not aware that things had gone so far. Have you told her of your love?"

"No, Father, I deemed it wiser not to speak for awhile and, indeed, had no thought of doing so without first consulting you; but things have taken so unlooked for a turn that I am sorely perplexed."

"What do you mean?"

"I mean that Térèse, who at first eagerly received any attention that I could offer, now openly spurns me. O, Father d'Ablon, you may not understand what I feel, but, reflect for an instant on my past trials, think of how severely my affections have suffered, and tell me why God demands such another bitter sacrifice."

"Pierre, my noble, strong-minded boy, is it you who speak thus? Should you or I presume to question God's inscrutable ways? Dare we censure the workings of His Divine will? Ah! no. And, at any rate, my child, yield not to such utter discouragement. Your misgivings may not be entirely groundless, but perhaps you exaggerate matters."

"But, think of it, Father, I have been shunned by a girl whose every word and act were true and artless, who said that she understood and trusted me and who, by her very glance, declared that she loved me."

"Slowly, Pierre, slowly. How know you that you did not invest her words with more than the intended meaning, that you did not read her glance amiss?"

The soldier stood still; these few words opened up a whole vista of possibilities and gradually he began to feel that perhaps he had been precipitate in his judgment and that Térèse did not care for him in the same measure as he had supposed. And yet, when he thought of the pure, guileless expression of her lustrous eyes and the speaking light that seemed to come from their very depths, carrying the supreme message from her honest heart, he was bewildered.

"Father," he said at last, "God forgive me for murmuring. I see that I should not have laid claim to what I had neither asked for nor been offered, but . . . the temptation was a sweet one, and I yielded. Now, I'll place all in God's hands, 'twill be infinitely better so; but Father, I shall not again visit Onondaga, because when I go there I risk meeting her, and why add further bitterness to my cup?"

"Now, my boy," said Father d'Ablon, putting his hand on Pierre's shoulder and holding him at arm's length, "will you take a bit of advice? Go to Onondaga whenever you may be asked to do so and, before entering the village, commend yourself to God and beg Him to inspire you, then proceed and act on impulse; thus, you cannot go astray. Have you faith in me, my son?"

"Implicit faith, Father. You've guided me for many

years and I've never had to repent of following your advice, so, with God's help, I'll follow it now. Remember, Father, no matter how weak the flesh, 'the spirit is willing.'"

Upon leaving his young friend, Father d'Ablon hastened to the chapel and implored God to guide him in directing the soul of Pierre Boudreau.

Chapter VII.

Orrewati.

The dawning of March seemed to bring new hope to the inmates of the fort at St. Mary's, for they felt sure that St. Joseph would attend to their entreaties, and that ere the close of the month dedicated to him by Holy Church, their appalling trouble would be in some degree mollified.

Assiduously, indeed, had they labored to make ready for a hasty flight. Provisions had been packed, boats secretly constructed and put in readiness to launch at a moment's notice, and for many a night no one had dared undress lest a sudden call find him unprepared. Moreover, the night watch had been increased, as, in addition to the four sentries appointed to patrol the enclosure, two were assigned to duty in the cupola which commanded an excellent view of the country for miles around.

Though there had been no outward cause for farther alarm, the people at the Fort knew that to relax their vigilance might prove fatal, so scrupulously they continued their long watch. The savages grew constantly more wary, and, by way of cutting off any contemplated retreat of the Frenchmen, they had concealed bands of Onondaga and Mohawk warriors in all parts of the forest, their poisoned arrows and well-whetted tomahawks ready to do dastardly work. Of course, the lake was unguarded, but it was of little use to station spies along its shores when its waters were choked with ice and navigation seemed utterly impossible. Indeed, so sure did the wily red men feel of their prey that they had now merely to decide upon the moment of attack, while on the other hand the intended victims, being hemmed in on all sides, could only continue to feign ignorance of their impending fate and commend themselves to the mercy of God.

On March 11, Father Le Mercier began a novena to St. Joseph, and the entire household of St. Mary's joined in it with unusual fervor. Late whispered rumors had led them to feel that the hour of the great crisis was at hand, but still they were harassed by awful uncertainty. On the ninth day of the novena Father Le Mercier asked Pierre Boudreau if he would be the bearer of a message to Fathers Chaumonot and Mesnard, who were then at the lodge in Onondaga.

"I meant to give you a letter," said the priest, "but time presses and you can just as well deliver the message verbally. Tell the Fathers that instead of going to Goyogouin (1) as they had intended, they must come to the Fort to-night, as I have a presentiment that danger is close upon us. Their absence from the village need awaken no suspicion, as it is known that they were to go to Goyogouin for a couple of days, and they can steal their way here. You understand, Pierre?"

"Yes, Father."

"Are you afraid to go alone? If so, I shall try to provide a companion for you."

"No, Father, I am not afraid. Why should they kill me singly if they contemplate a general massacre?"

Pierre had spoken truly; he did not fear to go, but it was his first trip to Onondaga since Térèse had spurned him and, crave as he did to once more look upon her, he felt that he could not endure another snub from the girl whom he still loved. However, Father d'Ablon's words of advice surged in upon his memory and stimulated him for the ordeal.

He reached Onondaga at noon and found the missionaries partaking of their frugal meal. His coming was none too early, as the priests had arranged to leave the next morning for Goyogouin; but, contrary to Pierre's expectations, they had no news to communicate. They said that everything was very quiet, but they thought that the savages were becoming

---

(1) A settlement in the land of the Cayugas.

more civil than they had been of late, which, of course, might be one of the worst of signs. Pierre did not remain long with the Fathers, and having assured them that, only for fear of arousing suspicion, he would wait and escort them on their night trip to Gannentaha, began his journey homeward.

When he had gone but a short distance, something impelled him to take the path leading past Orrewati's cabin and, almost unhesitatingly, he started that way, singing the while a bright, cheery tune quite out of harmony with his trend of thought. On, on he walked, apparently heedless of his surroundings and feigning to perfection a nonchalance that he could not feel. Orrewati's wigwam stood close to the roadside and, as the soldier neared it, he saw a squaw appear at the entrance. It was Gannendaris and, when she beckoned him to enter, he was struck mute with astonishment. However, he required no second invitation and, as he passed within the tent, he felt like one walking in a dream.

Squatting on a mat with his back propped against the wall, blankets rolled up cushion-fashion and placed so as to add as much as possible to his comfort, was Orrewati, who, when Pierre appeared, extended him a cordial greeting. An unnaturally dull expression on the old man's face indicated that he was not in his usual rugged health, and Pierre's experienced eye detected this at first glance, but he made no comment.

"Thy merry song caught my ear," said the old Iroquois, "and, when Gannendaris discovered thee to be the singer, I bade her call thee hither. 'Tis many moons since we have met."

"Yes," replied Pierre, quite at a loss to know what to say next. His head was in somewhat of a whirl and, for the moment, his tact forsook him, but Orrewati broke the silence.

"Hast business in Onondaga?" he inquired, and Pierre, feeling that his response must be non-committal, answered:

"Yes, as you probably know, the Fathers over at the lodge were to go to Goyogouin to-morrow, and I wished to see them before they would leave the village."

"Didst meet them?"

"Yes, I found them at dinner."

At this juncture Orrewati summoned Térèse who, till then, had cautiously remained in the background, and bade her bring him some tobacco. She did so and when she greeted Pierre her glance thrilled him, for in her eyes he beheld the same old light that had so often enraptured him.

"Fill up thy pipe, friend, I cannot enjoy mine, but I can watch thee smoke;" said the old man, offering his guest some tobacco. Pierre did as requested and the Iroquois continued:

"There has been some great disturbance here," rubbing his hand across his forehead, "and the strength has left my limbs; but an old man can not be as fleet of foot as when he was a boy."

"No, age begets weakness; but no man who has spent a useful life, need regret growing old." Pierre's words seemed to set the Onondaga thinking, and a moment or so elapsed before he replied but, when he did, it was with the air of one who spoke from purest conviction.

"Friend," he said, "my life has been well spent. When I was young I spared not my strength nor energy but fought our enemies with untiring zeal, wielded the tomahawk and aimed the arrow with uncommon skill, dyed my scalping-knife with the blood of many a foe, brought back from the hunt rich skins, and from the lakes and streams abundant fish, and when the hatchet was buried (1) and the calumet brought forth, no one smoked it with greater joy than I. And now, when sickness weakens me and age stiffens my stout limbs, the great Areskoüe frowns not because I can no longer tread the war-path, but smiles on me for work well done; and I, weary of bloodshed and scheming and strife, long for the day when I shall enter the happy hunting-ground, where my fathers wait to bid me welcome."

During the foregoing conversation Térèse had stood close by and Pierre, though attentive to his host's remarks, turned from time to time seemingly to follow the clouds of blue smoke, which issuing from his lips floated upward, breaking into

---

(1) To bury the hatchet was to proclaim peace. The *calumet* was the pipe of peace.

fantastic outlines, but in reality, to feast his eyes upon Térèse, whose graceful attitude he could not but note. When Orrewati had finished speaking, the girl sat down beside him and, affectionately stroking his broad, sinewy hand, asked why he would not tell Pierre the nature of his illness. "Thou knowest, Orrewati," she added, "that M. Boudreau was a medicine-man before he came into our country, and thou hast heard of how he cured the sick at the Fort." Orrewati seemed too fatigued to speak, but begged Térèse to describe the way in which he had suffered, and this she eagerly did, giving Pierre an accurate account of the severe and sudden illness by which Orrewati had been attacked two weeks previously, and adding that he would not permit Tawichkaron, the juggler, to visit him, and that she and Gannendaris had cared for him as best they could.

Pierre was interested in the recital, doubly so because of his fair informant, and asked if he might feel the sick man's pulse. Orrewati offered no resistance, and then when the young soldier had listened to the Indian's heart, he said:

"I advise that you remain perfectly quiet and avoid all excitement. Just at present, rest will do more for you than any medicine;" and Pierre made a move as if to go. He was grateful that no medicine was required lest, should he administer it, some suspicious pagan accuse him of poisoning the old Onondaga.

"Leave us not yet," pleaded Orrewati, "thy song, as thou camest hither, seemed to revive my spirit. Wouldst repeat it?" Pierre's heart had sunk when he saw that there was no possible prospect of having a word with Térèse, but when Orrewati made this request, a sudden light flashed upon the young man's mind, so with a pleasant smile, he acceded and, to a sweet melody, sang in French the words: "My Christian friend, when last we met, why did you scorn me so? Can I no longer claim your friendship? Have I done aught to merit your contempt? Answer, for my heart is troubled; speak, while there yet is time."

Térèse still sat at Orrewati's side, and, as the soldier's clear tenor notes rang out, her heart beat faster and faster and her cheeks burned like glowing coals. When Pierre ceased singing he turned to Orrewati.

"Will the maiden not let us hear her sweet voice?" he asked.

The Indian nodded assent, and, without requiring any urging, Térèse began to hum a Mohawk lullaby, and, as she proceeded, gradually introduced, in broken French, words that thrilled Pierre's heart, for they explained that prudence had dictated her apparent indifference towards him, but that her friendship was still unchanged. She also warned him that some awful fate, she knew not what, awaited all the inmates of the Fort.

"Beautiful!" exclaimed Pierre in Iroquois when Térèse's last limpid notes had died away.

"Ah! yes," said Orrewati, seemingly heedless of the fact that the girl had not sung in her native tongue, "and the music of your voices has cheered and soothed an old man's heart." If Orrewati's kindliness was not sincere, at least it was admirably feigned, and after a moment's silence, Pierre advanced and, extending his hand, warmly shook that of the Onondaga. He could see the light of good feeling shining in the old man's countenance, and experienced genuine regret at leaving him, but duty forbade him to longer delay.

Térèse walked with him to the entrance of the wigwam, and as he lingered a moment, looking straight into her eyes, those eyes in which he now could read the secret that he had so longed to know, he was seized with a desire to tell her what was in his heart, but the notion was only momentary; they were parting the best of friends, parting with the hope of meeting in the great hereafter, and there she would know why he had never told her of his love. When he presented his hand she did not ignore it as on a previous occasion, but clasped it fervently and, with quivering lips and trembling voice, framed the simple word, "Adieu," and, as she stood leaning against the cabin door watching his retreating figure, in her eyes was a look of mingled suffering and joy and in her heart a prayer.

Presently Orrewati called and in a trice she was in her accustomed place beside him.

"Art in pain, Orrewati?" she asked, looking tenderly into his ruddy face.

"No, child, but that same queer feeling is again creeping over me. Strange that the man who could slay a bear or a wolf can not fight off a feeling." As he spoke he raised his hand to his head, and Térèse saw his face grow rapidly darker whilst the veins in his forehead swelled as though they would burst, and then the massive head drooped upon her shoulder. The girl flinched not under the heavy weight and, after a few moments, the sick man revived.

"Térèse, wilt stay by me?" he asked. "I want thee near. Somehow it seems as though I had no longer any hold upon myself, and when thou art close to me I feel—safer."

"Then, Orrewati, I shall stay by thee." Her words reassured him and he smiled calmly and soon fell into a restful slumber and then, for the first time since Pierre's departure, Térèse could commune with her thoughts.

Had she seen Pierre Boudreau for the last time? That there was some diabolical plot hatched against the Frenchmen she knew, and she concluded that the Mohawks and Onondagas might perhaps combine in making a terrific attack upon them, because she was sure that both tribes had been represented at the secret council, while attending which Orrewati had been taken so suddenly and violently ill. But oh! if any great misfortune were to befall the Fathers what would become of her? Must she live on for the rest of her days amid scenes of barbarity, bloodshed and paganism? Must she be forever deprived of spiritual consolation, and see her people relapse into the loathsome vices from which the missionaries had uplifted them? Must she see the only man she ever loved become the victim of some awful fate which she was powerless to avert? And was not Orrewati, who had so jealously befriended and guarded her, succumbing to an apparently mortal disease?

Such painful ruminations were beyond even her Indian endurance, and scalding tears welled up into her eyes and rolled down her burning cheeks. What were all her former troubles when compared to these? But, in her almost overwhelming sadness, she had one bit of comfort, which was the conviction that Orrewati was not in league against her friends, even though he was then in no condition to aid them. She marvelled at the late change in him. Since the day when Aharihon had expired, a sort of child-like gentleness had settled upon Orrewati, and though the same as usual with others, his affection for her seemed to have increased. She longed to probe his heart and see if she could find therein the slightest inclination towards Christianity, but only a short while previously Echon (1) had bade her say naught to Orrewati till the latter would have spoken. Early in the evening Orrewati awoke, and Térèse, while waiting upon him, said:

"I hear some men of the village approaching, but they must not talk to thee to-night, thou art too weak to bear with them."

Before Orrewati could reply, five stalwart Onondagas stalked unceremoniously into the cabin, shaking the clinging snow from their moccasined feet, and, without awaiting an invitation, squatted on the floor and proceeded to warm their hands before the cheerful pine blaze. In a few moments Orrewati gave Térèse a significant glance, one which she knew must be obeyed, and wrapping her bear-skin about her, she summoned Gannendaris, and together they left the tent.

To Térèse, who was laboring under a severe nervous strain, the clear, crisp air was wonderfully invigorating, and as she walked along leaning upon Gannendaris' strong arm, it seemed as if she were imbibing new life.

"We must not go too far," she remarked after they had proceeded quite a distance, "as I would be near in case Orrewati should need me. Tell me, Gannendaris, dost not deem him very ill?"

"Yes," answered the squaw shaking her old head very regretfully, "I fear he soon will die, and then what will befall poor Gannendaris?"

Térése was about to reply when her attention was suddenly arrested by the sight of two figures creeping stealthily along

---

(1) Father Chaumonot's Indian name.

and endeavoring to keep within the shadow of the great waving pines, and instinctively she clung closer to the old slave who, being absorbed in her own gloomy thoughts, noticed not the reason of her young mistress' impulsive movement. Térèse had occasion to dread an evening encounter with any of the pagan Onondagas, because her unusual beauty had more than once elicited from them flattery of a most repugnant sort, but, after a moment, she observed that these men were trying to avoid rather than meet her and she felt infinitely relieved. Poor Tèrèse, little did she dream that they were friends, friends with whom, less than twenty-four hours later, she would crave in vain to speak. Presently she bade the old squaw turn homeward and, as they neared the cabin, they heard several voices raised in ardent discussion, but Térèse's appearance put an effectual quietus upon the coarse, burly fellows who had so boisterously aired their views.

The girl found Orrewati flushed with excitement, though otherwise calm as usual, and when he saw her enter a look of pleasant relief flitted over his dark face. The other Onondagas were lounging about smoking, and the cabin presented anything but its usually neat appearance, earthen bowls, pots and kettles being scattered around in bewildering confusion and bits of tobacco strewn all over the floor. As Orrewati afterwards explained, he had invited his guests to smoke and prepare themselves some *sagamite* and the reigning disorder was the result. The men did not remain long after Térèse returned, for they soon became conscious of the utter uselessness of trying to flatter her.

That night was a restless one for Orrewati and neither Térèse nor Gannendaris had much sleep, though their combined attentions seemed to afford the old man no relief, as he appeared to suffer more from anxiety.

(To be continued.)

ASPIRATIONS.

BY JAMES RAYMOND PERRY.

WHO has not dreamed of wearing laurels won
  By captains in the shock of battle rude?
Of buckling on the sword of Washington
  With his calm fortitude?

Who has not sighed for Raphael's gift divine
  To paint the faces of an angel throng?
Or Titian's power to make the canvas shine
  With colors rich and strong?

Who has not felt his bosom thrill with pride
  And joy at some sweet act of Christian grace,
That had an influence for good so wide
  It lifted all the race?

Who has not felt, with quickening of the breath,
  That for the truth he, too, could suffer loss
Of life and meet a martyr's painful death,
  With Christ upon the cross?

MISSION NOTES.

Under date of September 30, 1899, the *London Tablet* in an article on "Missions in the Far East," furnishes its readers with authentic reports, calculated to at the same time edify and encourage. "The opening up to civilization of the Far East," we are quoting, "the last great sealed mass of continent, is evidently destined to play as great a part in the history of the twentieth century as that of Africa in the nineteenth. Never since the discovery of the New World has there been so large an introduction of barbaric man to contact with Europe, never since then have regions so vast and so populous been thrown open to the commerce, the curiosity, the all-pervading influence of the white man. 'The White Man's Burden' must be shouldered along with the white man's prerogative and the birthright of civilization is in its highest sense primacy of service. It is only by the diffusion of the light of the Gospel among those dark regions of the earth that the Old World, Europe, will acquire a title to its regency over them. In Farther Asia the pioneers of Christianity have not waited for the armed invasion of the nations to carry its message to the swarming millions so long awaiting it. From statistics prefixed to the report of the Foreign Missions of the Rue du Bac in Paris we learn that in those regions including China, Corea, Japan, Indo-China, Burma and three stations in Hindostan, the Catholic population numbers 1,204,352 as compared with 180,046 of Christian sects, while the Pagan baptisms for the year amounted to 72,700 adults and 193,363 infants. In Japan there are over 60,000 Catholics, in Corea 35,000, in Mantchooria 25,000 and in Sze-cheun not far from 100,000. In the same countries there are 32 Bishops, 1,070 European and 584 native priests, with 4,611 churches and chapels, 40 seminaries, 2,985 schools, and 9,020 children receiving instruction. In Northern Mantchooria, a vast province, 900 miles in length by 750 in width, with a population of from eight to ten millions, we read of new Mission Stations being opened, of the acquisition of land for the sites of churches, and of 1,080 confessions in one year in a station with a Catholic population of 1,700."

The writer then goes on to enumerate some of the trials lately undergone by the missionaries and their people. "The intervention of the European Powers," he says, "was visited on the unoffending Christians in massacre and plunder, in which various classes of the population, votaries of secret societies, brigands and thieves and marauders in general participated. In East Szechuen 10,000 of Mgr. Chouvellon's flock have lost everything they had in the world and are absolutely destitute. Two missionaries are prisoners and seventeen neophytes have earned the palm of martyrdom by dying for their faith. In Southern Szechuen half the province has been overrun, and in two of the prefectures there does not remain a single Christian outside the towns. In Kwang-si, stations were looted and the missionaries were put to flight, but here swift retribution overtook the rebels, who were wiped out by tens of thousands as soon as the Imperial troops appeared upon the scene. The prompt intervention of the German troops, too, brought to exemplary punishment the murderers of Fathers Nies and Heule in Southern Shan-tung, victims both of the animosity of the sect of 'Great Knife.'"

Persecution, of course, shall forever continue the inheritance of our faith. Christianity made its advent among the nations red with the blood of martyrs, and the advance guard of the Church in heathendom stands ready for sacrifice. Whilst China, even at this late day in the period of its conversion, is still the almost daily scene of new terrors and barbarous cruelty, it is consoling to note that many of the wrongs done our missionaries are the deeds of hordes of robbers, and no more the work of the Chinese Government than was the recent wrecking of churches in Paris the work of the French Republic. Sometimes, too, unfounded rumors of wholesale slaughter find their way to Europe and needlessly alarm friends of the heroes engaged as apostles in the Far East. The following letter from Mgr. Chausse, Prefect Apostolic of Kouang-tong, lays some such fears and goes on to describe a flourishing condition of affairs. The letter can be found in full in *Les Missions Catholiques* of September 29, 1899. "It was no small surprise for me to read in different papers from France that the Mission of Kouang-tong was destroyed and that the murder of Father Chanès brought about its destruction. Pardon me if I tell you that the Bishop of Canton and the missionaries themselves, though on the very spot, were the only persons to know nothing of the news. The mistake, however, is easily explained. For a long time back the papers are full of very inexact reports about the Far East. The mistake is fortunate inasmuch as it gives me an opportunity to make known the prosperous condition of the Mission of Kouang-tong in the present perilous times and widespread revolution throughout China. Before the cruel death of our esteemed brother we had forty or fifty thousand candidates under instruction in the province. These now number about sixty or seventy thousand. The Mission, therefore, is a long remove from destruction. On the contrary, I quite believe that for the present we could hardly even wish for more success. Unfortunately our means are very limited, our resources are altogether unequal to the task of instructing this multitude. Imagine, if you can, sixty or seventy thousand pupils scattered over all France! What an army of professors would be needed? What care, what indefatigable zeal would be required to only eradicate from these souls the ill effects of paganism's polluting touch? Count, my Christian friends, and you will begin to somewhat understand the measure of devotedness which the conversion of even a hundred pagans demands. And now about Pak-tong where Father Chanès met his death. After his murder the bandits lingered some days in the neighborhood to sack and pillage pagan as well as Christian settlements. They even built a fort and looked forward to a long enjoyment of their bloody successes. But, alas for them! everything here below has an end. At the opening of November, the commander-in-chief of the Wai-tchaw troops arrived at Pak-tong with 1500 soldiers. He had been despatched to seize and punish the guilty. The brigands flew to the mountains. He occupied their town. In one engagement 500 of the enemy were slain, twenty-three were taken prisoners, carried back to Pak-tong and publicly beheaded. This signal victory struck terror into all the surrounding country. The robbers were hanged as fast as they were caught, every morning as many as ten to fifteen dangled from posts in front of the prison gates. The sub-prefect and the military mandarin who had basely connived at the death of the Missionary Father Chanès took poison to escape the penalty of the law. I have sent Father Laurent to Pak-tong to fill the place made vacant by the death of our martyred Father Chanès.

"After all this noise and disturbance perfect quiet is again restored throughout the province. For the time being persecution is over, religion is everywhere making rapid progress. Still, however, there is a wide field for reform. Things are in a ferment. Calls to arms, brigandage, piracy are more then ever the order of the day. The rivers and harbors abound with pirates; the woods and roads, with brigands. Secret societies are doing their worst and murders grow daily more frequent."

Father Escande, in *Les Missions Catholiques*, writes from Pondicherry: "Our Lord has ready against the Day of Judgment words of thanks and congratulation for my generous benefactors. In the meantime let this poor missionary do them the homage of sincerest gratitude. The names sent with contributions have been given in baptism to as many sometimes as eight little heathens. Not a few of our benefactors have more spiritual children than they think. Some of them live in heaven; some live here in Pondicherry. Those already safe with God can never forget to whom they owe the surpassing favor; those yet on earth can never lose memory of their duty to thank and pray God's blessing on the heads of kind friends."

Here is another extract from a touching letter addressed by Father Guéno of Annam in Cochin-China to *Les Missions Catholiques:* "I suffer these hardships for the good God of all, asking Him in return for the single favor of being able to present to Him at the year's end a rich harvest of converts. They are plentiful now and still more are coming. Since January I have gathered in more than eighty children. These little ones were in circumstances so destitute that for the most part their baptism and entrance into paradise were simultaneous. We can hope that these elect, the first fruits of coming harvests, will not forget in heaven the pious souls whose alms purchased for them eternal blessedness."

Acknowledgment is made of the following contributions:

For the Most Needy Mission:
J. F. B., Allegheny, Mich . $5 00

For Rev. Father Lobo, India:
B. T., Philadelphia $10 00

THE AFTERMATH.

BY EDWIN L. SABIN.

OVER the seas they are bringing them home—
    The lads who gaily left us.
Bringing them back, no more to roam—
    Oh, War, you have sore bereft us!
Captain and private, they now are one
    In rank and in estimation.
How empty is title, when all is done,
    And mourns the heart of a nation!

THE PILGRIM
OF
OUR LADY OF MARTYRS

XV. YEAR.   DECEMBER, 1899.   No. 12.

TRANSEAMUS USQUE BETHLEHEM.

(*St. Luke, II, 15.*)

BY H. M.

In robes of earth
   That hide His worth
  The Saviour leaves the skies,
   To Bethlehem's town
   He hath come down,
  And in a manger lies.
And soon o'er Arabia's sands shall gleam
  The wondrous star's bright beam,
And Kings will leave their throne to bring
  Rich offerings to their King.
   Transeamus Bethlehem!
   To greet our Infant King.

   To sing His birth
   Have come to earth
  The angels of the Lord,
   Good will they bring
   And peace they sing—
  The blessings of the Word.
Far out on the hills the shepherds hear
  The tidings of good cheer
Then quickly haste they down to bring
  Love's offerings to their King.
   Transeamus Bethlehem!
   To greet our Infant King.

TÉRÈSE AND PIERRE.
BY K. A. HENNESSY.
(Concluded.)
CHAPTER VIII.
An Eventful Night.

BY morning Orrewati was very weak and Térèse was therefore in a state of pitiable solicitude. She concluded that the excitement of the previous night had been too much for his undermined strength and, moreover, felt sure that his guests had communicated some news that had seriously disturbed him. At length she ventured to inquire.

"Orrewati," she said, "methinks thou hast heard something that annoys thee. Wilt not confide it to Térèse? Who has any better right to know what troubles thee?"

"No one," he promptly replied, "but others might be more concerned with what I have to tell. Thou knowest of the banquet to be given to-night at Gannentaha?"

"Yes," answered Térèse, but she did not add that, under no circumstances, would she attend it and leave her kind protector so miserable.

"Well, something terrible is to follow."

"What meanest thou?" exclaimed the girl, trembling with excitement. "Is it aught that concerns the inmates of the Fort?" Orrewati nodded in the affirmative.

"Do they mean to *kill* the Fathers and Frenchmen?"

"Yes."

Térèse made no reply but, throwing up her hands, uttered a low groan and fell heavily to the ground. For some minutes she did not speak and then, rising to her knees, she clasped her hands and whispered a short but fervent prayer. None of this had been lost upon Orrewati who watched her every move.

"Thou art grieved to hear of this, Térèse?" he asked, as she came nearer.

"Grieved beyond the telling, Orrewati; and thou?" The last two words had escaped her almost unconsciously, but she made no effort to recall them; and when the old man, with all the sincerity of which he was capable, said: "I too, am sorry," her heart gave a sudden throb of delight. Now she knew from his own lips that which, for the past few weeks, she had felt sure was so, that Orrewati was not hostile to her friends.

"I've expected this for many a day," resumed the old warrior, "in fact, there was a time when I hoped and voted for it. But that time is passed, though our men know it not, else I would not now possess their secret. Knowest thou when I changed, Térèse?"

"No," she replied as a sweet, sad smile lit up her face.

"At first, when thou didst so openly defy me and declare that thou wouldst continue to frequent the chapel; and again, on the day when thou didst care for and defend thy father's slayer, and that, even before knowing that he had not meant to kill Gonaterezon. For many moons hadst thou been the brightness of my life, but never, till that day, did I resolve to think, believe and pray as thou dost; for the Great Spirit who can put such goodness in thy mind and heart is the one that Orrewati chooses for his God."

At these words every trace of sadness vanished from Térèse's face and her supreme delight shut out, for one moment, all thought of the crushing sorrow that had weighed her down to earth.

"Then thou art, at heart, a Christian?" she asked.

"Yes, and but for the hope that when this blow was about to fall I could ward it off, I would now be a baptized Christian. But I knew that any intercourse with the blackgowns would deprive me of the confidence of our elders, and that I could therefore learn naught of their plans. And yet, now that I know all, I am forced to lie here helpless while, for want of a word of warning, those good men must perish."

"Speak not thus, Orrewati, there yet is time: surely we can do something for them."

"Thou, child, canst do naught. Thou art known to be

their friend and any advance on thy part would draw down suspicion on thee and them. From sunrise this morning till banquet time to-night they are to be well spied so that none may escape the general slaughter." Orrewati's voice had grown gradually weaker and was now merely a hoarse whisper, so Térèse bade him talk no more till he would have rested, and ere long he fell into a quiet sleep.

Meantime the girl prayed as she had never done before, prayed that God would avert the impending danger, that the hands of the would-be murderers might be stayed, that the Fathers might be spared to continue their work of love, and that Pierre Boudreau might not be robbed of his fair young life.

"What shall I do?" she mused. "Now that I know the secret of Orrewati's heart, know that he is ripe for baptism, I find myself alone. The friend to whom I would announce the great news is not now at hand, no blackgown is near to pour the saving waters upon Orrewati's head, for, dared I summon them hither at this moment, I could not, since they are miles away. Gannendaris says they left at dawn for Goyogouin; some of the Hurons told her so when she went to draw water this morning. Oh! if Pierre could know all!"

Thus it was that Térèse planned and prayed, her very soul writhing in anguish. Suddenly she thought that could she but attend the banquet she might meet some white men there, because she knew that a number of them would be present, and that, without arousing any suspicion among the Indians, she could in the course of merry-making, whisper her secret to one of the Frenchmen, and surely a late warning would be better than none. But, no sooner had the idea developed than she remembered Orrewati's delicate condition and how entirely he depended upon her and she reproached herself for having even thought of leaving him.

"No, I cannot do it," she murmured. "I must risk confiding the message to one of the Christian Huron women who will attend the banquet, though I feel it would remain safer here;" and clasping her hands over her bosom, she heaved a sigh that seemed to come from the innermost depths of her heart.

"And yet," she soliloquized, as she endeavored to reason

the matter out, "Orrewati's life, though in danger, is not in immediate peril and, while I owe him deep gratitude it must also be my duty to warn those whose lives, perhaps before to-morrow's sunrise, will have been mercilessly mowed down. Ah yes, if I can avert the danger, I must. 'Twill be safer for me to act than to trust my secret with another in these dark, treacherous times. I shall see what Orrewati will advise."

Térèse was truly sick at heart. Her anguish increased momentarily and, at length, a nervous restlessness so overcame her that she felt impelled to keep constantly moving and, when not upon her knees rocking to and fro praying with all the ardor of her pure, earnest soul, she was patrolling the cabin taxing her overwrought brain in an effort to devise some plausible mode of action. After a while Orrewati awoke, seemingly refreshed by his rest, and calling Térèse to him, said:

"Child, these Frenchmen must be warned of their danger, and I know no way in which the news could more safely reach them than through thee. Thou must attend the banquet to-night."

Térèse paused a moment as if weighing his words, and then, "Thou hast anticipated me, Orrewati," she said, "the same thought had occurred to me, but—I dread to leave thee."

"Fear not for that, child, my wants are few and my life is of little note compared to theirs. I could die happy to-night did I but know that they were safe, that thou wouldst not suffer in want of my protection, and could I but feel the purifying waters of baptism flow upon my brow. Térèse, what if a blackgown could not come to me?"

"If thou wert dying and none of the Fathers could reach thee, I could act for them."

"They are not near now, Térèse, so, before thou leavest me to-night, wilt baptize me?"

"Oh! I could not, Orrewati, unless thou wert really about to die."

"But, Térèse, suppose that thou shouldst return to this cabin to-night and find Orrewati cold, stiff and lifeless;

wouldst not grieve to know that he could never enter the Christian's heaven nor see the Christian's God?"

Impulsively Térèse dropped on her knees beside him. "In that case, Orrewati, the Christian's God would not refuse thee entrance to His kingdom, because thy strong desire would have opened for thee the gates of heaven. But, tell me, why speakest thou so? Art feeling weaker than thy wont?"

With unfeigned tenderness she bathed his face and hands, brushed the coarse hair from his broad, low brow and raised him to a sitting posture. "Thou wilt feel better so," she said, "the change will rest thee."

The day had been a grey one, the sky being overhung with dull clouds, and occasional flurries of snow heralding the approach of a heavy storm; therefore, by the middle of the afternoon, darkness had spread its wings over the prosperous Indian village of Onondaga, wherein many braves and their squaws were busy preparing for the banquet to be given at Gannentaha some hours later. For that early darkness and the steady snowfall that followed many an ejaculation of thanksgiving was offered.

Térèse had begun her preparations for the event and a sort of hopeful excitement had, in a measure, superseded the harrowing anguish which, for hours previously, had had possession of her soul.

"After all," she reasoned, "I have prayed and prayed and surely not in vain. God must hear me. He will not desert the men who have been so true to Him. But,—Orrewati disturbs me. Can his end be near, that he talked as he did to-day? Suppose he were to die while I would be away to-night. But no, God would not permit it, not when I am on an errand of charity. While it is yet early I shall dress for the feast, so that when Orrewati wakes, I may sit and talk with him to the last."

Thus did Térèse muse as she carefully divided her sleek black hair, finer by many degrees than that of the average Iroquois woman, and, making the greater part of it into two shining plaits, drew what remained into a small coil on the top of her head, and ornamented the little coiffure with multicolored beads and several small, arrow-shaped sticks that had been carefully whittled and painted. Neither her hair nor face bore any trace of bear grease or other repulsive unguent, without the abundant use of which no Iroquois belle would consider her toilet complete, and the expression of her lustrous black eyes, which were larger by far than those of many of her dusky sisters, seemed to have been mellowed by the suffering through which she had recently passed. She donned her best moccasins and leggings, her most richly beaded jacket and brightest blanket skirt, about her neck she suspended numberless strings of glass beads that hung in graduated circles, the longest reaching below her waist, and on her shapely arms she placed a profusion of bracelets.

Meantime, at her mistress's request, Gannendaris had gone out to one of the distant lodges to ask its inmates to stop that evening at Orrewati's cabin on their way to Gannentaha, that Térèse might join them. Gannendaris, though a pagan, was loyal to her master and his ward, and Térèse, who had great consideration for the old squaw, had said, as the latter departed :

"Thou hast no need to hurry back, I shall not require thy services ; thou mayest remain and rest awhile, returning with our friends when they come hither."

Though yet early it had become quite dark, and Térèse having completed the donning of her festive attire, stood looking wistfully at Orrewati, who still slumbered on. Then as though an idea had suddenly occurred to her, she thrust her hand inside the neck of her jacket, fumbled for a moment and drew out the small, rudely carved wooden cross which had belonged to her dead mother. She would leave it with Orrewati for the night, it might comfort him in her absence Poor Orrewati, weak and helpless since the day when, in the council chamber, he had fallen ill and was carried to his cabin by four stalwart Indians, how sad to see his once powerful limbs paralyzed, his ruddy old face becoming wan and wasted and his skilful hands hanging limp and listless at his side. Poor Orrewati !

A rap on the outer door interrupted Térèse's train of thought, and caused her to start to her feet. It was indeed an unusual sound and typical of a certain conventionality totally unknown among Indians. What could it mean? As she opened the door a tall figure confronted her and, despite the darkness, she could distinguish a towering head-dress of feathers and a face luminous with warpaint. "Térèse," whispered a voice too soft and well-tempered to be that of any Indian, a voice, the accents of which were like sweetest music to Térèse's ear, and, involuntary swaying in her effort to be calm, she fell forward into a pair of outstretched arms. She did not scream, she did not faint; but, for a moment, it seemed as if she could neither think nor speak; and then, struggling to her feet, she said: "Pierre, God has sent thee." She led him in, motioned him to sit down and proceeded at once to tell him all she knew. He listened with eagerness but showed no surprise until she mentioned Orrewati's desire to become a Christian, and related how he had insisted that she attend the banquet in order to thus find a chance to warn the white men of their impending fate. Pierre told her that the rumor of it had reached them the day before, just after they had finished their novena to St. Joseph, and that the banquet was to be the screen that would shield their contemplated escape.

"But," he added, "they are watching us closely, so closely that, except in this disguise, I could not have ventured hither; but God favored my designs and permitted me to come once more to . . . " he hesitated, and Térèse asked:

"To what, Pierre?"

"To look again upon the woman I love."

"Pierre!" exclaimed the girl in a rapture of wild delight, "Pierre, canst truly love a child of the dark forest?"

"With all my heart, Térèse. And you, can you say that you love me a little?"

"No, Pierre, for such would not be true, because I love thee much and dearly."

"And would you trust your life to me, Térèse? Believe me, my love for you is no idle fancy. Since first I knew you it has been constantly growing, till now it has become so great and deep that without you, I could not be happy.

Would you then, to make me happy, fly with us to-night far from your forest home, far from the woodland that you love, to live in some distant clime and be my wife, the mistress of my home? If we be overtaken in our flight the Onondagas may slay us, but, God is good, and there is a chance of our success. Could you, would you take the risk, Térèse?"

"Would I, Pierre?" As she spoke she stood erect and the fire's ruddy glow cast its reflection full upon her sweet face as, with eyes and hands uplifted, she exclaimed: "God knows I would! But . . . what of Orrewati? Thou, Pierre, hast my heart, but Orrewati's soul is very dear to me."

Scarcely had she uttered the last words when a peculiar sound issued from the inner chamber. For a second both listened intently and neither spoke, then Pierre whispered:

"Is it Orrewati? If so, I like not such breathing." They hastened to the old man's side and Térèse, bending over him, called him by name, but he gave no signs of consciousness and the girl looked toward her companion in mute appeal.

"The last is near," said Pierre in answer to her questioning glance. "Hast hot water at hand, Térèse?" She pointed to a pot on the fire and Pierre, taking a long scarf from around his neck, wrung it out of the water and applied it to the soles of the Indian's feet, Térèse standing by like one dazed. But while Pierre's experienced hands were busy caring for the victim, she seemed to recover herself and suddenly exclaimed:

"And now, look to his soul, Pierre."

"Bring water, and I shall baptize him," he said, "but hasten, there is not a moment to lose."

In bewilderment Térèse looked about the cabin and, snatching up a wooden bowl, disappeared only to return in an instant with it filled with snow. Pierre took a large handful, squeezed it above the dying man's head and, while a tiny stream of purest water flowed upon his brow, pronounced the words: "I baptize thee, Joseph, in the name of the Father, and of the Son, and of the Holy Ghost. Amen." Meantime Térèse had knelt and, taking from Orrewati's bosom the small wooden cross which she had placed there but an hour previously, put it in his hands and, clasping her own about them, held the precious symbol within the death-chilled palms, till Pierre had finished the simple but significant ceremony. Then Orrewati's breathing grew slower and fainter and when, in a few moments, his spirit took flight, two tear-stained faces looked down upon his mortal remains and thanked God that the noble soul was now within His precious keeping.

Chapter IX.

A Flower Transplanted.

Never in the history of Gannentaha had such hilarious excitement prevailed as upon the night of March 20, 1658, when, in a large cabin situated at a short distance from the Fort, Frenchmen and Indians gathered to make merry and partake of a great banquet.

The birch walls were profusely decorated with pine branches, and in each of the four corners of the oblong structure there blazed a cheerful fire, that did duty not only in the way of preparing the refreshment to be served to one and all, but in illuminating the vast apartment. Excitement reigned supreme. The Indians in their gaudiest and best attire, the men hideous in war-paint and feathers, the women resplendent with glittering trinkets and well greased faces, vied with one another in their efforts to amuse the white men who, in their turn, would not be outdone in affability.

The uproar had an almost deafening effect upon the latter, but they nevertheless encouraged it and made every effort to have it well sustained, being actuated by no less a motive than a struggle for life. Therefore did M. Dupuy flatter the red men's vanity by presenting strings of wampum to those who would shout loudest and longest, and to others who, by their grotesque contortions, could win the most boisterous applause; therefore did Jules Dupont beat a drum till the muscles of his arm ached from the exertion; and for the same reason, did Guillaume Beauchamp perform acrobatic feats, thereby eliciting prolonged cheers, whilst Fathers Le Mercier, d'Ablon, Frémin and Ragueneau, with some Onondaga elders, wended their way in and out of the motley crowd dispensing the greasy food which so tickled the savage palate. Dancing prevailed to such an extent that there was little room for squatting, but that did not prevent the dusky guests from patronizing the four fires, grabbing the food as soon as it was cooked, and partaking more plentifully than nature could sanction.

When all had had more than their fill the frightful noise began to gradually diminish till, after a while, it subsided entirely and, where but a short while before such dire confusion had prevailed, silence reigned and the gluttonous savages lay in heaps about the floor of the banquet-chamber, overcome by fatigue and sleeping from sheer exhaustion. But the white men slumbered not, and those of them who had not already stolen out of the long cabin where the atmosphere had grown well nigh intolerable, were cautiously picking their way over the bodies of their enemies and making their exit as rapidly as possible. They too must have succumbed to the fatigue which almost overpowered them, had they not known that to do so might mean that they would awake in eternity.

In the meantime under cover of the unearthly noise reigning in the pandemonium, Fathers Chaumonot and Mesnard, who were supposed to be at Goyogouin, aided by the Frenchmen who did not attend the banquet, had been working with unremitting ardor, and had succeeded in carrying from the Fort the two newly constructed long boats, besides four canoes made in Iroquois and four in Algonquin style, and in launching and loading the same. Then, at about eleven o'clock, when the auspicious moment had come, the fifty-three Frenchmen of Gannentaha, including the missionaries, boarded their small craft and, in the name of God, embarked upon a voyage which might, at any moment, be brought to an abrupt and bloody close. But they were taking a last chance and they made the venture under the auspices of One Who ever hearkens to those who earnestly appeal to Him.

Lake Gannentaha was gorged with floating ice and the little fleet made pitifully slow progress, but all worked with an energy born of desperation—worked for life. In one of the long boats that took the lead could be distinguished a face beautiful indeed, but dark by contrast with those about it, and Pierre Boudreau's strong right arm encircled the waist of its owner, who was none other than Térèse, the Mohawk, the young Frenchman's affianced wife.

On the morning of March 21st dismay and consternation prevailed where on the previous night all had been excitement and festivity, and, upon examining the cage that they had supposed held their coveted prey, the wily, blood-thirsty Onondagas discovered that it was empty and that the precious birds had flown. With lightning rapidity the news was circulated, and searching parties were dispatched in different directions through the woods, while other detachments clambered to the top of the neighboring heights and peering out into the distance, looked in vain for the objects of their contemplated vengeance. The lake, they felt convinced, could have afforded no means of escape as they considered its waters impassable and looked upon the miniature icebergs moving slowly between its shores, as insurmountable obstacles. Moreover they supposed the Frenchmen to be without boats of any kind and therefore, sorely baffled, they began to prepare new weapons with which to repel the attack which they feared the white men, returning with auxiliary troops, would make upon them.

Meanwhile the refugees toiled relentlessly on amid dangers the most appalling, and at length, ten days after their hazardous escape from Gannentaha, entered Lake Ontario where they were obliged to use their hatchets and cut their way through the ice (1); and, after innumerable trials, including the shipwreck and drowning of three of the party, the dauntless wayfarers reached Montreal on April 3rd, and Tadoussac on the 17th. (2)

At the latter place they spent the feast of Easter, on which day Pierre and Térèse, after untold suffering and sorrow, were united in holy matrimony, and when Father d'Ablon, who put the seal upon their mutual happiness, had concluded the ceremony, he said: "My dear children, God has at last

---

(1) *Relations des Jésuites.* (Quebec Edition.) Year 1658, chap. II. p. 8.
(2) Ibid.

brought you safely out of darkness and danger and given you to each other, and I earnestly pray that you may ever be happy in the sunshine of His love."

On the following Tuesday the party reached Quebec, where one and all were hailed as having returned from the dead, and whence M. and Mme. Boudreau sailed on the first vessel that left for France.

Ere long Pierre installed his wife in a beautiful home in Lyons, and surrounded her with comforts and luxuries that would naturally overwhelm one of simple tastes, but the innate tact which, from the first, he had remarked in her, came to her rescue and, within a surprisingly short time, she became fully acquainted with the requirements of highly civilized life and, what is more, met them most successfully. Her husband's old friends were charmed with the sweet simplicity of her manner and each succeeding day increased Pierre's love and admiration for his hard-earned treasure. One evening after they had returned from a reception at which Térèse had met the cream of Lyons' society, Pierre looked fondly at his wife, exclaiming:

"And so my transplanted lily languishes not for her native soil?"

"Not in the least, and how dost thou account for it?" she asked, turning her great brown eyes full upon his handsome face.

"I think it is undoubtedly because of your French ancestry," he proudly replied.

"But I," she said, her pretty head drooping gracefully to one side and a piquant smile playing about the corners of her mouth, "*know*, and I thank God for it, that it is because I am safe and happy with the man I love."

SHRINE NOTES.

With this number of the PILGRIM OF OUR LADY OF MARTYRS we close the XVth volume, the first having been published in the year 1885. For twelve years it was really a supplement to the *Messenger of the Sacred Heart*, and was actually called the *Little Messenger*, the chief object for which it was originally intended occupying during all that time only one-third or, at most, one-half of its pages, the rest being taken up with information about the Apostleship of Prayer in League with the Sacred Heart. In 1896 it was found necessary to give more space to the things concerning the League, and to issue the *Messenger* Supplement in conjunction with the *Messenger* itself. On the other hand it was deemed opportune to enlarge the proper work of the PILGRIM, and to devote it entirely to the interests of the Shrine of Our Lady of Martyrs, at Auriesville, N. Y., the cause of the Beatification of Father Isaac Jogues and of his companions who labored, suffered and died at Auriesville, and to the history of missions past and present, chiefly of those which were first established in the territory now occupied by the United States and Canada.

Accordingly during the past three years the PILGRIM has been devoted exclusively to these objects, and on this account its circulation has been restricted to readers who are interested in these things, nor have we as yet made any special effort to extend its circulation, except occasionally to ask our subscribers to make it known to their friends. By their kind co-operation during the past summer, the number of its subscribers, which had been decreasing for awhile, was promptly raised to a number sufficient to enable us to continue publishing it without loss to the various interests for which it has been founded. Some have shown themselves particularly zealous in making it known to their friends, and we have not failed to express to them our gratitude. Entering as we are on a year which we hope to make the most important one as yet passed for both the Shrine of Our Lady of Martyrs and for the cause of those who have hallowed it by their labors and death, we appeal with confidence to every subscriber to help us to obtain a sufficient number of subscribers not only for the maintenance of the PILGRIM, but also to make it a means of supporting the Shrine and of providing resources for the expenses of the process which must be instituted for the beatification of those whom all the world considers, and whom we would fain have our Holy Church proclaim from her altars, as martyrs for the faith.

To justify this appeal we need only say that, besides the interest which attaches to the Shrine and the cause of Father Jogues, we propose next year beginning with our January number to make the PILGRIM more entertaining and instructive than ever. The history of the early missions in the United States and Canada will be given in a series of chapters based upon the famous Jesuit Relations, and edifying narratives about the lives and doings of pioneer missionary men and women on our shores will also be given. Points about the process of beatification and accounts of the virtues of Father Jogues and his companions will make one very interesting series of articles; chapters on the virtues of the Blessed Virgin Mary another series, and to the Shrine annals we shall add some brief editorial comments and notices of books, pamphlets and magazines which concern the topics suitable for the PILGRIM. The usual verse and story will not be omitted.

The PILGRIM costs but 50 cents a year. At this rate 3,000 subscribers are needed to make it clear expenses, and yield a revenue of a few hundred dollars for the Shrine and other objects each year. We have not at present quite 2,000. If each subscriber, when renewing a subscription, would for this year add one more for some friend we would soon have the desired number. We should hesitate before making this appeal, but for the fact that the PILGRIM contains so much and costs so little. Moreover, since we have had to incur so much expense the past season, and must look forward to more still, if we hope to make the ceremony of crowning the statue of Our Lady of Martyrs worthy of such an event, we must take some means of obtaining the necessary money, and what means could be more acceptable to our readers than to increase the circulation of the PILGRIM, since everyone who subscribes to it has the double satisfaction of knowing that his subscription is devoted to a good cause, and of deriving benefit from the study of the magazine he receives in return?

Some of the subscriptions lately sent us for six months have not reached us, no doubt because the card in which the silver quarters had been wrapped were lost in the mails. Should some of our subscribers know of any person whose subscription has thus been lost, we shall be grateful if they will let us know it, so that we may remedy the matter.

This number has been delayed by the fire which a few weeks ago destroyed the composing and press room in which the PILGRIM is printed, and we thank our subscribers for being patient in spite of the delay.

The Index of the PILGRIM for 1899 will be published and inserted in loose sheet in the January number.

URSULINE MONASTERY, QUEBEC, NOVEMBER 4, 1899.
REV. FATHER JOHN J. WYNNE, S.J., NEW YORK:
Dear Reverend Father:

I have delayed answering yours of 27th inst. until I received some information from the present Curé of S^a Foye (alias Notre Dame de Foye) near Quebec, the Abbé Arthur Scott, who is half Scotch and half French-Canadian like myself.

Regarding the disappearance and migrations of the real statue (i. e. the first copy sent from Belgium) there is no record whatsoever extant.

The Hurons transferred their residence from N. D. de Foye to Lorette (the first of the name in Canada, now called Ancienne Lorette) in December 1673. Father Chaumonot, always possessed with the desire of having a *facsimile* of the *Santa Casa* in New France, set to work immediately to realize his plan, and to obtain a copy of the Madonna of Loretto, in Italy. Having set all his heart and soul on this new sanctuary, he no doubt willingly enough transferred his statue of Notre Dame de Foye to Father Lamberville, either in 1673 or later. Father Lamberville was stationed at Lorette in 1689 and 1690.

The proximity of two pilgrimages (four or five miles distant from one another) would have been hurtful to either or to both.

As to the type of the statue, it is easy to ascertain it from the description of it given by several writers on the shrine of Foye, v.g., Father Bonneux, Dinant, 1693.

The Jesuits of Dinant sent copies of the same statue to other missions of the Society. Father Bonnart, S.J., missionary at Lorette, in his Relation of 1675, published a few years ago in the *Abeille*, a College Journal edited by the pupils of the Seminary of Quebec, mentions a statue of the Blessed Virgin and Child which was borne in procession at the dedication of the Sanctuary of Loretto, in 1674. It had been sent to the Mission by the City of Nancy (no date), and had been carved out of the oak tree in which the miraculous statue of Notre Dame de Foye was found. The statue had disappeared, but the act of homage accompanying it still existed and will be published in my historical study of N. D. de Lorette. This latter statue has evidently been replaced by a silver one now existing in the treasury of Lorette, and of which I send you enclosed a photograph. The following are the differences existing between it and the miraculous image of Dinant.

1. The Infant Jesus (in the original) holds a globe in his right hand.

2. His right leg is crossed over the left one and the Blessed Virgin holds his right foot in her left hand.

The latter characteristic (i. e. the holding of one of the Infant's feet in the left hand of his Mother) is found in all statues of Notre Dame de Foye.

At Ste. Foye there exists to-day a wooden statue of our Lady artistically carved in 1716 by a former curé of the parish, Monsieur Le Prevost. It is of the same type as the original of the enclosed photo, excepting the hands of the Divine Infant, whose right hand rests on his own breast, and whose left is drawn to his waist. The sculptor must have executed his design from memory or from hearsay.

I shall publish in my article the text of the letter sent in 1672 by the Jesuits of Dinant in recognition of the vow of the Hurons to Our Lady of Foye. From this document it seems manifest that the faith signified by the title of *Virgo fidelis* is, not so much the fidelity of the Martyr, as the theological virtue.

Abbé Scott tells me he will write a short article for a review called "*Bulletin des Recherches Historique.*" If it contains any valuable information, I shall send it to you.

Wishing you prompt success in the cause of beatification of the Jesuit Martyrs, for which I pray every day, I remain

Yours devotedly in SS. Corde Jesu,

L. St. G. Lindsay.

CONTRIBUTIONS TO THE SHRINE.

J. McK., Philadelphia, Pa.	$1.00	C. H., New York.	5.00
M. L. S. H., Buffalo, N. Y.	5.00	J. F., New York.	5.00
A. W. B., Atlantic City, N. J.	13.50	F. E. M., Philadelphia, Pa.	.50

MORAD.

BY CHARLES J. MULLALY, S. J.

IT was evening on the northern border of Arabia. The sun was fast sinking, and the tents of the Caleb tribe, resplendent with their many-colored trimmings, shone brightly against a barren background of trackless sand. Far to the west the heights of Pisgah and Nebo might be seen, standing like two mighty sentinels guarding the eastern approaches of Roman Judea. The scene, vast and wild with its stretch of mountains and apparently endless plains, was truly an imposing one.

As we pass along the narrow, sandy street of the Arab encampment—for here our story opens—meeting group after group of these wanderers of the Desert, who are lying lazily around their open tents and discoursing on the idle news of their camp, let us stop at a small pavilion at the western extremity of the tented settlement and see if the humdrum of desert life is the subject of its occupants' conversation. Drawing aside the curtain, we behold a slight-built, dark-eyed Arab child, apparently seven years of age, intently engaged in conversation with an aged Caleb, whose snow-white locks and beard, shriveled but yet kindly face, tell us that the destroying angel of Death is not far distant.

"Senoral," the child is saying, "you have never told me all you know of mother. You always put me off, saying 'she's gone away, but will soon return.' Where is she, Senoral? I asked old Menha to-day, and she told me that I would never see my mother again. Is this true, Senoral?"

"Morad, my child," said the old man, with tears in his eyes, "I have feared all along to tell you the story of your mother, but now I see I must—you are getting old enough and should know it. Listen, child, and I shall tell you.

"Three years ago to-day, your father and mother left the camp on the bank of Lake Saloometh to visit the tribe of Lened. They left you with me, for Halah, your father, feared to take you with them; he seemed to know beforehand that something wrong would happen. One dark and stormy night, two weeks afterwards, a tribesman of Lened, wounded and bleeding, his horse foaming and exhausted, reached the camp telling us that your father and all the men of the Lened tribe had been slain in a sudden attack by the fierce Pilanales, and that Wiona, your mother, with the other women and children, had been carried off into slavery. When the news spread from tent to tent, the wildest excitement followed. That very night, before the moon pierced the clouds in the middle heaven, two hundred armed men rode from the camp, swearing to avenge the death of your father, and the destruction of the Lened tribe, as well as to rescue Wiona and the Lened women and children from the hands of their fierce captors. For nine days they followed them through the desert. Night and day they pushed on, stopping only now and then to rest their wearied horses; but fast as they rode, they could not overtake the fleeing enemy, for the cursed demons had too great a start. At last, at the Desert of Arak, they were forced to turn back, disheartened and disappointed, for they feared to leave the women and children unprotected in the camp. Time and time again, child, have I inquired from friendly Southern tribes of the captives' whereabouts, but all I could learn was that most of the women had been sold into Syria.

"If we could find mother, could we get her back?" asked Morad eagerly.

"If she is in Syria, yes; for they will readily sell her, provided we offer sufficient ransom. But alas, Morad, I know not where she is! Child, it breaks my poor old heart to see you without father or mother. Would to the gods Wiona were here! You know not what a mother you had. Kindness and goodness were her very nature. How well I remember her when a child, nine or ten years old, going with her father to the Sea of the West, when he went to sell our camel hair to the merchants of Judea. When she came back to the desert, her spirit had changed, there seemed a mystery about her that no one could fathom. No longer did she love to play with the children of the camp, but for hours sat silent and sad in her father's tent.

"One day I called her to me and asked her what had happened that her young heart was so changed. 'Wiona,' I asked, 'why are you so sad at times? What has happened? You know Senoral loves you, and is worried when he sees his little darling weeping alone.' Poor child! she began to cry, telling me that she wept to see our people so wicked. 'They are not as good as they should be, Senoral.'

"'Wiona, we are not wicked,' I said. 'How can you say this, child? We adore the gods as other nations do; when we fight, we fight only in self-defense. Do you say that Father is wicked, that Senoral is wicked? Oh, my little darling, you do not know what wickedness is.'

"'O Senoral,' she said, clasping me around the neck, 'I met at Ascalon, a kind, beautiful lady, with a child whose features were as fair as the golden morning. As she saw me standing alone—for father was busy with the merchants—she called me to her and asked me about the desert, the tents and the sand. She told me, when I asked her where she lived, that she was returning from Egypt with her husband and child, and that they were going into Galilee. O Senoral, her voice was as sweet as the softest wind, and her child was so beautiful that I could not take my eyes from him. How gentle and kind they were! She told me, Senoral, of the great God that lives above the clouds and how He loves the good and hates the crimes of the wicked. She also told me that this great God was soon going to save His people and let them come to Him, since now no one can enter His happy kingdom because of the wickedness of men. Father then came and called me, but before I left her, she whispered to me 'Wiona, serve that great God and you shall be happy and be among those He saves.'

"Poor Wiona!" continued the old man, "how I wish she were here to bring you up a brave and good child of the desert."

"Senoral, is there no way of finding where mother is?" asked the boy with tears in his eyes.

"Yes, if the Sibyl of Rabbath Ammon is still alive, she can tell us, for she knows all things, past, present and to come. We are nearer the temple now than we have been in thirty-five years. I think, child, she will readily tell us when she learns that Wiona is one of the Caleb tribe, for the father of the Sibyl was a member of our tribe."

"Did she know mother, Senoral? Did the Pilanales tell her what they did with the captives?" asked the child, wonderingly.

"No, no! Morad, the Sibyl knows all things from the gods. They tell her anything she wishes to know. She dwells, if still alive, at Rabbath Ammon, with the priest of the god Thabal. Thirty-five years ago I was sent by my brother Shaba, our great chief, to consult her as to whether we should go to war or not against our enemy, the Magael. She counseled war, and although many were lost in battle, still in the end we were victorious."

"How far from here is Rabbath Ammon?" asked Morad.

"But a child's journey. If I were not so old I would go myself and ask her."

"O Senoral, let me go. I'm seven years old; I walk now almost the whole day with the camels. The Sibyl will tell me when she knows that I am a poor little Caleb child looking for my mother. May I? Do let me, Senoral. 'Tis to find mother, mother, Senoral."

The old man, with tears streaming down his wrinkled cheeks, hesitated to answer. He clasped the boy in his aged arms and thought for a moment, then said, "Yes, go, child. May the Desert god help you to find your mother! You are strong enough. You are a brave child for your age. Yes, you may go to-morrow. But, come Morad; if you will start before the sun awakes, you had better come to sleep, for the moon is fast climbing the heavens."

* * * * * *

The moon was still shining and the faintest trace of light in the eastern sky showed that the dawn was not far off, when an aged man, accompanied by a small boy, might be seen noiselessly stealing along the narrow street of the still sleeping camp. It was Senoral leading his young charge to the boundary of the settlement to direct him on his way.

"Ah, the end at last!" exclaimed the old man. "Morad, my child, the path is a wild and desert one. If you keep far from the border line, and always have the mountains on your left, you will be safe. When you reach Rabbath Ammon tell the priest you come from Senoral, the brother of the great Shaba, the Caleb chief who helped to build the temple. This, child, will insure your admittance to the Sibyl. Good-by! May the god of the Desert help you to find your mother!"

He had hardly finished when the child darted off into the fading moonlight like a young deer. Fainter and fainter grew the sound of his footsteps until at last they entirely died away.

(To be continued)

NOTES OF INTEREST.

——On November 13, the faithful of Angers flocked in crowds to their cathedral to honor the memory of Mgr. Freppel, once their devoted bishop. The present bishop, Mgr. Rumeau, had invited the city to assist at the erection of a memorial tablet, to perpetuate the virtues of his illustrious predecessor in the See of Angers. What manner of man Mgr. Freppel was can best be gathered from the following panegyric of Mgr. Rumeau. "After a study of the life and works of Mgr. Freppel, we are at a loss to know what to admire most in him, the writer, the preacher, the trained soldier or the patriot. But we can hardly lose sight of the fact that he was first of all a bishop, and a bishop of colossal proportions. As a watchful, vigilant and untiring pastor he actually multiplied himself to govern his vast and important diocese. His vigorous constitution enabled him to display in the care of his children a consuming energy. On the principle, 'that a bishop in our times has no right to take a rest,' he often subjected his habitually good health to dangerous and severe strains. His prudent foresight never failed him. At the right moment he stood in the breach to give notice of danger, to meet an attack, to hold positions already won by hard fighting. This is the reason why he gave a tremendous impetus to works of every description. This is why he undertook so many new projects, why he made his influence felt in every quarter at once, communicating to different branches of religious work a power of energy, a vigor of strength, a breath of prosperity, that made for the Church of Augers a most enviable reputation. To work these seeming marvels he had received from heaven, among other gifts, a nature of the choicest kind. He betrayed at times the first symptoms of an impetuous and imperious character; and, yet, no one was ever quicker to acknowledge and correct his own mistakes. Nobody, not even an adversary, ever disputed his superior intelligence, his rightmindedness, his loyalty and goodness of heart. His was a heart that knew no rancor, even when the strife raged fiercest. In a word, he was wanting in none of the qualities that go to make up a perfect man. One of his friends, Louis Veuillot, a stout champion of the faith like himself, felt able to without flattery pay him this tribute of praise, ' He was a man and he combined within himself the strength of many men.' "

——Francis Veuillot, in *L' Univers* of November 9th, graphically describes an incident that had place during a recent trip through Brittany. The occasion was the unveiling at Lesneven of a statue raised to the memory of the illustrious General Le Flo. The statue is of bronze. The general is represented in full uniform, his head uncovered, his eyes raised and looking straight to the front, his whole bearing that of a true and simple soldier. His left hand rests on the hilt of his sword, a heavy cloak thrown across his shoulders falls in graceful folds to his feet. Four bas-reliefs in white marble, carved with art and true to life, ornament the pedestal. They are sketches of events in his career as a soldier and statesman. The sculptor, Godebski, made a present of this beautiful work of art to the city. Speeches were made by the mayor of the city, by other distinguished citizens, and by representatives from the French and Russian governments. Like all ceremonies of the kind, this ended with a sumptuous banquet. The procession from the public square to the dining-hall was imposing and picturesque. The route lay through patches of paved streets and fields, half city and half country, past the modest homes of the peasantry and the more pretentious dwellings of the townspeople, hung with a profusion of flags. The various officials, clad in sombre black flashing with medals and decorations of honor, were in strange and charming contrast with the peasants and farmers, who lined the way to enjoy the novel parade of city finery. The gay headdress of the Breton peasants lent the scene a delicious touch of antiquity, while the short jackets and round hats of the farmers were the object of all eyes. An air of cordial simplicity united with all the grandeur of state-splendor to fashion a scene impressive in the extreme. The banquet was as much of a success as the rest of the day's proceedings, and the pious author takes occasion to remark that in the midst of the decorations the crucifix was conspicuous. "The image of the Saviour," he gracefully writes, "presided over this feast, set in honor of a patriot and Christian soldier." The writer concludes his article thus: "They say that Brittany is a land of barren fields, and some writers hold it in little esteem. With these I have no quarrel. But I have myself seen it, this rugged country of the sturdy Bretons; rich, beyond the telling, in brave soldiers and devoted priests; and I love it; yes, I love it!"

ADDRESS OF THE FRENCH CARDINALS TO HIS HOLINESS ON THE OCCASION OF HIS RECENT ENCYCLICAL TO THE CLERGY OF FRANCE:

MOST HOLY FATHER:

The Encyclical of September 8, addressed to the bishops and priests of France, is a new and striking proof of the enduring and fond love entertained by Your Holiness for our country. We deem it our duty to express to you our deep gratitude, and we lay at your feet the homage of emotions, stirred by this act of kindness in the hearts of all the bishops and all the priests of France, so honored in receiving from the Vicar of Jesus Christ encouragement and advice best fitted to their wants in the present difficult circumstances. The French cardinals feel certain that they are only the faithful spokesmen of their colleagues in the Episcopacy, and of all the priests who under their direction work for the spread of God's glory in their land, when they assure Your Paternity that, after receiving with the most filial respect your instructions of September 8, they will ponder them with most serious attention and will with unflagging zeal endeavor to put them into effect. The Pontifical letter is for them a clear and sound summary of the doctrine taught by Saints, Fathers and Doctors of the Church, by Popes and Councils, concerning the high dignity of the priesthood and the perfection towards which the ministers of the altar ought to continually strive. They likewise find in it rules for conduct, admirably well adapted to the difficulties of the hour. It discovers to them the secret of uniting with timely and courageous energy, that prudence, moderation and discretion without which the best intentions are fruitless of good or even hurtful to causes they purpose helping. Last of all, it reminds them that neither the vicissitudes of time, nor social changes, nor the particular needs of this or that age can ever, if we really want to spread the Kingdom of Jesus Christ, weigh against our bounden duty to save the souls entrusted to our care, to be useful at one and the same time to the Church and to our country, to speak, and act, and behave everywhere and always like men of God. With this expression of our sincerest gratitude for the new and signal favor for which the Church of France is indebted to Your Holiness, and humbly praying you to again impart to our country, to our dioceses and to ourselves your paternal blessing, we subscribe ourselves your most obedient, devoted and affectionate sons in our Lord Jesus Christ.

———Our Holy Father Pope Leo XIII., gave audience on October 23, to one hundred and fifty English pilgrims. These were the advance guard of a vast army of pilgrims, which the Catholic Association of Great Britain intends to muster in Rome for the Jubilee year. After remarking that this was the third English pilgrimage received during his reign, and after showering compliments on the Duke of Norfolk, His Holiness continued : " This display, my sons, of filial affection is extremely dear to us. In coming to Rome, to kneel at the feet of the Vicar of Jesus Christ, you acquit yourselves of a solemn and public act of faith, and you offer the world a noble example of sincere attachment to the Holy See. You likewise make open profession of that obedience, which is free from prejudice, from passion, and from hastiness, and is due him who holds supreme authority and the divine commission to guide and govern the Church. May your conduct, with heaven's blessing, have many imitators ! Many of you belong to Catholic Ireland. O, how rich in high traditions that blessed isle ! What lasting proofs of devotion and generosity we to-day receive from her sons ! We are heartily glad to see you all united here at the central point of Catholic unity, in the presence of your common father, an army of brothers arrayed under the standard of the same faith. To one and all we make sincere acknowledgment of our gratification and pleasure.

To one and all we counsel obedience to your respective pastors and steadfast perseverance in good. And for pledge of our paternal affection we, from the bottom of our heart, grant to all here present, to your far-distant families, to your parents and your friends, the apostolic benediction."

MISSION NOTES.

——Under date of October 28 *L'Univers* prints this letter from Angora: "The choice of Mgr. Emmanuellian for Patriarch of the Armenian Catholics was ratified by the Sultan on October 13. He was born at Telermen, near Mardin in Armenia, January 16, 1829. He commenced his ecclesiastical studies in the seminary at Bjimmar, and finished them at Rome, in the College of the Propaganda. Soon after his ordination he was made Vicar-General, and in 1881 Bishop of Cæserea. Mgr. Emmanuellian's remarkable talent, his unbounded goodness of heart, his long experience in the ministry, and his solid virtue justify the confidence reposed in him by the Sultan and the Catholics of Armenia, as well as the almost unanimous vote of his colleagues in the Episcopate, assembled together in Synod at Constantinople for the election of a successor to Mgr. Azarian. In the person of Mgr. Emmanuellian we have a patriarch in the old and time-honored sense of the word, a holy religious, pious, austere towards himself, kind towards all, aiming in all his actions at the accomplishment of good and the conquest of hearts for Christ. The new patriarch, in accordance with a custom originally introduced to bear witness to the attachment and loyalty of the Armenians to the Holy See, added to his name of Paul that of Peter. Under this twofold name, for a shield of strength, we can predict for the new head of the Catholic Church in Armenia the most happy and successful results. He has our warmest best wishes and our most fervent prayers."

——For the edification of our readers we subjoin this clipping from the *Semaine Religieuse* of Auch. "It is now ten years since Bourbaki, the chivalric leader of the Turks in Africa, and then of the Zouaves, stopped at Lourdes on his way to the springs at Cauterets, to do homage to the Virgin of the Grotto. When near the Gave, he halted and stood like one in a trance. He saw pass at no great distance an aged litter-carrier, whose features recalled the outlines of an old comrade in arms. This latter was helping a patient, and, noticing the astonishment of the pilgrim, cried out to him in a voice far above the surrounding noises, ' No, no ; you are making no mistake ! Just wait where you are till I return !' Bourbaki had, indeed, made no mistake. The litter-carrier was no other than General de Geslin, governor of Paris during the presidency of MacMahon. A few minutes later the two friends embraced, and the self-constituted servant of the sick said to his old companion in arms, ' I am convinced that when you saw me pass with the litter and the straps of a carrier you wrote me down an old woman, a softy.' ' What, I write you down an old woman, a softy? No, never ; a thousand times, never ! I knew you well, and never yet have I caught you in a nobler or grander act than the one I have just seen you perform.' For a whole quarter of an hour the two generals, with all the precision of military bearing, stood, one beside the other, in full view of the snow white Lady of the Rock. Then grasping hands they waved a fond farewell and disappeared in the direction of the village."

———We are indebted to *Les Missions Catholiques* for the following statistics and items. They are gleanings from the letter of an Oblate of Mary Immaculate, a resident missionary, we presume, in South Africa. Southern Africa, in Church language, is divided into two Vicariates Apostolic and two Prefectures. The Vicariates are Natal and Orange Free State ; the Prefectures, Basutoland and The Transvaal. Natal, which twenty-five years ago had a Catholic population of only 800, now numbers 12,000. The proportion, however, is small when one reflects that the colony contains more than a million infidels. The principal missions are Durban, Pietermaritzburg, Estcourt, Ladysmith, Newcastle, Oakford, Kokstat and Umtata. The native Kaffirs are sunk in polygamy and have no fancy for a religion that teaches self-denial and imposes unpleasant duties. Besides, Protestant ministers, who got the start of Catholic missionaries by many years, have filled the minds of the natives with false notions of our holy religion. One even went so far as to preach in public that polygamy was not opposed to Christianity, bolstering up his assertion with this empty question, "Why must savages be denied the right to have several wives in face of the example set by Abraham, Isaac and other patriarchs of the Old Law?" The argument reminds us of an incident that took place lately in Egypt. One day a good Catholic Copt asked the

Schismatic bishop of Minieh why he sanctioned divorce. "With us," said the Catholic, "it is never allowed; and yet you say that you have the same religion as ours and obey the same laws." "What difference does it make?" said the bishop. "It is all right. You see, you follow the New Testament; we follow the Old, and *it* allows divorce. We both have the word of God for rule and guide." A very convenient settlement, indeed; and one that ought to commend itself to those of our separated brethren, who are at present looking for a way out of the woods.

The other Vicariate, that of the Orange Free State, contains as many as 4,500 Catholics, with 14,000 heretics and more than a million native pagans. Kimberley is the residence of the Vicar, a Mgr. Gaughran, of Irish extraction. In this city nearly half the Catholics of the Vicariate live. At Bloemfontein, the capital of the State, the Sisters of the Holy Family have a flourishing school with more than a hundred boarders. Mafeking and Taunys, Jaegersfontein, Harrismith and Beaconsfield are some of the most important missions.

Basutoland, separated from Natal by the Drakensberg Mountains, is inhabited almost entirely by negroes. Missionary work among them is trying in the extreme, and up to 1883 was attended with very little success. That year the mission was consecrated to the Sacred Heart and results have since been most gratifying. In a single year the missionaries have been able to register more conversions than the previous twenty-five years together witnessed. At the present writing the Catholics of Basutoland number 6,000.

The Transvaal, the second of the two Prefectures Apostolic, is the home of the Boers and the centre of a world's attention to-day. Missions are established at Pretoria, Barbeton, Johannesburg, Pontchefstroom, Lydenburg and Vleeschfontein. Of these Johannesburg is by far the most important. It is a city of 100,000 inhabitants and three out of the six thousand Catholics in the Transvaal make it their headquarters. The hostility of the Boers to the true religion is too well known to need comment. It must, however, in fairness be stated that the past ten years have witnessed a small revolution in their sentiments. They have from contact with Catholics outgrown many of their prejudices and begin, at last, to entertain some regard for priests and sisters. The municipal hospital in Johannesburg, a distinctively State institution, is in the hands of the Sisters of the Holy Family and presents the hopeful and rather unusual spectacle of a Protestant government's confidence in the charity of a Catholic sisterhood. The lot of the Boers is a heavy one. Since 1835, when slavery was abolished by the English in Cape Colony, they have repeatedly struck camp for the interior to escape trouble. Carrying their slaves with them, they founded the Orange Free State in 1836; and in 1853, the republic of the Transvaal. Their hatred of the true faith never abandoned them and, in keeping with the spirit of their Dutch ancestors, they steadfastly refused to recognize Catholicity. They say that the first visit of a priest to Pontchefstroom threw this Huguenot stronghold into a panic. A fanatical minister wrote at the time, "Woe to you, Pontchefstroom, woe to you; the devil is dropped down on you, and his anger is hot!" The magistrate of the republic scented danger and summoned the priest for a hearing. He treated him to a long dissertation on the laws of the country and concluded by threatening him with immediate expulsion, if he dared exercise his ministry. The priest coolly answered that, as he had honored Pontchefstroom with a visit at the invitation of some Catholic friends to bless a marriage and baptize a few children, he thought it his duty to proceed this far, at any rate, in his ministry. "When that's over," he added, "if you are really anxious to escort me to the border, I shall interpose no objection. Quite the contrary. I shall be grateful to you for the attention. I am a poor man, and I can hardly pay for the luxury of a trip home on horseback, much less in a carriage." Everything happened as he wished. Calvinists are slow to shake off prejudices, and the Boers are no exception to the rule. Our missionaries write that the only apparent change in their dispositions is a certain religious indifference, encouraged by the mercenary spirit of their ministers. Very little hope, therefore, attaches to their conversion as a nation. Individuals among them are quite friendly and even this small favor is a very decided improvement on the scorn and hatred encountered everywhere only a few years ago. Our schools and convents exert a wide influence for good and are doing much to better the condition of affairs. Parents begin to know and appreciate the high quality of Catholic education and readily entrust their children to our care. Herein lies our hope. These children must, under such influences, grow up better able than their fathers to rise superior to prejudice and meet the malicious lies spread broadcast by our enemies. The present war, of course, is a setback to missionary work. Our establishments at Kimberley, Mafeking and Ladysmith are exposed to all the hardships and dangers inseparable from towns in a state of siege. The churches are in many localities wholly abandoned, the entire population having either taken to flight or enlisted in the ranks of war. The missionaries in the meantime are kept busy with works of charity and with works of the ministry among the soldiers of both armies.

——The *Revue des deux Mondes* for September contained an article from the pen of Mme. Isabelle Massieu, on Burmah. In this article she informs her French readers that the English government, besides donating the ground for the various Catholic schools, pays one half of the building expenses, just as it does for Protestant establishments.

The lieutenant governor of Burmah, a staunch Protestant, speaking of the zeal and self-sacrifice of the Catholic missionaries told the writer, "Although they do not profess our religion, yet we all entertain for them the greatest admiration and deepest respect. *If England possessed such apostles, she would own the world.* Our missioners know not how to sacrifice themselves ; they do not devote themselves entirely to their work ! They do not forget their temporal interests ; but they prepare the way for us in the same manner as our merchants."

"A new hospital for lepers draws the sick together, and solicits material assistance, in spite of a similar asylum founded by the Wesleyans. Leprosy in Burmah puts on its most hideous and repulsive forms. One hundred and six men and fifty-four women receive assistance and encouragement from Fathers Wehinger and Martin. Few among the patients are Catholics, but all are touched by the care and devotion displayed by the Fathers at all hours, and won by the goodness of heart which evidently comes from above. They realize that there is a God greater than the one they have thus far known, who alone can inspire such abnegation. The calm, the quiet, the gentleness of the older inmates of the asylum, strike the new comers, and of their own accord they ask to be instructed in the religion which renders men so good."

FROM THE MISSIONS.

St. Mary's Mission, Alma P. O., Washington,
October 20, 1899.

Dear Rev. Father, P. C.:

I am travelling, and having no good pen to write, I take my pencil. I know you have been good to my poor mission and think you are willing to do what you can for me. I will speak to you to-day about one part of the work going on here during the winter, especially at St. Mary's Mission and may be you can get some generous people interested in it and able to help. In such a large mission, one hundred miles in all directions from St. Mary's, it is impossible to gather the people every Sunday. We have then to be on the road as much as possible to visit in every direction. When I have been all around, the people I have been visiting first have been abandoned for a long time, and when I am alone, as we cannot be always two here, many places are not visited once a year. To-day it is not a question only of an Indian mission as in the start, but the whites are all over settling in any place they can find way in the mountains, and it may take one two, three or more days to go and visit a poor Catholic family. They are busy at home and have no time to come to church. This is the story of every one of them. The Indians are rather easier to gather once in a while at the mission and once in a while in the chapels I have been building for nearly each tribe. Besides, we have 700 infidel Indians in two tribes and I have really no time to take care of them, as this work alone would busy one father all the time, if we want to convert them. Now how are we going to instruct the children and make Catholics out of the new generations? The visits around the country amount to nothing as far as teaching is concerned and we have no school. The school would settle the question, but for the present the only thing we can do is to gather the boys at the mission during winter in order to prepare them for the first communion. This is the work I was going to speak to you about. Whites as well as Indians and half-breeds ought to be sending their children to the mission, where they can learn something about their religion. The Indians have built a good house with a kitchen and three rooms where a family passes the winter and is doing the cooking for the children. There, too, they pass the nights. In my parlor we teach them. Some stay in the camp and come only for school hours, but this many parents, and by far the greater number, cannot do. They are supposed to give the food of the children and the clothing, because we have no help for the work. How many again, whites as well as Indians, cannot even do that much and then we have to refuse these poor children as we cannot support them.

Would it not be a great charity to send us help for these poor children so that we could keep them in the winter and prepare them well for the sacraments. We teach them to serve Mass, catechism, hymns, to sing the High Mass, the High Mass for the dead and the Benediction of the Blessed Sacrament. The best that come out of it form our choir for the church; without this winter teaching we could not have any ceremonies in the church and no choir of any kind. We teach, besides, music. Some play the organ pretty well, and we are forming also a brass band. The best of them are to be graduated Catechists in order to baptize in camps away from the mission, to assist dying people, and also to be leaders of prayers in the chapels on Sunday where the priest cannot be, etc. I do not see any better, more useful work, to be done in this mission, awaiting the day Providence will judge good for regular schools. The means to carry on the work as it ought to be and extend it as it is necessary, are all depending on the charity. Poor abandoned children! They grow up and it is too late. As I am alone a great part of the time, I need a good man who could take care of the boys and teach them in my absence. This is what I have been doing the other winters.

Who knows, perhaps you may find some charitable people who would think of us. Even masses here are hard to get. I think you were the last to send me any.

In union with your holy SS.

Your Reverence's Servant in Xto.

E. DE ROUGE, S. J.

FOR THE CHALICE.

Nine various pieces of jewelry, from a friend of the shrine.
Gold ring and breast pin, C. D. and M. F., Parkersburg, W. Va.
Various pieces of jewelry, F. Liston, N. Y.

www.ingramcontent.com/pod-product-compliance
Lightning Source LLC
Chambersburg PA
CBHW030342230426
43664CB00007BA/507